CHILTON'S REPAIR & TUNE-UP GUIDE
DATSUN 1973 to 1980

510 & 1200 1973 • 610 1973-76 • 710 1974-77 • B210 1974-78
F10 1976-78 • 200SX 1977-80 • 810 1977-80 • 510 1978-80
210 1979-80 • 310 1979-80

Managing Editor KERRY A. FREEMAN, S.A.E.
Senior Editor RICHARD J. RIVELE, S.A.E.
Editor LANCE A. EALEY

President WILLIAM A. BARBOUR
Executive Vice President JAMES A. MIADES
Vice President and General Manager JOHN P. KUSHNERICK

CHILTON BOOK COMPANY
Radnor, Pennsylvania
19089

SAFETY NOTICE

Proper service and repair procedures are vital to the safe, reliable operation of all motor vehicles, as well as the personal safety of those performing repairs. This book outlines procedures for servicing and repairing vehicles using safe, effective methods. The procedures contain many NOTES, CAUTIONS and WARNINGS which should be followed along with standard safety procedures to eliminate the possibility of personal injury or improper service which could damage the vehicle or compromise its safety.

It is important to note that repair procedures and techniques, tools and parts for servicing motor vehicles, as well as the skill and experience of the individual performing the work vary widely. It is not possible to anticipate all of the conceivable ways or conditions under which vehicles may be serviced, or to provide cautions as to all of the possible hazards that may result. Standard and accepted safety precautions and equipment should be used when handling toxic or flammable fluids, and safety goggles or other protection should be used during cutting, grinding, chiseling, prying, or any other process that can cause material removal or projectiles.

Some procedures require the use of tools specially designed for a specific purpose. Before substituting another tool or procedure, you must be completely satisfied that neither your personal safety, nor the performance of the vehicle will be endangered.

Although information in this guide is based on industry sources and is as complete as possible at the time of publication, the possibility exists that the manufacturer made later changes which could not be included here. While striving for total accuracy, Chilton Book Company cannot assume responsibility for any errors, changes, or omissions that may occur in the compilation of this data.

PART NUMBERS

Part numbers listed in this reference are not recommendations by Chilton for any product by brand name. They are references that can be used with interchange manuals and aftermarket supplier catalogs to locate each brand supplier's discrete part number.

ACKNOWLEDGMENTS

Chilton Book Company thanks Nissan Motor Corporation in U.S.A., Gardena, California 90247, for assistance in the preparation of this book.

CONTENTS

Quick Reference Specifications For Your Vehicle

Fill in this chart with the most commonly used specifications for your vehicle. Specifications can be found in Chapters 1 through 3 or on the tune-up decal under the hood of the vehicle.

 ## Tune-Up

Firing Order_____

Spark Plugs:

    Type_____

    Gap (in.)_____

Point Gap (in.)_____

Dwell Angle (°)_____

Ignition Timing (°)_____

    Vacuum (Connected/Disconnected)_____

Valve Clearance (in.)

    Intake_____   Exhaust_____

Capacities

Engine Oil (qts)

    With Filter Change_____

    Without Filter Change_____

Cooling System (qts)_____

Manual Transmission (pts)_____

    Type_____

Automatic Transmission (pts)_____

    Type_____

Front Differential (pts)_____

    Type_____

Rear Differential (pts)_____

    Type_____

Transfer Case (pts)_____

    Type_____

FREQUENTLY REPLACED PARTS

Use these spaces to record the part numbers of frequently replaced parts.

PCV VALVE

Manufacturer_____

Part No._____

OIL FILTER

Manufacturer_____

Part No._____

AIR FILTER

Manufacturer_____

Part No._____

General Information and Maintenance

HOW TO USE THIS BOOK

This book is structured in ten easy to follow chapters, using as little mechanic's jargon as possible and highlighting important procedures with scores of illustrations. Everything from engine rebuilding to replacing your radiator cap is covered. Of course, even the best mechanic won't attempt a repair without the proper tools. That's why operations like rebuilding your transmission or differential assembly are not included here—they require a range of special tools which are too expensive to be useful to the average shade-tree mechanic.

Before tangling with any repairs, read through the entire section and make sure you have the time, tools and replacement parts necessary. This will save you the frustration of hoofing it down to the bus stop Monday morning because you forgot a widget or a what-cha-ma-call-it while making repairs Sunday afternoon.

Each section begins with a brief description of the particular system and a smattering of the theory behind it. When repairs involve a high level of technical know-how, we tell you how to remove the part and replace it with a new or overhauled unit. In this way you can shave dollars off your regular labor costs.

A few basic mechanic's rules should be mentioned here. First, whenever the left side of the vehicle is referred to, it means the driver's side of the car. The right side is the passenger's side. Second, most screws and nuts and bolts are removed by turning them counterclockwise and tightened by turning clockwise. Never crawl under a car supported only by a floor or bumper jack . . . **use support stands!** Never smoke or position an exposed flame near a battery or any part of the fuel system. Common sense is your best safeguard against injury.

TOOLS AND EQUIPMENT

The following list contains the basic tools needed to perform most of the procedures described in this guide. Your Datsun is built with metric screws and bolts; if you don't already have a set of metric wrenches—buy them. Standard wrenches are either too loose or too tight a fit on metric fasteners.

1. Metric sockets, also a $^{13}/_{16}$ in. spark plug socket. If possible, buy various length socket drive extensions. One break in this department is that the metric sockets available in the US will all fit the ratchet handles and extensions you may already have ($\frac{1}{4}$, $\frac{3}{8}$, and $\frac{1}{2}$ in. drive).

2. Set of metric combination (one end open and one box) wrenches.

3. Spark plug wire gauge.

4. Flat feeler gauge for breaker points and valve lash checking.

5. Slot and phillips heads screwdrivers.

6. Timing light, preferably a DC battery hook-up type.

7. Dwell/tachometer.

8. Oil can filler spout.

9. Oil filter strap wrench. Makes removal of a tight filter much simpler. Never use to install filter.

10. Pair of channel lock pliers. Always handy to have.

11. Two sturdy jackstands—cinder blocks, bricks, and other makeshift supports are just not safe.

In addition to these basic tools, there are several other tools and gauges you may find useful. These include:

1. A compression gauge. The screw-in type is slower to use but eliminates the possibility of a faulty reading due to escaping pressure.

2. A manifold vacuum gauge.

3. A test light.

4. An induction meter. This is used for determining whether or not there is current in a wire. These are handy for use if a wire is broken somewhere in a wiring harness.

As a final note, you will probably find a torque wrench necessary for all but the most basic work. The beam type models are perfectly adequate, although the newer click type are more precise.

NOTE: *Datsun special tools referred to in this guide are available through Kent-Moore Corporation, 29784 Little Mack, Roseville, Michigan 48066. For Canada, contact Kent-Moore of Canada, Ltd., 2395 Cawthra Mississauga, Ontario, Canada L5A 3P2.*

SERVICING YOUR CAR SAFELY

It is virtually impossible to anticipate all of the hazards involved with automotive maintenance and service, but care and common sense will prevent most accidents.

The rules of safety for mechanics range from "don't smoke around gasoline," to "use the proper tool for the job." The trick to avoiding injuries is to develop safe work habits and take every possible precaution.

Dos

• Do keep a fire extinguisher and first aid kit within easy reach.

• Do wear safety glasses or goggles when cutting, drilling, grinding or prying, even if you have 20–20 vision. If you wear glasses for the sake of vision, they should be made of hardened glass that can serve also as safety glasses, or wear safety goggles over your regular glasses.

• Do shield your eyes whenever you work around the battery. Batteries contain sulphuric acid. In case of contact with the eyes or skin, flush the area with water or a mixture of water and baking soda and get medical attention immediately.

• Do use safety stands for any undercar service. Jacks are for raising vehicles; safety stands are for making sure the vehicle stays raised until you want to come down. Whenever the car is raised, block the wheels remaining on the ground and set the parking brake.

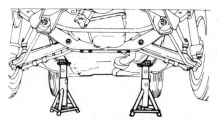

Always use support stands when working under your car

• Do use adequate ventilation when working with any chemicals or hazardous materials. Like carbon monoxide, the asbestos dust resulting from brake lining wear can be poisonous in sufficient quantities.

• Do disconnect the negative battery cable when working on the electrical system. The secondary ignition system can contain up to 40,000 volts.

• Do follow manufacturer's directions whenever working with potentially hazardous materials. Both brake fluid and antifreeze are poisonous if taken internally.

• Do properly maintain your tools. Loose hammerheads, mushroomed punches and chisels, frayed or poorly grounded electrical cords, excessively worn screwdrivers, spread wrenches (open end), cracked sockets, slipping ratchets, or faulty droplight sockets can cause accidents.

• Do use the proper size and type of tool for the job being done.

• Do when possible, pull on a wrench handle rather than push on it, and adjust your stance to prevent a fall.

• Do be sure that adjustable wrenches are tightly closed on the nut or bolt and pulled so that the face is on the side of the fixed jaw.

• Do select a wrench or socket that fits the nut or bolt. The wrench or socket should sit straight, not cocked.

• Do strike squarely with a hammer; avoid glancing blows.

• Do set the parking brake and block the drive wheels if the work requires the engine running.

Don'ts

• Don't run an engine in a garage or anywhere else without proper ventilation—EVER! Carbon monoxide is poisonous; it takes a long time to leave the human body and you can build up a deadly supply of it in your system by simply breathing in a little every day. You may not realize you are slowly poisoning yourself. Always use power vents, windows, fans or open the garage doors.

• Don't work around moving parts while wearing a necktie or other loose clothing. Short sleeves are much safer than long, loose sleeves; hard-toed shoes with neoprene soles protect your toes and give a better grip on slippery surfaces. Jewelry such as watches, fancy belt buckles, beads or body adornment of any kind is not safe working around a car. Long hair should be hidden under a hat or cap.

• Don't use pockets for toolboxes. A fall or bump can drive a screwdriver deep into your body. Even a wiping cloth hanging from the back pocket can wrap around a spinning shaft or fan.

• Don't smoke when working around gasoline, cleaning solvent or other flammable material.

• Don't smoke when working around the battery. When the battery is being charged, it gives off explosive hydrogen gas.

• Don't use gasoline to wash your hands; there are excellent soaps available. Gasoline may contain lead, and lead can enter the body through a cut, accumulating in the body until you are very ill. Gasoline also removes all the natural oils from the skin so that bone dry hands will suck up oil and grease.

• Don't service the air conditioning system unless you are equipped with the necessary tools and training. The refrigerant, R-12, is extremely cold when compressed, and when released into the air will instantly freeze any surface it contacts, including your eyes. Although the refrigerant is normally non-toxic, R-12 becomes a deadly poisonous gas in the presence of an open flame. One good whiff of the vapors from burning refrigerant can be fatal.

HISTORY

The first Datsun automobile was produced in 1913. The original name of the company, D.A.T., was derived from the last initials of the three founders. Datson, for son of D.A.T., was used later and finally evolved into Datsun. Since the first few cars were imported in 1960, Datsun has moved up to second place in imported sales.

This guide covers all Datsun coupes, sedans, hatchbacks and station wagons from 1973 to 1980. The 240-280Z(X) sports cars and the Datsun line of pick–up trucks are covered in separate Chilton books. Years and models covered are: the 1973 510, 1973 1200, the B210 from 1974 to 1978, the 610 from 1973 to 1976 and the 710 from 1974 to 1977. Also covered are the F10 from 1976 to 1978, the 810 from 1977 to 1980, the 200SX from 1977 to 1980, the new 510 from 1978 to 1980, the 310 for 1979 and 1980, and 210 from 1979 to 1980.

SERIAL NUMBER IDENTIFICATION

Chassis

The chassis serial number is stamped into the firewall. The model designation, such as

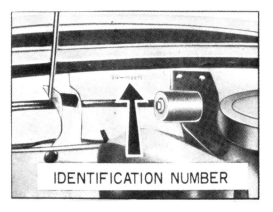

IDENTIFICATION NUMBER

B210, precedes the serial number. The chassis number is also located on a dashboard plate which is visible through the windshield.

Vehicle Identification Plate

The vehicle identification plate is attached to the firewall. This plate gives the vehicle model, engine displacement in cc, SAE horsepower rating, wheelbase, engine number, and chassis number.

Vehicle identification plate

Engine

The engine number is stamped on the right side top edge of the cylinder block on all models except the 1980 200SX. Its engine number is stamped on the left side top of the engine block. The engine serial number is preceded by the engine model code.

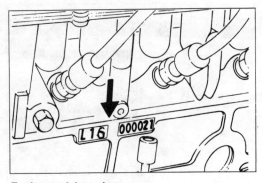

Engine serial number

Transmission

The transmission serial number is stamped on the front upper face of the transmission case on manual transmissions, or on the right side of the transmission case on automatic transmissions. On the F10 and the 310 transaxles, the transmission/transaxle number is stamped on the front upper face of the transmission case.

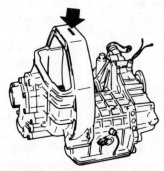

Transmission number location: F10, 310

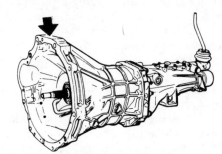

Manual transmission number location

ROUTINE MAINTENANCE

Air Cleaner

All Datsuns covered in this guide are equipped with a disposable paper cartridge air cleaner element. At every tuneup, or sooner if the car is operated in a dusty area, undo the wing nut, remove the housing top, and withdraw the element. Check the element. Replace the filter if it is extremely dirty. Loose dust can sometimes be removed by striking the filter against a hard surface several times or by blowing through it with compressed air. The filter should be replaced every 24,000 miles. Before installing either the original or a replacement filter, wipe out the inside of the air cleaner housing with a clean rag or paper towel. Install the paper air cleaner filter, seat the top cover on the bottom housing, and tighten the wing nut.

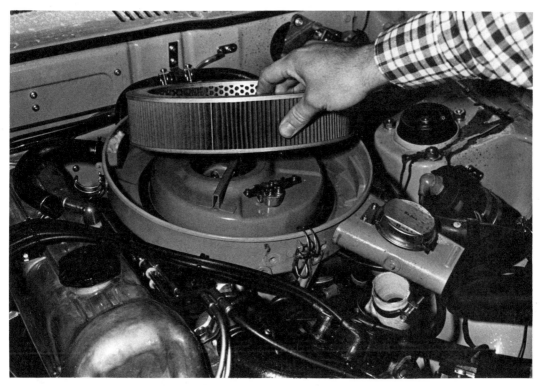

Your engine breathes too, don't strangle it with a dirty air filter

NOTE: *Some flat, cartridge type air cleaner elements have the word "UP" printed on them. Be sure the side with "UP" on it faces up.*

Air Induction Valve Filter

This filter is located in the air cleaner of late model Datsuns, both fuel injected and carburetor models. To replace it, remove the screws and remove the valve filter case. Install the new filter, paying attention to which direction the valve is facing so that exhaust gases will not flow backwards through the system.

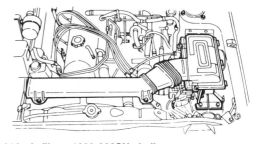

810 air filter; 1980 200SX similar

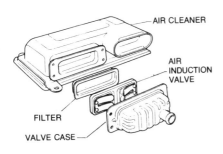

Air induction valve filter, 810, 1980 200SX

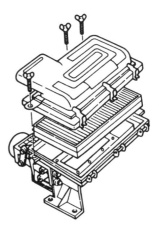

Exploded view of 810 air filter; 1980 200SX similar

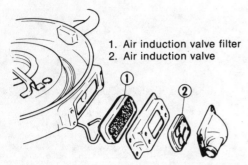

1. Air induction valve filter
2. Air induction valve

Air induction valve filter, carburetor models

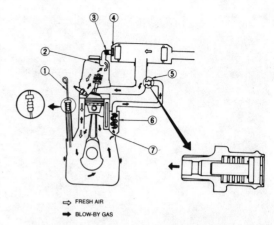

⇨ FRESH AIR
➡ BLOW-BY GAS

1. Seal type oil level gauge
2. Baffle plate
3. Flame arrester
4. Filter
5. P.C.V. valve
6. Steel net
7. Baffle plate

210, 310 PCV valve location; others similar

Positive Crankcase Ventilation Valve

This valve feeds crankcase blow-by gases into the intake manifold to be burned with the normal air/fuel mixture. The PCV valve should be replaced every 24,000 miles. Make sure that all PCV connections are tight. Check that the connecting hoses are clear and not clogged. Replace any brittle or broken hoses.

To replace the valve, which is located in the intake manifold directly below the carburetor:

1. Squeeze the hose clamp with pliers and remove the hose.

2. Using a wrench, unscrew the PCV valve and remove the valve.

3. Disconnect the ventilation hoses and flush with solvent.

4. Install the new PCV valve and replace the hoses and clamp.

PCV valve (arrow). On the late models, there are so many hoses in the way, the valve is hard to spot

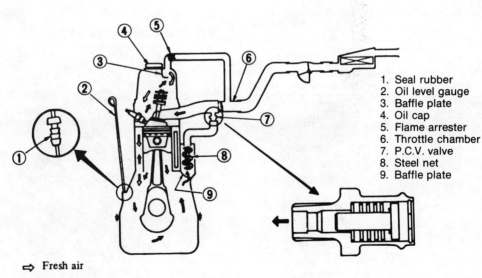

1. Seal rubber
2. Oil level gauge
3. Baffle plate
4. Oil cap
5. Flame arrester
6. Throttle chamber
7. P.C.V. valve
8. Steel net
9. Baffle plate

⇨ Fresh air
➡ Blow-by gas

810 PCV valve location; 1980 200SX similar

Fuel Evaporative Emissions System

Check the evaporation control system every 12,000 miles. Check the fuel and vapor lines for proper connections and correct routing as well as condition. Replace damaged or deteriorated parts as necessary. Remove and check the operation of the check valve on pre-1975 models in the following manner.

1. With all the hoses disconnected from the valve, apply air pressure to the fuel tank side of the valve. The air should flow through the valve and exit the crankcase side of the valve. If the valve does not behave in the above manner, replace it.

2. Apply air pressure to the crankcase side valve. Air should not pass to either of the two outlets.

3. When air pressure is applied to the carburetor side of the valve, the air should pass through to exit out the fuel tank and/or the crankcase side of the valve.

On 1975 and later models, the flow guide valve is replaced with a carbon filled canister which stores fuel vapors until the engine is started and the vapors are drawn into the combustion chambers and burned.

To check the operation of the carbon canister purge control valve, disconnect the rubber hose between the canister control valve and the T-fitting, at the T-fitting. Apply vacuum to the hose leading to the control valve.

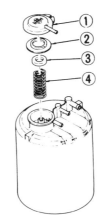

1. Cover
2. Diaphragm
3. Retainer
4. Diaphragm spring

1975–80 carbon canister fuel evaporative emissions system

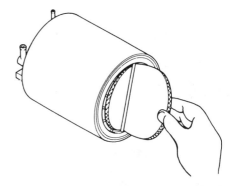

The carbon canister has a replaceable filter in the bottom

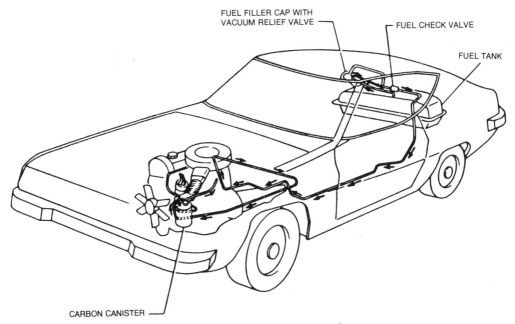

FUEL FILLER CAP WITH VACUUM RELIEF VALVE

FUEL CHECK VALVE

FUEL TANK

CARBON CANISTER

Evaporative emissions schematic

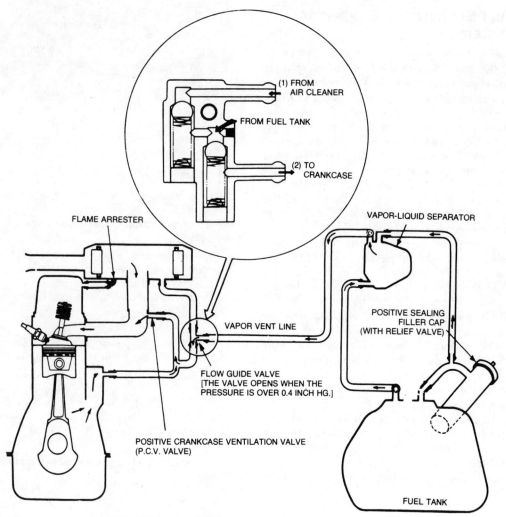

1973–74 check valve fuel evaporative emissions system

The vacuum condition should be maintained indefinitely. If the control valve leaks, remove the top cover of the valve and check for a dislocated or cracked diaphragm. If the diaphragm is damaged, a repair kit containing a new diaphragm, retainer, and spring is available and should be installed.

The carbon canister has an air filter in the bottom of the canister. The filter element should be checked once a year or every 12,000 miles; more frequently if the car is operated in dusty areas. Replace the filter by pulling it out of the bottom of the canister and installing a new one.

Heat Control Valve

The heat control valve, or Early Fuel Evaporative System, is a thermostatically operated valve in the exhaust manifold. It closes when the engine is warming up to direct hot exhaust gases to the intake manifold, in order to pre-heat the incoming air/fuel mixture. If it sticks shut, the result will be frequent stalling during warmup, especially in cold or damp weather. If it sticks open, the result will be a rough idle after the engine is warm.

The heat control valve should be checked for free operation every six months or 6,000 miles. Simply give the counterweight a twirl (engine cold) to make sure that no binding exists. If the valve sticks, apply a heat control solvent to the ends of the shaft. This type of solvent is available in auto parts stores. Sometimes lightly rapping the end of the shaft with a hammer (engine hot) will break it loose. If this fails, the components will have to be removed from the car for repair.

NOTE: *The 1980 carbureted engines do*

not use the heat control valve. Instead, these engines warm the fuel mixture by a coolant passage under the carburetor. No maintenance is required.

Belts

TENSION CHECKING, ADJUSTING, AND REPLACEMENT

Check the belts driving the fan, air pump, air conditioning compressor, and the alternator for cracks, fraying, wear, and tension every 6,000 miles. It is recommended that the belts be replaced every 24 months or 24,000 miles. Belt deflection at the midpoint of the longest span between pulleys should not be more than $7/16$ of an inch with 22 lbs of pressure applied to the belt.

To adjust the tension on all components except the air conditioning compressor, power steering pump, and some late model air pumps, loosen the pivot and mounting bolts of the component which the belt is driving, then, using a wooden lever, pry the component toward or away from the engine until the proper tension is achieved.

CAUTION: *An overtight belt will wear out the pulley bearings on the assorted components.*

Tighten the component mounting bolts securely. If a new belt is installed, recheck the tension after driving about 1,000 miles.

NOTE: *The replacement of the inner belt on multi-belted engines may require the removal of the outer belts.*

Belt tension adjustments for the factory installed air conditioning compressor and power steering pump are made at the idler pulley. The idler pulley is the smallest of the three pulleys. At the top of the slotted bracket holding the idler pulley there is a bolt which is used to either raise or lower the pulley. To free the bolt for adjustment, it is necessary to loosen the lock nut in the face of the idler pulley. After adjusting the belt tension, tighten the lock nut in the face of the idler pulley.

NOTE: *1980 California Datsuns come equipped with special fan belts which, if loose, generate friction heat by slipping and shrink, taking up the slack.*

The optional air conditioning drive belt is adjusted in a similar fashion.

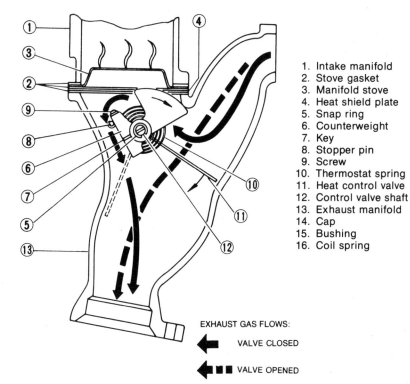

1. Intake manifold
2. Stove gasket
3. Manifold stove
4. Heat shield plate
5. Snap ring
6. Counterweight
7. Key
8. Stopper pin
9. Screw
10. Thermostat spring
11. Heat control valve
12. Control valve shaft
13. Exhaust manifold
14. Cap
15. Bushing
16. Coil spring

EXHAUST GAS FLOWS:

← VALVE CLOSED

←■■ VALVE OPENED

Heat control valve (early fuel evaporative system) A-series engine

How to Spot Worn V-Belts

V-Belts are vital to efficient engine operation—they drive the fan, water pump and other accessories. They require little maintenance (occasional tightening) but they will not last forever. Slipping or failure of the V-belt will lead to overheating. If your V-belt looks like any of these, it should be replaced.

Cracking or weathering

This belt has deep cracks, which cause it to flex. Too much flexing leads to heat build-up and premature failure. These cracks can be caused by using the belt on a pulley that is too small. Notched belts are available for small diameter pulleys.

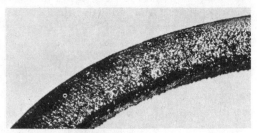

Softening (grease and oil)

Oil and grease on a belt can cause the belt's rubber compounds to soften and separate from the reinforcing cords that hold the belt together. The belt will first slip, then finally fail altogether.

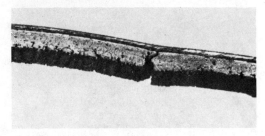

Glazing

Glazing is caused by a belt that is slipping. A slipping belt can cause a run-down battery, erratic power steering, overheating or poor accessory performance. The more the belt slips, the more glazing will be built up on the surface of the belt. The more the belt is glazed, the more it will slip. If the glazing is light, tighten the belt.

Worn cover

The cover of this belt is worn off and is peeling away. The reinforcing cords will begin to wear and the belt will shortly break. When the belt cover wears in spots or has a rough jagged appearance, check the pulley grooves for roughness.

Separation

This belt is on the verge of breaking and leaving you stranded. The layers of the belt are separating and the reinforcing cords are exposed. It's just a matter of time before it breaks completely.

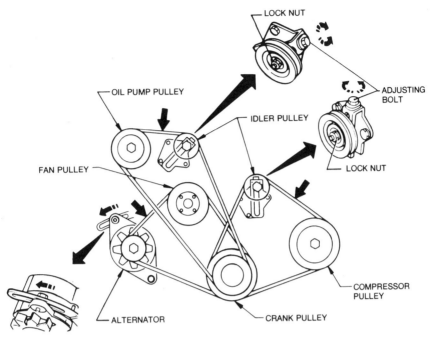

810 1980 fan belt configuration. Note idler pulleys

Cooling System

Your Datsun's internal combustion engine generates power by the controlled explosion of a mixture of gasoline and air in the combustion chamber of each cylinder. The piston of each cylinder is at the top of its upward travel when the explosion occurs and subsequently is forced downward, creating mechanical power. But not all of the force of the ignited fuel mixture is expended in forcing the piston down; some is released as heat, and the job of the cooling system is to effectively remove that heat from the engine before it raises the cylinder head and block temperature too greatly.

To drain the cooling system, allow the

Always handle a warm radiator cap with a heavy rag to avoid scalds

engine to cool down BEFORE ATTEMPTING TO REMOVE THE RADIATOR CAP. Then turn the cap until it hisses. Wait until all pressure is off the cap before removing it completely. To avoid burns and scalding, always handle a warm radiator cap with a heavy rag. After the radiator cap is off, drain the radiator by loosening the petcock or plug at the bottom of the radiator. See "Coolant" section under "Fluid Level Checks" in this chapter for refilling procedures.

Air Conditioning

This book contains no repair or maintenance procedures for the air conditioning system. It is recommended that any such repairs be left to the experts, whose personnel are well aware of the hazards and who have the proper equipment.

CAUTION: *The compressed refrigerant used in the air conditioning system expands into the atmosphere at a temperature of −21.7° F or lower. This will freeze any surface, including your eyes, that it contacts. In addition, the refrigerant decomposes into a poisonous gas in the presence of flame. Do not open or disconnect any part of the air conditioning system.*

SIGHT GLASS CHECK

You can safely make a few simple checks to determine if your air conditioning system

The sight glass is located in the head of the receiver-dryer (arrow)

needs service. The tests work best if the temperature is warm (about 70° F).

NOTE: *If your vehicle is equipped with an after-market air conditioner, the following system check may not apply. You should contact the manufacturer of the unit for instructions on systems checks.*

1. Place the automatic transmission in Park or the manual transmission in Neutral. Set the parking brake.

2. Run the engine at a fast idle (about 1,500 rpm) either with the help of a friend, or by temporarily readjusting the idle speed screw.

3. Set the controls for maximum cold with the blower on high.

4. Locate the sight glass in one of the sys-

tem lines. Usually it is on the left alongside the top of the radiator.

5. If you see bubbles, the system must be recharged. Very likely there is a leak at some point.

6. If there are no bubbles, there is either no refrigerant at all or the system is fully charged. Feel the two hoses going to the belt-driven compressor. If they are both at the same temperature, the system is empty and must be recharged.

7. If one hose (high-pressure) is warm and the other (low-pressure) is cold, the system may be all right. However, you are probably making these tests because you think there is something wrong, so proceed to the next step.

8. Have an assistant in the car turn the fan control on and off to operate the compressor clutch. Watch the sight glass.

9. If bubbles appear when the clutch is disengaged and disappear when it is engaged, the system is properly charged.

10. If the refrigerant takes more than 45 seconds to bubble when the clutch is disengaged, the system is overcharged. This usually causes poor cooling at low speeds.

CAUTION: *If it is determined that the system has a leak, it should be corrected as soon as possible. Leaks may allow moisture to enter and cause a very expensive rust problem.*

NOTE: *Exercise the air conditioner for a few minutes, every two weeks or so, during the cold months. This avoids the possibility of the compressor seals drying out from lack of lubrication.*

Hoses

HOSE REPLACEMENT

Remove the radiator cap and drain the radiator into a clean pan if you are going to reuse the old coolant. Remove the hose clamps and remove the hose by either cutting it off or twisting it to break its seal on the radiator and engine coolant inlets. When installing the new hose, do not overtighten the hose clamps or you might cut the hose. Refill the radiator with coolant, run the engine with the radiator cap on and then recheck the coolant level.

Fluid Level Checks

ENGINE OIL

The best time to check the engine oil is before operating the engine or after it has been

How to Spot Bad Hoses

Both the upper and lower radiator hoses are called upon to perform difficult jobs in an inhospitable environment. They are subject to nearly 18 psi at under hood temperatures often over 280°F., and must circulate nearly 7500 gallons of coolant an hour—3 good reasons to have good hoses.

Swollen hose

A good test for any hose is to feel it for soft or spongy spots. Frequently these will appear as swollen areas of the hose. The most likely cause is oil soaking. This hose could burst at any time, when hot or under pressure.

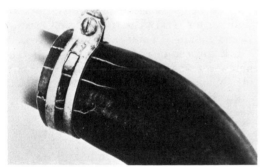

Cracked hose

Cracked hoses can usually be seen but feel the hoses to be sure they have not hardened; a prime cause of cracking. This hose has cracked down to the reinforcing cords and could split at any of the cracks.

Frayed hose end (due to weak clamp)

Weakened clamps frequently are the cause of hose and cooling system failure. The connection between the pipe and hose has deteriorated enough to allow coolant to escape when the engine is hot.

Debris in cooling system

Debris, rust and scale in the cooling system can cause the inside of a hose to weaken. This can usually be felt on the outside of the hose as soft or thinner areas.

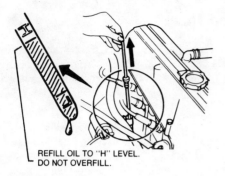

REFILL OIL TO "H" LEVEL.
DO NOT OVERFILL.

Oil dipstick markings

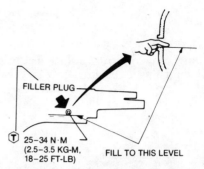

FILLER PLUG

25–34 N·M
(2.5–3.5 KG-M,
18–25 FT-LB)   FILL TO THIS LEVEL

Transmission oil should be level with the bottom of the filler plug on manual transmissions

sitting for at least 10 minutes in order to gain an accurate reading. This will allow the oil to drain back in the crankcase. To check the engine oil level, make sure that the vehicle is resting on a level surface, remove the oil dipstick, wipe it clean and reinsert the stick firmly for an accurate reading. The oil dipstick has two marks to indicate high and low oil level. If the oil is at or below the "low level" mark on the dipstick, oil should be added as necessary. The oil level should be maintained in the safety margin, neither going above the "high level" mark or below the "low level" mark.

TRANSMISSION

Manual

Check the level of the lubricant in the transmission every 3,000 miles. The lubricant level should be even with the bottom of the filler hole. Hold in on the filler plug when unscrewing it. When you are sure that all of the threads of the plug are free of the transmission case, move the plug away from the case slightly. If lubricant begins to flow out of the transmission, then you know it is full. If not, add SAE90 gear oil as necessary. It is recommended that the transmission lubricant be changed every 24,000 miles.

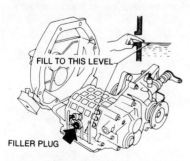

FILL TO THIS LEVEL

FILLER PLUG

Transmission filler plug location and oil level; F10, 310

Automatic

Check the level of the automatic transmission fluid every 2,000 miles. There is a dipstick at the right rear of the engine under the hood. It has a scale on each side, one for COLD and the other for HOT. The transmission is considered hot after 15 miles of highway driving.

Park the car on a level surface with the engine running. If the transmission is not hot, shift into Drive, Low, then Neutral or Park. Set the handbrake and block the wheels.

Remove the dipstick, wipe it clean, then reinsert it firmly. Remove the dipstick and check the fluid level on the appropriate scale. The level should be at the "Full" mark.

If the level is below the "Full" mark, add Type A or DEXRON® type automatic transmission fluid as necessary, with the engine

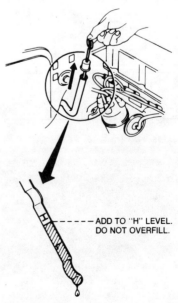

ADD TO "H" LEVEL.
DO NOT OVERFILL.

Remove the automatic transmission dipstick with engine warm and idling in Park

running, through the dipstick tube. Do not overfill, as this may cause the transmission to malfunction and damage itself.

BRAKE AND CLUTCH MASTER CYLINDER

Check the levels of brake fluid in the brake and clutch master cylinder reservoirs every 3,000 miles. The fluid level should be maintained to a level not below the bottom line on the reservoirs and not above the top line. Any sudden decrease in the level in either of the three reservoirs (two for the brakes and one for the clutch) indicates a probable leak in that particular system and the possibility of a leak should be checked out.

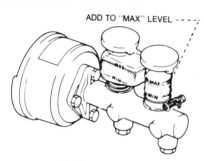

Brake master cylinder

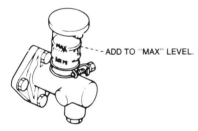

Clutch master cylinder

COOLANT

Check the coolant level every time you change the oil. Check for loose connections and signs of deterioration of the coolant hoses. Maintain the coolant level 3 in. below the level of the filler neck when the engine is cold. Add a mixture of 70% to 50% water and 30% to 50% ethylene glycol antifreeze as necessary. Never remove the radiator cap when the vehicle is hot or overheated. Wait until it has cooled. Place a thick cloth over the radiator cap to shield yourself from the heat and turn the radiator cap *slightly* until the sound of escaping pressure can be heard. *Do not turn any more.* Allow the pressure to release gradually. When no more pressure can be heard escaping, then remove the cap with

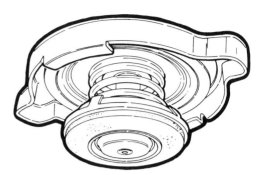

Check the rubber gasket on the cap when checking the coolant level

the heavy cloth *cautiously*. Never add cold water to an overheated engine while the engine is not running. Run the engine until it reaches normal operating temperature after filling the radiator to make sure that the thermostat has opened and all air is bled from the system.

REAR AXLE

Check the rear axle lubricant every 6,000 miles. Remove the filler plug in the axle housing. The lubricant should be up to the bottom of the filler hole with the vehicle resting on a level surface. Add SAE90 gear oil as necessary to bring the lubricant up to the proper level.

STEERING GEAR

Check the level of the lubricant in the steering gear every 12,000 miles. If the level is low, check for leakage. An oily film is not considered a leak; solid grease must be present. Change the lubricant every 36,000 miles. Use steering gear lubricant. The lubricant is added and checked through the filler plug hole in the top of the steering gear.

POWER STEERING RESERVOIR

Some models of the Datsun 810 and 200SX are equipped with power steering.

Check the oil level in the reservoir by checking the side of the dipstick marked "HOT" after running the vehicle, or the side

Fill the power steering pump to the correct level

marked "COLD" when the car has not been used. In each case, fluid should reach the appropriate full line. Check the fluid level often. When refilling, use DEXRON® ATF. The unit holds approximately 1½ qts. See chapter 8, "Suspension and Steering" for system bleeding procedures.

BATTERY

The battery is located in the engine compartment. Routinely check the battery electrolyte level and specific gravity. A few minutes

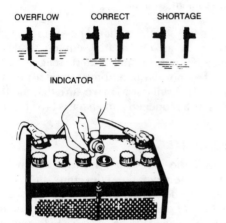

Make sure the electrolyte in the battery is level with the bottoms of the filler holes

Periodically clean the battery posts and connections

occasionally spent monitoring battery condition is worth saving hours of frustration when your car won't start due to a dead battery. Only distilled water should be used to top up the battery, as tap water, in many areas, contains harmful minerals. Two tools which will facilitate battery maintenance are a hydrometer and a squeeze bulb filler. These are cheap and widely available at automotive parts stores, hardware stores, etc. The specific gravity of the electrolyte should be between 1.27 and 1.20. Keep the top of the battery clean, as a film of dirt can sometimes completely discharge a battery. A solution of baking soda and water may be used to clean the top surface, but be careful to flush this off with clear water and that none of the solution enters the filler holes. Clean the battery posts and clamps with a wire brush to eliminate corrosion deposits. Special clamp and terminal cleaning brushes are available for just this purpose. Lightly coat the posts and clamps with petroleum jelly or chassis grease after cleaning them.

Tires

Check the air pressure in your tires every few weeks. Make sure that the tires are cool, as you will get a false reading when the tires are heated because air pressure increases with temperature. A decal tells you the proper tire pressure for the standard equipment tires. Naturally, when you replace tires you will want to get the correct tire pressures

When bands appear as shown, your tire tread is below 1/16 inch. Tire should be replaced

Capacities

Year	Model	Engine Crankcase		Transmission (pts)			Drive Axle (pts)	Gas Tank (gals)	Cooling System (qts)
		With Filter	Without Filter	4-Spd	5-Spd	Automatic (total capacity)			
1973	510	4.5	4	3.7	—	11.4	1.75	11.9	7.2
	1200	3.6	2.6	2.5	—	11.8	1.8	10/10.5 (sedan)	5.2
	610	5.0	4.5	4.25	—	11.8	1.75/2.75 (wagon)	13.8/14.5 (sedan)	9.0
1974	B210	3.45	—	2.5	—	11.8	1.8	11.5	5.5
	610	4.5	—	4.25	—	10.9	1.75/2.2 (wagon)	14.5/13.5 (wagon)	6.88
	710	4.45	—	4.25	—	10.9	2.75	13.25	7
1975	B210	4.2	3.7	2.7	—	11.4	1.89	11.5	6.25 ④
	610	4.5	4.0	4.25	—	11.8	1.75/2.75 (wagon)	14.5/13.7 (wagon)	7.25
	710	5.0	4.5	4.25	—	11.8	2.75	13.2/11.8 (wagon)	7.25
1976	610	4.5	4.0	4.25	—	11.8	1.75/2.2 (wagon)	14.5/13.75 (wagon)	7.25
1976–77	710	4.5	4.0	4.25 ①	—	11.8	2.75	13.25/11.8 (wagon)	7.25
1976–78	B210	3.8	3.4	2.75	3.6	11.8	1.8	11.5	6.25 ④
	F10	3.6	3.2	4.9	4.9	—	—	10.6/9.1 (wagon)	7
1977–78	810	6.0	5.5	3.6	—	11.8	2.75/2.2 (wagon)	15.9/14.5 (wagon)	11
1977–79	200SX	4.5	4.0	—	3.6	11.8	2.75	15.9	7.9
1978–79	510	4.5	4.0	3.6	3.6	11.8	2.4	13.2	9.4
1979–80	210	②	—	③	2.5	11.8	1.8	13.25	6.25 ④
	310	3.4	2.8	4.9	4.9	—	—	13.25	6.25
	810	5.9	5.25	3.7	4.25	11.8	2.0	15.9/14.5 (wagon)	11

Capacities (cont.)

Year	Model	Engine Crankcase		Transmission (pts)			Drive Axle (pts)	Gas Tank (gals)	Cooling System (qts)
		With Filter	Without Filter	4-Spd	5-Spd	Automatic (total capacity)			
1980	510	⑤	—	3.15	3.6	11.8	2.4	13.25	9.25
	200SX	4.4	4.1	—	4.25	11.8	2.4	14/15.9 (hatchback)	10

① 3.6 pts., 1977
② A12A, A14 engines: 3.46 qts.
   A15 engine: 3.25 qts.
③ A12A engine: 2.5 pts.
   A14 engine: 2.75 pts.
④ Automatic transmission: 6 qts.
⑤ L20B engine: 4.5 qts.
   Z20S engine: 4.65 qts.

for the new ones from the dealer or manufacturer. It pays to buy a tire pressure gauge to keep in the car, since those at service stations are usually inaccurate or broken.

While you are checking the tire pressure, take a look at the tread. The tread should be wearing evenly across the tire. Excessive wear in the center of the tread could indicate overinflation. Excessive wear on the outer edges could indicate underinflation. An irregular wear pattern is usually a sign of incorrect front wheel alignment or wheel balance. A front end that is out of alignment will usually pull the car to one side of a flat road when the steering wheel is released. Incorrect wheel balance will produce vibration in the steering wheel, while unbalanced rear wheels will result in floor or trunk vibration.

Rotating the tires every 6,000 miles or so will result in increased tread life. Use the correct pattern for your tire switching. Most automotive experts agree that radial tires are better all around performers, giving longer wear and better handling. An added benefit which you should consider when purchasing tires is that radials have less rolling resistance and can give up to a 10% increase in fuel economy over a bias-ply tire.

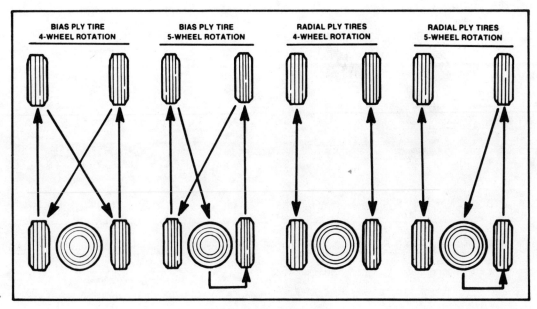

Tire rotation patterns

Tires of different construction should never be mixed. Always replace tires in sets of four or five when switching tire types and never substitute a belted tire for a bias-ply, a radial for a belted tire, etc. An occasional pressure check and periodic rotation could make your tires last much longer than a neglected set and maintain the safety margin which was designed into them.

Fuel Filter

The fuel filter on all models is a disposable plastic unit. It's located on the right inner fender. The filter should be replaced at least every 24,000 miles. A dirty filter will starve the engine and cause poor running.

REPLACEMENT

1. Locate fuel filter on right-side of the engine compartment.

NOTE: *The 810 and the 1980 200SX have electric fuel pumps. The pressure must be released on these before you can change the fuel filter. Refer to Chapter 4 under "Fuel Pump: Testing" for the procedures.*

2. Disconnect the inlet and outlet hoses from the fuel filter. Make certain that the inlet hose (bottom) doesn't fall below the fuel tank level or the gasoline will drain out.

3. Pry the fuel filter from its clip and replace the assembly.

4. Replace the inlet and outlet lines; secure the hose clamps to prevent leaks.

5. Start the engine and check for leaks.

Fuel filter (arrow). This is a 1978 510; others are similar

LUBRICATION

Oil and Fuel Recommendations

Your Datsun is designed to operate on regular low lead or lead-free fuel. The octane ratings are listed on the inside of the fuel filler door, but these need only be checked when traveling outside of the United States. Should you find the regular gasoline available, say in Mexico, to be of too low an octane, mix enough Premium to raise the octane level. No benefit will be derived from running a higher octane gasoline than that recommended.

Oil must be selected with regard to the anticipated temperatures during the period before the next oil change. Using the chart, select the oil viscosity for the lowest expected temperature and you will be assured of easy cold starting and sufficient engine protection. The oil you pour into your Datsun engine should have the designation "SE" marked on the top of its container. Under the classification system adopted by the American Petroleum Institute (API) in May, 1970, "SE" is the highest designation for passenger car use. The "S" stands for passenger car and the second letter denotes a more specific application. "SA" oil, for instance, contains no additives and is suitable only for very light-duty usage. Oil designated "MS" (motor severe) may also be used, since this was the highest classification under the old API rating system.

Oil Viscosity Selection Chart

	Anticipated Temperature Range	SAE Viscosity
Multi-grade	Above 32° F	10W—40 10W—50 20W—40 20W—50 10W—30
	May be used as low as −10° F	10W—30 10W—40
	Consistently below 10° F	5W—20 5W—30
Single-grade	Above 32° F	30
	Temperature between +32° F and −10° F	10W

Oil Changes

The mileage figures given in your owner's manual are the Datsun recommended intervals for oil and filter changes assuming average driving. If your Datsun is being used under dusty, polluted, or off-road conditions, change the oil and filter sooner than specified. The same thing goes for cars driven in stop-and-go traffic or only for short distances.

Always drain the oil after the engine has been running long enough to bring it to operating temperature. Hot oil will flow easier and more contaminants will be removed along with the oil than if it were drained cold. You will need a large capacity drain pan, which you can purchase at any store which sells automotive parts. Another necessity is containers for the used oil. You will find that plastic bottles, such as those used for bleach or fabric softener, make excellent storage jugs. One ecologically desirable solution to the used oil disposal problem is to find a co-operative gas station owner who will allow you to dump your used oil into his tank. Another is to keep the oil for use around the house as a preservative on fences, railroad tie borders, etc.

Datsun recommends changing both the oil and filter during the first oil change and the filter every other oil change thereafter. For the small price of an oil filter, it's cheap insurance to replace the filter at every oil change. One of the larger filter manufacturers points out in its advertisements that not changing the filter leaves one quart of dirty oil in the engine. This claim is true and should be kept in mind when changing your oil.

CHANGING YOUR ENGINE OIL

1. Run the engine until it reaches normal operating temperature.

2. Jack up the front of the car and support it on safety stands if necessary to gain access to the filter.

3. Slide a drain pan of at least 6 quarts capacity under the oil pan.

4. Loosen the drain plug. Turn the plug out by hand. By keeping an inward pressure on the plug as you unscrew it, oil won't escape past the threads and you can remove it without being burned by hot oil.

5. Allow the oil to drain completely and then install the drain plug. Don't overtighten the plug, or you'll be buying a new pan or a trick replacement plug for buggered threads.

The oil filter on L-series engines is easily located on the right hand side of the block

A strap wrench will make oil filter removal easier. Do not install a filter with a strap wrench

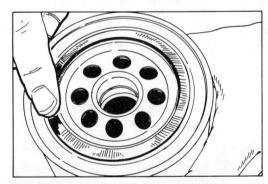

Apply a light coat of oil to the rubber gasket on the oil filter before installing it

6. Using a strap wrench, remove the oil filter. Keep in mind that it's holding about one quart of dirty, hot oil.

7. Empty the old filter into the drain pan and dispose of the filter.

8. Using a clean rag, wipe off the filter adapter on the engine block. Be sure that the rag doesn't leave any lint which could clog an oil passage.

9. Coat the rubber gasket on the filter with fresh oil. Spin it onto the engine *by*

hand; when the gasket touches the adapter surface give it another ½–¾ turn. No more, or you'll squash the gasket and it will leak.

10. Refill the engine with the correct amount of fresh oil. See the "Capacities" chart.

11. Crank the engine over several times and then start it. If the oil pressure "idiot light" doesn't go out or the pressure gauge shows zero, shut the engine down and find out what's wrong.

12. If the oil pressure is OK and there are no leaks, shut the engine off and lower the car.

TRANSMISSION

Manual

Change the transmission lubricant in your manual transmission every 36,000 miles as follows:

1. Park the car on a level surface and apply the parking brake. Jack up the car and support it on stands.

2. Remove the oil filler plug (the upper one).

3. Place a drain pan under the drain plug in the transmission bottom pan.

4. Slowly remove the drain plug keeping an upward pressure on it until you can quickly pull it out.

5. Allow all of the old gear oil to drain and then replace the plug. Don't overtighten it.

6. Fill the transmission with SAE 90 gear oil. Refill with the quantity shown in the "Capacities" chart. An oil suction gun or squeeze bulb filler are handy for this chore and can be used for the rear axle, too.

7. Replace the filler plug and lower the car.

Automatic

The transmission fluid in an automatic transmission should be changed every 24,000 miles of normal driving or every 12,000 miles of driving under abnormal or severe conditions. The fluid should be drained immediately after the vehicle has been driven, but before it has had the chance to cool. Follow the procedure given below:

1. Drain the automatic transmission fluid from the transmission into a large drain pan, by removing the transmission bottom pan screws, pan, and gasket.

2. Thoroughly clean the bottom pan and position a new gasket on the pan mating surface. Use petroleum jelly on the gasket to seal it. Install the bottom pan and secure it with the attaching screws, tightening them to 3–5 ft lbs.

3. Pour the same amount of Type A DEXRON® automatic transmission fluid, which was drained from the oil pan, in through the filler pipe. Make sure that the funnel, container, hose, or any other item used to assist in filling the transmission is clean.

4. Start the engine. Do NOT race it. Allow the engine to idle for a few minutes.

5. Place the selector lever in Park and apply the parking brake. With the transmission fluid at operating temperatures, check the fluid level; add fluid to bring the level to the "FULL" mark on the dip-stick.

REAR AXLE

Change the gear oil in the rear axle every 36,000 miles as follows:

1. With the car on a level surface, jack up the rear and support it with stands.

2. Slide a drain pan under the drain plug, remove the plug, and allow the oil to drain out.

3. Install the drain plug, but don't overtighten it. Remove the filler plug.

4. Refill the rear axle with SAE 90 gear oil up to the level of the filler plug.

5. Install the filler plug and lower the car.

Chassis Greasing

Datsun doesn't install lubrication fittings in lube points on the steering linkage or suspension. You can buy metric threaded fittings to grease these points or use a pointed, rubber tip end on your grease gun. Lubricate all joints equipped with a plug every 24,000 miles. Replace the plugs after lubrication.

PUSHING, TOWING AND JUMP STARTING

All cars sold with manual transmission through 1975, and 1976 and later 49 States

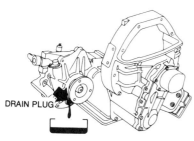

Location of the transmission drain plug on the F10, 310

Jump Starting a Dead Battery

The chemical reaction in a battery produces explosive hydrogen gas. This is the safe way to jump start a dead battery, reducing the chances of an accidental spark that could cause an explosion.

Jump Starting Precautions

1. Be sure both batteries are of the same voltage.
2. Be sure both batteries are of the same polarity (have the same grounded terminal).
3. Be sure the vehicles are not touching.
4. Be sure the vent cap holes are not obstructed.
5. Do not smoke or allow sparks around the battery.
6. In cold weather, check for frozen electrolyte in the battery.
7. Do not allow electrolyte on your skin or clothing.
8. Be sure the electrolyte is not frozen.

Jump Starting Procedure

1. Determine voltages of the two batteries; they must be the same.
2. Bring the starting vehicle close (they must not touch) so that the batteries can be reached easily.
3. Turn off all accessories and both engines. Put both cars in Neutral or Park and set the handbrake.
4. Cover the cell caps with a rag—do not cover terminals.
5. If the terminals on the run-down battery are heavily corroded, clean them.
6. Identify the positive and negative posts on both batteries and connect the cables in the order shown.
7. Start the engine of the starting vehicle and run it at fast idle. Try to start the car with the dead battery. Crank it for no more than 10 seconds at a time and let it cool off for 20 seconds in between tries.
8. If it doesn't start in 3 tries, there is something else wrong.
9. Disconnect the cables in the reverse order.
10. Replace the cell covers and dispose of the rags.

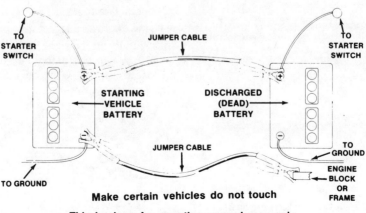

Make certain vehicles do not touch

This hook-up for negative ground cars only

and Canada cars with manual transmissions can be pushed started. 1976 and later cars sold in California with catalytic converters may not be pushed started, since doing so may damage the converter. Cars with automatic transmissions may not be push started. Check to make sure that the bumpers of both vehicles are aligned so neither will be damaged. Be sure that all electrical system components are turned off (headlights, heater blower, etc.). Turn on the ignition switch. Place the shift lever in third or fourth gear and push in the clutch pedal. At about 15 mph, signal the driver of the pushing vehicle to fall back, depress the accelerator pedal and release the clutch pedal slowly. The engine should start.

The manufacturer advises against trying to tow-start your Datsun for fear of ramming the tow-vehicle when the engine starts.

Both manual and automatic Datsuns may be towed for short distances and at speeds no more than 20 mph. If the car must be towed a great distance, it should be done with either the drive wheels off the ground or the driveshaft(s) disconnected.

Jump starting is the favored method of starting a car with a dead battery. Make sure that the cables are properly connected, negative-to-negative and positive-to-positive, or you stand a chance of damaging the electrical systems of both cars.

JACKING

Never use the tire changing jack for anything other than that. If you intend to use this tool to perform your own maintenance, a good scissors or small hydraulic jack and two sturdy jackstands would be a wise purchase. Always chock the wheels when changing a tire or working beneath the car. It cannot be overemphasized, CLIMBING UNDER A CAR SUPPORTED BY JUST THE JACK IS EXTREMELY DANGEROUS.

Tune-Up

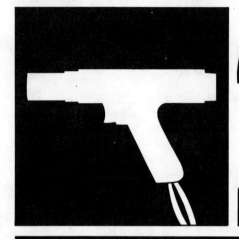

The following procedures are specific ones for your Datsun. To help you should the car need more than a regular tune-up. See Chapter 11, "Troubleshooting," for engine troubleshooting procedures.

TUNE-UP PROCEDURES

The following procedures will show you exactly how to tune your Datsun. For 1973–79 models, Datsun recommends a tune-up, including distributor points (unless equipped with electronic ignition), and spark plugs every 12,000 miles.

In 1980, Datsun began using a new, more durable spark plug in all models sold in the United States. Datsun recommends that the new plugs be replaced every 30,000 miles or 24 months, which ever comes first. Certain 1980 Canadian Datsuns still use the conventional 12 month, 12,000 mile spark plugs. All United States 1980 models have electronic ignition systems, so there are no breaker points and condenser to replace.

Even though the manufacturer suggests a 30,000 mile, 24 month spark plug replacement span for 1980 U.S.A. models, it would be wise to remove the plugs and inspect them every 12,000 miles.

If you're experiencing some specific problem with your engine, turn to Chapter 11, "Troubleshooting," and follow the programmed format until you pinpoint the trouble. If you're just doing a tune-up to restore your Datsun's pep and economy, proceed with the following steps.

It might be noted that the tune-up is a good time to take a look around the engine compartment for problems in the making, such as oil and fuel leaks, deteriorating radiator or heater hoses, loose and/or frayed fan belts, etc.

Spark Plugs

A typical spark plug consists of a metal shell surrounding a ceramic insulator. A metal electrode extends downward through the center of the insulator and protrudes a small distance. Located at the end of the plug and attached to the side of the outer metal shell is the side electrode. The side electrode bends in at a 90 degree angle so that its tip is even with, and parallel to, the tip of the center electrode. The distance between these two electrodes (measured in thousandths of an inch) is called the spark plug gap. The spark plug in no way produces a spark but merely provides a gap across which the current can arc. The coil produces anywhere from 20,000

Tune-Up Specifications

When analyzing compression test results, look for uniformity among cylinders, rather than specific pressures.

| Year | Model | Spark Plug | | Distributor | | Ignition Timing (deg) | | Fuel Pump Pressure (psi) | Idle Speed (rpm) | | Valve Clearance (in.) | | Percentage of CO at Idle |
		Type	Gap (in.)	Point Dwell (deg)	Point Gap (in.)	MT	AT		MT	AT ①	In	Ex	
1973	510	BP-6ES	0.028–0.031	49–55	0.018–0.022	5B @ 800	5B @ 650	2.6–3.4	800	650	0.008 cold, 0.010 hot	0.010 cold, 0.012 hot	1.5
	1200	BP-5ES	0.032–0.036	49–55	0.018–0.022	5B @ 700	5B @ 600	2.6	800	650	0.010 cold, 0.014 hot	0.010 cold, 0.014 hot	1.5
	610	BP-6ES	0.028–0.031	49–55	0.018–0.022	5B @ 800	5B @ 650	2.6–3.4	800	650	0.008 cold, 0.010 hot	0.010 cold, 0.012 hot	1.5
1974	610	B6ES	0.028–0.031	49–55	0.017–0.022	12B @ 750	12B @ 650	3–3.8	750	650	0.010 hot	0.012 hot	3.0
	710	B6ES	0.028–0.031	49–55	0.017–0.022	12B @ 800	12B @ 650	2.6–3.4	800	650	0.010 hot	0.012 hot	1.5
	B210	BP5ES	0.031–0.035	49–55	0.017–0.022	5B @ 800	5B @ 650	3.4	800	650	0.014 hot	0.014 hot	1.5
1975	B210 (Federal)	BP-5ES	0.031–0.035	49–55	0.017–0.022	10B	10B	3.8	700	650	0.014 hot	0.014 hot	2.0
	610 (Federal)	BP-6ES	0.031–0.035	49–55	0.017–0.022	12B	12B	3.8	750	650	0.010 hot	0.012 hot	2.0
	710 (Federal)	BP-6ES	0.031–0.035	49–55	0.017–0.022	12B	12B	3.8	750	650	0.010 hot	0.012 hot	2.0
	B210 (California)	BP-6ES	0.031–0.035	Electronic	②	10B	10B	3.8	750	650	0.014 hot	0.014 hot	2.0
	710, 610 (California)	BP-6ES	0.031–0.035	Electronic	②	12B	12B	3.8	750	650	0.010 hot	0.012 hot	2.0
1976	B210 (Federal)	BP-5ES	0.031–0.035	49–55	0.017–0.022	10B	10B	3.8	700	650	0.014 hot	0.014 hot	2.0

Year	Model	Spark Plug	Plug Gap	Distributor	Point Gap								
	B210 (California)	BP-5ES	0.031–0.035	Electronic	②	10B	10B	3.8	700	650	0.014 hot	0.014 hot	2.0
	610, 710 (Federal)	BP-6ES	0.031–0.035	49–55	0.018–0.022	12B	12B	3.8	750	650	0.010 hot	0.012 hot	2.0
	610, 710 (California)	BP-6ES	0.039–0.043	Electronic	②	12B	12B	3.8	750	650	0.010 hot	0.012 hot	2.0
	F10 (Federal)	BP-5ES	0.031–0.035	49–55	0.018–0.022	10B	—	3.8	700	—	0.014 hot	0.014 hot	2.0
	F10 (California)	BP-5ES	0.031–0.035	Electronic	②	10B	—	3.8	700	—	0.014 hot	0.014 hot	2.0
1977	B210 (Federal)	BP-5ES	0.039–0.043	49–55	0.018–0.022	10B	8B	3.8	700	650	0.014 hot	0.014 hot	2.0
	B210 (California)	BP-5ES	0.039–0.043	Electronic	②	10B	10B	3.8	700	650	0.014 hot	0.014 hot	2.0
	710 (Federal)	BP-6ES	0.039–0.043	49–55	0.018–0.022	12B	12B	3.8	750	650	0.010 hot	0.012 hot	2.0
	710 (California)	BP-6ES	0.039–0.043	Electronic	②	12B	12B	3.8	600	600	0.010 hot	0.012 hot	1.0
	F10 (Federal)	BP-5ES	0.039–0.043	49–55 ②	0.018–0.022 ②	10B	—	3.8	700	—	0.014 hot	0.014 hot	2.0
	200SX (Federal)	BP-6ES	0.039–0.043	49–55	0.018–0.022	10B ③	12B	3.8	600	600	0.010 hot	0.012 hot	1.0
1977–78	F10 (California) (1978 Federal)	BP-5ES	0.039–0.043	Electronic	②	10B	—	3.8	700	—	0.014 hot	0.014 hot	2.0
1977–79	200SX (1977 California)	BP-6ES	0.039–0.043	Electronic	②	9B ③	12B	3.8	600	600	0.010 hot	0.012 hot	1.0
1978	B210 (except FU)	BP-5ES	0.039–0.043	Electronic	②	10B	8B ⑨	3.9	700	650	0.014	0.014	2.0
	B210 (FU model)	BP-5EQ	0.043–0.051	Electronic	②	5B	—	3.9	700	—	0.014	0.014	1.0

Tune-Up Specifications (cont.)

When analyzing compression test results, look for uniformity among cylinders, rather than specific pressures.

| Year | Model | Spark Plug | | Distributor | | Ignition Timing (deg) | | Fuel Pump Pressure (psi) | Idle Speed (rpm) | | Valve Clearance (in.) | | Percentage of CO at Idle |
		Type	Gap (in.)	Point Dwell (deg)	Point Gap (in.)	MT	AT		MT	AT ①	In	Ex	
1977–80	810	BP-6ES	0.039–0.043	Electronic	②	10B	10B	36 EFI	700	650	0.010 hot 0.008 cold	0.012 hot 0.010 cold	1.0/0.5 Cal.
1978–79	510	BP-6ES	0.039–0.043	Electronic	②	12B ④	12B	3.8	600	600	0.010 hot	0.012 hot	1.0
1979	210	BP-5ES ⑪	0.039–0.043 ⑫	Electronic	②	10B ⑥ ⑩	8B ⑥	3.8	700	650	0.014 hot	0.014 hot	2.0
	310	BP-5ES	0.039–0.043	Electronic	②	10B ⑥	—	3.8	700	—	0.014 hot	0.014 hot	2.0
1980	210	BP-5ES	0.039–0.043	Electronic	②	10B ⑤	8B	3.8	700	650	0.014 hot	0.014 hot	2.0
	310	BP-5ES	0.039–0.043	Electronic	②	8B	—	3.8	750	—	0.014 hot	0.014 hot	2.0
	200SX	BP-6ES	0.031–0.035	Electronic	②	8B ⑦	8B ⑦	⑧ EFI	700	700	0.012 hot	0.012 hot	1.3
	510	BP-6ES	0.031–0.035	Electronic	②	8B ⑦	8B ⑦	3.8	600	600	0.012 hot	0.012 hot	1.5

NOTE: Emission control requires a very precise approach to tune-up. Timing and idle speed are peculiar to the engine and its application, rather than to the engine alone. Data for the particular application is on a sticker in the engine compartment on all late models. If the sticker disagrees with this chart, use the sticker figure. The results of any adjustments or modifications should be checked with a CO meter. On many 1980 cars, CO levels are not adjustable.

EFI: electronic fuel injection

① In Drive
② Electronic ignition—reluctor gap: 0.008–0.016 in. (1975–78); 0.012–0.020 in. (1979–80)
③ California models: 12B
④ 1979 Federal: 11B
⑤ A14 engine: 8B
⑥ California models: 5B
⑦ California models: 6B
⑧ At idle: 30 psi
   Accelerator fully depressed: 37 psi
⑨ California: 10B
⑩ FU model: 5B
⑪ FU model: BP-5EQ
⑫ FU model: 0.043–0.051 in.

NOTE: FU models are Hatchbacks with 5-speed transmissions sold in the U.S.A. except for California.

to 40,000 volts, which travels to the distributor where it is distributed through the spark plug wires to the spark plugs. The current passes along the center electrode and jumps the gap to the side electrode, and, in so doing, ignites the air/fuel mixture in the combustion chamber.

Spark plug life and efficiency depend upon the condition of the engine and the temperatures to which the plug is exposed. Combustion chamber temperatures are affected by many factors such as compression ratio of the engine, air/fuel mixtures, exhaust emission equipment, and the type of driving you do. Spark plugs are designed and classified by number according to the heat range at which they will operate most efficiently.

Spark Plug Heat Range

While spark plug heat range has always seemed to be somewhat of a mystical subject for many people, in reality the entire subject is quite simple. Basically, it boils down to this; the amount of heat the plug absorbs is determined by the length of the lower insulator. The longer the insulator (or the farther it extends into the engine), the hotter the plug will operate; the shorter the insulator the cooler it will operate. A plug that absorbs little heat and remains too cool will quickly accumulate deposits of oil and carbon since it is not hot enough to burn them off. This leads to plug fouling and consequently to misfiring. A plug that absorbs too much heat will have no deposits, but, due to the excessive heat, the electrodes will burn away quickly and in some instances, preignition may result. Preignition takes place when plug tips get so hot that they glow sufficiently to ignite the fuel/air mixture before the actual spark oc-

curs. This early ignition will usually cause a pinging during low speeds and heavy loads. In severe cases, the heat may become high enough to start the fuel/air mixture burning throughout the combustion chamber rather than just to the front of the plug as in normal operation. At this time, the piston is rising in the cylinder making its compression stroke. The burning mass is compressed and an explosion results, forcing the piston back down in the cylinder while it is still trying to go up. Obviously, something must go, and it does—pistons are often damaged.

The general rule of thumb for choosing the correct heat range when picking a spark plug is: if most of your driving is long distance, high speed travel, use a colder plug; if most of your driving is stop and go, use a hotter plug. Factory-installed plugs are, of course, compromise plugs, since the factory has no way of knowing what sort of driving you do. It should be noted that most people never have occasion to change their plugs from the factory-recommended heat range.

REMOVAL AND INSTALLATION

NOTE: *The 1980 California model 200SX and 510's equipped with the Z20 engine have two spark plugs in each cylinder. All eight plugs should be replaced at every tune-up for maximum fuel efficiency and power. Unplug and remove each spark plug one at a time from the high tension harness to avoid confusing the wiring.*

1. Grasp the spark plug boot and pull it straight out. Don't pull on the wire. If the boot(s) are cracked, replace them.

2. Place the spark plug socket firmly on the plug. Turn the spark plug out of the cylinder head in a counterclockwise direction.

NOTE: *The Datsun cylinder head is alumi-*

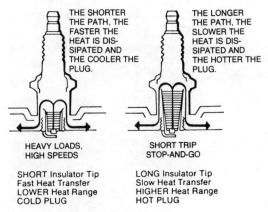

THE SHORTER THE PATH, THE FASTER THE HEAT IS DISSIPATED AND THE COOLER THE PLUG.

THE LONGER THE PATH, THE SLOWER THE HEAT IS DISSIPATED AND THE HOTTER THE PLUG.

HEAVY LOADS, HIGH SPEEDS

SHORT TRIP STOP-AND-GO

SHORT Insulator Tip
Fast Heat Transfer
LOWER Heat Range
COLD PLUG

LONG Insulator Tip
Slow Heat Transfer
HIGHER Heat Range
HOT PLUG

Spark plug heat range

Twist and pull the boot, not the wire

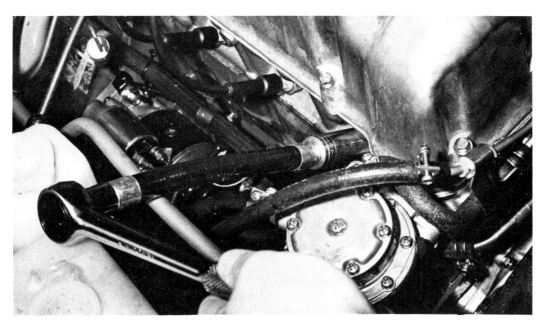

Keep the socket straight on the plug to avoid breaking it

num, which is easily stripped. Remove plugs only when the engine is cold.

If removal is difficult, loosen the plug only slightly and drip penetrating oil onto the threads. Allow the oil time enough to work and then unscrew the plug. Proceeding in this manner will prevent damaging the threads in the cylinder head. Be sure to keep the socket straight to avoid breaking the ceramic insulator.

3. Continue and remove the remaining spark plugs.

4. Inspect the plugs using the "Color Insert" section illustrations and then clean or discard them according to condition.

New spark plugs come pre-gapped, but double check the setting or reset them if you desire a different gap. The recommended spark plug gap is listed in the "Tune-Up Specifications" chart. Use a spark plug wire gauge for checking the gap. The wire should pass through the electrode with just a slight drag. Never attempt to adjust the plug gap with a flat-bladed feeler gauge; a false reading will result. Using the electrode bending tool on the end of the gauge, bend the side electrode to adjust the gap. Never attempt to adjust the center electrode. Lightly oil the threads of the replacement plug and install it hand-tight. It is a good practice to use a

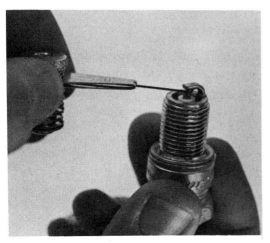

Check the spark plug gap with a wire gauge

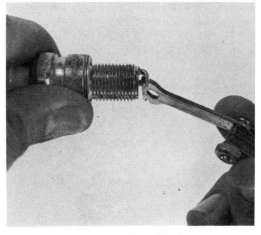

Bend the electrode to adjust the plug gap

torque wrench to tighten the spark plugs on any car and especially on the Datsun, since the head is aluminum. Torque the spark plugs to 14–22 ft lbs. Install the ignition wire boots firmly on the spark plugs.

CHECKING AND REPLACING SPARK PLUG CABLES

Visually inspect the spark plug cables for burns, cuts, or breaks in the insulation. Check the spark plug boots and the nipples on the distributor cap and coil. Replace any damaged wiring. If no physical damage is obvious, the wires can be checked with an ohmmeter for excessive resistance. Remove the distributor cap and leave the wires connected to the cap. Connect one lead of the ohmmeter to the corresponding electrode inside the cap and the other lead to the spark plug terminal (remove it from the spark plug for the test). Replace any wire which shows over 50,000 ohms. Generally speaking, however, resistance should not run over 35,000 ohms and 50,000 ohms should be considered the outer limits of acceptability. Test the coil wire by connecting the ohmmeter between the center contact in the cap and either of the primary terminals at the coil. If the total resistance of the coil and cable is more than 25,000 ohms, remove the cable from the coil and check the resistance of the cable alone. If the resistance is higher than 15,000 ohms, replace the cable. It should be remembered that wire resistance is a function of length, and that the longer the cable, the greater the resistance. Thus, if the cables on your car are longer than the factory originals, resistance will be higher and quite possibly outside of these limits.

When installing a new set of spark plug cables, replace the cables one at a time so there will be no mixup. Start by replacing the longest cable first. Install the boot firmly

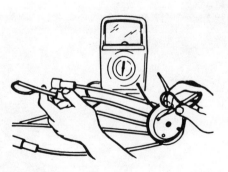

Check the spark plug cable resistance with an ohmmeter

over the spark plug. Route the wire exactly the same as the original. Insert the nipple firmly into the tower on the distributor cap. Repeat the process for each cable.

Breaker Points and Condenser

NOTE: *Certain 1975–77 and virtually all 1978 and later Datsuns are equipped with electronic, breakerless ignition systems. See the following section for maintenance procedures.*

The dual breaker point distributor was used on the 510 and 610 in 1973 as part of the emissions control system. The point sets are wired parallel in the primary ignition circuit. The two sets have a phase difference of 7°, making one a retard set and the other an advance. Ignition timing is advanced or retarded depending on which set is switching. Which set the engine operates on is controlled by a relay which in turn is connected to throttle position, temperature, and transmission switches. The dual points are adjusted with a feeler gauge in the same manner as the single point distributor.

INSPECTION OF THE POINTS

1. Disconnect the high-tension wire from the top of the distributor and the coil.

2. Remove the distributor cap by prying off the spring clips on the sides of the cap.

3. Remove the rotor from the distributor shaft by pulling it straight up. Examine the condition of the rotor. If it is cracked or the metal tip is excessively worn or burned, it should be replaced. Clean the tip with fine emery paper.

4. Pry open the contacts of the points with a screwdriver and check the condition of the contacts. If they are excessively worn, burned or pitted, they should be replaced.

5. If the points are in good condition, adjust them and replace the rotor and the distributor cap. If the points need to be replaced, follow the replacement procedure given below.

REPLACEMENT OF THE BREAKER POINTS AND CONDENSER

1. Remove the coil high-tension wire from the top of the distributor cap. Remove the distributor cap and place it out of the way. Remove the rotor from the distributor shaft by pulling up.

2. On single point distributors, remove the condenser from the distributor body. On

early dual-point distributors, you will find that one condenser is virtually impossible to reach without removing the distributor from the engine. To do this, first note and mark the position of the distributor on the small timing scale on the front of the distributor. Then mark the position of the rotor in relation to the distributor body. Do this by simply replacing the rotor on the distributor shaft and marking the spot on the distributor body where the rotor is pointing. Be careful not to turn the engine over while performing this operation.

3. Remove the distributor on dual point models by removing the small bolt at the rear of the distributor. Lift the distributor out of the block. It is now possible to remove the rear condenser. Do not crank the engine with the distributor removed.

4. On single point distributors, remove the points assembly attaching screws and then remove the points. A magnetic screwdriver or one with a holding mechanism will come in handy here, so that you don't drop a screw into the distributor and have to remove the entire distributor to retrieve it. After the points are removed, wipe off the cam and apply new cam lubricant. If you don't, the points will wear out in a few thousand miles.

5. On dual point distributors, you will probably find it easier to simply remove the points assemblies while the distributor is out of the engine. Install the new points and condensers. You can either set the point gap now or later after you have reinstalled the distributor.

6. On dual point models, install the distributor, making sure the marks made earlier are lined up. Note that the slot for the oil pump drive is tapered and will only fit one way.

7. On single point distributors, slip the new set of points onto the locating dowel and install the screws that hold the assembly onto the plate. Don't tighten them all the way yet, since you'll only have to loosen them to set the point gap.

8. Install the new condenser on single point models and attach the condenser lead to the points.

9. Set the point gap and dwell (see the following sections).

ADJUSTMENT OF THE BREAKER POINTS WITH A FEELER GAUGE

Single Point Distributor

1. If the contact points of the assembly are not parallel, bend the stationary contact so that they make contact across the entire surface of the contacts. Bend only the stationary bracket part of the point assembly; not the movable contact.

2. Turn the engine until the rubbing block of the points is on one of the high points of the distributor cam. You can do this by either turning the ignition switch to the start position and releasing it quickly ("bumping" the engine) or by using a wrench on the bolt which holds the crankshaft pulley to the crankshaft.

3. Place the correct size feeler gauge between the contacts (see the Tune-Up Chart). Make sure that it is parallel with the contact surfaces.

4. With your free hand, insert a screwdriver into the eccentric adjusting screw, then twist the screwdriver to either increase or decrease the gap to the proper setting.

5. Tighten the adjustment lockscrew and recheck the contact gap to make sure that it

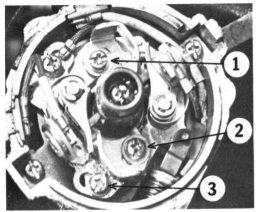

On dual point distributors, #1 and #2 are the mounting screws. Do not loosen #3, the phase adjusting screw

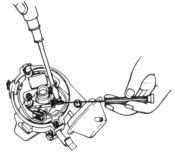

All single point distributor gaps are adjusted with the eccentric screw

didn't change when the lockscrew was tightened.

6. Replace the rotor and distributor cap, and the high-tension wire which connects the top of the distributor and the coil. Make sure that the rotor is firmly seated all the way onto the distributor shaft and that the tab of the rotor is aligned with notch in the shaft. Align the tab in the base of the distributor cap with the notch in the distributor body. Make sure that the cap is firmly seated on the distributor and that the retainer clips are in place. Make sure that the end of the high-tension wire is firmly placed in the top of the distributor and the coil.

Dual Point Distributor

The two sets of breaker points are adjusted with a feeler gauge in the same manner as those in a single point distributor, except that you do the actual adjusting by twisting a screwdriver in the point set notch. Check the "Tune-Up Specifications" chart for the correct setting; both are set to the same opening.

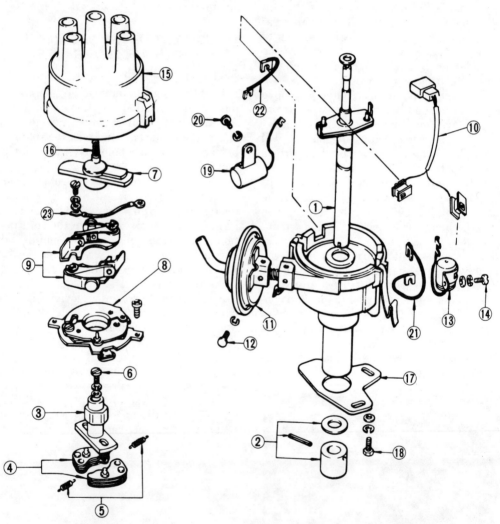

1. Shaft assembly	9. Breaker points	17. Retaining plate
2. Collar set assembly	10. Connector assembly	18. Bolt
3. Cam assembly	11. Vacuum control assembly	19. Condenser
4. Governor weight assembly	12. Screw	20. Screw
5. Governor spring set	13. Condenser	21. Lead wire
6. Screw	14. Screw	22. Lead wire
7. Rotor	15. Distributor cap	23. Ground wire
8. Breaker plate	16. Carbon point assembly	

Dual point distributor components (1973—510 and 610)

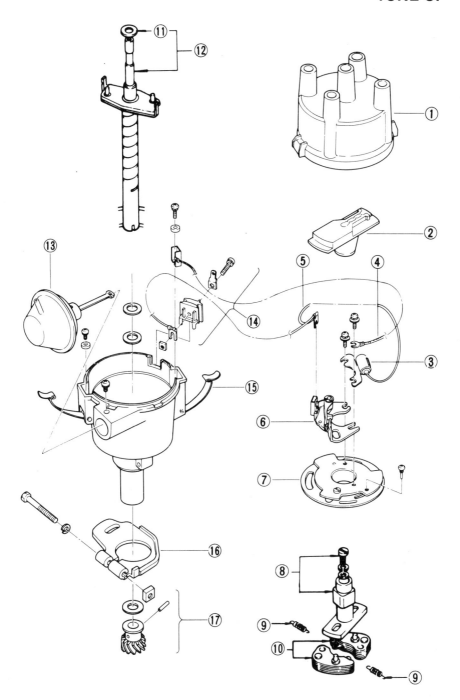

1. Cap
2. Rotor
3. Condenser
4. Ground wire
5. Lead wire
6. Breaker points
7. Breaker plate
8. Cam assembly
9. Governor spring
10. Governor weight
11. Thrust washer
12. Shaft assembly
13. Vacuum control assembly
14. Terminal assembly
15. Clamp
16. Retaining plate
17. Gear set

Single point distributor components

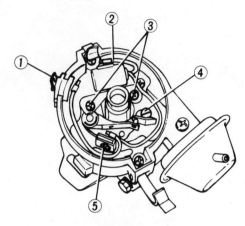

1. Primary lead terminal
2. Ground lead wire
3. Set screw
4. Adjuster
5. Screw

Single point distributor

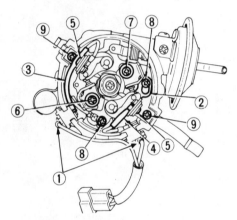

1. Lead wire terminal set screws
2. Adjuster plate
3. Primary lead wire—advanced points
4. Primary lead wire—retarded points
5. Primary lead wire set screw
6. Set screw—advanced points
7. Set screw—retarded points
8. Adjuster plate set screws
9. Breaker plate set screws

Dual point distributor. This view shows two screws (8) which must not be disturbed when adjusting or replacing points

Dwell Angle

The dwell angle or cam angle is the number of degrees that the distributor cam rotates while the points are closed. There is an inverse relationship between dwell angle and point gap. Increasing the point gap will decrease the dwell angle and vice versa. Checking the dwell angle with a meter is a far more

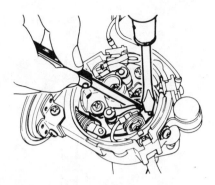

Point gap on the dual point distributor is adjusted by twisting a screwdriver in the notch

accurate method of measuring point opening than the feeler gauge method.

After setting the point gap to specification with a feeler gauge as described above, check the dwell angle with a meter. Attach the dwell meter according to the manufacturer's instruction sheet. The negative lead is grounded and the positive lead is connected to the primary wire terminal which runs from the coil to the distributor. Start the engine, let it idle and reach operating temperature, and observe the dwell on the meter. The reading should fall within the allowable range. If it does not, the gap will have to be reset or the breaker points will have to be replaced.

ADJUSTMENT OF THE BREAKER POINTS WITH A DWELL METER

Single Point Distributor

1. Adjust the points with a feeler gauge as previously described.

2. Connect the dwell meter to the ignition circuit as according to the manufacturer's instructions. One lead of the meter is connected to a ground and the other lead is connected to the distributor post on the coil. An adapter is usually provided for this purpose.

3. If the dwell meter has a set line on it, adjust the meter to zero the indicator.

4. Start the engine.

NOTE: *Be careful when working on any vehicle while the engine is running. Make sure that the transmission is in Neutral and that the parking brake is applied. Keep hands, clothing, tools and the wires of the test instruments clear of the rotating fan blades.*

5. Observe the reading on the dwell me-

ter. If the reading is within the specified range, turn off the engine and remove the dwell meter.

NOTE: *If the meter does not have a scale for 4 cylinder engines, multiply the 8 cylinder reading by two.*

6. If the reading is above the specified range, the breaker point gap is too small. If the reading is below the specified range, the gap is too large. In either case, the engine must be stopped and the gap adjusted in the manner previously covered.

After making the adjustment, start the engine and check the reading on the dwell meter. When the correct reading is obtained, disconnect the dwell meter.

7. Check the adjustment of the ignition timing.

Dual Point Distributor

Adjust the point gap of a dual point distributor with a dwell meter as follows:

1. Disconnect the wiring harness of the distributor from the engine wiring harness.

2. Using a jumper wire, connect the black wire of the engine side of the harness to the black wire of the distributor side of the harness (advance points).

3. Start the engine and observe the reading on the dwell meter. Shut the engine off and adjust the points accordingly as previously outlined for single point distributors.

4. Disconnect the jumper wire from the black wire of the distributor side of the wiring harness and connect it to the yellow wire (retard points).

5. Adjust the point gap as necessary.

6. After the dwell of both sets of points is correct, remove the jumper wire and connect the engine-to-distributor wiring harness securely.

Use the terminals provided (arrows) for jumper wire connections

DATSUN ELECTRONIC IGNITION

In 1975, in order to comply with California's tougher emissions laws, Datsun introduced electronic ignition systems for all models sold in that state. Since that time, the Datsun electronic ignition system has undergone a metamorphosis from a standard transistorized circuit (1975–78) to an Intergrated Circuit system (IC), 1979–80, to the special 1980 dual spark plug system used in 510 and 200SX California models.

The electronic ignition system differs from the conventional breaker points system in form only; its function is exactly the same—to supply a spark to the spark plugs at precisely the right moment to ignite the compressed gas in the cylinders and create mechanical movement.

Located in the distributor, in addition to the normal rotor cap, is a spoked rotor (reluctor) which fits on the distributor shaft where the breaker points cam is found on nonelectronic ignitions. The rotor (reluctor) revolves with the top rotor cap and, as it passes a pickup coil inside the distributor body, breaks a high flux phase which occurs while the space between the reluctor spokes passes the pickup coil. This allows current to flow to the pickup coil. Primary ignition current is then cut off by the electronic ignition unit, allowing the magnetic field in the ignition coil to collapse, creating the spark which the distributor passes on to the spark plug.

The 1979–80 IC ignition system uses a ring type pickup coil which surrounds the reluctor instead of the single post type pickup coil on earlier models.

The dual spark plug ignition system used on 1980 510 and 200SX vehicles in California with Z20 engines uses two ignition coils and each cylinder has two spark plugs which fire simultaneously. In this manner the engine is able to consume large quantities of recirculated exhaust gas which would cause a single spark plug cylinder to misfire and idle roughly.

Because no points or condenser are used, and because dwell is determined by the electronic unit, no adjustments are necessary. Ignition timing is checked in the usual way, but unless the distributor is disturbed it is not likely to ever change very much.

Service consists of inspection of the distributor cap, rotor, and ignition wires, replacing when necessary. These parts can be expected to last for at least 40,000 miles. In addition, the reluctor air gap should be checked periodically.

1. The distributor cap is held on by two clips. Release them with a screwdriver and lift the cap straight up and off, with the wires attached. Inspect the cap for cracks, carbon tracks, or a worn center contact. Replace it if necessary, transferring the wires one at a time from the old cap to the new.

2. Pull the ignition rotor (not the spoked reluctor) straight up to remove. Replace it if its contacts are worn, burned, or pitted. Do not file the contacts. To replace, press it firmly onto the shaft. It only goes on one way, so be sure it is fully seated.

3. Before replacing the ignition rotor, check the reluctor air gap. *Use a non-magnetic feeler gauge.* Rotate the engine until a reluctor spoke is aligned with the pick-up coil (either bump the engine around with the starter, or turn it with a wrench on the crankshaft pulley bolt). The gap should measure 0.008–0.016 in. through 1978, or 0.012–0.020 in. for 1979–80. Adjustment, if necessary, is made by loosening the pickup coil mounting screws and shifting the coil either closer to or farther from the reluctor. On 1979–80 models, center the pickup coil (ring) around the reluctor. Tighten the screws and recheck the gap.

4. Inspect the wires for cracks or brittleness. Replace them one at a time to prevent crosswiring, carefully pressing the replacement wires into place. The cores of electronic wires are more susceptible to breakage than those of standard wires, so treat them gently.

Troubleshooting

1975–78

The main differences between the 1975–77 and 1978 systems are: (1) the 1975–77 system uses an external ballast resistor located next to the ignition coil, and (2) the earlier system uses a wiring harness with individual eyelet connectors to the electronic unit, while the later system uses a multiple plug connector. You will need an accurate voltmeter and ohmmeter for these tests, which must be performed in the order given.

1. Check all connections for corrosion, looseness, breaks, etc., and correct if necessary. Clean and gap the spark plugs.

2a. Disconnect the harness (connector or plug) from the electronic unit. Turn the ignition switch On. Set the voltmeter to the DC 50v range. Connect the positive (+) voltmeter lead to the black/white wire terminal, and the negative (−) lead to the black wire terminal. Battery voltage should be obtained. If not, check the black/white and black wires for continuity; check the battery terminals for corrosion; check the battery state of charge.

2b. Next, connect the voltmeter + lead to the blue wire and the − lead to the black wire. Battery voltage should be obtained. If not, check the blue wire for continuity; check the ignition coil terminals for corrosion or looseness; check the coil for continuity. On 1975–77 models, also check the external ballast resistor.

3. Disconnect the distributor harness wires from the ignition coil ballast resistor on 1975–77 models, leaving the ballast resistor-to-coil wires attached. On 1978 models, disconnect the ignition coil wires. Connect the leads of an ohmmeter to the ballast resistor outside terminals (at each end) for 1975–77, and to the two coil terminals for 1978. With the ohmmeter set in the X1 range, the following model years should show a reading of 1.6–2.0 ohms: 1976 710, 610; 1977 810, 710.

The following models should show a reading of approximately 0 ohms: 1975 B-210, 710; 1976 B-210; 1977 F10, B-210; 1978 B-210, F10, 810, 200SX. The maximum allowable limit for the 1.6–2.0 ohm range models is 2.0 ohms. The limit for the 0 ohm models is 1.8 ohms. If a reading higher than the limit is received, replace the ignition coil assembly.

4. Disconnect the harness from the electronic control unit. Connect an ohmmeter to the red and the green wire terminals. Resistance should be 720 ohms. If far more or far less, replace the distributor pick-up coil.

5. Disconnect the anti-dieseling solenoid connector (see Chapter 4). Connect a voltmeter to the red and green terminals of the electronic control harness. When the starter is cranked, the needle should deflect slightly. If not, replace the distributor pick-up coil.

6. Reconnect the ignition coil and the electronic control unit. Leave the anti-dieseling solenoid wire disconnected. Unplug the high tension lead (coil to distributor) from the distributor and hold it 1/8–1/4 in. from the cylinder head with a pair of insulated pliers and a heavy glove. When the engine is cranked, a spark should be observed. If not, check the lead, and replace if necessary. If still no spark, replace the electronic control unit.

7. Reconnect all wires.

1976–77: connect the voltmeter + lead to the blue electronic control harness connector and the − lead to the black wire. The harness should be attached to the control unit.

1978: connect the voltmeter + lead to the − terminal of the ignition coil and the − lead to ground.

As soon as the ignition switch is turned On, the meter should indicate battery voltage. If not, replace the electronic control unit.

1979–80

1. Make a check of the power supply circuit. Turn the ignition OFF. Disconnect the connector from the top of the IC unit. Turn the ignition ON. Measure the voltage at each terminal of the connector in turn by touching the probe of the positive lead of the voltmeter to one of the terminals, and touching the probe of the negative lead of the voltmeter to a ground, such as the engine. In each case, battery voltage should be indicated. If not, check all wiring, the ignition switch, and all connectors for breaks, corrosion, discontinuity, etc., and repair as necessary.

2. Check the primary windings of the ignition coil. Turn the ignition OFF. Disconnect the harness connector from the negative coil terminal. Use an ohmmeter to measure the resistance between the positive and negative coil terminals. If resistance is 0.84–1.02 ohms (1.04–1.27 ohms, 200SX, 510–1980 California) the coil is OK. Replace if far from this range.

If the power supply, circuits, wiring, and coil are in good shape, check the IC unit and pick-up coil, as follows:

3. Turn the ignition OFF. Remove the distributor cap and ignition rotor. Use an ohmmeter to measure the resistance between the two terminals of the pick-up coil, where they attach to the IC unit. Measure the resistance by reversing the polarity of the probes. If approximately 400 ohms are indicated, the pick-up coil is OK, but the IC unit is bad and must be replaced. If other than 400 ohms are measured, go to the next Step.

4. Be certain the two pin connector to the IC unit is secure. Turn the ignition ON. Measure the voltage at the ignition coil negative terminal. Turn the ignition OFF.

CAUTION: *Remove the tester probe from the coil negative terminal before switching the ignition OFF, to prevent burning out the tester.*

If zero voltage is indicated, the IC unit is bad and must be replaced. If battery voltage is indicated, proceed.

5. Remove the IC unit from the distributor:

   a. Disconnect the battery ground (negative) cable.

   b. Remove the distributor cap and ignition rotor.

   c. Disconnect the harness connector at the top of the IC unit.

   d. Remove the two screws securing the IC unit to the distributor.

   e. Disconnect the two pick-up coil wires from the IC unit.

   CAUTION: *Pull the connectors free with a pair of needlenosed pliers. Do not pull on the wires to detach the connectors.*

   f. Remove the IC unit.

6. Measure the resistance between the terminals of the pick-up coil. It should be approximately 400 ohms. If so, the pick-up coil is OK, and the IC unit is bad. If not approximately 400 ohms, the pick-up coil is bad and must be replaced.

7. With a new pick-up coil installed, install the IC unit. Check for a spark at one of the spark plugs (see Step 4.1 in the Troubleshooting Section at the end of this Chapter). If a good spark is obtained, the IC unit is OK. If not, replace the IC unit.

1980 200SX, 510 (CALIFORNIA)

Complete step 1, under 1979–80, above. Complete step 2, under 1979–80, above: the resistance should be between 1.04–1.27 ohms. If not, replace ignition coil(s).

NOTE: *The manufacturer does not give a complete system of tests for the 1980 200SX/510 California ignition system. Therefore, before attempting anything else, try this spark performance test:*

1. Turn the ignition switch to the "OFF" position.

2. On the 510, disconnect the anti-dieseling solenoid valve connector to cut off the fuel supply to the engine. On the 200SX, disconnect the electronic fuel injection (EFI) fusible link (see Chapter 4).

3. Disconnect the high tension cable from the distributor. Hold the cable with insulated pliers to avoid getting shocked. Position the wire about a ¼ of an inch from the engine block and have an assistant turn over the engine using the starter. A spark should jump from the cable to the engine block. If not, there is probably something amiss with

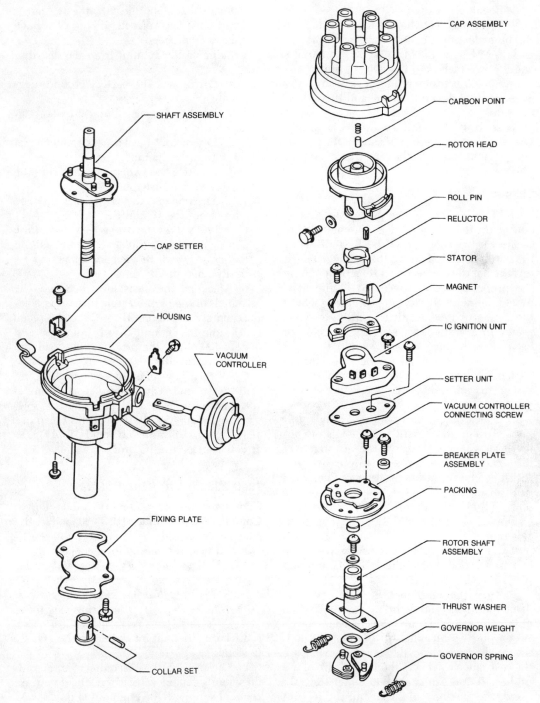

Z-series engine dual spark plug, dual coil distributor (California 1980 only)

the ignition system. Further testing should be left to your Datsun dealer.

Ignition Timing

CAUTION: *When performing this or any other operation with the engine running, be very careful of the alternator belt and pulleys. Make sure that your timing light wires don't interfere with the belt.*

Ignition timing is an important part of the tune-up. It is always adjusted after the points are gapped (dwell angle changed), since altering the dwell affects the timing. Three basic types of timing lights are available, the neon, the DC, and the AC powered. Of the

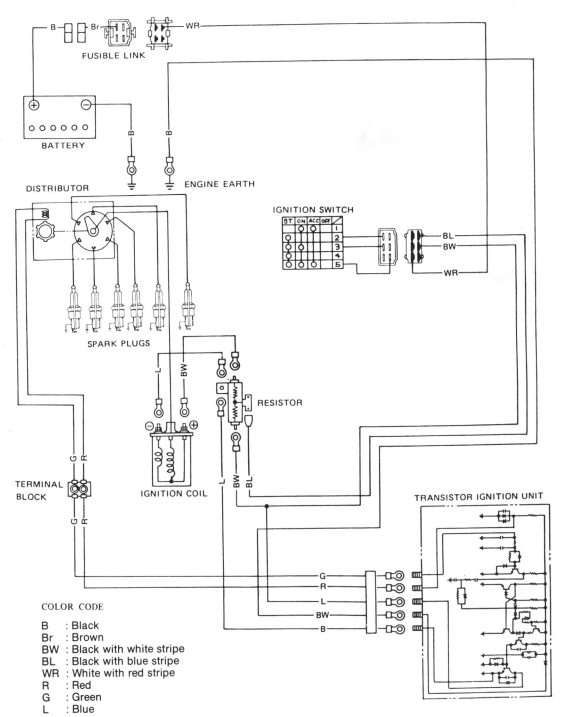

1975–78 electronic ignition schematic for six cylinder (four cylinder similar)

COLOR CODE

B : Black
Br : Brown
BW : Black with white stripe
BL : Black with blue stripe
WR : White with red stripe
R : Red
G : Green
L : Blue

three, the DC light is the most frequently used by professional tuners. The bright flash put out by the DC light makes the timing marks stand out on even the brightest of days. Another advantage of the DC light is that you don't need to be near an electrical outlet. Neon lights are available for a few

dollars, but their weak flash makes it necessary to use them in a fairly dark work area. One neon light lead is attached to the spark plug and the other to the plug wire. The DC light attaches to the spark plug and the wire with an adapter and two clips attach to the battery posts for power. The AC unit is simi-

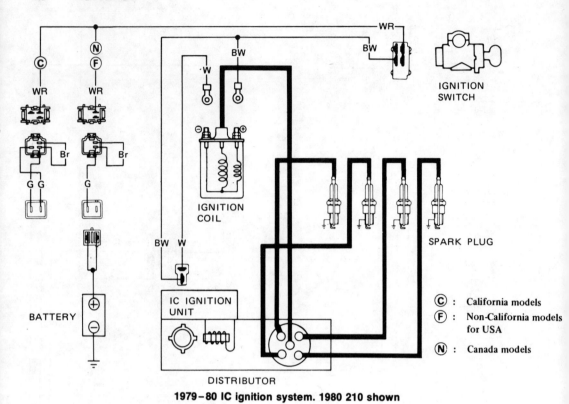

WR

BW

BW

IGNITION
SWITCH

W

C

N

F

WR

WR

Br

Br

G G

G

IGNITION
COIL

SPARK PLUG

BATTERY

BW W

IC IGNITION
UNIT

DISTRIBUTOR

C : California models

F : Non-California models
for USA

N : Canada models

1979–80 IC ignition system. 1980 210 shown

1. Cap assembly
2. Rotor head assembly
3. Roll pin
4. Reluctor
5. Pick-up coil
6. Contactor
7. Breaker plate assembly
8. Packing
9. Rotor shaft
10. Governor spring
11. Governor weight
12. Shaft assembly
13. Cap setter
14. Vacuum controller
15. Housing
16. Fixing plate
17. O-ring
18. Collar

Exploded view of 1975–78 electronic ignition distributor

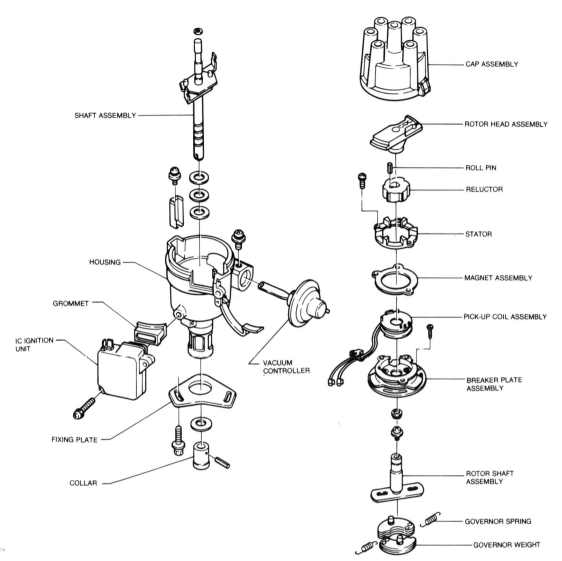

CAP ASSEMBLY

ROTOR HEAD ASSEMBLY

ROLL PIN

RELUCTOR

STATOR

MAGNET ASSEMBLY

PICK-UP COIL ASSEMBLY

BREAKER PLATE ASSEMBLY

ROTOR SHAFT ASSEMBLY

GOVERNOR SPRING

GOVERNOR WEIGHT

SHAFT ASSEMBLY

HOUSING

GROMMET

IC IGNITION UNIT

FIXING PLATE

COLLAR

VACUUM CONTROLLER

1979–80 IC type distributor. 1980 810 (six cylinder) shown

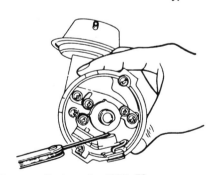

Air gap adjustment—1975–78

lar, except that the power cable is plugged into a house outlet.

Ignition timing is the measurement, in degrees of crankshaft rotation, of the point at which the spark plugs fire in each of the cyl-inders. It is measured in degrees before or after Top Dead Center (TDC) of the com-pression stroke. Ignition timing is controlled by turning the distributor body in the engine.

Ideally, the air/fuel mixture in the cylinder will be ignited by the spark plug just as the piston passes TDC of the compression stroke. If this happens, the piston will be beginning its downward motion of the power stroke just as the compressed and ignited air/fuel mixture starts to expand. The expan-sion of the air/fuel mixture then forces the piston down on the power stroke and turns the crankshaft.

Because it takes a fraction of a second for the spark plug to ignite the mixture in the cylinder, the spark plug must fire a little before the piston reaches TDC. Otherwise, the mixture will not be completely ignited as the piston passes TDC and the full power of the explosion will not be used by the engine.

The timing measurement is given in degrees of crankshaft rotation before the piston reaches TDC (BTDC). If the setting for the ignition timing is 5° BTDC, the spark plug must fire 5° before each piston reaches TDC. This only holds true, however, when the engine is at idle speed.

As the engine speed increases, the pistons go faster. The spark plugs have to ignite the fuel even sooner if it is to be completely ignited when the piston reaches TDC. To do this, the distributor has a means to advance the timing of the spark as the engine speed increases. This is accomplished by centrifugal weights within the distributor and a vacuum diaphragm, mounted on the side of the distributor. It is necessary to disconnect the vacuum line from the diaphragm when the ignition timing is being set.

If the ignition is set too far advanced (BTDC), the ignition and expansion of the fuel in the cylinder will occur too soon and tend to force the piston down while it is still traveling up. This causes engine ping. If the ignition spark is set too far retarded, after TDC (ATDC), the piston will have already passed TDC and started on its way down when the fuel is ignited. This will cause the piston to be forced down for only a portion of its travel. This will result in poor engine performance and lack of power.

The timing is best checked with a timing light. This device is connected in series with the No. 1 spark plug. The current which fires the spark plug also causes the timing light to flash.

The timing marks are located at the front crankshaft pulley and consist of a notch on the crankshaft pulley and a scale of degrees of crankshaft rotation attached to the front cover.

When the engine is running, the timing light is aimed at the marks on the flywheel pulley and the pointer.

IGNITION TIMING ADJUSTMENT

NOTE: *Datsun does not give ignition timing adjustments for 1980 California Datsuns. The procedure has been discontinued.*

NOTE: *Refer to Chapter 4 "Emission Controls and Fuel System" for the procedure to*

check and adjust the phase timing of the two sets of points on 1973 models.

1. Set the dwell to the proper specification.

2. Locate the timing marks on the crankshaft pulley and the front of the engine.

3. Clean off the timing marks so that you can see them.

4. Use chalk or white paint to color the mark on the crankshaft pulley and the mark on the scale which will indicate the correct timing when aligned with the notch on the crankshaft pulley.

5. Attach a tachometer to the engine.

6. Attach a timing light to the engine, according to the manufacturer's instructions.

7. Leave the vacuum line connected to the distributor vacuum diaphragm on all models except 1979 210 wagons with automatic transmissions and the A15 engine and 1980 A-series engines.

8. Check to make sure that all of the wires clear the fan and then start the engine. Allow the engine to reach normal operating temperature.

9. Adjust the idle to the correct setting.

10. Aim the timing light at the timing marks. If the marks that you put on the pulley and the engine are aligned when the light flashes, the timing is correct. Turn off the engine and remove the tachometer and the timing light. If the marks are not in alignment, proceed with the following steps.

11. Turn off the engine.

12. Loosen the distributor lockbolt just enough so that the distributor can be turned with a little effort.

13. Start the engine. Keep the wires of the timing light clear of the fan.

14. With the timing light aimed at the

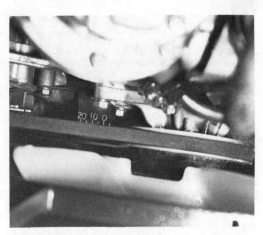

Timing marks, L-series engines

pulley and the marks on the engine, turn the distributor in the direction of rotor rotation to retard the spark, and in the opposite direction of rotor rotation to advance the spark. Align the marks on the pulley and the engine with the flashes of the timing light. Tighten the hold-down bolt.

Valve Lash

Valve adjustment determines how far the valves enter the cylinder and how long they stay open and closed.

If the valve clearance is too large, part of the lift of the camshaft will be used in removing the excessive clearance. Consequently, the valve will not be opening as far as it should. This condition has two effects: the valve train components will emit a tapping sound as they take up the excessive clearance and the engine will perform poorly because the valves don't open fully and allow the proper amount of gases to flow into and out of the engine.

If the valve clearance is too small, the intake valves and the exhaust valves will open too far and they will not fully seat on the cylinder head when they close. When a valve seats itself on the cylinder head, it does two things: it seals the combustion chamber so that none of the gases in the cylinder escape and it cools itself by transferring some of the heat it absorbs from the combustion in the cylinder to the cylinder head and to the engine's cooling system. If the valve clearance is too small, the engine will run poorly because of the gases escaping from the combustion chamber. The valves will also become overheated and will warp, since they cannot transfer heat unless they are touching the valve seat in the cylinder head.

NOTE: *While all valve adjustments must be made as accurately as possible, it is better to have the valve adjustment slightly loose than slightly tight, as a burned valve may result from overly tight adjustments.*

VALVE ADJUSTMENT—1200, B210, F10, 210, AND 310

1. Run the engine until it reaches normal operating temperature. Oil temperature, not water temperature, is critical to valve adjustment. With this in mind, make sure the engine is fully warmed up since this is the only way to make sure the parts have reached their full expansion. Generally speaking, this takes around fifteen minutes. After the en-

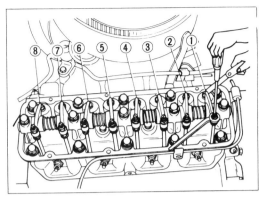

Adjusting A-series valve clearances

gine has reached normal operating temperature, shut it off.

2. Purchase a new valve cover gasket before removing the valve cover. The new silicone gasket sealers are just as good or better if you can't find a gasket.

3. Note the location of any hoses or wires which may interfere with valve cover removal, disconnect them and move them aside. Then, remove the bolts which hold the valve cover in place.

4. After the valve cover has been removed, the next step is to get the number one piston at TDC on the compression stroke. There are at least two ways to do it; you can bump the engine over with the starter or turn it over by using a wrench on the front pulley attaching bolt. The easiest way to find TDC is to turn the engine over slowly with a wrench (after first removing no. 1 plug) until the piston is at the top of its stroke and the TDC timing mark on the crankshaft pulley is in alignment with the timing mark pointer. At this point, the valves for no. 1 should be closed.

NOTE: *Make sure both valves are closed with the valve springs up as high as they will go. An easy way to find the compression stroke is to remove the distributor cap and see toward which spark plug lead the rotor is pointing. If the rotor points to number one spark plug lead, number one cylinder is on its compression stroke. When the rotor points to number two spark plug lead, number two cylinder is on its compression stroke, etc.*

5. With no. 1 piston at TDC of the compression stroke, check the clearance on valves Nos. 1, 2, 3, and 5 (counting from the front to the rear).

6. To adjust the clearance, loosen the locknut with a wrench and turn the adjuster

with a screwdriver while holding the locknut. The correct size feeler gauge should pass with a slight drag between the rocker arm and the valve stem.

7. Turn the crankshaft one full revolution to position the no. 4 piston at TDC of the compression stroke. Adjust valves nos. 4, 6, 7, and 8 in the same manner as the first four.

8. Replace the valve cover.

VALVE ADJUSTMENT—1973–79 510, 610, 710, 1977–79, 200SX

1. The valves are adjusted with the engine at normal operating temperature. Oil temperature, and the resultant parts expansion, is much more important than water temperature. Run the engine for at least fifteen minutes to ensure that all the parts have reached their full expansion. After the engine is warmed up, shut it off.

2. Purchase either a new gasket or some silicone gasket seal before removing the camshaft cover. Note the location of any wires and hoses which may interfere with cam cover removal, disconnect them and move them aside. Then remove the bolts which hold the cam cover in place and remove the cam cover.

3. Place a wrench on the crankshaft pulley bolt and turn the engine over until the valves for No. 1 cylinder are closed. When both cam lobes are pointing up, the valves are closed. If you have not done this before, it is a good idea to turn the engine over slowly several times and watch the valve action until you have a clear idea of just when the valve is closed.

4. Check the clearance of the intake and exhaust valves. You can differentiate between them by lining them up with the tubes of the intake and exhaust manifolds. The correct size feeler gauge should pass between

Valve lash adjustment, L-series engines

the base circle of the cam and the rocker arm with just a slight drag. Be sure the feeler gauge is inserted *straight* and not on an angle.

5. If the valves need adjustment, loosen the locking nut and then adjust the clearance with the adjusting screw. You will probably find it necessary to hold the locking nut while you turn the adjuster. After you have the correct clearance, tighten the locking nut and recheck the clearance. Remember, it's better to have them too loose than too tight, especially exhaust valves.

6. Repeat this procedure until you have checked and/or adjusted all the valves. Keep in mind that all that is necessary is to have the valves closed and the camshaft lobes pointing up. It is not particularly important what stroke the engine is on.

7. Install the cam cover gasket, the cam cover, and any wires and hoses which were removed.

VALVE ADJUSTMENT—810

1977 810 engines must be "overnight" cold before the valves can be adjusted. They must not be operated for about eight hours before adjustment. 1978–80 810 engines are adjusted hot.

NOTE: *Skip steps 7 and 8 if you have a 1978–80 810: Complete steps 7 and 8 if you have a 1977 810.*

1. Note the locations of all hoses or wires that would interfere with valve cover removal, disconnect them and move them aside. Then, remove the six bolts which hold the valve cover in place.

2. Bump one end of the cover sharply to loosen the gasket and then pull the valve cover off the engine vertically.

3. Crank the engine with the starter until both No. 1 cylinder valves (No. 1 is at the front) are closed (the lobes are pointed upward), and the timing mark on the crankshaft pulley is lined up approximately as it would be when the No. 1 spark plug fires.

4. Adjust the No. 1 cylinder intake valve to 0.008 in. (0.20 mm). First loosen the pivot locking nut and then insert the feeler gauge between the cam and cam follower. Adjust the pivot screw until there is a slight pull on the gauge when it is inserted *straight* between the cam and follower. Then, tighten the locking nut, recheck the adjustment, and correct as necessary.

5. Repeat the procedure for the No. 1 cyl-

inder exhaust valve, but use a 0.010 in. (0.25 mm) gauge.

You can differentiate between the intake and exhaust valves by lining them up with the tubes of the intake and exhaust manifolds.

6. Repeat Steps 4 and 5 for the other cylinders, going in the firing order of 1-5-3-6-2-4. Turn the engine ahead ⅓ turn before adjusting the valves for each cylinder so that the lobes will point upward.

7. Reinstall the valve cover gasket and hoses, start the engine, and operate it until it is fully warmed up.

8. Repeat the entire valve adjustment procedure using the gauges specified in the "Tune-Up" chart, but do not loosen the locking nuts unless the gauge indicates that adjustment is required.

9. When all valves are at hot specifications, clean all traces of old gasket material from the valve cover and the head. Install the new gasket in the valve cover with sealer and install the valve cover. Tighten the valve cover bolts evenly in several stages going around the cover to ensure a good seal. Reconnect all hoses and wires securely and operate the engine to check for leaks.

VALVE ADJUSTMENT—1980 510 AND 200SX WITH Z20 ENGINES

1. The valves must be adjusted with the engine warm, so start the car and run the engine until the needle on the temperature gauge reaches the middle of the gauge. After the engine is warm, shut it off.

2. Purchase either a new gasket or some silicone gasket sealer before removing the camshaft cover. Counting on the old gasket to be in good shape is a losing proposition; always use new gaskets. Note the location of any wires and hoses which may interfere with cam cover removal, disconnect them and move them to one side. Remove the bolts holding the cover in place and remove the cover. Remember, the engine will be hot, so be careful.

3. Place a wrench on the crankshaft pulley bolt and turn the engine over until the first cam lobe behind the camshaft timing chain sprocket is pointing straight down.

NOTE: *If you decide to turn the engine by "bumping" it with the starter, be sure to disconnect the high tension wire from the coil(s) to prevent the engine from accidentally starting and spewing oil all over the engine compartment.*

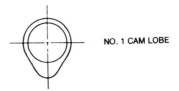

Z-series engines: cam lobe pointing straight down

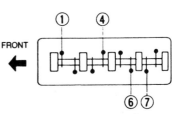

Primary adjustment, Z-series engines

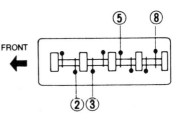

Secondary adjustment, Z-series engines

CAUTION: *Never attempt to turn the engine by using a wrench on the camshaft sprocket bolt; there is a one to two turning ratio between the camshaft and the crankshaft which will put a tremendous strain on the timing chain.*

4. See the illustration marked "Primary adjustment" and adjust valves (1), (4), (6), and (7) to 0.012 in. using a flate-bladed feeler gauge. The feeler gauge should pass between the valve stem end and the rocker arm screw with a very slight drag. Insert the feeler gauge *straight*, not at an angle.

5. If the clearance is not within specified value, loosen the rocker arm lock nut and turn the rocker arm screw to obtain the proper clearance. After correct clearance is obtained, tighten the lock nut.

6. Turn the engine over so that the first cam lobe behind the camshaft timing chain sprocket is pointing straight up and adjust the valves marked (2), (3), (5), and (8) in the "Secondary adjustment" illustration. They, too, should have a clearance of 0.012 in.

7. Install the cam cover gasket, the cam cover and any wires and hoses which were removed.

Carburetor

This section contains only tune-up adjustment procedures for carburetors. Descriptions, adjustments, and overhaul procedures for carburetors can be found in Chapter 4.

When the engine in your Datsun is running, the air-fuel mixture from the carburetor is being drawn into the engine by a partial vacuum which is created by the movement of the pistons downward on the intake stroke. The amount of air-fuel mixture that enters into the engine is controlled by the throttle plate(s) in the bottom of the carburetor. When the engine is not running the throttle plate(s) is closed, completely blocking off the bottom of the carburetor from the inside of the engine. The throttle plates are connected by the throttle linkage to the accelerator pedal in the passenger compartment of the Datsun. When you depress the pedal, you open the throttle plates in the carburetor to admit more air-fuel mixture to the engine.

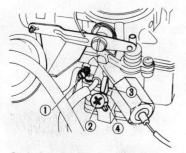

1 Throttle adjusting screw

2 Idle adjusting screw

3 Idle limiter cap

4 Stopper

Carburetor adjusting screws

Mixture screw (arrow). Note limiter tab

When the engine is not running, the throttle plates are closed. When the engine is idling, it is necessary to have the throttle plates open slightly. To prevent having to hold your foot on the pedal when the engine is idling, an idle speed adjusting screw was added to the carburetor linkage.

The idle adjusting screw contacts a lever (throttle lever) on the outside of the carburetor. When the screw is turned, it either opens or closes the throttle plates of the carburetor, raising or lowering the idle speed of the engine. This screw is called the curb idle adjusting screw.

IDLE SPEED AND MIXTURE ADJUSTMENT (CARBURETED ENGINES)

NOTE: *1980 model Datsuns require a CO Meter to adjust their mixture ratios, therefore, no procedures concerning this adjustment are given. Also, many California model Datsuns have a plug over their mixture control screw. It is suggested that in both of these cases, mixture adjustment be left to a qualified technician.*

1. Start the engine and allow it to run until it reaches normal operating temperature.

2. Allow the engine idle speed to stabilize by running the engine at idle for at least two minutes.

3. If you have not done so already, check and adjust the ignition timing to the proper setting.

4. Shut off the engine and connect a tachometer.

5. Disconnect and plug the air hose between the three way connector and the check valve, if equipped. On 1980 models, disconnect the air induction hose and plug the pipe. With the transmission in Neutral, check the idle speed on the tachometer. If the reading

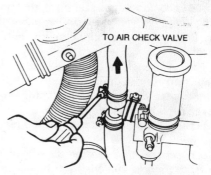

TO AIR CHECK VALVE

Disconnecting air hose between three way connector and check valve, 1978 510 shown

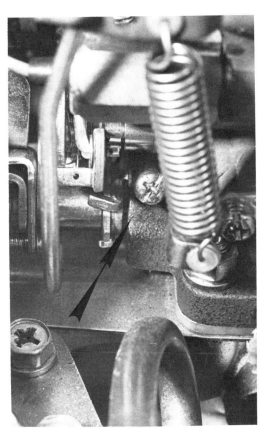

Idle speed screw (arrow)

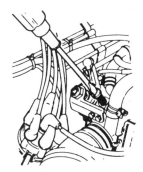

810 idle speed screw

stall it. Go on to step 10 for all 1975–79 models.

8. On 1973–74 models, turn the mixture screw back out to the point midway between the two extreme positions where the engine began losing rpm to achieve the fastest and smoothest idle.

9. Adjust the curb idle speed to the proper specification, on 1973–74 models, with the idle speed adjusting screw.

10. Install the air hose. If the engine speed increases, reduce it with the idle speed screw.

Electronic Fuel Injection (E.F.I.)—810, 1980 200SX

These cars use a rather complex fuel injection system which is controlled by a series of temperature, altitude (for California) and air flow sensors which feed information into a central control unit. The control unit then relays an electronic signal to the injector nozzle at each cylinder, which allows a predetermined amount of fuel into the combustion chamber. To adjust the mixture controls on these units requires a CO meter and several special Datsun tools, therefore we will confine ourselves to idle speed adjustment.

1. Start the engine and run it until the water temperature indicator points to the middle of the temperature gauge. It might be quicker to take a short spin down the road and back.

2. Open the engine hood. Run the engine at about 2,000 rpm for a few minutes with the transmission in Neutral and all accessories off. If you have not already done so, check the ignition timing and make sure it is correct. Hook up a tachometer. For automatic transmission, set parking brake, block wheels and set shift selector in Drive position.

is correct, continue on to Step 6 for 1973–79 Datsuns. For 1980 and certain California models, proceed to step 10 below if the idle is correct. If the idle is not correct, for all models, turn the idle speed adjusting screw clockwise with a screwdriver to increase idle speed or counterclockwise to decrease it.

6. With the automatic transmission in Drive (wheels blocked and parking brake on) or the manual transmission in Neutral, turn the mixture screw out until the engine rpm starts to drop due to an overly rich mixture.

7. Turn the screw until just before the rpm starts to drop due to an overly lean mixture. Turn the mixture screw in until the idle speed drops 60–70 rpm with manual transmission, or 15–25 rpm with automatic transmission (in Drive) for 1975–76 B210, 610, all FU models and 710; 35–45 rpm with manual transmission or 10–20 rpm with automatic for 1977–78 B210, 1979 210; 35–45 rpm (all transmissions) for 1977–79 F10; 45–55 rpm for all 1977 710's, and 1978–79 510's and 200 SX's. If the mixture limiter cap will not allow this adjustment, remove it, make the adjustment, and re-in-

3. Run the engine at idle speed and disconnect the hose from the air induction pipe, then plug the pipe. Allow the engine to run for about a minute at idle speed.

4. Check the idle against the specifications given earlier in this chapter. Adjust the idle speed by turning the idle speed adjusting screw, located near the air cleaner on the 200SX. Turn the screw clockwise for slower idle speed and counterclockwise for faster idle speed.

5. Connect hose and disconnect the ta-chometer. If idle speed increases, adjust it with the idle speed adjusting screw.

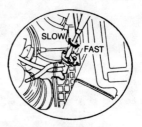

Z-series engine idle speed screw

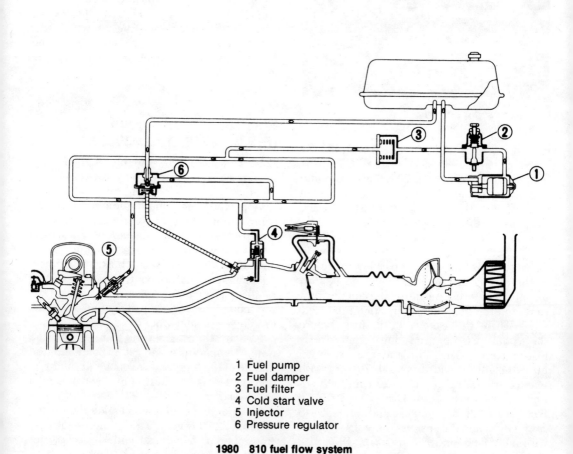

1 Fuel pump
2 Fuel damper
3 Fuel filter
4 Cold start valve
5 Injector
6 Pressure regulator

1980   810 fuel flow system

Engine and Engine Rebuilding

ENGINE ELECTRICAL

Distributor

REMOVAL

1. Unfasten the retaining clips and lift the distributor cap straight up. It will be easier to install the distributor if the wiring is not disconnected from the cap. If the wires must be removed from the cap, mark their positions to aid in installation.

2. Disconnect the distributor wiring harness.

3. Disconnect the vacuum lines.

4. Note the position of the rotor in relation to the base. Scribe a mark on the base of the distributor and on the engine block to facilitate reinstallation. Align the marks with the direction the metal tip of the rotor is pointing.

5. Remove the bolt(s) which holds the distributor to the engine.

6. Lift the distributor assembly from the engine.

INSTALLATION

1. Insert the distributor shaft and assembly into the engine. Line up the mark on the distributor and the one on the engine with the metal tip of the rotor. Make sure that the vacuum advance diaphragm is pointed in the same direction as it was pointed originally. This will be done automatically if the marks on the engine and the distributor are lined up with the rotor.

2. Install the distributor hold-down bolt and clamp. Leave the screw loose enough so that you can move the distributor with heavy hand pressure.

3. Connect the primary wire to the coil. Install the distributor cap on the distributor housing. Secure the distributor cap with the spring clips.

4. Install the spark plug wires if removed. Make sure that the wires are pressed all the way into the top of the distributor cap and firmly onto the spark plug.

5. Adjust the point dwell and set the ignition timing.

NOTE: *If the crankshaft has been turned or the engine disturbed in any manner (i.e., disassembled and rebuilt) while the distributor was removed, or if the marks were not drawn, it will be necessary to initially time the engine. Follow the procedure given below.*

INSTALLATION—ENGINE DISTURBED

1. It is necessary to place the No. 1 cylinder in the firing position to correctly install the distributor. To locate this position, the igni-

tion timing marks on the crankshaft front pulley are used.

2. Remove the No. 1 cylinder spark plug. Turn the crankshaft until the piston in the No. 1 cylinder is moving up on the compression stroke. This can be determined by placing your thumb over the spark plug hole and feeling the air being forced out of the cylinder. Stop turning the crankshaft when the timing marks that are used to time the engine are aligned.

3. Oil the distributor housing lightly where the distributor bears on the cylinder block.

4. Install the distributor so that the rotor, which is mounted on the shaft, points toward the No. 1 spark plug terminal tower position when the cap is installed. Of course you won't be able to see the direction in which the rotor is pointing if the cap is on the distributor. Lay the cap on the top of the distributor and make a mark on the side of the distributor housing just below the No. 1 spark plug terminal. Make sure that the rotor points toward that mark when you install the distributor.

5. When the distributor shaft has reached the bottom of the hole, move the rotor back and forth slightly until the driving lug on the end of the shaft enters the slots cut in the end

Firing Order

To avoid confusion, replace the spark plug wires one at a time.

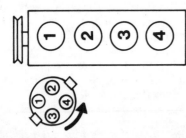

L16,L18 engine

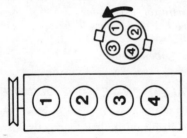

A-series engines

of the oil pump shaft and the distributor assembly slides down into place.

6. When the distributor is correctly installed, the breaker points should be in such.

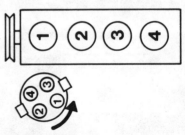

L20B engine

L24 engine

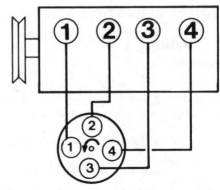

Z20E, Z20S engines (non-California)

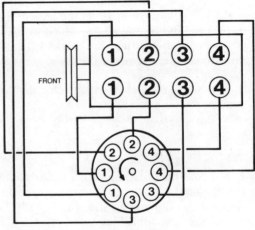

Z20E, Z20S engines (California)

a position that they are just ready to break contact with each other. This is accomplished by rotating the distributor body after it has been installed in the engine. Once again, line up the marks that you made before the distributor was removed from the engine.

7. Install the distributor hold-down bolt.

8. Install the spark plug into the No. 1 spark plug hole and continue from Step 3 of the preceding distributor installation procedure.

Alternator

ALTERNATOR PRECAUTIONS

To prevent damage to the alternator and regulator, the following precautionary measures must be taken when working with the electrical system.

1. Never reverse battery connections.

2. Booster batteries for starting must be connected properly. Make sure that the positive cable of the booster battery is connected to the positive terminal of the battery that is getting the boost. This applies to both negative and ground cables.

3. Disconnect the battery cables before using a fast charger; the charger has a tendency to force current through the diodes in the opposite direction for which they are designed. This burns out the diodes.

4. Never use a fast charger as a booster for starting the vehicle.

5. Never disconnect the voltage regulator while the engine is running.

6. Do not ground the alternator output terminal.

7. Do not operate the alternator on an open circuit with the field energized.

8. Do not attempt to polarize an alternator.

REMOVAL AND INSTALLATION

1. Disconnect the negative batter terminal.

2. Disconnect the two lead wires and connector from the alternator.

3. Loosen the drive belt adjusting bolt and remove the belt.

4. Unscrew the alternator attaching bolts and remove the alternator from the vehicle.

5. Install the alternator in the reverse order of removal.

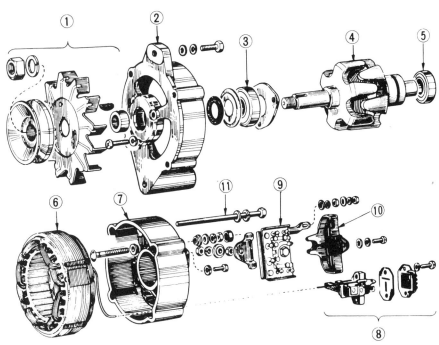

1. Pulley assembly
2. Front cover
3. Front bearing
4. Rotor
5. Rear bearing
6. Stator
7. Rear cover
8. Brush assembly
9. Diode set plate assembly
10. Diode cover
11. Through-bolt

Exploded view of 1200, B210, and F10 alternator

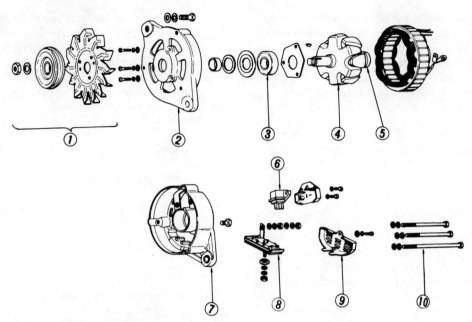

1. Pulley assembly
2. Front cover
3. Front bearing
4. Rotor
5. Rear bearing
6. Brush assembly
7. Rear cover
8. Diode set plate assembly
9. Diode cover
10. Through-bolts

Exploded view of the alternator used on pre-1978 510, 610, 710 and 200SX

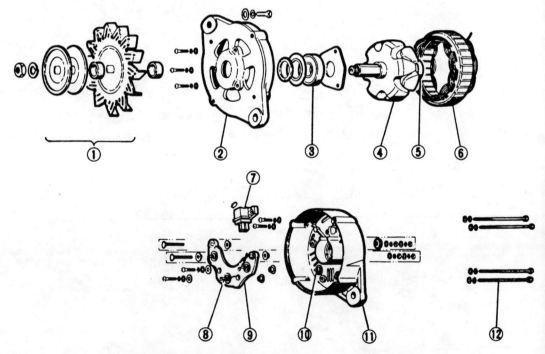

1. Pulley assembly
2. Front cover
3. Front bearing
4. Rotor
5. Rear bearing
6. Stator assembly
7. Brush assembly
8. Diode
9. SR holder
10. Diode
11. Rear cover
12. Through bolts

Exploded view of 1977 810 alternator

Alternator connections—integral regulator alternator

Regulator

REMOVAL AND INSTALLATION

NOTE: *1978–80 models are equipped with integral regulator alternators. Since the regulator is part of the alternator, no adjustments are possible or necessary.*

1. Disconnect the negative battery terminal.

2. Disconnect the electrical lead connector of the regulator.

3. Remove the two mounting screws and remove the regulator from the vehicle.

4. Install the regulator in the reverse order of removal.

ADJUSTMENT

1. Adjust the voltage regulator core gap by loosening the screw which is used to secure the contact set on the yoke, and move the contact up or down as necessary. Retighten

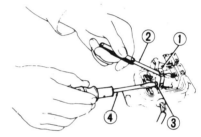

| 1. Contacts | 3. Adjusting screw |
| 2. Feeler gauge | 4. Phillips screwdriver |

Adjusting the core gap

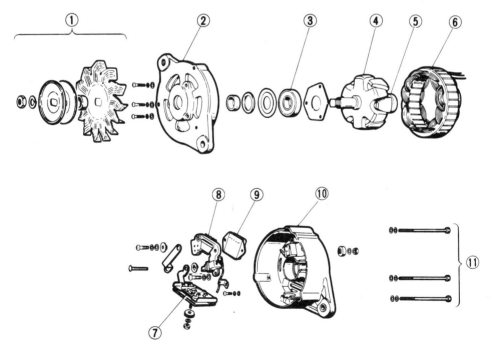

1. Pulley assembly	5. Rear bearing	8. Brush assembly
2. Front cover	6. Stator	9. IC voltage regulator
3. Front bearing	7. Diode (Set plate)	10. Rear cover
4. Rotor	assembly	11. Through bolt

Integral regulator-type alternator

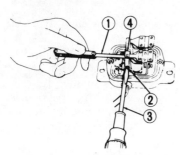

1. Feeler gauge   3. Phillips screwdriver
2. Screw   4. Upper contact

Adjusting the point gap

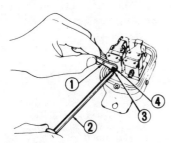

1. Wrench   3. Adjusting screw
2. Phillips screwdriver 4. Locknut

Adjusting the regulated voltage

the screw. The gap should be 0.024–0.039 in.

2. Adjust the point gap of the voltage regulator coil by loosening the screw used to secure the upper contact and move the upper contact up or down. The gap for 1973–75 models and the 1976 B-210 is 0.012–0.016 in. The point gap for all other models is 0.014–0.018 in.

3. The core gap and point gap on the charge relay coil is or are adjusted in the same manner as previously outlined for the voltage regulator coil. The core gap is to be set at 0.032–0.039 in. and the point gap adjusted to 0.016–0.024 in.

4. The regulated voltage is adjusted by loosening the locknut and turning the adjusting screw clockwise to increase, or counterclockwise to decrease the regulated voltage. The voltage should be between 14.3–15.3 volts at 68° F.

Starter

Datsun began using a gear reduction starter in some 1978 Canadian and United States models. The differences between the gear reduction and conventional starters are: the gear reduction starter has a set of ratio reduction gears while the conventional starter does

not; the brushes on the gear reduction starter are located on a plate behind the starter drive housing, while the conventional starter's brushes are located in its rear cover. The extra gears on the gear reduction starter make the starter pinion gear turn at about half the speed of the starter, giving the starter twice the turning power of a conventional starter.

REMOVAL AND INSTALLATION

1. Disconnect the negative battery cable from the battery.
2. Disconnect the starter wiring at the starter, taking note of the positions for correct reinstallation.
3. Remove the bolts attaching the starter to the engine and remove the starter from the vehicle.
4. Install the starter in the reverse order of removal.

Note the wire locations before removing the starter

BRUSH REPLACEMENT
Non-Reduction Gear Type

1. With the starter out of the vehicle, remove the bolts holding the solenoid to the top of the starter and remove the solenoid.
2. To remove the brushes, remove the two thru-bolts, and the two rear cover attaching screws and remove the rear cover.
3. Disconnect the electrical leads and remove the brushes.
4. Install the brushes in the reverse order of removal.

Alternator and Regulator Specifications

Model	Year	Alternator Identification Number	Rated Output @ 5000 RPM	Output @ 2500 RPM (not less than)	Brush Length (in.)	Brush Spring Tension (oz)	Regulated Voltage
B210	1973–74	LT135-13B	35	14	0.571	8.99–12.17	14.3–15.3
		LT150-05 ③	50	28	0.571	8.99–12.17	14.3–15.3
	1975–76	LT150-19	50	37.5	0.295	9.0–12.2	14.3–15.3
	1977	LT150-26	50	37.5	0.295	9.0–12.2	14.3–15.3
	1978	LR150-36 ①	50	40	0.295	9.0–12.2	14.3–15.3
810	1977	LT160-39	60	40	0.310	9.0–12.2	14.3–15.3
	1978–79	LR160-42 ①	60	40	0.280	8.99–12.17	14.4–15.0
	1980	LR160-42B ①	60	50	0.295	8.99–12.17	14.4–15.0
710	1973–75	LT150-13	50	37.5	0.571	8.80	14.3–15.3
	1976	LT150-13	50	37.5	0.295	9.0–12.2	14.3–15.3
	1977	LT150-25	50	37.5	0.295	9.0–12.2	14.3–15.3
610	1973–74	LT150-05B	50	37.5	0.571	8.8–12.32	14.3–15.3
	1975–77	LT150-13	50	37.5	0.310	9.0–12.2	14.3–15.3
200SX	1977–79	LR150-35 ①	50	40	0.295	8.99–12.17	14.4–15.0
	1980	LR160-47 ①	60	45	0.295	8.99–12.17	14.4–15.0
1200	1973	LT135-13B	35	14	0.571	8.80–12.32	14.3–15.3
510	1973	LT150-05B	50	14	0.571	8.99–12.17	14.3–15.3
	1978–79	LR150-35 ①	50	40	0.295	8.99–12.17	14.4–15.0
		LR160-47 ① ③	60	41	0.295	8.99–12.17	14.4–15.0
	1980	LR150-52 ①	50	40	0.295	8.99–12.17	14.4–15.0
210	1979–80	LR150-36 ①	50	40	0.295	8.99–12.17	14.4–15.0
F-10	1976–77	LT150-26	50	37.5	0.295	9.0–12.2	14.3–15.3
	1978	LR150-36 ①	50	40	0.295	8.99–12.7	14.3–15.3
		LR160-46 ① ②	60	45	0.295	8.99–12.17	14.4–15.0
310	1979–80	LR160-46 ①	60	40	0.295	8.99–12.17	14.4–15.0

① Uses integral voltage regulator
② With air conditioning
③ Optional

Reduction Gear Type

1. Remove the starter. Remove the solenoid.

2. Remove the through bolts and the rear cover. The rear cover can be pried off with a screwdriver, but be careful not to damage the O-ring.

3. Remove the starter housing, armature, and brush holder from the center housing. They can be removed as an assembly.

4. Remove the positive side brush from its holder. The positive brush is insulated from the brush holder, and its lead wire is connected to the field coil.

5. Carefully lift the negative brush from the commutator and remove it from the holder.

6. Installation is the reverse.

STARTER DRIVE REPLACEMENT
Non-Reduction Gear Type

1. With the starter motor removed from the vehicle, remove the solenoid from the starter.

2. Remove the two thru-bolts and separate the gear case from the yoke housing.

3. Remove the pinion stopper clip and the pinion stopper.

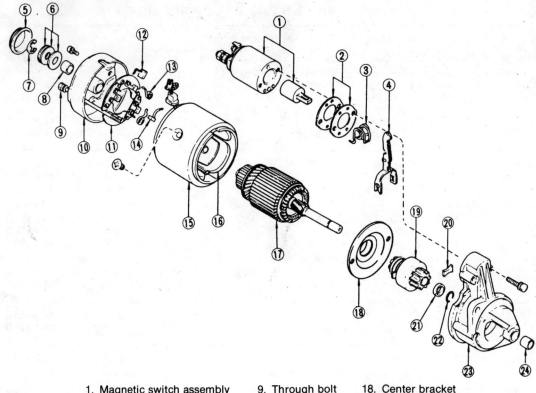

1. Magnetic switch assembly
2. Dust cover
   (Adjusting washer)
3. Torsion spring
4. Shift lever
5. Dust cover
6. Thrust washer
7. E-ring
8. Rear cover metal
9. Through bolt
10. Rear cover
11. Brush holder
12. Brush (−)
13. Brush spring
14. Brush (+)
15. Yoke
16. Field coil
17. Armature
18. Center bracket
19. Pinion assembly
20. Dust cover
21. Pinion stopper
22. Stopper clip
23. Gear case
24. Gear case metal

Exploded view of non-reduction gear starter

4. Slide the starter drive off the armature shaft.

5. Install the starter drive and reassemble the starter in the reverse order of removal.

Reduction Gear Type

1. Remove the starter.

2. Remove the solenoid and the shift lever.

3. Remove the bolts securing the center housing to the front cover and separate the parts.

4. Remove the gears and starter drive.

5. Installation is the reverse.

BATTERY

Refer to Chapter One for details on battery maintenance.

REMOVAL AND INSTALLATION

1. Disconnect the negative (ground) cable from the terminal, and then the positive cable. Special pullers are available to remove the cable clamps.

NOTE: *To avoid sparks, always disconnect the ground cable first, and connect it last.*

2. Remove the battery hold-down clamp.

3. Remove the battery, being careful not to spill the acid.

NOTE: *Spilled acid can be neutralized with a baking soda/water solution. If you somehow get acid into your eyes, flush it out with lots of water and get to a doctor.*

4. Clean the battery posts thoroughly before reinstalling, or when installing a new battery.

5. Clean the cable clamps, using a wire brush, both inside and out.

6. Install the battery and the hold-down

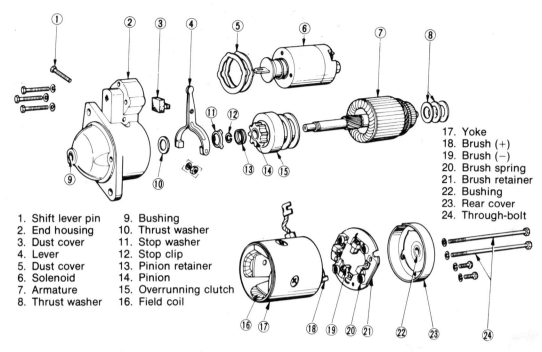

1. Shift lever pin
2. End housing
3. Dust cover
4. Lever
5. Dust cover
6. Solenoid
7. Armature
8. Thrust washer
9. Bushing
10. Thrust washer
11. Stop washer
12. Stop clip
13. Pinion retainer
14. Pinion
15. Overrunning clutch
16. Field coil
17. Yoke
18. Brush (+)
19. Brush (−)
20. Brush spring
21. Brush retainer
22. Bushing
23. Rear cover
24. Through-bolt

Exploded view of 610, 710 starter

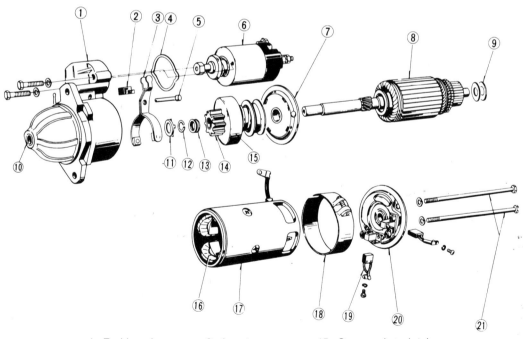

1. End housing
2. Dust cover
3. Lever
4. Dust cover
5. Pin
6. Solenoid
7. Center bracket
8. Armature
9. Thrust washer
10. Bushing
11. Stop washer
12. Stop clip
13. Pinion retainer
14. Pinion
15. Overrunning clutch
16. Field coil
17. Yoke
18. Brush cover
19. Brush
20. Rear cover
21. Through-bolt

Exploded view of 1200 and B210 starter

Battery and Starter Specifications

All cars use 12 volt, negative ground electrical systems

Year	Model	Battery Amp Hour Capacity	Lock Test Amps	Lock Test Volts	Lock Test Torque (ft-lbs)	No Load Test Amps	No Load Test Volts	No Load Test RPM	Brush Spring Tension (oz)	Min Brush Length (in)
All	1200	45	420	6.3	6.5 MT	60	12	7,000	56	0.26
					7.2 AT	60	12	6,000	29	0.37
1973	510	50, 60	430 MT	6.0	6.3	60	12	7,000	64	0.24
			540 AT	5.0	6.0	60	12	6,000	64	0.24
All	610, 710	50, 60	430 MT	6.0	6.3	60	12	7,000	49–64	0.47
			540 AT	5.0	6.0	60	12	6,000	49–64	0.47
All	F10	60	Not Recommended			60	12	7,000	49–64	0.47
All	B210	60	420	6.3	6.5	60	12	7,000	49–64	0.47
			—	—	—	60	12	6,000 ①	29	0.37
			—	—	—	100	12	4,300 RG	56–70	0.43
1977–79	200SX	60	—	—	—	60 MT	12	7,000	49–64	0.47
						60 AT	12	6,000	49–64	0.47
						100 RG	12	4,300	56–70	0.43
1978	510	60	—	—	—	60 MT	12	7,000	49–64	0.47
						60 AT	12	6,000	49–64	0.47
						100 RG	12	4,300	56–70	0.43
1979–80	510	60	—	—	—	60 MT	11.5	7,000	50–64	0.47
						60 AT	11.5	6,000	50–64	0.47
						100 RG	11	3,900	56–70	0.43
All	210, 310	60	—	—	—	60	11.5	7,000	50–64	0.47
						100 RG	11	3,900	56–70	0.43
1977–79	810	60	—	—	—	100 RG	12	4,300	56–70	0.43
1980	200SX	60	—	—	—	60 MT	11.5	7,000	50–64	0.47
						60 AT	11.5	6,000	50–64	0.47
						100 RG	11	3,900	56–70	0.43
	810	60	—	—	—	100 RG	11	3,900	56–70	0.43

MT: Manual Transmission
AT: Automatic Transmission
RG: Reduction Gear type starter
① 1974 Automatic Transmission models only
—: Not Recommended

clamp or strap. Connect the positive, and then the negative cable. Do not hammer them in place. The terminals should be coated lightly (externally) with grease to prevent corrosion. There are also felt washers impregnated with an anti-corrosion sub-stance which are slipped over the battery posts before installing the cables; these are available in auto parts stores.

CAUTION: *Make absolutely sure that the battery is connected properly before you turn on the ignition switch. Reversed po-*

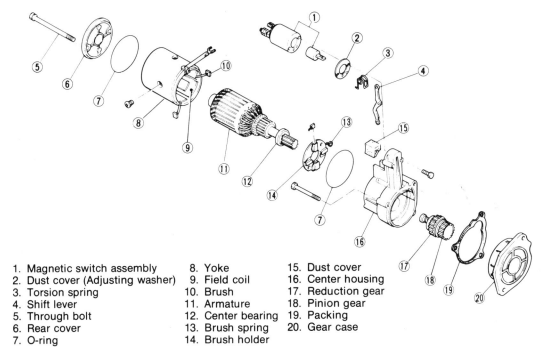

1. Magnetic switch assembly
2. Dust cover (Adjusting washer)
3. Torsion spring
4. Shift lever
5. Through bolt
6. Rear cover
7. O-ring
8. Yoke
9. Field coil
10. Brush
11. Armature
12. Center bearing
13. Brush spring
14. Brush holder
15. Dust cover
16. Center housing
17. Reduction gear
18. Pinion gear
19. Packing
20. Gear case

Gear reduction starter

larity can burn out your alternator and regulator within a matter of seconds.

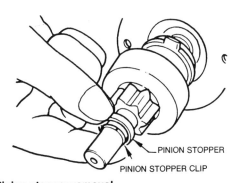

PINION STOPPER
PINION STOPPER CLIP

Pinion stopper removal

ENGINE MECHANICAL

Design

There are four different engine families used in the models covered in this book. All of the engines are of the inline-water-cooled variety, and all of them use a cast iron block and an aluminum cylinder head.

The A12, A12A, A13, A14 and A15 series of engines are used in the 1200, and B210, the 210, the F10 and the 310. The main difference between these engines is displace-

ment, which becomes greater as the number after the prefix "A" becomes greater. All of the A series engines are overhead valve engines. The camshaft is placed high in the cylinder block allowing short pushrods. Valve train reciprocating weight is reduced and higher engine speeds are possible. As with all 1973–80 Datsun four cylinder engines, the A series motors have five main crankshaft bearings with a center bearing thrust washer.

The L16, L18, and L20B engines are used in the 610, 510(1973, 1978–79), 710, and the 1977–79 200SX. These engines are all overhead camshaft designs, and like the A-series, are all essentially the same engine with different displacements. They have five main bearings with the thrust washer on the center bearing.

The new Z20E (electronic fuel injection) and Z20S (carburetor) engines are four cylinder, overhead camshaft engines with cast iron blocks, cross flow aluminum cylinder heads and hemi-spherical combustion chambers. The Z20E is used in the 1980 200SX while the Z20S is used in 1980 United States 510's. The California models of both of these engines have two spark plugs per cylinder which fire simultaneously, effectively burning all of the recirculated exhaust gases and improving idling and performance. The Z20 series engines have five main bearings with the thrust washer on the center bearing.

The 810 is the only one of the Datsun sedans to use a six-cylinder engine, a detuned version of the engine found in the Z-car. This engine is known as the L24 and is an overhead camshaft inline six-cylinder. Datsun's six-cylinder engines were developed from their OHC four cylinders, and share a great many similarities. Essentially, the L24 engine is stretched version of the L20B found in the sedans. Besides the extra two cylinders, the major difference is that the L24 engine is fuel injected while the L20B uses a carburetor. The L24 has a cast iron block, aluminum head and seven main bearings.

Engines are referred to by model designation codes throughout this book. Use the "Engine Identification" chart for the identification of engines by model, number of cylinders, displacement, and camshaft location.

Engine Removal and Installation—All Engines Except F10, 310

The engine and transmission are removed together and then separated when out of the car.

1. Mark the location of the hinges on the hood. Unbolt and remove the hood.

2. Disconnect the battery cables. Remove the battery from the models with the L16 engine and Z20E California models with air conditioning.

Engine I.D. Table

Number of Cylinders	Displacement cu in. (cc)	Type	Engine Model Code
4	97.3 (1,595)	OHC	L16
4	71.5 (1,171)	OHV	A12
4	108.0 (1,770)	OHC	L18
4	78.59 (1,288)	OHV	A13
4	119.1 (1,952)	OHC	L20B
4	85.24 (1,397)	OHV	A14
6	146 (2,393)	OHC	L24
4	75.48 (1,237)	OHV	A12A
4	90.80 (1,488)	OHV	A15
4	119.1 (1,952)	OHC	Z20S, Z20E

3. Drain the coolant and automatic transmission fluid.

4. Remove the grille on 510, 610, and 710 models. Remove the radiator and radiator shroud after disconnecting the automatic transmission coolant tubes.

5. Remove the air cleaner.

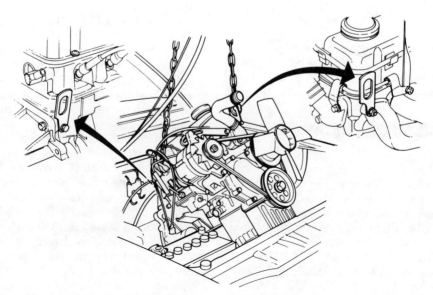

Removing the engine. The A13 is shown, but all engines are removed in a similar manner

6. Remove the fan and pulley.

7. Disconnect:
   a. water temperature gauge wire;
   b. oil pressure sending unit wire;
   c. ignition distributor primary wire;
   d. starter motor connections;
   e. fuel hose;
   f. alternator leads;
   g. heater hoses;
   h. throttle and choke connections.
   i. engine ground cable
   j. thermal transmitter wire.
   k. wire to fuel cut-off solenoid
   l. vacuum cut solenoid wire

NOTE: *A good rule of thumb when disconnecting the rather complex engine wiring of today's cars is to put a piece of masking tape on the wire and on the connection you removed the wire from, then mark both pieces of tape 1,2,3, etc. When replacing wiring, simply match the pieces of tape.*

CAUTION: *On models with air conditioning, it is necessary to remove the compressor and the condenser from their mounts. DO NOT ATTEMPT TO UNFASTEN ANY OF THE AIR CONDITIONER HOSES. See chapter one for additional warnings.*

8. Disconnect the power brake booster hose from the engine.

9. Remove the clutch operating cylinder and return spring.

10. Disconnect the speedometer cable from the transmission. Disconnect the backup light switch and any other wiring or attachments to the transmission. On cars with the L18 and L20B engine, disconnect the parking brake cable at the rear adjuster.

11. Disconnect the column shift linkage. Remove the floorshift lever. On 1200, Z20 and B210 models, remove the boot, withdraw the lock pin, and remove the lever from inside the car.

12. Detach the exhaust pipe from the exhaust manifold. Remove the front section of the exhaust system.

13. Mark the relationship of the driveshaft flanges and remove the driveshaft.

14. Place a jack under the transmission. Remove the rear crossmember. On 1200 and B210 models, remove the rear engine mounting nuts.

15. Attach a hoist to the lifting hooks on the engine (at either end of the cylinder head). Support the engine.

16. Unbolt the front engine mounts. Tilt the engine by lowering the jack under the transmission and raising the hoist.

17. Reverse the procedure to install the engine.

Engine Removal and Installation—F10, 310

The engine and transmission must be removed as a single unit. Since the F10 and 310 are front wheel drive cars, this is a fairly involved procedure.

1. Mark the location of the hinges on the hood and then remove the hood.

2. Disconnect the battery cables and remove the battery.

3. Drain the coolant from the radiator and remove the radiator and radiator hoses.

4. Remove the air cleaner and all attendant hoses and lines.

5. Disconnect the following:
   a. Ignition coil ground wire and high tension lead
   b. Wires to the distributor at the block connector
   c. Carburetor throttle linkage
   d. Fusible links
   e. Engine harness connectors
   f. Fuel line to the carburetor and the fuel return hose

Gearshift lever removal: B210, 1200, 1980 510, 200SX

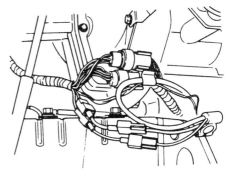

F10 engine harness connector

General Engine Specifications

Year	Model	Type (model)	Engine Displacement Cu In. (cc)	Carburetor Type	Horsepower (SAE) @ rpm	Torque @ rpm (ft lbs)	Bore x Stroke (in.)	Compression Ratio	Normal Oil Pressure (psi)
1973	510 1600 Sedan	OHC 4 (L16)	97.3 (1595)	Dual throat downdraft	96 @ 5,600	100 @ 3,600	3.27 x 2.90	8.5 : 1	54–57
	1200 Sedan 1200 Coupe	OHV 4 (A12)	71.5 (1171)	Dual throat downdraft	69 @ 6,000	70 @ 4,000	2.87 x 2.76	8.5 : 1	54–60
	610 1800 Sedan 610 1800 Hardtop 610 1800 Wagon	OHC 4 (L18)	108.0 (1770)	Dual throat downdraft	105 @ 6,000	108 @ 3,600	3.35 x 3.307	8.5 : 1	50–57
1974	710 Sedan 710 Hardtop	OHC 4 (L18)	108 (1770)	Dual throat downdraft	105 @ 6,000	108 @ 3,600	3.35 x 3.07	8.5 : 1	50–57
	B210 Sedan, Coupe	OHV 4 (A13)	78.59 (1288)	Dual throat downdraft	75 @ 6,000	77 @ 3,600	2.87 x 3.03	8.5 : 1	43–50
1974–75	610 Sedan 610 Hardtop 610 Wagon	OHC 4 (L20B)	119.1 (1952)	Dual throat downdraft	110 @ 5,600	112 @ 3,600	3.35 x 3.39	8.5 : 1	50–57
1975	710 Sedan 710 Hardtop 710 Wagon	OHC 4 (L20B)	119.1 (1952)	Dual throat downdraft	100 @ 5,600	100 @ 3,600	3.35 x 3.39	8.5 : 1	50–57
	B210 Sedan, Coupe	OHV 4 (A14)	85.24 (1397)	Dual throat downdraft	78 @ 6,000	75 @ 4,000	3.09 x 3.03	8.5 : 1	43–50
1976	610	OHC 4 (L20B)	119.1 (1952)	Dual throat downdraft	112 @ 5,600	108 @ 3,600	3.35 x 3.39	8.5 : 1	50–57
1976–77	710	OHC 4 (L20B)	119.1 (1952)	Dual throat downdraft	110 @ 5,600	112 @ 5,600	3.35 x 3.39	8.5 : 1	50–57

Year	Model	Engine No. Cyl. (Code)	Displacement cu in (cc)	Carburetion	Horsepower @ rpm	Torque @ rpm	Bore x Stroke	Compression Ratio	Oil Pressure
	F10	OHV 4 (A14)	85.2 (1397)	Dual throat downdraft	80 @ 6,000	83 @ 3,600	2.99 x 3.03	8.5 : 1	43–50
1977–78	200SX	OHC 4 (L20B)	119.1 (1952)	Dual throat downdraft	97 @ 5,600	102 @ 3,200	3.35 x 3.39	8.5 : 1	50–57
	810	OHC 6 (L24)	146 (2393)	Electronic fuel injection	154 @ 5,600	155 @ 4,400	3.27 x 2.90	8.6 : 1	50–57
1978	510	OHC 4 (L20B)	119.1 (1952)	Dual throat downdraft	97 @ 5,600	102 @ 3,200	3.35 x 3.39	8.5 : 1	50–57
1979	200SX, 510	OHC 4 (L20B)	119.1 (1952)	Dual throat downdraft	92 @ 5,600	107 @ 3,200	3.35 x 3.39	8.5 : 1	50–57
1979–80	810	OHC 6 (L24)	146 (2393)	Electronic fuel injection	120 @ 5,200	125 @ 4,400	3.27 x 2.90	8.9 : 1	50–60
	310	OHV 4 (A14)	85.2 (1397)	Dual throat downdraft	65 @ 5,600	75 @ 3,600	2.99 x 3.03	8.9 : 1	43–50
	210	OHV 4 (A12A)	75.5 (1237)	Dual throat downdraft	58 @ 5,600	67 @ 3,600	2.95 x 2.75	8.5 : 1	43–50
		OHV 4 (A14)	85.3 (1397)	Dual throat downdraft	65 @ 5,600	75 @ 3,600	2.99 x 3.03	8.5 : 1	43–50
		OHV 4 (A15)	90.8 (1488)	Dual throat downdraft	67 @ 5,200	80 @ 3,200	2.99 x 3.23	8.9 : 1	43–50
1980	200SX	OHC 4 (Z20E)	119.1 (1952)	Electronic fuel injection	100 @ 5,200	112 @ 3,200	3.35x3.39	8.5 : 1	50–60
	510	OHC 4 (Z20S)	119.1 (1952)	Dual throat downdraft	92 @ 5,200	112 @ 2,800	3.35x3.39	8.5 : 1	50–60

NOTE: Specifications given are for United States except California.

Crankshaft and Connecting Rod Specifications

All measurements given in inches

Engine Model	Crankshaft				Connecting Rod Bearings		
	Main Brg Journal Dia	Main Brg Oil Clearance	Shaft End-Play	Thrust on No.	Journal Dia	Oil Clearance	Side Clearance
L16	2.1631–2.1636	0.001–0.003	0.002–0.006	3	1.9670–1.9675	0.001–0.003	0.008–0.012
A12	1.9671–1.9668	0.001–0.002	0.002–0.006	3	1.7701–1.7706	0.001–0.002	0.008–0.012
L18	2.1631–2.1636	0.001–0.002	0.002–0.007	3	1.9670–1.9675	0.001–0.002	0.008–0.012
L20B	2.3599–2.360	0.0008–0.002	0.002–0.007	3	1.9660–1.9670	0.001–0.002	0.008–0.012
L18 (710)	2.3599–2.360	0.0008–0.002	0.002–0.007	3	1.967–1.9675	0.001–0.002	0.008–0.012
A13	1.966–1.967	0.0008–0.002	0.002–0.006	3	1.7701–1.7706	0.0008–0.002	0.008–0.012
A14 (1975–78)	1.966–1.967	0.0008–0.002	0.002–0.006	3	1.7701–1.7706	0.0008–0.002	0.008–0.012
A12A, A14, A15 (1979–80)	1.9666–1.9671	0.001–0.0035	0.002–0.0059	3	1.7701–1.7706	0.0012–0.0031	0.008–0.012
Z20S, Z20E	2.1631–2.1636	0.0008–0.0024	0.002–0.0071	3	1.967–1.9675	0.001–0.0022	0.008–0.012
L24	2.1631–2.1636	0.001–0.003	0.002–0.007	Center	1.9670–1.9675	0.001–0.002	0.008–0.012

Piston and Ring Specifications
All measurements in inches

Engine Model	Piston Clearance	Ring Gap			Ring Side Clearance		
		Top Compression	Bottom Compression	Oil Control	Top Compression	Bottom Compression	Oil Control
L16	0.001–0.002	0.010–0.016	0.006–0.012	0.012–0.035	0.002–0.003	0.001–0.003	—
A12	0.001–0.002	0.008–0.014	0.008–0.014	0.012–0.035	0.002–0.003	0.002–0.003	0.002–0.003
L18	0.001–0.002	0.014–0.022	0.012–0.020	0.012–0.035	0.002–0.003	0.002–0.003	—
A13	0.001–0.002	0.008–0.014	0.008–0.014	0.012–0.035	0.002–0.003	0.002–0.003	—
L20B	0.001–0.002	0.010–0.016	0.012–0.020	0.012–0.035	0.002–0.003	0.001–0.003	—
A14 1975–78	0.0009–0.002	0.008–0.014	0.006–0.012	0.012–0.035	0.002–0.003	0.001–0.002	Combined ring
A12A, A14, A15 (1979–80)	0.001–0.002	0.008–0.014	0.006–0.012	0.012–0.035	0.002–0.003	0.001–0.002	—
Z20E, Z20S	0.001–0.002	0.0098–0.016	0.006–0.012	0.012–0.035	0.002–0.003	0.001–0.0025	—
L24	0.001–0.002	0.010–0.016	0.006–0.012	0.012–0.035	0.002–0.003	0.001–0.003	—

—Not applicable

Valve Specifications

Model	Seat Angle (deg)	Spring Test Pressure lbs @ in.		Free Length (in.)		Stem-to-Guide Clearance (in.)		Stem Diameter (in.)	
		Outer	Inner	Outer	Inner	Intake	Exhaust	Intake	Exhaust
L16, L18, L20B	45° ②	47@1.58	27@1.38	1.97	1.77	0.0008–0.0021	0.0016–0.0029	0.3136–0.3142	0.3128–0.3134
A12, A13, A14 (1973–78)	45°	52.7@1.52	—	1.83	—	0.0006–0.0018	0.0016–0.0028	0.3138–0.3144	0.3128–0.3134
A12A, A14, A15 (1979–80)	45°30′	52.7@1.19	—	1.83	—	0.0006–0.0018	0.0016–0.0028	0.3138–0.3144	0.3128–0.3134
L24	45° ③	47@1.58	27@1.38	1.968	1.766	0.0008–0.0021	0.0016–0.0029	0.3136–0.3142	0.3128–0.3134
Z20E, Z20S	45°	50.7@1.58	24@1.39	1.959	1.736	0.0008–0.0021	0.0016–0.0029	0.3136–0.3142	0.3128–0.3134

① Valves closed
② 45°30′, 1975 710
③ 45°30′, 1979–80 810

Torque Specifications
All readings in ft lbs

Engine Model	Cylinder Head Bolts	Main Bearing Bolts	Rod Bearing Bolts	Crankshaft Pulley Bolt	Flywheel to Crankshaft Bolts	Manifolds	
						Intake	Exhaust
L16	43	33–40	23–27	87–116	101–116	9–12	9–12
A12	40–43	36–43	25–26	108–116	47–54	7–10	7–10
L18	47–62	33–40	33–40	87–116	101–116	9–12	9–12
A13	54–58	36–43	23–27	108–145	54–61	7–10	7–10
L20B	51–61	33–40	33–40	87–116	101–116	9–12	9–12
L24	51–61	33–40	33–40	101–116	94–108	②	
A12A, A14, A15	51–54	36–43	23–27	108–145	58–65 ①	11–14	11–14
Z20E, Z20S	51–58	33–40	33–40	87–116	101–116	12–15	12–15

① 1975–78 A14: 54–61 ft-lbs.
② M8 bolt: 11–18 ft-lbs.
  M10 bolt: 25–33 ft-lbs.
  M8 nut: 9–12 ft-lbs.

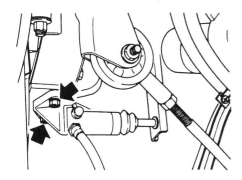

F10 slave cylinder. 310 similar

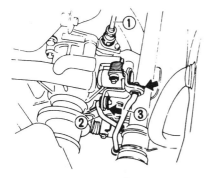

1. Speedometer cable
2. Shift rod
3. Select rod

Speedometer cable and shift rod removal: F10, 310

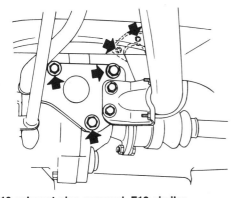

310 exhaust pipe removal. F10 similar

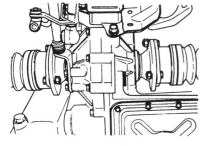

Axle shaft removal F10, 310

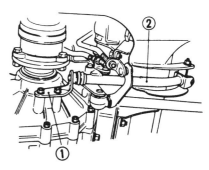

1. Link support
2. Radius link

F10 radius link support

g. Heater hoses and all vacuum hoses

h. Air pump hoses

NOTE: *On models with air conditioning, it is necessary to remove the compressor and the condenser from their mounts. DO NOT ATTEMPT TO UNFASTEN ANY OF THE AIR CONDITIONER HOSES. See chapter one for additional warnings.*

6. Remove the slave cylinder from the clutch housing.

7. Unhook the speedometer cable from the transmission and remove the shift linkage from the transmission.

8. Unbolt the exhaust pipe from the exhaust manifold. There are three bolts which attach the pipe to the manifold and bolts which attach the pipe support to the engine.

9. Unbolt the axle shafts from the differential.

10. Remove the buffer rods from the engine. Do not alter the length of the rods.

11. Unbolt the engine from the engine mounts. Unbolt the transmission mount.

12. Attach a sling to the engine and remove it.

13. Installation is the reverse of removal. If the buffer rod length has not been altered, it should still be correct.

Cylinder Head

REMOVAL AND INSTALLATION

NOTE: *To prevent distortion or warping of the cylinder head, allow the engine to cool completely before removing the head bolts.*

A12, A12A, A13, A14 and A15 Overhead Valve Engines

To remove the cylinder head on OHV engines:

1. Drain the coolant.

2. Disconnect the battery ground cable.

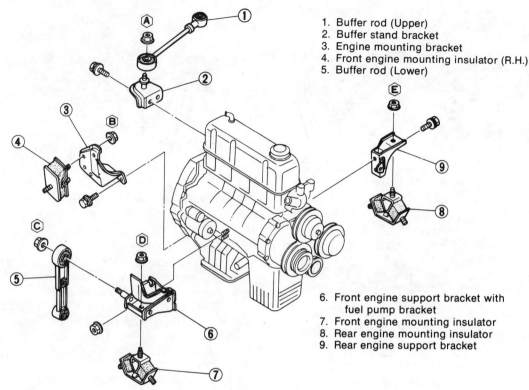

1. Buffer rod (Upper)
2. Buffer stand bracket
3. Engine mounting bracket
4. Front engine mounting insulator (R.H.)
5. Buffer rod (Lower)

6. Front engine support bracket with fuel pump bracket
7. Front engine mounting insulator
8. Rear engine mounting insulator
9. Rear engine support bracket

Exploded view—310 engine attachment points

3. Remove the upper radiator hose. Remove the water outlet elbow and the thermostat.

4. Remove the air cleaner, carburetor, rocker arm cover, and both manifolds.

5. Remove the spark plugs.

6. Disconnect the temperature gauge connection.

7. Remove the head bolts and remove the head and rocker arm assembly together. Rap the head with a mallet to loosen it from the block. Remove the head and discard the gasket.

8. Remove the pushrods, keeping them in order.

To replace the cylinder head on OHV engines:

1. Make sure that head and block surfaces are clean. Check the cylinder head surface with a straightedge and a feeler gauge for flatness. If the head is warped more than 0.004 in., it must be trued. If this is not done, there will probably be a leak. The block surface should also be checked in the same way. If the block is warped more than 0.004 in., it must be trued.

2. Install a new head gasket. Most gaskets have a TOP marking. Make sure that the proper head gasket is used on the A12 so that no water passages are blocked off.

3. Install the head. Install the pushrods in their original locations. Install the rocker arm assembly. Loosen the rocker arm adjusting screws to prevent bending the pushrods when tightening the head bolts. Tighten the head bolts finger tight. One of the head bolts

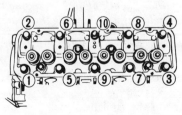

A-series cylinder head bolt loosening sequence

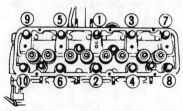

A-series cylinder head torque tightening sequence

is smaller in diameter than the others. This bolt should be inserted in hole number one, center in the illustration.

CAUTION: *The above mentioned bolt is thinner than the others because it acts as the oil passageway for the rocker components. It must be inserted in the correct hole or the valve train will seize up after a few hundred miles.*

4. Refer to the "Torque Specifications" chart for the correct head bolt torque. Tighten the bolts to one third of the specified torque in the order shown in the head bolt tightening sequence illustration. Torque the rocker arm mounting bolts to 15–18 ft lbs.

5. Tighten the bolts to two thirds of the specified torque in sequence.

6. Tighten the bolts to the full specified torque in sequence.

7. Adjust the valves to the cold setting.

8. Reassemble the engine. Intake and exhaust manifold bolt torque for 1200 A12 engine is 7–10 ft-lbs., for all others 11–14 ft-lbs. Fill the cooling system. Start the engine and run it until normal temperature is reached. Remove the rocker arm cover. Torque the bolts in sequence once more. Check the valve clearances.

9. Retorque the head bolts after 600 miles of driving. Check the valve clearances after torquing, as this may disturb the settings.

L16, L18, and L20B Overhead Camshaft Engines

1. Crank the engine until the No. 1 piston is TDC of the compression stroke and disconnect the negative battery cable, drain the cooling system and remove the air cleaner and attending hoses.

2. Remove the alternator.

3. Disconnect the carburetor throttle linkage, the fuel line and any other vacuum lines or electrical leads, and remove the carburetor.

4. Disconnect the exhaust pipe from the exhaust manifold.

5. Remove the fan and fan pulley.

6. Remove the spark plugs to protect

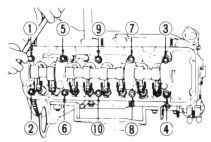

L-series engine cylinder head bolt loosening sequence

them from damage. Lay the spark plugs aside and out of the way.

7. Remove the rocker cover.

8. Remove the water pump.

9. Remove the fuel pump.

10. Remove the fuel pump drive cam.

11. Mark the relationship of the camshaft sprocket to the timing chain with paint or chalk. If this is done, it will not be necessary to locate the factory timing marks. Before removing the camshaft sprocket, it will be necessary to wedge the chain in place so that it will not fall down into the front cover. The factory procedure is to wedge the timing chain in place with the wooden wedge shown here. The problem with this procedure is that it may allow the chain tensioner to move out far enough to cock itself against the chain. If this happens, you'll find that the chain won't go back over the sprocket after you've put the sprocket back on. In this case, you'll have to remove the front cover and push the tensioner back. After you've wedged the chain, unbolt the camshafts sprocket and remove it.

12. Loosen and remove the cylinder head bolts. You will need a 10 mm allen wrench to remove the head bolts. Keep the bolts in order since they are different sizes. Lift the cylinder head assembly from the engine. Re-

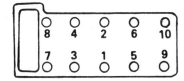

L-series head torque tightening sequence (4 cylinder)

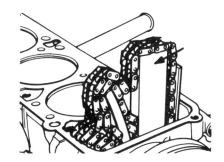

Wedge the chain with a wooden block (arrow). If you don't you'll be fishing for the chain in the crankcase (overhead cam engines)

70 ENGINE AND ENGINE REBUILDING

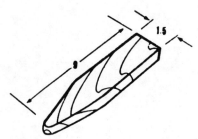

Dimensions of wooden wedge used to hold chain in place

move the intake and exhaust manifolds as necessary.

13. Thoroughly clean the cylinder block and head mating surfaces and install a new cylinder head gasket. Check for head and block warpage; see the preceding A-series engine section for instructions. Do not use sealer on the cylinder head gasket.

14. With the crankshaft turned so that the No. 1 piston is at TDC of the compression stroke (if not already done so as mentioned in Step 1), make sure that the camshaft sprocket timing mark and the oblong groove in the plate are aligned.

15. Place the cylinder head in position on the cylinder block, being careful not to allow any of the valves to come in contact with any of the pistons. Do not rotate the crankshaft or camshaft separately because of possible damage which might occur to the valves.

16. Temporarily tighten the two center right and left cylinder head bolts to 14.5 ft lbs.

17. Install the camshaft sprocket together with the timing chain to the camshaft. Make sure the marks you made earlier line up with each other. If you get into trouble, see "Timing Chain Removal and Installation" for timing procedures.

18. Install the cylinder head bolts. Note that there are two sizes of bolts used; the longer bolts are installed on the driver's side of the engine with a smaller bolt in the center position. The remaining small bolt are installed on the opposite side of the cylinder head.

19. Tighten the cylinder head bolts in three stages: first to 29 ft lbs, second to 43 ft lbs, and lastly to 47–62 ft lbs.

Tighten the cylinder head bolts on all models in the proper sequence.

20. Install and assemble the remaining components of the engine in the reverse order of removal. Adjust the valves. Fill the cooling system; start the engine and run it

until normal operating temperature is reached. Retorque the cylinder head bolts to specifications, then readjust the valves. Retorque the head bolts again after 600 miles, and readjust the valves at that time.

L24 Overhead Camshaft Engine

1. Crank the engine until the No. 1 piston is at TDC of the compression stroke, disconnect the battery, and drain the cooling system.

2. Remove the radiator hoses and the heater hoses. Unbolt the alternator mounting bracket and move the alternator to one side, if necessary.

3. If the car is equipped with air-conditioning, unbolt the compressor and place it to one side. *Do not disconnect the compressor lines. Severe injury could result.*

4. Remove the power steering pump.

5. Remove the spark plug leads from the spark plugs.

6. Remove the cold start valve and the fuel pipe as an assembly. Remove the throttle linkage.

7. Remove all lines and hoses from the intake manifold. Mark them first so you will know where they go.

8. Unbolt the exhaust manifold from the exhaust pipe. The cylinder head can be removed with both the intake and exhaust manifolds in place.

9. Remove the camshaft cover.

10. Mark the relationship of the camshaft

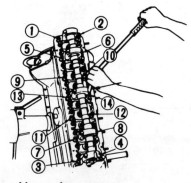

L24 head loosening sequence

O 12	O 8	O 4	O 2	O 6	O 10	O 14
11 O	7 O	3 O	1 O	5 O	9 O	13 O

L24 head tightening sequence

sprocket to the timing chain with paint. There are timing marks on the chain and the sprocket which should be visible when no. 1 piston is at TDC, but the marks are quite small and not particularly useful.

11. Before removing the camshaft sprocket, it will be necessary to wedge the chain in place so that it will not fall down into the front cover. The factory procedure is to wedge the timing chain in place with the wooden wedge shown here. The problem with this procedure is that it may allow the chain tensioner to move out far enough to cock itself against the chain. If this happens, you'll find that the chain won't go back over the sprocket after you've put the sprocket back on. In this case, you'll have to remove the front cover and push the tensioner back. After you've wedged the chain, unbolt the camshaft sprocket and remove it.

12. Remove the cylinder head bolts. They require an allen wrench type socket adapter. Keep the bolts in order as two different sizes are used.

13. Lift off the cylinder head. You may have to tap it *lightly* with a hammer.

To install the cylinder head:

14. Install a new head gasket and place the head in position on the block.

15. Install the head bolts in their original locations.

16. Torque the head bolts in three stages: first to 29 ft lbs, then to 43 ft lbs, then to 62 ft lbs.

17. Reinstall the camshaft sprocket in its original location. The chain is installed at the same time as the sprocket. Make sure the marks you made earlier line up. If the chain has slipped, or the engine has been disturbed, correct the timing as described under "Timing Chain Removal and Installation."

18. Reinstall all ancillary parts, coolant, etc.

19. Adjust the valves as described in chapter 2.

20. After 600 miles of driving, retorque the head bolts and readjust the valves.

Z20E, Z20S, Overhead Camshaft Engine

1. Complete steps 1 through 5 under L24 Overhead Camshaft Engine. Observe the following note for step 5.

NOTE: *The spark plug leads should be marked, however it would be wise to mark them yourself, especially the dual spark plug California models.*

2. Disconnect the throttle linkage, the air cleaner or its intake hose assembly (fuel injection). Disconnect the fuel line, the return fuel line and any other vacuum lines or electrical leads. On the Z20S, remove the carburetor to avoid damaging it while removing the head.

NOTE: *A good rule of thumb when disconnecting the rather complex engine wiring of today's automobiles is to put a piece of masking tape on the wire or hose and on the connection you removed the wire or hose from, then mark both pieces of tape 1, 2, 3, etc. When replacing wiring, simply match the pieces of tape.*

3. Remove the E.G.R. tube from around the rear of the engine.

4. Remove the exhaust air induction tubes from around the front of the engine on Z20S engines and from the exhaust manifold on Z20E engines.

5. Unbolt the exhaust manifold from the exhaust pipe. On the Z20S, remove the fuel pump.

6. On the Z20E, remove the intake manifold supports from under the manifold. Remove the P.C.V. valve from around the rear of the engine if necessary.

7. Remove the spark plugs to protect them from damage. Remove the valve cover.

8. Mark the relationship of the camshaft sprocket to the timing chain with paint or chalk. If this is done, it will not be necessary to locate the factory timing marks. Before removing the camshaft sprocket, it will be necessary to wedge the chain in place so that it will not fall down into the front cover. The factory procedure is to wedge the timing chain in place with the wooden wedge shown here. The problem with this procedure is that it may allow the chain tensioner to move out far enough to cock itself against the chain. If this happens, you'll find that the chain won't go back over the sprocket after you've put the sprocket back on. In this case, you'll have to remove the front cover and push the tensioner back. After you've wedged the chain, unbolt the camshaft sprocket and remove it.

9. Working from both ends in, loosen the cylinder head bolts and remove them. Remove the bolts securing the cylinder head to the front cover assembly.

10. Lift the cylinder head off the engine block. It may be necessary to tap the head lightly with a copper or brass mallet to loosen it.

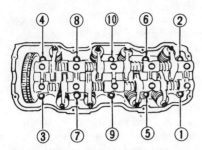

Z20 engine cylinder head loosening sequence

To install the cylinder head:

11. Thoroughly clean the cylinder block and head surfaces and check both for warpage. See A12, etc. Overhead Valve Engines cylinder head removal section for procedure. (Step 1 of assembly process).

12. Fit the new head gasket. Don't use sealant. Make sure that no open valves are in the way of raised pistons, and do not rotate the crankshaft or camshaft separately because of possible damage which might occur to the valves.

13. Temporarily tighten the two center right and left cylinder head bolts to 14 ft-lbs.

14. Install the camshaft sprocket together with the timing chain to the camshaft. Make sure the marks you made earlier line up with each other. If you get into trouble, see "Timing Chain Removal and Installation" for timing procedures.

15. Install the cylinder head bolts and torque them to 20 ft-lbs., then 40 ft-lbs., then 58 ft-lbs. in the order shown in the illustration.

16. Assemble the rest of the components in the reverse order of disassembly.

NOTE: *It is always wise to drain the crankcase oil after the cylinder head has been installed to avoid coolant contamination.*

OVERHAUL

Cylinder head overhaul should be referred to a competent automotive machine shop.

Valve guides and seats are removable and oversizes are available from Datsun. For procedures, see overhaul section at the end of this chapter.

Rocker Shaft
REMOVAL AND INSTALLATION
A12, A12A, A13, A14, A15 Engines

1. Remove rocker cover.
2. Loosen rocker adjusting bolts and push adjusting screws away from pushrods.
3. Unbolt and remove the rocker shaft assembly.
4. To install, reverse the above. Tighten the rocker shaft bolts to 14–18 ft-lbs. in a circular sequence. Adjust the valves.

NOTE: *Both the intake and the exhaust valve springs are the uneven pitch type. That is, the springs have narrow coils at the bottom and wide coils at the top. The narrow coils (painted white) must be the side making contact on the cylinder head surface.*

For overhead camshaft engine rocker removal and installation, see Camshaft Removal and Installation section in this chapter.

Intake Manifold
REMOVAL AND INSTALLATION—ALL EXCEPT 810 and 1980 200SX/510

1. Remove the air cleaner assembly together with all of the attending hoses.
2. Disconnect the throttle linkage and fuel and vacuum lines from the carburetor.
3. The carburetor can be removed from the manifold at this point or can be removed as an assembly with the intake manifold.
4. On the A series engines, disconnect the intake and exhaust manifold unless you are removing both. Loosen the intake manifold attaching nuts, working from the two ends toward the center, and then remove them.

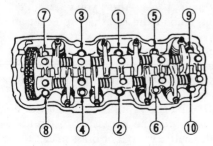

Z20 engine head tightening sequence

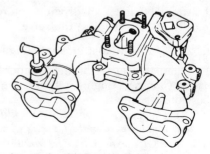

A-series engine intake manifold

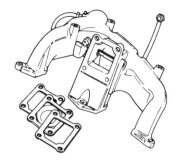

A-series engine exhaust manifold

Removing the A-series intake and exhaust manifolds as a unit

5. Remove the intake manifold from the engine.

6. Install the intake manifold in the reverse order of removal.

L24 ENGINE (810) INTAKE MANIFOLD REMOVAL AND INSTALLATION

1. Disconnect all hoses to the air cleaner and remove the air cleaner.

2. Disconnect all air, water vacuum and fuel hoses to the intake manifold. Remove the cold start valve and fuel pipe as an assembly. Remove the throttle linkage.

3. Remove the B.P.T. valve control tube

L-series engine intake manifold (4 cylinder)

from the intake manifold. Remove the EGR hoses.

4. Disconnect all electrical wiring to the fuel injection unit. Note the location of the wires and mark them in some manner to facilitate reinstallation.

5. Make sure all wires, hoses, lines, etc. are removed. Unbolt the intake manifold. Keep the bolts in order since they are of two different sizes.

6. Installation is the reverse of removal. Use a new gasket, clean both sealing surfaces, and torque the bolts in several stages, working from the center outward.

1980 200SX/510 INTAKE MANIFOLD REMOVAL AND INSTALLATION

1. Drain the coolant.

2. On the fuel injected engine, remove the air cleaner hoses. On the carbureted engine, remove the air cleaner.

3. Remove the radiator hoses from the manifold.

4. For the carbureted engine, remove the fuel, air and vacuum hoses from the carburetor. Remove the throttle linkage and remove the carburetor.

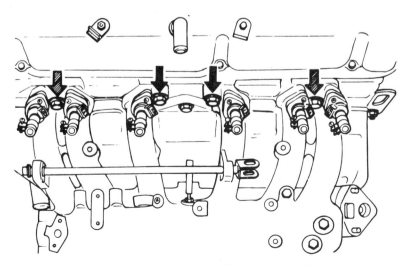

L24 engine intake manifold securing bolts

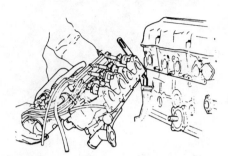

Z20E: remove the manifold with injectors, etc., still attached

5. Remove the throttle cable and disconnect the fuel pipe and the return fuel line on fuel injection engines. Plug the fuel pipe to prevent spilling fuel.

NOTE: *When unplugging wires and hoses, mark each hose and its connection with a piece of masking tape, then match-code the two pieces of tape with the numbers 1,2,3,etc. When assembling, simply match the pieces of tape.*

6. Remove all remaining wires, tubes, the air cleaner bracket (carbureted engines) and the E.G.R. and P.C.V. tubes from the rear of the intake manifold. Remove the air induction pipe from the front of the carbureted engine. Remove the manifold supports on the fuel injected engine.

7. Unbolt and remove the intake manifold. On fuel injected engines, remove the manifold with injectors, E.G.R. valve, fuel tubes, etc., still attached.

Installation is the reverse of removal. Use a new intake manifold gasket.

Exhaust Manifold

REMOVAL AND INSTALLATION

1. Remove the air cleaner assembly, if necessary for access. Remove the heat shield, if present.

2. Disconnect the exhaust pipe from the exhaust manifold. Disconnect the intake manifold from the exhaust manifold (A-series engines only) unless you are removing both.

3. Remove all temperature sensors, air induction pipes and other attachments from the manifold.

4. Loosen and remove the exhaust manifold attaching nuts and remove the manifold from the engine.

5. Install the exhaust manifold in the reverse order of removal.

Timing Chain Cover

REMOVAL AND INSTALLATION

A12, A12A, A13, A14, A15 Overhead Valve Engines

1. Remove the radiator. Loosen the alternator adjustment and remove the belt. Loosen the air pump adjustment and remove the belt on engines with the air pump system.

2. Remove the fan and water pump.

3. Bend back the locktab from the crankshaft pulley nut. Remove the nut by affixing a heavy wrench and rapping the wrench with a hammer. The nut must be unscrewed in the opposite direction of normal engine rotation. Pull off the pulley.

4. It is recommended that the oil pan be removed or loosened before the front cover is removed.

5. Unbolt and remove the timing chain cover.

6. Replace the crankshaft oil seal in the cover. Most models use a felt seal.

7. Reverse the procedure to install, using new gaskets. Apply sealant to both sides of the timing cover gasket. Front cover bolt torque is 4 ft lbs, water pump bolt torque is 7–10 ft lbs, and oil pan bolt torque is 4 ft lbs.

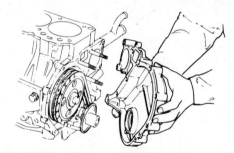

Removing the A-series engine timing cover

L16, L18, L20B, L24, Z20S and Z20E Overhead Camshaft Engines

NOTE: *It may be necessary to remove the cylinder head to perform this operation if you cannot cut the front of the head gasket cleanly as described in step 10. If so, you will need a new head gasket.*

1. Disconnect the negative battery cable from the battery, drain the cooling system, and remove the radiator together with the upper and lower radiator hoses.

2. Loosen the alternator drive belt adjusting screw and remove the drive belt. Remove the bolts which attach the alternator

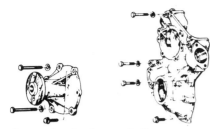

L-series engine front cover bolts

bracket to the engine and set the alternator aside out of the way.

3. Remove the distributor.

4. Remove the oil pump attaching screws, and take out the pump and its drive spindle.

5. Remove the cooling fan and the fan pulley together with the drive belt.

6. Remove the water pump.

7. Remove the crankshaft pulley bolt and remove the crankshaft pulley.

8. Remove the bolts holding the front cover to the front of the cylinder block, the four bolts which retain the front of the oil pan to the bottom of the front cover, and the two bolts which are screwed down through the front of the cylinder head and into the top of the front cover.

9. Carefully pry the front cover off the front of the engine.

10. Cut the exposed front section of the oil pan gasket away from the oil pan. Do the same to the gasket at the top of the front cover. Remove the two side gaskets and clean all of the mating surfaces.

11. Cut the portions needed from a new oil pan gasket and top front cover gasket.

12. Apply sealer to all of the gaskets and position them on the engine in their proper places.

13. Apply a light coating of grease to the crankshaft oil seal and carefully mount the front cover to the front of the engine and install all of the mounting bolts.

Tighten the 8 mm bolts to 7–12 ft lbs and the 6 mm bolts to 3–6 ft lbs. Tighten the oil pan attaching bolts to 4–7 ft lbs.

14. Before installing the oil pump, place the gasket over the shaft and make sure that the mark on the drive spindle faces (aligned) with the oil pump hole.

Install the oil pump after priming it with oil. For oil pump installation procedures, see "Oil Pump Removal and Installation" in this chapter.

Timing Chain and Camshaft

REMOVAL AND INSTALLATION

A12, A12A, A13, A14, A15 Overhead Valve Engines

It is recommended that this operation be done with the engine removed from the vehicle.

1. Remove the timing chain cover.

2. Unbolt and remove the chain tensioner.

3. Remove the camshaft sprocket retaining bolt.

4. Pull off the camshaft sprocket, easing off the crankshaft sprocket at the same time. Remove both sprockets and chain as an assembly. Be careful not to lose the shims and oil slinger from behind the crankshaft sprocket.

5. Remove the distributor, distributor drive spindle, pushrods, and valve lifters.

NOTE: *The lifters cannot be removed until the camshaft has been removed.*

Remove the oil pump and pump driveshaft.

When removing the A-series engine timing cover it is necessary to loosen or remove the oil pan

A-series engine camshaft locating plate correctly installed

6. Unbolt and remove the camshaft locating plate.

7. Remove the camshaft carefully. This will be easier if the block is inverted to prevent the lifters from falling down.

8. The camshaft bearings can be pressed out and replaced. They are available in undersizes, should it be necessary to regrind the camshaft journals.

9. Reinstall the camshaft. If the locating plate has an oil hole, it should be to the right of the engine. The locating plate is marked with the word LOWER and an arrow. Locating plate bolt torque is 3–4 ft lbs. Be careful to engage the drive pin in the rear end of the camshaft with the slot in the oil pump driveshaft.

10. Camshaft end-play can be measured after temporarily replacing the camshaft sprocket and securing bolt.

The standard end-play specifications for the A12 engine are 0.001–0.003 in. with a service limit (largest allowable end-play limit) of 0.004 in. The A12A, A13, A14 and A15 engines have standard end-play specifications of 0.0004–0.002 in. with a service limit of 0.004 in. If the end-play is excessive, replace the locating plate. New plates are available in several sizes.

11. If the crankshaft or camshaft has been replaced, install the sprockets temporarily and make sure that they are parallel. Adjust by shimming under the crankshaft sprocket.

12. Assemble the sprockets and chain, aligning them.

13. Turn the crankshaft until the keyway and the No. 1 piston is at top dead center. Install the sprockets and chain. The oil slinger behind the crankshaft sprocket must be replaced with the concave surface to the front. If the chain and sprocket installation is correct, the sprocket marks must be aligned between the shaft centers when the No. 1 pis-

ton is at top dead center. Engine camshaft sprocket retaining bolt torque is 33–36 ft lbs.

14. The rest of the reassembly procedure is the reverse of disassembly. Engine chain tensioner bolt torque is 4–6 ft lbs.

Timing Chain and Tensioner
REMOVAL AND INSTALLATION
L16, L18, L20B, L24, Z20E and Z20S Overhead Camshaft Engines

1. Before beginning any disassembly procedures, position the no. 1 piston at TDC on the compression stroke.

2. Remove the front cover as previously outlined. Remove the camshaft cover and remove the fuel pump if it runs off a cam lobe in front of the camshaft sprocket.

3. With the No. 1 piston at TDC, the timing marks on the camshaft sprocket and the timing chain should be visible. Mark both of them with paint. Also mark the relationship of the camshaft sprocket to the camshaft. At this point you will notice that there are three sets of timing marks and locating holes in the sprocket. They are for making adjustments to compensate for timing chain stretch. See the following "Timing Chain Adjustment" for more details.

4. With the timing marks on the cam sprocket clearly marked, locate and mark the

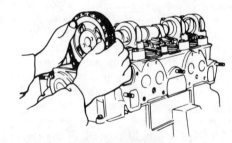

Removing the camshaft sprocket

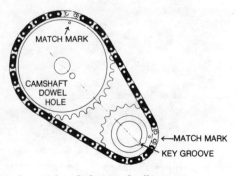

A-series engine timing mark alignment

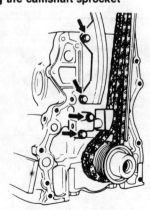

Tensioner and chain guide removal

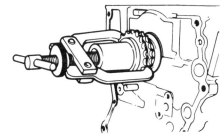

Crankshaft sprocket removal

1. Fuel pump drive cam
2. Chain guide
3. Chain tensioner
4. Crank sprocket
5. Cam sprocket
6. Chain guide

Timing chain and sprocket alignment—L-series engine

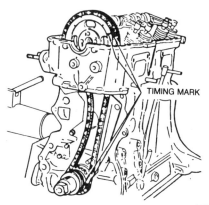

TIMING MARK

Timing chain and sprocket alignments—Z20 engines

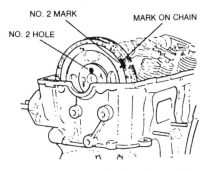

NO. 2 MARK

MARK ON CHAIN

NO. 2 HOLE

Use the No. 2 mark and hole to align camshaft—Z20 engines

timing marks on the crankshaft sprocket. Also mark the chain timing mark. Of course, if the chain is not to be re-used, marking it is useless.

5. Unbolt the camshaft sprocket and remove the sprocket along with the chain. As you remove the chain, hold it where the chain tensioner contacts it. When the chain is removed, the tensioner is going to come apart. Hold on to it and you won't lose any of the parts. There is no need to remove the chain guide unless it is being replaced.

6. Install the timing chain and the camshaft sprocket together after first positioning the chain over the crankshaft sprocket. Position the sprocket so that the marks made earlier line up. This is assuming that the engine has not been disturbed. The camshaft and crankshaft keys should both be pointing upward. If a new chain and/or gear is being installed, position the sprocket so that the timing marks on the chain align with the marks on the crankshaft sprocket and the camshaft sprocket (with both keys pointing up). The marks are on the right-hand side of the sprockets as you face the engine. The L16 and L18 have 42 pins between the mating marks of the chain and sprockets when the chain is installed correctly. The L20B has 44 pins. The L24 engine used in the 810 has 42

pins between timing marks. The Z20E and Z20S engines do not use the pin counting method for finding correct valve timing. Instead, position the key in the crankshaft sprocket so that it is pointing upward and install the camshaft sprocket on the camshaft with its dowel pin at the top using the number 2 mounting hole and timing mark. The painted links of the chain should be on the right hand side of the sprockets as you face the engine. See the illustration.

NOTE: *The factory manual refers to the pins you are to count in the L-series engines as links, but in America, this is not correct. Count the pins. There are two pins per link. This is an important step. If you do not get the exact number of pins between the timing marks, valve timing will be incorrect and the engine will either not run at all, in which case you may stand the chance of bending the valves, or the engine will run very feebly.*

7. Install the chain tensioner. Install the remaining components in the reverse order of disassembly.

TIMING CHAIN ADJUSTMENT

L16, L18, L20B, L24, Z20E and Z20S Overhead Camshaft Engines

When the timing chain stretches excessively, the valve timing will be adversely affected. There are three sets of holes and timing marks on the camshaft sprocket.

If the stretch of the chain roller links is excessive, adjust the camshaft sprocket location by transferring the set position of the camshaft sprocket from the factory position of no. 1 or no. 2 to one of the other positions as follows:

1. Turn the crankshaft until the no. 1 piston is at TDC on the compression stroke. Examine whether the camshaft sprocket location notch is to the left of the oblong groove on the camshaft retaining plate. If the notch in the sprocket is to the left of the groove in the retaining plate, then the chain is stretched and needs adjusting.

2. Remove the camshaft sprocket together with the chain and reinstall the sprocket and chain with the locating dowel on the camshaft inserted into either the no. 2 or 3 hole of the sprocket. The timing mark on the timing chain must be aligned with the mark on the sprocket. The amount of modification is 4 degrees of crankshaft rotation for each mark.

3. Recheck the valve timing as outlined in Step 1. The notch in the sprocket should be to the right of the groove in the camshaft retaining plate.

4. If and when the notch cannot be brought to the right of the groove, the timing chain is worn beyond repair and must be replaced.

Camshaft

REMOVAL AND INSTALLATION

L16, L18, L20B, and L24 Overhead Camshaft Engines

1. Removal of the cylinder head from the engine is optional. Remove the camshaft sprocket from the camshaft together with the timing chain.

2. Loosen the valve rocker pivot locknut and remove the rocker arm by pressing down on the valve spring.

3. Remove the two retaining nuts on the camshaft retainer plate at the front of the cylinder head and carefully slide the camshaft out of the camshaft carrier.

4. Lightly coat the camshaft bearings with clean motor oil and carefully slide the camshaft in place in the camshaft carrier.

5. Install the camshaft retainer plate with the oblong groove in the face of the plate facing toward the front of the engine.

6. Check the valve timing as outlined under "Timing Chain Removal and Installation" and install the timing sprocket on the camshaft, tightening the bolt together with the fuel pump cam to 86–116 ft lbs.

7. Install the rocker arms by pressing down the valve springs with a screwdriver and install the valve rocker springs.

8. Install the cylinder head, if it was removed, and assemble the rest of the engine in the reverse order of removal.

Z20E, Z20S Camshaft Removal and Installation

1. Removal of the cylinder head from the engine is optional. Remove the camshaft

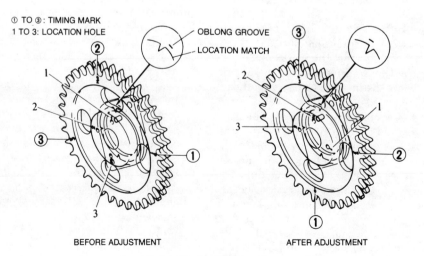

TO ③: TIMING MARK
1 TO 3: LOCATION HOLE

OBLONG GROOVE
LOCATION MATCH

BEFORE ADJUSTMENT   AFTER ADJUSTMENT

Timing chain adjustment

sprocket from the camshaft together with the timing chain. After setting No. 1 piston at TDC on its compression stroke.

2. Loosen the bolts holding the rocker shaft assembly in place and remove the six center bolts. Do not pull the four end bolts out of the rocker assembly because they hold the unit together.

CAUTION: *When loosening the bolts, work from the ends in and loosen all of the bolts a little at a time so that you do not strain the camshaft or the rocker assembly. Remember, the camshaft is under pressure from the valve springs.*

3. After removing the rocker assembly, remove the camshaft.

NOTE: *Keep the disassembled parts in order.*

If you need to disassemble the rocker unit, assemble as follows.

4. Install the mounting brackets, valve rockers and springs observing the following considerations.

The two rocker shafts are different. Both have punch marks in the ends that face the front of the engine. The rocker shaft that goes on the side the intake manifold has two slits in its end just below the punch mark. The exhaust side rocker shaft does not have slits.

The rocker arms for the intake and exhaust valves are interchangeable between cylinders one and three and are identified by the mark "1". Similarly, the rockers for cylinders two and four are interchangeable and are identified by the mark "2".

The rocker shaft mounting brackets are also coded for correct placement with either an "A" or a "Z" plus a number code. See the illustration for proper placement.

To install the camshaft and rocker assembly:

5. Place the camshaft on the head with its dowel pin pointing up.

6. Fit the rocker assembly on the head, making sure you mount it on its knock pin.

7. Torque the bolts to 11–18 ft-lbs, in several stages working from the middle bolts and moving outwards on both sides.

NOTE: *Make sure the engine is on TDC compression stroke for no. 1 piston or you may damage some valves.*

See the section on timing chain installation. Adjust the valves.

Pistons and Connecting Rods
REMOVAL AND INSTALLATION
All Engines

1. Remove the cylinder head.

2. Remove the oil pan.

3. Remove any carbon buildup from the cylinder wall at the top end of the piston travel with a ridge reamer tool.

4. Position the piston to be removed at the bottom of its stroke so that the connecting rod bearing cap can be reached easily from under the engine.

5. Unscrew the connecting rod bearing cap nuts and remove the cap and lower half of the bearing.

6. Push the piston and connecting rod up and out of the cylinder block with a length of wood. Use care not to scratch the cylinder wall with the connecting rod or the wooden tool.

7. Keep all of the components from each cylinder together and install them in the cylinder from which they were removed.

8. Coat the bearing face of the connecting rod and the outer face of the pistons with engine oil.

9. See the illustrations for the correct placement of the piston rings for your model and year Datsun.

10. Turn the crankshaft until the rod journal of the particular cylinder you are working on is brought to the TDC position.

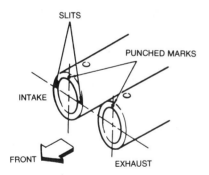

Note the difference in rocker shafts—Z20 engines

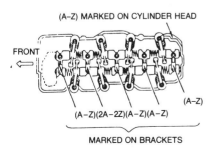

Rocker shaft mounting brackets are assembled in this order—Z20 engines

11. With the piston and rings clamped in a ring compressor, the notched mark on the head of the piston toward the front of the engine, and the oil hole side of the connecting rod toward the fuel pump side of the engine, push the piston and connecting rod assembly into the cylinder bore until the big bearing end of the connecting rod contacts and is seated on the rod journal of the crankshaft. Use care not to scratch the cylinder wall with the connecting rod.

12. Push down farther on the piston and turn the crankshaft while the connecting rod rides around on the crankshaft rod journal. Turn the crankshaft until the crankshaft rod journal is at BDC (bottom dead center).

13. Align the mark on the connecting rod bearing cap with that on the connecting rod and tighten the bearing cap bolts to the specified torque.

14. Install all of the piston/connecting rod assemblies in the manner outlined above and assemble the oil pan and cylinder head to the engine in the reverse order of removal.

PISTON AND CONNECTING ROD IDENTIFICATION AND POSITIONING

The pistons are marked with a number or "F" in the piston head. When installed in the engine the number or "F" markings are to be facing toward the front of the engine.

The connecting rods are installed in the engine with the oil hole facing toward the fuel pump side (right) of the engine.

NOTE: *It is advisable to number the pistons, connecting rods, and bearing caps in some manner so that they can be rein-*

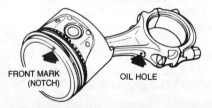

Piston and rod positioning—Z-series, L-series engines

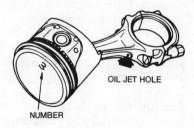

Piston and rod positioning—A-series engines

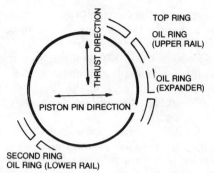

Piston ring placement—L20B, L24, Z20 engines

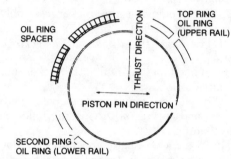

Piston ring placement—A-series engines

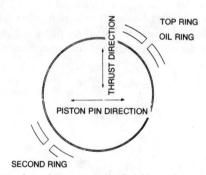

Piston ring placement—L16, L18 engines

stalled in the same cylinder, facing in the same direction from which they are removed.

ENGINE LUBRICATION

Oil Pan

REMOVAL AND INSTALLATION

All Engines

To remove the oil pan it will be necessary to unbolt the motor mounts and jack the engine to gain clearance. Drain the oil, remove the attaching screws, and remove the oil pan and gasket. Install the oil pan in the reverse order with a new gasket, tightening the screws to 4–7 ft lbs.

Rear Main Oil Seal

REPLACEMENT

In order to replace the rear main oil seal, the rear main bearing cap must be removed. Removal of the rear main bearing cap requires the use of a special rear main bearing cap puller. Also, the oil seal is installed with a special crankshaft rear oil seal drift. Unless these or similar tools are available to you, it is recommended that the oil seal be replaced by a Datsum service center.

1. Remove the engine and transmission assembly from the vehicle.

2. Remove the transmission from the engine. Remove the oil pan.

3. Remove the clutch from the flywheel.

4. Remove the flywheel from the crankshaft.

5. Remove the rear main bearing cap together with the bearing cap side seals.

6. Remove the rear main oil seal from around the crankshaft.

7. Apply lithium grease around the sealing lip of the oil seal and install the seal around the crankshaft using a suitable tool.

8. Apply sealer to the rear main bearing cap as indicated, install the rear main bearing cap, and tighten the cap bolts to 33–40 ft lbs.

9. Apply sealant to the rear main bearing cap side seals and install the side seals, driving the seals into place with a suitable drift.

10. Assemble the engine and install it in the vehicle in the reverse order of removal.

Oil Pump

The oil pump is mounted externally on the engine, this eliminates the need to remove the oil pan in order to remove the oil pump. The A-series oil pump is actually part of the oil filter mounting bracket. The L-series and Z-series oil pumps are mounted in the timing chain cover.

REMOVAL AND INSTALLATION

1973–79 All Models, 1980 210, 310

1. Remove the distributor on the L16, L18, L20B and L24 engines.

2. Drain the engine oil.

3. Remove the front stabilizer bar if it is in the way of removing the oil pump.

4. Remove the splash shield.

5. Remove the oil pump body with the drive spindle assembly.

Removing A-series engine oil pump

Removing Z-series, L-series oil pump

6. Install the A-series oil pump in the reverse order of removal. On the L-series engines, turn the crankshaft so that the No. 1 piston is at TDC of the compression stroke.

7. Fill the pump housing with engine oil, then align the punch mark on the spindle with the hole in the oil pump.

8. With a new gasket placed over the drive spindle, install the oil pump and drive spindle assembly so that the projection on the top of the drive spindle is located in the 11:25 o'clock position.

9. Install the distributor with the metal tip of the rotor pointing toward the No. 1 spark plug tower of the distributor cap.

10. Assemble the remaining components in the reverse order of removal.

1980 All Models, Except 210, 310

CAUTION: *Before attempting to remove the oil pump on 1980 models, you must perform the following procedures:*

a. Drain the oil from the oil pan.

b. Turn the crankshaft so that No. 1 piston is at TDC on its compression stroke.

c. Remove the distributor cap and mark the position of the distributor rotor in rela-

tion to the distributor base with a piece of chalk.

1. Remove the front stabilizer bar, if so equipped.

2. Remove the splash shield.

3. Remove the oil pump body with the drive spindle assembly.

4. To install, fill the pump housing with engine oil, align the punch mark on the spindle with the hole in the oil pump. No. 1 piston should be at TDC on its compression stroke.

5. With a new gasket placed over the drive spindle, install the oil pump and drive spindle assembly, making sure the tip of the drive spindle fits into the distributor shaft notch securely. The distributor rotor should be pointing to the match mark you made earlier.

NOTE: *Great care must be taken not to disturb the distributor rotor while installing the oil pump, or the ignition timing will be wrong.*

Assemble the remaining components in the reverse order of removal.

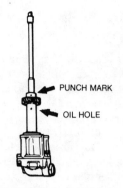

Z-series, L-series oil pump alignment

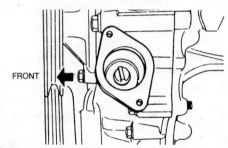

Position of the distributor drive spindle—L-series engines

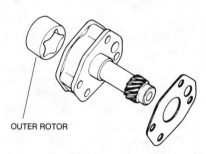

Exploded view of A-series engine oil pump

1. Oil pump body
2. Inner rotor and shaft
3. Outer rotor
4. Oil pump cover
5. Regulator valve
6. Regulator spring
7. Washer
8. Regulator cap
9. Cover gasket

Exploded view of Z-series, L-series engine oil pump

ENGINE COOLING

Radiator

REMOVAL AND INSTALLATION

NOTE: *On some models it may be necessary to remove the front grille.*

1. Drain the engine coolant into a clean container. On fuel injected models, remove the air cleaner inlet pipe.

2. Disconnect the upper and lower radiator hoses and the expansion tank hose.

3. Disconnect the automatic transmission oil cooler lines after draining the transmission. Cap the lines to keep dirt out of them.

4. If the fan has a shroud, unbolt the shroud and move it back, hanging it over the fan.

5. Remove the radiator mounting bolts and the radiator.

6. Installation is the reverse of removal. Fill the automatic transmission to the proper level. Fill the cooling system.

Water Pump

REMOVAL AND INSTALLATION

All Engines

1. Drain the engine coolant into a clean container.

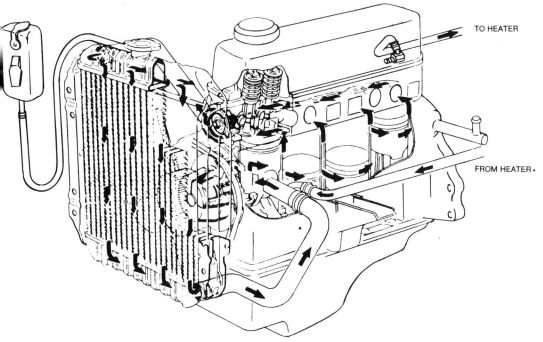

TO HEATER

FROM HEATER.

A-series engine cooling system

2. Loosen the four bolts retaining the fan shroud to the radiator and remove the shroud.

3. Loosen the belt, then remove the fan and pulley from the water pump hub.

4. Remove the bolts retaining the pump and remove the pump together with the gasket from the front cover.

5. Remove all traces of gasket material and install the water pump in the reverse order with a new gasket and sealer. Tighten the bolts uniformly.

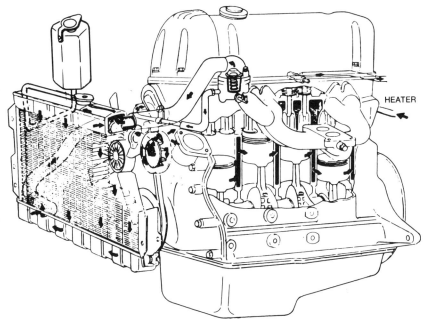

HEATER

L-series engine cooling system (4 cylinder)

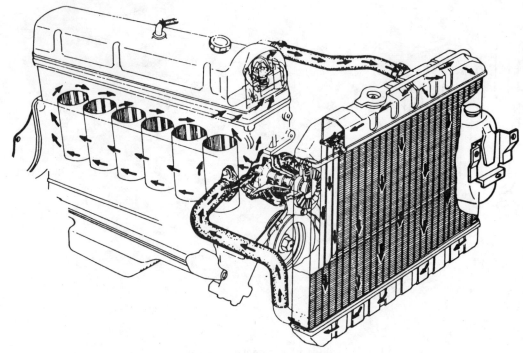

Cooling system—L24 engine

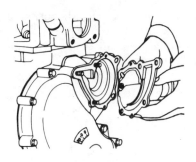

A-series engine water pump removal

Thermostat

REMOVAL AND INSTALLATION

All Engines

1. Drain the engine coolant into a clean container so that the level is below the thermostat housing.

2. Disconnect the upper radiator hose at the water outlet.

3. Loosen the two securing nuts and remove the water outlet, gasket, and the thermostat from the thermostat housing.

4. Install the thermostat in the reverse order of removal, using a new gasket with sealer and with the thermostat spring toward the inside of the engine.

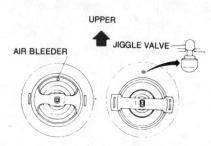

1980 A-series thermostat: place jiggle valve toward top

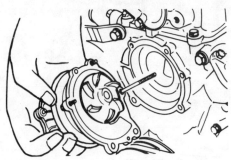

L-series, Z-series engines water pump removal

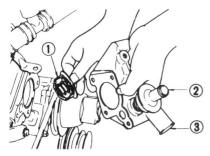

1. Thermostat
2. Air check valve
3. Water outlet

A-series thermostat removal

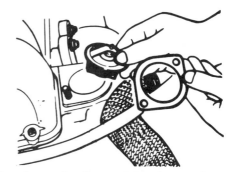

L-series engine thermostat replacement

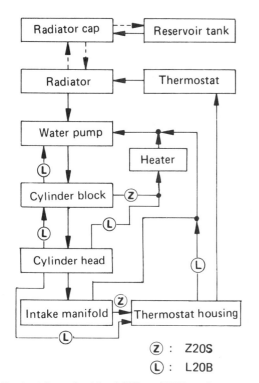

Ⓩ : Z20S
Ⓛ : L20B

Coolant flow chart for L20B and Z20 engines

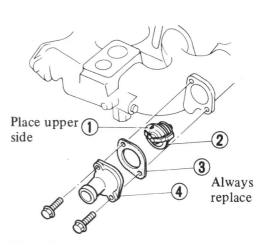

Place upper side ①
②
③
④
Always replace

Z20 engine thermostat location. Note jiggle valve

ENGINE REBUILDING

Most procedures involved in rebuilding an engine are fairly standard, regardless of the type of engine involved. This section is a guide to accepted rebuilding procedures. Examples of standard rebuilding practices are illustrated and should be used along with specific details concerning your particular engine, found earlier in this chapter.

The procedures given here are those used by any competent rebuilder. Obviously some of the procedures cannot be performed by the do-it-yourself mechanic, but are provided so that you will be familiar with the services that should be offered by rebuilding or machine shops. As an example, in most instances, it is more profitable for the home mechanic to remove the cylinder heads, buy the necessary parts (new valves, seals, keepers, keys, etc.) and deliver these to a machine shop for the necessary work. In this way you will save the money to remove and install the cylinder head and the mark-up on parts.

On the other hand, most of the work involved in rebuilding the lower end is well within the scope of the do-it-yourself mechanic. Only work such as hot-tanking, actually boring the block or Magnafluxing (invisible crack detection) need be sent to a machine shop.

Tools

The tools required for basic engine rebuilding should, with a few exceptions, be those included in a mechanic's tool kit. An accurate torque wrench, and a dial indicator (reading in thousandths) mounted on a universal base should be available. Special tools, where required, are available from the major tool suppliers. The services of a competent automotive machine shop must also be readily available.

Precautions

Aluminum has become increasingly popular for use in engines, due to its low weight and excellent heat transfer characteristics. The following precautions must be observed when handling aluminum (or any other) engine parts:
—Never hot-tank aluminum parts.
—Remove all aluminum parts (identification tags, etc.) from engine parts before hot-tanking (otherwise they will be removed during the process).

—Always coat threads lightly with engine oil or anti-seize compounds before installation, to prevent seizure.
—Never over-torque bolts or spark plugs in aluminum threads. Should stripping occur, threads can be restored using any of a number of thread repair kits available (see next section).

Inspection Techniques

Magnaflux and Zyglo are inspection techniques used to locate material flaws, such as stress cracks. Magnaflux is a magnetic process, applicable only to ferrous materials. The Zyglo process coats the material with a fluorescent dye penetrant, and any material may be tested using Zyglo. Specific checks of suspected surface cracks may be made at lower cost and more readily using spot check dye. The dye is sprayed onto the suspected area, wiped off, and the area is then sprayed with a developer. Cracks then will show up brightly.

Overhaul

The section is divided into two parts. The first, Cylinder Head Reconditioning, assumes that the cylinder head is removed from the engine, all manifolds are removed, and the cylinder head is on a workbench. The camshaft should be removed from overhead cam cylinder heads. The second section, Cylinder Block Reconditioning, covers the block, pistons, connecting rods and crankshaft. It is assumed that the engine is mounted on a work stand, and the cylinder head and all accessories are removed.

Procedures are identified as follows:

Unmarked—Basic procedures that must be performed in order to successfully complete the rebuilding process.

Starred (*)—Procedures that should be performed to ensure maximum performance and engine life.

Double starred (**)—Procedures that may be performed to increase engine performance and reliability.

When assembling the engine, any parts that will be in frictional contact must be pre-lubricated, to provide protection on initial start-up. Any product specifically formulated for this purpose may be used. NOTE: *Do not use engine oil. Where semi-permanent* (locked but removable) installation of bolts or nuts is desired, threads should be cleaned and located with Loctite® or a similar product (non-hardening).

Repairing Damaged Threads

Several methods of repairing damaged threads are available. Heli-Coil® (shown here), Keenserts® and Microdot® are among the most widely used. All involve basically the same principle—drilling out stripped threads, tapping the hole and installing a pre-wound insert—making welding, plugging and oversize fasteners unnecessary.

Two types of thread repair inserts are usually supplied—a standard type for most Inch Coarse, Inch Fine, Metric Coarse and Metric Fine thread sizes and a spark plug type to fit most spark plug port sizes. Consult the individual manufacturer's catalog to determine exact applications. Typical thread repair kits will contain a selection of pre-wound threaded inserts, a tap (corresponding to the outside diameter threads of the insert) and an installation tool. Spark plug inserts usually differ because they require a tap equipped with pilot threads and a combined reamer/tap section. Most manufacturers also supply blister-packed thread repair inserts separately in addition to a master kit containing a variety of taps and inserts plus installation tools.

Before effecting a repair to a threaded hole, remove any snapped, broken or damaged bolts or studs. Penetrating oil can be used to free frozen threads; the offending item can be removed with locking pliers or with a screw or stud extractor. After the hole is clear, the thread can be repaired, as follows:

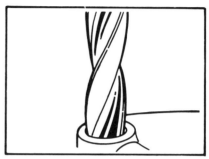
Drill out the damaged threads with specified drill. Drill completely through the hole or to the bottom of a blind hole

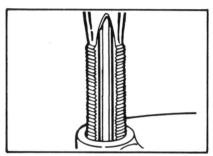
With the tap supplied, tap the hole to receive the thread insert. Keep the tap well oiled and back it out frequently to avoid clogging the threads

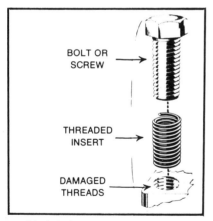
Damaged bolt holes can be repaired with thread repair inserts

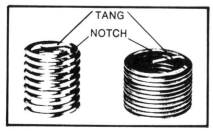
Standard thread repair insert (left) and spark plug thread insert (right)

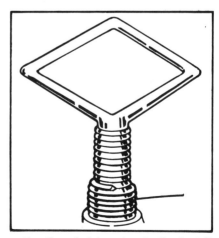
Screw the threaded insert onto the installation tool until the tang engages the slot. Screw the insert into the tapped hole until it is ¼–½ turn below the top surface. After installation break off the tang with a hammer and punch

Standard Torque Specifications and Fastener Markings

The Newton-metre has been designated the world standard for measuring torque and will gradually replace the foot-pound and kilogram-meter. In the absence of specific torques, the following chart can be used as a guide to the maximum safe torque of a particular size/grade of fastener.

- There is no torque difference for fine or coarse threads.
- Torque values are based on clean, dry threads. Reduce the value by 10% if threads are oiled prior to assembly.
- The torque required for aluminum components or fasteners is considerably less.

U. S. BOLTS

SAE Grade Number	1 or 2			5			6 or 7		

Bolt Markings

Manufacturer's marks may vary—number of lines always 2 less than the grade number.

Usage	Frequent			Frequent			Infrequent		
Bolt Size (inches)—(Thread)	Maximum Torque			Maximum Torque			Maximum Torque		
	Ft-Lb	kgm	Nm	Ft-Lb	kgm	Nm	Ft-Lb	kgm	Nm
¼—20	5	0.7	6.8	8	1.1	10.8	10	1.4	13.5
—28	6	0.8	8.1	10	1.4	13.6			
5/16—18	11	1.5	14.9	17	2.3	23.0	19	2.6	25.8
—24	13	1.8	17.6	19	2.6	25.7			
3/8—16	18	2.5	24.4	31	4.3	42.0	34	4.7	46.0
—24	20	2.75	27.1	35	4.8	47.5			
7/16—14	28	3.8	37.0	49	6.8	66.4	55	7.6	74.5
—20	30	4.2	40.7	55	7.6	74.5			
½—13	39	5.4	52.8	75	10.4	101.7	85	11.75	115.2
—20	41	5.7	55.6	85	11.7	115.2			
9/16—12	51	7.0	69.2	110	15.2	149.1	120	16.6	162.7
—18	55	7.6	74.5	120	16.6	162.7			
5/8—11	83	11.5	112.5	150	20.7	203.3	167	23.0	226.5
—18	95	13.1	128.8	170	23.5	230.5			
¾—10	105	14.5	142.3	270	37.3	366.0	280	38.7	379.6
—16	115	15.9	155.9	295	40.8	400.0			
7/8— 9	160	22.1	216.9	395	54.6	535.5	440	60.9	596.5
—14	175	24.2	237.2	435	60.1	589.7			
1— 8	236	32.5	318.6	590	81.6	799.9	660	91.3	894.8
—14	250	34.6	338.9	660	91.3	849.8			

METRIC BOLTS

NOTE: *Metric bolts are marked with a number indicating the rela-tive strength of the bolt. These numbers have nothing to do with size.*

Description	Torque ft-lbs (Nm)			
Thread size x pitch (mm)	Head mark—4		Head mark—7	
6 x 1.0	2.2–2.9	(3.0–3.9)	3.6–5.8	(4.9–7.8)
8 x 1.25	5.8–8.7	(7.9–12)	9.4–14	(13–19)
10 x 1.25	12–17	(16–23)	20–29	(27–39)
12 x 1.25	21–32	(29–43)	35–53	(47–72)
14 x 1.5	35–52	(48–70)	57–85	(77–110)
16 x 1.5	51–77	(67–100)	90–120	(130–160)
18 x 1.5	74–110	(100–150)	130–170	(180–230)
20 x 1.5	110–140	(150–190)	190–240	(160–320)
22 x 1.5	150–190	(200–260)	250–320	(340–430)
24 x 1.5	190–240	(260–320)	310–410	(420–550)

NOTE: *This engine rebuilding section is a guide to accepted rebuilding procedures. Typical examples of standard rebuilding procedures are illustrated. Use these procedures along with the detailed instructions earlier in this chapter, concerning your particular engine.*

Cylinder Head Reconditioning

Procedure	Method
Remove the cylinder head:	See the engine service procedures earlier in this chapter for details concerning specific engines.
Identify the valves:	Invert the cylinder head, and number the valve faces front to rear, using a permanent felt-tip marker.
Remove the rocker arms (OHV engines only):	Remove the rocker arms with shaft(s) or balls and nuts. Wire the sets of **rockers**, balls and nuts together, and identify according to the corresponding valve.
Remove the camshaft (OHC engines only):	See the engine service procedures earlier in this chapter for details concerning specific engines.
Remove the valves and springs:	Using an appropriate valve spring compressor (depending on the configuration of the cylinder head), compress the valve springs. Lift out the keepers with needlenose pliers, release the compressor, and remove the valve, spring, and spring retainer. See the engine service procedures earlier in this chapter for details concerning specific engines.

Cylinder Head Reconditioning

Procedure	*Method*

Check the valve stem-to-guide clearance:

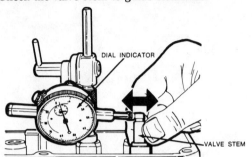

Check the valve stem-to-guide clearance

Clean the valve stem with lacquer thinner or a similar solvent to remove all gum and varnish. Clean the valve guides using solvent and an expanding wire-type valve guide cleaner. Mount a dial indicator so that the stem is at 90° to the valve stem, as close to the valve guide as possible. Move the valve off its seat, and measure the valve guide-to-stem clearance by rocking the stem back and forth to actuate the dial indicator. Measure the valve stems using a micrometer, and compare to specifications, to determine whether stem or guide wear is responsible for excessive clearance.
NOTE: *Consult the Specifications tables earlier in this chapter.*

De-carbon the cylinder head and valves:

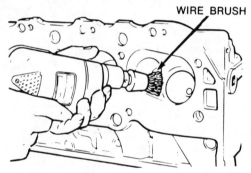

Remove the carbon from the cylinder head with a wire brush and electric drill

Chip carbon away from the valve heads, combustion chambers, and ports, using a chisel made of hardwood. Remove the remaining deposits with a stiff wire brush.
NOTE: *Be sure that the deposits are actually removed, rather than burnished.*

Hot-tank the cylinder head (cast iron heads only):
CAUTION: *Do not hot-tank aluminum parts.*

Have the cylinder head hot-tanked to remove grease, corrosion, and scale from the water passages.
NOTE: *In the case of overhead cam cylinder heads, consult the operator to determine whether the camshaft bearings will be damaged by the caustic solution.*

Degrease the remaining cylinder head parts:

Clean the remaining cylinder head parts in an engine cleaning solvent. Do not remove the protective coating from the springs.

Check the cylinder head for warpage:

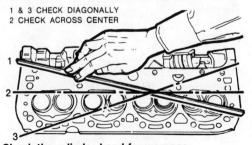

Check the cylinder head for warpage

Place a straight-edge across the gasket surface of the cylinder head. Using feeler gauges, determine the clearance at the center of the straight-edge. If warpage exceeds .003″ in a 6″ span, or .006″ over the total length, the cylinder head must be resurfaced.
NOTE: *If warpage exceeds the manufacturer's maximum tolerance for material removal, the cylinder head must be replaced.* When milling the cylinder heads of V-type engines, the intake manifold mounting position is altered, and must be corrected by milling the manifold flange a proportionate amount.

Cylinder Head Reconditioning

Procedure	Method

*Knurl the valve guides:

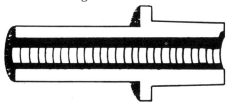

Cut-away view of a knurled valve guide

*Valve guides which are not excessively worn or distorted may, in some cases, be knurled rather than replaced. Knurling is a process in which metal is displaced and raised, thereby reducing clearance. Knurling also provides excellent oil control. The possibility of knurling rather than replacing valve guides should be discussed with a machinist.

Replace the valve guides:
NOTE: *Valve guides should only be replaced if damaged or if an oversize valve stem is not available.*

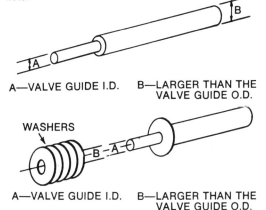

A—VALVE GUIDE I.D.   B—LARGER THAN THE VALVE GUIDE O.D.

WASHERS

A—VALVE GUIDE I.D.   B—LARGER THAN THE VALVE GUIDE O.D.

Valve guide installation tool using washers for installation

See the engine service procedures earlier in this chapter for details concerning specific engines. Depending on the type of cylinder head, valve guides may be pressed, hammered, or shrunk in. In cases where the guides are shrunk into the head, replacement should be left to an equipped machine shop. In other cases, the guides are replaced using a stepped drift (see illustration). Determine the height above the boss that the guide must extend, and obtain a stack of washers, their I.D. similar to the guide's O.D., of that height. Place the stack of washers on the guide, and insert the guide into the boss.
NOTE: *Valve guides are often tapered or beveled for installation.* Using the stepped installation tool (see illustration), press or tap the guides into position. Ream the guides according to the size of the valve stem.

Replace valve seat inserts:

Replacement of valve seat inserts which are worn beyond resurfacing or broken, if feasible, must be done by a machine shop.

Resurface (grind) the valve face:

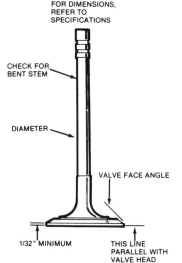

FOR DIMENSIONS, REFER TO SPECIFICATIONS

CHECK FOR BENT STEM

DIAMETER

VALVE FACE ANGLE

1/32" MINIMUM   THIS LINE PARALLEL WITH VALVE HEAD

Critical valve dimensions

Using a valve grinder, resurface the valves according to specifications given earlier in this chapter.
CAUTION: *Valve face angle is not always identical to valve seat angle.* A minimum margin of

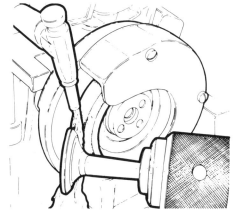

Valve grinding by machine

Cylinder Head Reconditioning

Procedure	Method
	$1/32''$ should remain after grinding the valve. The valve stem top should also be squared and resurfaced, by placing the stem in the V-block of the grinder, and turning it while pressing lightly against the grinding wheel. NOTE: *Do not grind sodium filled exhaust valves on a machine. These should be hand lapped.*
Resurface the valve seats using reamers or grinder: 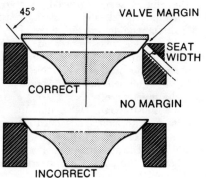 Valve seat width and centering  Reaming the valve seat with a hand reamer	Select a reamer of the correct seat angle, slightly larger than the diameter of the valve seat, and assemble it with a pilot of the correct size. Install the pilot into the valve guide, and using steady pressure, turn the reamer clockwise. CAUTION: *Do not turn the reamer counterclockwise.* Remove only as much material as necessary to clean the seat. Check the concentricity of the seat (following). If the dye method is not used, coat the valve face with Prussian blue dye, install and rotate it on the valve seat. Using the dye marked area as a centering guide, center and narrow the valve seat to specifications with correction cutters. NOTE: *When no specifications are available, minimum seat width for exhaust valves should be $5/64''$, intake valves $1/16''$.* After making correction cuts, check the position of the valve seat on the valve face using Prussian blue dye.
	To resurface the seat with a power grinder, select a pilot of the correct size and coarse stone of the proper angle. Lubricate the pilot and move the stone on and off the valve seat at 2 cycles per second, until all flaws are gone. Finish the seat with a fine stone. If necessary the seat can be corrected or narrowed using correction stones.
Check the valve seat concentricity: 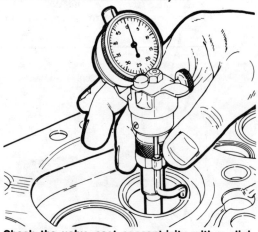 Check the valve seat concentricity with a dial gauge	Coat the valve face with Prussian blue dye, install the valve, and rotate it on the valve seat. If the entire seat becomes coated, and the valve is known to be concentric, the seat is concentric.
	*Install the dial gauge pilot into the guide, and rest of the arm on the valve seat. Zero the gauge, and rotate the arm around the seat. Run-out should not exceed .002''.

Cylinder Head Reconditioning

Procedure	Method
*Lap the valves: NOTE: *Valve lapping is done to ensure efficient sealing of resurfaced valves and seats.*	*Invert the cylinder head, lightly lubricate the valve stems, and install the valves in the head as numbered. Coat valve seats with fine grinding compound, and attach the lapping tool suction cup to a valve head. NOTE: *Moisten the suction cup.* Rotate the tool between the palms, changing position and lifting the tool often to prevent grooving. Lap the valve until a smooth, polished seat is evident. Remove the valve and tool, and rinse away all traces of grinding compound.

Lapping the valves by hand

**Fasten a suction cup to a piece of drill rod, and mount the rod in a hand drill. Proceed as above, using the hand drill as a lapping tool.
CAUTION: *Due to the higher speeds involved when using the hand drill, care must be exercised to avoid grooving the seat.* Lift the tool and change direction of rotation often.

HAND DRILL

ROD

Home-made valve lapping tool

SUCTION CUP

Check the valve springs:	Place the spring on a flat surface next to a square. Measure the height of the spring, and rotate it against the edge of the square to measure distortion. If spring height varies (by comparison) by more than $1/16''$ or if distortion exceeds $1/16''$, replace the spring.

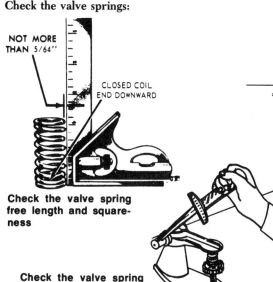

NOT MORE THAN 5/64''

CLOSED COIL END DOWNWARD

Check the valve spring free length and square-ness

**In addition to evaluating the spring as above, test the spring pressure at the installed and compressed (installed height minus valve lift) height using a valve spring tester. Springs used on small displacement engines (up to 3 liters) should be ∓ 1 lb of all other springs in either position. A tolerance of ∓ 5 lbs is permissible on larger engines.

Check the valve spring test pressure

Cylinder Head Reconditioning

Procedure	Method
*Install valve stem seals: 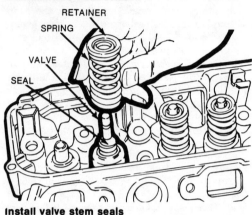 **Install valve stem seals**	* Due to the pressure differential that exists at the ends of the intake valve guides (atmospheric pressure above, manifold vacuum below), oil is drawn through the valve guides into the intake port. This has been alleviated somewhat since the addition of positive crankcase ventilation, which lowers the pressure above the guides. Several types of valve stem seals are available to rocker arms and balls, and install them on the the stem and guide boss, while others require that the boss be machined. Recently, Teflon guide seals have become popular. Consult a parts supplier or machinist concerning availability and suggested usages. NOTE: *When installing seals, ensure that a small amount of oil is able to pass the seal to lubricate the valve guides; otherwise, excessive wear may result.*
Install the valves:	See the engine service procedures earlier in this chapter for details concerning specific engines. Lubricate the valve stems, and install the valves in the cylinder head as numbered. Lubricate and position the seals (if used) and the valve springs. Install the spring retainers, compress the springs, and insert the keys using needle-nose pliers or a tool designed for this purpose. NOTE: *Retain the keys with wheel bearing grease during installation.*
Check valve spring installed height: 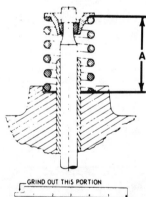 Measure the valve spring installed height (A) with a modified steel rule 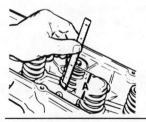 Valve spring installed height (A)	Measure the distance between the spring pad and the lower edge of the spring retainer, and compare to specifications. If the installed height is incorrect, add shim washers between the spring pad and the spring. CAUTION: *Use only washers designed for this purpose.*
Install the camshaft (OHC engines only) and check end-play:	See the engine service procedures earlier in this chapter for details concerning specific engines.

Cylinder Head Reconditioning

Procedure	Method
Inspect the rocker arms, balls, studs, and nuts (OHV engines only): 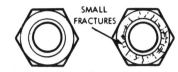 **Stress cracks in the rocker nuts**	Visually inspect the rocker arms, balls, studs, and nuts for cracks, galling, burning, scoring, or wear. If all parts are intact, liberally lubricate the rocker arms and balls, and install them on the cylinder head. If wear is noted on a rocker arm at the point of valve contact, grind it smooth and square, removing as little material as possible. Replace the rocker arm if excessively worn. If a rocker stud shows signs of wear, it must be replaced (see below). If a rocker nut shows stress cracks, replace it. If an exhaust ball is galled or burned, substitute the intake ball from the same cylinder (if it is intact), and install a new intake ball. NOTE: *Avoid using new rocker balls on exhaust valves.*
Replacing rocker studs (OHV engines only): AS STUB BEGINS TO PULL UP, IT WILL BE NECESSARY TO REMOVE THE NUT AND ADD MORE WASHERS 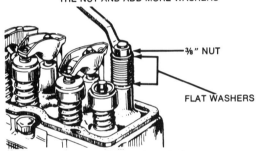 ⅜" NUT FLAT WASHERS **Extracting a pressed-in rocker stud** 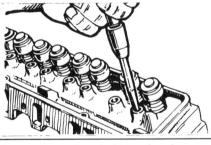 **Ream the stud bore for oversize rocker studs**	In order to remove a threaded stud, lock two nuts on the stud, and unscrew the stud using the lower nut. Coat the lower threads of the new stud with Loctite, and install. Two alternative methods are available for replacing pressed in studs. Remove the damaged stud using a stack of washers and a nut (see illustration). In the first, the boss is reamed .005–.006" oversize, and an oversize stud pressed in. Control the stud extension over the boss using washers, in the same manner as valve guides. Before installing the stud, coat it with white lead and grease. To retain the stud more positively drill a hole through the stud and boss, and install a roll pin. In the second method, the boss is tapped, and a threaded stud installed.
Inspect the rocker shaft(s) and rocker arms (OHV engines only) 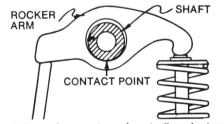 ROCKER ARM — SHAFT CONTACT POINT **Check the rocker arm-to-rocker shaft contact area**	Remove rocker arms, springs and washers from rocker shaft. NOTE: *Lay out parts in the order as they are removed.* Inspect rocker arms for pitting or wear on the valve contact point, or excessive bushing wear. Bushings need only be replaced if wear is excessive, because the rocker arm normally contacts the shaft at one point only. Grind the valve contact point of rocker arm smooth if necessary, removing as little material as possible. If excessive material must be removed to smooth and square the arm, it should be replaced. Clean out all oil holes and passages in rocker shaft. If shaft is grooved or worn, replace it. Lubricate and assemble the rocker shaft.

Cylinder Head Reconditioning

Procedure	Method
Inspect the pushrods (OHV engines only):	Remove the pushrods, and, if hollow, clean out the oil passages using fine wire. Roll each pushrod over a piece of clean glass. If a distinct clicking sound is heard as the pushrod rolls, the rod is bent, and must be replaced.
	*The length of all pushrods must be equal. Measure the length of the pushrods, compare to specifications, and replace as necessary.
Inspect the valve lifters (OHV engines only): 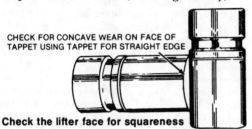 CHECK FOR CONCAVE WEAR ON FACE OF TAPPET USING TAPPET FOR STRAIGHT EDGE **Check the lifter face for squareness**	Remove lifters from their bores, and remove gum and varnish, using solvent. Clean walls of lifter bores. Check lifters for concave wear as illustrated. If face is·worn concave, replace lifter, and carefully inspect the camshaft. Lightly lubricate lifter and insert it into its bore. If play is excessive, an oversize lifter must be installed (where possible). Consult a machinist concerning feasibility. If play is satisfactory, remove, lubricate, and reinstall the lifter.
*Testing hydraulic lifter leak down (OHV engines only):	Submerge lifter in a container of kerosene. Chuck a used pushrod or its equivalent into a drill press. Position container of kerosene so pushrod acts on the lifter plunger. Pump lifter with the drill press, until resistance increases. Pump several more times to bleed any air out of lifter. Apply very firm, constant pressure to the lifter, and observe rate at which fluid bleeds out of lifter. If the fluid bleeds very quickly (less than 15 seconds), lifter is defective. If the time exceeds 60 seconds, lifter is sticking. In either case, recondition or replace lifter. If lifter is operating properly (leak down time 15–60 seconds), lubricate and install it.

Cylinder Block Reconditioning

Procedure	Method
Checking the main bearing clearance: 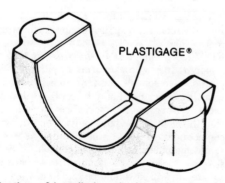 PLASTIGAGE® **Plastigage® installed on the lower bearing shell**	Invert engine, and remove cap from the bearing to be checked. Using a clean, dry rag, thoroughly clean all oil from crankshaft journal and bearing insert. NOTE: *Plastigage® is soluble in oil; therefore, oil on the journal or bearing could result in erroneous readings.* Place a piece of Plastigage along the full length of journal, reinstall cap, and torque to specifications. NOTE: *Specifications are given in the engine specifications earlier in this chapter.* Remove bearing cap, and determine bearing clearance by comparing width of Plastigage to the scale on Plastigage envelope. Journal taper is determined by comparing width of the Plastigage strip near its ends. Rotate crankshaft 90° and retest, to determine journal eccentricity. NOTE: *Do not rotate crankshaft with Plastigage*

Cylinder Block Reconditioning

Procedure	Method

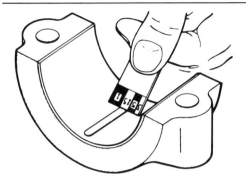

Measure Plastigage® to determine main bearing clearance

installed. If bearing insert and journal appear intact, and are within tolerances, no further main bearing service is required. If bearing or journal appear defective, cause of failure should be determined before replacement.

* Remove crankshaft from block (see below). Measure the main bearing journals at each end tiwce (90° apart) using a micrometer, to determine diameter, journal taper and eccentricity. If journals are within tolerances, reinstall bearing caps at their specified torque. Using a telescope gauge and micrometer, measure bearing I.D. parallel to piston axis and at 30° on each side of piston axis. Subtract journal O.D. from bearing I.D. to determine oil clearance. If crankshaft journals appear defective, or do not meet tolerances, there is no need to measure bearings; for the crankshaft will require grinding and/or undersize bearings will be required. If bearing appears defective, cause for failure should be determined prior to replacement.

Check the connecting rod bearing clearance:

Connecting rod bearing clearance is checked in the same manner as main bearing clearance, using Plastigage. Before removing the crankshaft, connecting rod side clearance also should be measured and recorded.

* Checking connecting rod bearing clearance, using a micrometer, is identical to checking main bearing clearance. If no other service is required, the piston and rod assemblies need not be removed.

Remove the crankshaft:

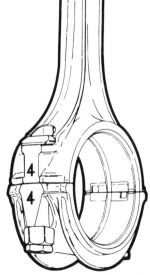

Using a punch, mark the corresponding main bearing caps and saddles according to position (i.e., one punch on the front main cap and saddle, two on the second, three on the third, etc.). Using number stamps, identify the corresponding connecting rods and caps, according to cylinder (if no numbers are present). Remove the main and connecting rod caps, and place sleeves of plastic tubing or vacuum hose over the connecting rod bolts, to protect the journals as the crankshaft is removed. Lift the crankshaft out of the block.

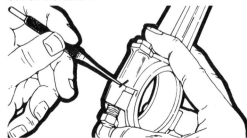

Match the connecting rod to the cylinder with a number stamp

Match the connecting rod and cap with scribe marks

Cylinder Block Reconditioning

Procedure	Method
Remove the ridge from the top of the cylinder: 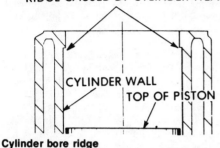 **Cylinder bore ridge**	In order to facilitate removal of the piston and connecting rod, the ridge at the top of the cylinder (unworn area; see illustration) must be removed. Place the piston at the bottom of the bore, and cover it with a rag. Cut the ridge away using a ridge reamer, exercising extreme care to avoid cutting too deeply. Remove the rag, and remove cuttings that remain on the piston. **CAUTION:** *If the ridge is not removed, and new rings are installed, damage to rings will result.*
Remove the piston and connecting rod:  **Push the piston out with a hammer handle**	Invert the engine, and push the pistons and connecting rods out of the cylinders. If necessary, tap the connecting rod boss with a wooden hammer handle, to force the piston out. **CAUTION:** *Do not attempt to force the piston past the cylinder ridge* (see above).
Service the crankshaft:	Ensure that all oil holes and passages in the crankshaft are open and free of sludge. If necessary, have the crankshaft ground to the largest possible undersize.
	** Have the crankshaft Magnafluxed, to locate stress cracks. Consult a machinist concerning additional service procedures, such as surface hardening (e.g., nitriding, Tuftriding) to improve wear characteristics, cross drilling and chamfering the oil holes to improve lubrication, and balancing.
Removing freeze plugs:	Drill a small hole in the middle of the freeze plugs. Thread a large sheet metal screw into the hole and remove the plug with a slide hammer.
Remove the oil gallery plugs:	Threaded plugs should be removed using an appropriate (usually square) wrench. To remove soft, pressed in plugs, drill a hole in the plug, and thread in a sheet metal screw. Pull the plug out by the screw using pliers.
Hot-tank the block: **NOTE:** *Do not hot-tank aluminum parts.*	Have the block hot-tanked to remove grease, corrosion, and scale from the water jackets. **NOTE:** *Consult the operator to determine whether the camshaft bearings will be damaged during the hot-tank process.*

Cylinder Block Reconditioning

Procedure	Method
Check the block for cracks:	Visually inspect the block for cracks or chips. The most common locations are as follows: Adjacent to freeze plugs. Between the cylinders and water jackets. Adjacent to the main bearing saddles. At the extreme bottom of the cylinders. Check only suspected cracks using spot check dye (see introduction). If a crack is located, consult a machinist concerning possible repairs.
	** Magnaflux the block to locate hidden cracks. If cracks are located, consult a machinist about feasibility of repair.
Install the oil gallery plugs and freeze plugs:	Coat freeze plugs with sealer and tap into position using a piece of pipe, slightly smaller than the plug, as a driver. To ensure retention, stake the edges of the plugs. Coat threaded oil gallery plugs with sealer and install. Drive replacement soft plugs into block using a large drift as driver.
	* Rather than reinstalling lead plugs, drill and tap the holes, and install threaded plugs.
Check the bore diameter and surface:	Visually inspect the cylinder bores for roughness, scoring, or scuffing. If evident, the cylinder bore must be bored or honed oversize to eliminate imperfections, and the smallest possible oversize piston used. The new pistons should be given to the machinist with the block, so that the cylinders can be bored or honed exactly to the piston size (plus clearance). If no flaws are evident, measure the bore diameter using a telescope gauge and micrometer, or dial gauge, parallel and perpendicular to the engine centerline, at the top (below the ridge) and bottom of the bore. Subtract the bottom measurements from the top to determine taper, and the parallel to the centerline measurements from the perpendicular measurements to determine eccentricity. If the measurements are not within specifications, the cylinder must be bored or honed, and an oversize piston installed. If the measurements are within specifications the cylinder may be used as is, with only finish honing (see below).

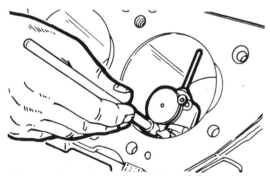

Measure the cylinder bore with a dial gauge

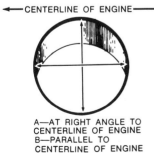

A—AT RIGHT ANGLE TO CENTERLINE OF ENGINE
B—PARALLEL TO CENTERLINE OF ENGINE

Cylinder bore measuring points

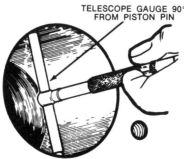

Measure the cylinder bore with a telescope gauge

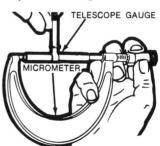

Measure the telescope gauge with a micrometer to determine the cylinder bore

Cylinder Block Reconditioning

Procedure	Method
	NOTE: *Prior to submitting the block for boring, perform the following operation(s).*
Check the cylinder block bearing alignment: 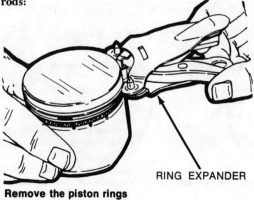 **Check the main bearing saddle alignment**	Remove the upper bearing inserts. Place a straightedge in the bearing saddles along the centerline of the crankshaft. If clearance exists between the straightedge and the center saddle, the block must be alignbored.
*Check the deck height:	The deck height is the distance from the crankshaft centerline to the block deck. To measure, invert the engine, and install the crankshaft, retaining it with the center main cap. Measure the distance from the crankshaft journal to the block deck, parallel to the cylinder centerline. Measure the diameter of the end (front and rear) main journals, parallel to the centerline of the cylinders, divide the diameter in half, and subtract it from the previous measurement. The results of the front and rear measurements should be identical. If the difference exceeds .005″, the deck height should be corrected. NOTE: *Block deck height and warpage should be corrected at the same time.*
Check the block deck for warpage:	Using a straightedge and feeler gauges, check the block deck for warpage in the same manner that the cylinder head is checked (see Cylinder Head Reconditioning). If warpage exceeds specifications, have the deck resurfaced. NOTE: *In certain cases a specification for total material removal (Cylinder head and block deck) is provided. This specification must not be exceeded.*
Clean and inspect the pistons and connecting rods: **Remove the piston rings** — RING EXPANDER	Using a ring expander, remove the rings from the piston. Remove the retaining rings (if so equipped) and remove piston pin. NOTE: *If the piston pin must be pressed out, determine the proper method and use the proper tools; otherwise the piston will distort.* Clean the ring grooves using an appropriate tool, exercising care to avoid cutting too deeply. Thoroughly clean all carbon and varnish from the piston with solvent. CAUTION: *Do not use a wire brush or caustic solvent on pistons.* Inspect the pistons for scuffing, scoring, cracks, pitting, or excessive ring groove wear. If wear is evident, the piston must be replaced. Check the connecting rod length by measuring the rod from the inside of the large end to the

Cylinder Block Reconditioning

Procedure	Method

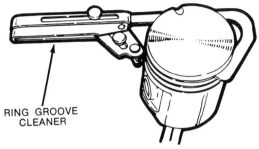

RING GROOVE
CLEANER

Clean the piston ring grooves

inside of the small end using calipers (see illustration). All connecting rods should be equal length. Replace any rod that differs from the others in the engine.

* Have the connecting rod alignment checked in an alignment fixture by a machinist. Replace any twisted or bent rods.

* Magnaflux the connecting rods to locate stress cracks. If cracks are found, replace the connecting rod.

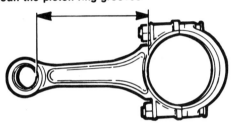

Check the connecting rod length (arrow)

Fit the pistons to the cylinders:

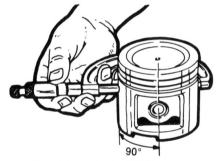

90°

Measure the piston prior to fitting

Using a telescope gauge and micrometer, or a dial gauge, measure the cylinder bore diameter perpendicular to the piston pin, 2½" below the deck. Measure the piston perpendicular to its pin on the skirt. The difference between the two measurements is the piston clearance. If the clearance is within specifications or slightly below (after boring or honing), finish honing is all that is required. If the clearance is excessive, try to obtain a slightly larger piston to bring clearance within specifications. Where this is not possible, obtain the first oversize piston, and hone (or if necessary, bore) the cylinder to size.

Assemble the pistons and connecting rods:

Install the piston pin lock-rings (if used)

Inspect piston pin, connecting rod small end bushing, and piston bore for galling, scoring, or excessive wear. If evident, replace defective part(s). Measure the I.D. of the piston boss and connecting rod small end, and the O.D. of the piston pin. If within specifications, assemble piston pin and rod.
CAUTION: *If piston pin must be pressed in, determine the proper method and use the proper tools; otherwise the piston will distort.*
Install the lock rings; ensure that they seat properly. If the parts are not within specifications, determine the service method for the type of engine. In some cases, piston and pin are serviced as an assembly when either is defective. Others specify reaming the piston and connecting rods for an oversize pin. If the connecting rod bushing is worn, it may in many cases be replaced. Reaming the piston and replacing the rod bushing are machine shop operations.

Cylinder Block Reconditioning

Procedure	Method

Clean and inspect the camshaft:

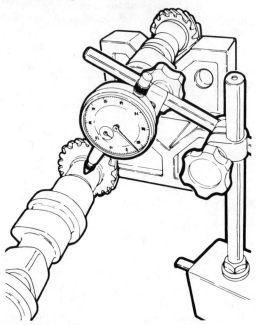

Check the camshaft for straightness

Degrease the camshaft, using solvent, and clean out all oil holes. Visually inspect cam lobes and bearing journals for excessive wear. If a lobe is questionable, check all lobes as indicated below. If a journal or lobe is worn, the camshaft must be reground or replaced.

NOTE: *If a journal is worn, there is a good chance that the bushings are worn.* If lobes and journals appear intact, place the front and rear journals in V-blocks, and rest a dial indicator on the center journal. Rotate the camshaft to check straightness. If deviation exceeds .001", replace the camshaft.

*Check the camshaft lobes with a micrometer, by measuring the lobes from the nose to base and again at 90° (see illustration). The lift is determined by subtracting the second measurement from the first. If all exhaust lobes and all intake lobes are not identical, the camshaft must be reground or replaced.

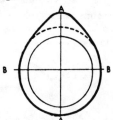

Camshaft lobe measurement

Replace the camshaft bearings (OHV engines only):

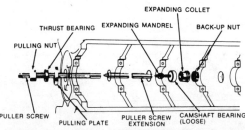

Camshaft bearing removal and installation tool (OHV engines only)

If excessive wear is indicated, or if the engine is being completely rebuilt, camshaft bearings should be replaced as follows: Drive the camshaft rear plug from the block. Assemble the removal puller with its shoulder on the bearing to be removed. Gradually tighten the puller nut until bearing is removed. Remove remaining bearings, leaving the front and rear for last. To remove front and rear bearings, reverse position of the tool, so as to pull the bearings in toward the center of the block. Leave the tool in this position, pilot the new front and rear bearings on the installer, and pull them into position: Return the tool to its original position and pull remaining bearings into position.

NOTE: *Ensure that oil holes align when installing bearings.* Replace camshaft rear plug, and stake it into position to aid retention.

Finish hone the cylinders:

Chuck a flexible drive hone into a power drill, and insert it into the cylinder. Start the hone, and move it up and down in the cylinder at a rate which will produce approximately a 60° cross-hatch pattern.

NOTE: *Do not extend the hone below the cylin-*

Cylinder Block Reconditioning

Procedure	*Method*

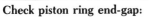

CROSS HATCH PATTERN

50°-60°

Cylinder bore after honing

der bore. After developing the pattern, remove the hone and recheck piston fit. Wash the cylinders with a detergent and water solution to remove abrasive dust, dry, and wipe several times with a rag soaked in engine oil.

Check piston ring end-gap:

Check the piston ring end gap

Compress the piston rings to be used in a cylinder, one at a time, into that cylinder, and press them approximately 1" below the deck with an inverted piston. Using feeler gauges, measure the ring end-gap, and compare to specifications. Pull the ring out of the cylinder and file the ends with a fine file to obtain proper clearance.
CAUTION: *If inadequate ring end-gap is utilized, ring breakage will result.*

Install the piston rings:

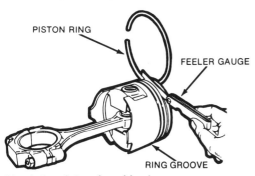

PISTON RING

FEELER GAUGE

RING GROOVE

Check the piston ring side clearance

Inspect the ring grooves in the piston for excessive wear or taper. If necessary, recut the grooves(s) for use with an overwidth ring or a standard ring and spacer. If the groove is worn uniformly, overwidth rings, or standard rings and spacers may be installed without recutting. Roll the outside of the ring around the groove to check for burrs or deposits. If any are found, remove with a fine file. Hold the ring in the groove, and measure side clearance. If necessary, correct as indicated above.
NOTE: *Always install any additional spacers above the piston ring.*
The ring groove must be deep enough to allow the ring to seat below the lands (see illustration). In many cases, a "go-no-go" depth gauge will be provided with the piston rings. Shallow grooves may be corrected by recutting, while deep grooves require some type of filler or expander behind the piston. Consult the piston ring sup-

Cylinder Block Reconditioning

Procedure	Method
	plier concerning the suggested method. Install the rings on the piston, lowest ring first, using a ring expander. NOTE: *Position the ring as specified by the manufacturer.* Consult the engine service procedures earlier in this chapter for details concerning specific engines.
Install the camshaft (OHV engines only):	Liberally lubricate the camshaft lobes and journals, and install the camshaft. CAUTION: *Exercise extreme care to avoid damaging the bearings when inserting the camshaft.* Install and tighten the camshaft thrust plate retaining bolts. See the engine service procedures earlier in this chapter for details concerning specific engines.
Check camshaft end-play (OHV engines only): **Check the camshaft end-play with a feeler gauge**	Using feeler gauges, determine whether the clearance between the camshaft boss (or gear) and backing plate is within specifications. Install shims behind the thrust plate, or reposition the camshaft gear and retest endplay. In some cases, adjustment is by replacing the thrust plate. See the engine service procedures earlier in this chapter for details concerning specific engines.
DIAL INDICATOR CAMSHAFT **Check the camshaft end-play with a dial indicator**	*Mount a dial indicator stand so that the stem of the dial indicator rests on the nose of the camshaft, parallel to the camshaft axis. Push the camshaft as far in as possible and zero the gauge. Move the camshaft outward to determine the amount of camshaft endplay. If the endplay is not within tolerance, install shims behind the thrust plate, or reposition the camshaft gear and retest. See the engine service procedures earlier in this chapter for details concerning specific engines.
Install the rear main seal:	See the engine service procedures earlier in this chapter for details concerning specific engines.
Install the crankshaft: 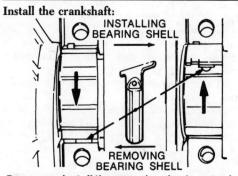INSTALLING BEARING SHELL REMOVING BEARING SHELL **Remove or install the upper bearing insert using a roll-out pin**	Thoroughly clean the main bearing saddles and caps. Place the upper halves of the bearing inserts on the saddles and press into position. NOTE: *Ensure that the oil holes align.* Press the corresponding bearing inserts into the main bearing caps. Lubricate the upper main bearings, and lay the crankshaft in position. Place a strip of Plastigage on each of the crankshaft journals, install the main caps, and torque to specifications. Remove the main caps, and compare the Plastigage to the scale on the Plastigage envelope. If clearances are within tolerances, remove the Plastigage, turn the crankshaft 90°, wipe off all oil and retest. If all clearances are correct, re-

Cylinder Block Reconditioning

Procedure	Method

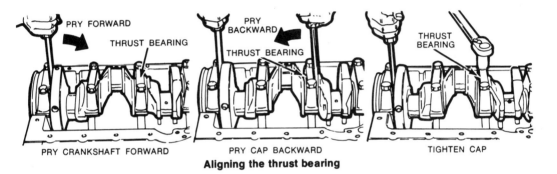

Home-made bearing roll-out pin

move all Plastigage, thoroughly lubricate the main caps and bearing journals, and install the main caps. If clearances are not within tolerance, the upper bearing inserts may be removed, without removing the crankshaft, using a bearing roll out pin (see illustration). Roll in a bearing that will provide proper clearance, and retest. Torque all main caps, excluding the thrust bearing cap, to specifications. Tighten the thrust bearing cap finger tight. To properly align the thrust bearing, pry the crankshaft the extent of its axial travel several times, the last movement held toward the front of the engine, and torque the thrust bearing cap to specifications. Determine the crankshaft end-play (see below), and bring within tolerance with thrust washers.

Aligning the thrust bearing

Measure crankshaft end-play:

Mount a dial indicator stand on the front of the block, with the dial indicator stem resting on the nose of the crankshaft, parallel to the crankshaft axis. Pry the crankshaft the extent of its travel rearward, and zero the indicator. Pry the crankshaft forward and record crankshaft end-play.

NOTE: *Crankshaft end-play also may be measured at the thrust bearing, using feeler gauges (see illustration).*

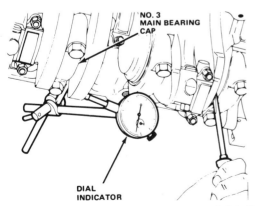

Check the crankshaft end-play with a dial indicator

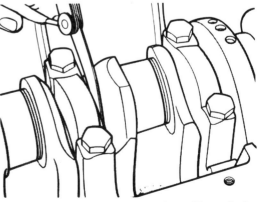

Check the crankshaft end-play with a feeler gauge

Cylinder Block Reconditioning

Procedure	*Method*
Install the pistons:	Press the upper connecting rod bearing halves into the connecting rods, and the lower halves into the connecting rod caps. Position the piston ring gaps according to specifications (see car section), and lubricate the pistons. Install a ring compresser on a piston, and press two long (8″) pieces of plastic tubing over the rod bolts. Using the tubes as a guide, press the pistons into the bores and onto the crankshaft with a wooden hammer handle. After seating the rod on the crankshaft journal, remove the tubes and install the cap finger tight. Install the remaining pistons in the same manner. Invert the engine and check the bearing clearance at two points (90° apart) on each journal with Plastigage.

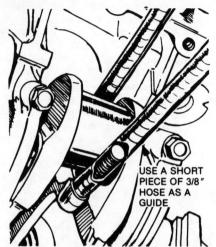

USE A SHORT PIECE OF 3/8″ HOSE AS A GUIDE

Use lengths of vacuum hose or rubber tubing to protect the crankshaft journals and cylinder walls during piston installation

NOTE: *Do not turn the crankshaft with Plastigage installed.* If clearance is within tolerances, remove *all* Plastigage, thoroughly lubricate the journals, and torque the rod caps to specifications. If clearance is not within specifications, install different thickness bearing inserts and recheck.

CAUTION: *Never shim or file the connecting rods or caps.* Always install plastic tube sleeves over the rod bolts when the caps are not installed, to protect the crankshaft journals.

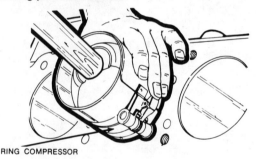

RING COMPRESSOR

Install the piston using a ring compressor

Check connecting rod side clearance:	Determine the clearance between the sides of the connecting rods and the crankshaft, using feeler gauges. If clearance is below the minimum tolerance, the rod may be machined to provide adequate clearance. If clearance is excessive, substitute an unworn rod, and recheck. If clearance is still outside specifications, the crankshaft must be welded and reground, or replaced.

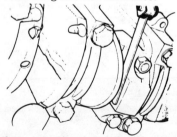

Check the connecting rod side clearance with a feeler gauge

Inspect the timing chain (or belt):	Visually inspect the timing chain for broken or loose links, and replace the chain if any are found. If the chain will flex sideways, it must be replaced. Install the timing chain as specified. Be sure the timing belt is not stretched, frayed or broken. NOTE: *If the original timing chain is to be reused, install it in its original position.*

Cylinder Block Reconditioning

Procedure	Method
Check timing gear backlash and runout (OHV engines):	Mount a dial indicator with its stem resting on a tooth of the camshaft gear (as illustrated). Rotate the gear until all slack is removed, and zero the indicator. Rotate the gear in the opposite direction until slack is removed, and record gear backlash. Mount the indicator with its stem resting on the edge of the camshaft gear, parallel to the axis of the camshaft. Zero the indicator, and turn the camshaft gear one full turn, recording the runout. If either backlash or runout exceed specifications, replace the worn gear(s).

Check the camshaft gear backlash

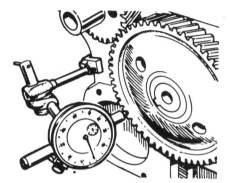

Check the camshaft gear run-out

Completing the Rebuilding Process

Following the above procedures, complete the rebuilding process as follows:

Fill the oil pump with oil, to prevent cavitating (sucking air) on initial engine start up. Install the oil pump and the pickup tube on the engine. Coat the oil pan gasket as necessary, and install the gasket and the oil pan. Mount the flywheel and the crankshaft vibration damper or pulley on the crankshaft. NOTE: *Always use new bolts when installing the flywheel.* Inspect the clutch shaft pilot bushing in the crankshaft. If the bushing is excessively worn, remove it with an expanding puller and a slide hammer, and tap a new bushing into place.

Position the engine, cylinder head side up. Lubricate the lifters, and install them into their bores. Install the cylinder head, and torque it as specified. Insert the pushrods (where applicable), and install the rocker shaft(s) (if so equipped) or position the rocker arms on the pushrods. Adjust the valves.

Install the intake and exhaust manifolds, the carburetor(s), the distributor and spark plugs. Adjust the point gap and the static ignition timing. Mount all accessories and install the engine in the car. Fill the radiator with coolant, and the crankcase with high quality engine oil.

Break-in Procedure

Start the engine, and allow it to run at low speed for a few minutes, while checking for leaks. Stop the engine, check the oil level, and fill as necessary. Restart the engine, and fill the cooling system to capacity. Check the point dwell angle and adjust the ignition timing and the valves. Run the engine at low to medium speed (800–2500 rpm) for approximately ½ hour, and retorque the cylinder head bolts. Road test the car, and check again for leaks.

Follow the manufacturer's recommended engine break-in procedure and maintenance schedule for new engines.

Emission Controls and Fuel System

EMISSION CONTROLS

There are three types of automotive pollutants; crankcase fumes, exhaust gases and gasoline evaporation. The equipment that is used to limit these pollutants is commonly called emission control equipment.

Crankcase Emission Controls

The crankcase emission control equipment consists of a positive crankcase ventilation valve (PCV), a closed or open oil filler cap and hoses to connect this equipment.

When the engine is running, a small portion of the gases which are formed in the combustion chamber during combustion leak by the piston rings and enter the crankcase. Since these gases are under pressure they tend to escape from the crankcase and enter into the atmosphere. If these gases were allowed to remain in the crankcase for any length of time, they would contaminate the engine oil and cause sludge to build up. If the gases are allowed to escape into the atmosphere, they would pollute the air, as they contain unburned hydrocarbons. The crankcase emission control equipment recycles these gases back into the engine combustion chamber where they are burned.

Crankcase gases are recycled in the following manner: while the engine is running, clean filtered air is drawn into the crankcase through the carburetor air filter and then through a hose leading to the rocket cover. As the air passes through the crankcase it picks up the combustion gases and carries them out of the crankcase, up through the PCV valve and into the intake manifold. After they enter the intake manifold they are drawn into the combustion chamber and burned.

The most critical component in the system is the PCV valve. This vacuum controlled valve regulates the amount of gases which are recycled into the combustion chamber. At low engine speeds the valve is partially closed, limiting the flow of gases into the intake manifold. As engine speed increases, the valve opens to admit greater quantities of the gases into the intake manifold. If the valve should become blocked or plugged, the gases will be prevented from escaping from the crankcase by the normal route. Since these gases are under pressure, they will find their own way out of the crankcase. This alternate route is usually a weak oil seal or gasket in the engine. As the gas escapes by the gasket, it also creates an oil leak. Besides causing oil leaks, a clogged PCV valve also allows these gases to remain in the crankcase

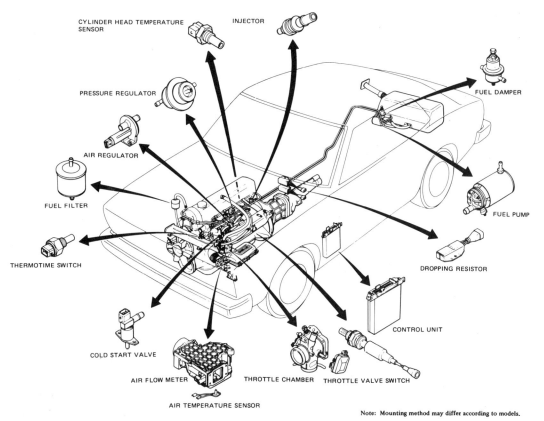

1980 810 emission control system. 1980 200SX similar

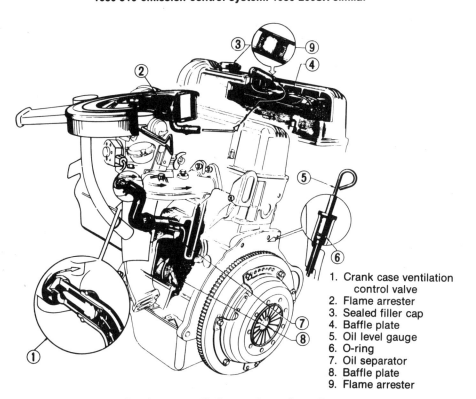

1. Crank case ventilation
   control valve
2. Flame arrester
3. Sealed filler cap
4. Baffle plate
5. Oil level gauge
6. O-ring
7. Oil separator
8. Baffle plate
9. Flame arrester

Crankcase ventilation system schematic

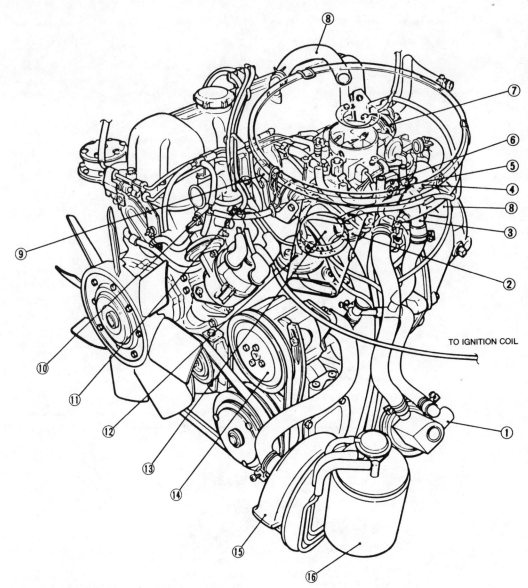

TO IGNITION COIL

1. Air control valve	7. Auto-choke	13. A.T.C. air cleaner
2. E.G.R. control valve	8. P.C.V. hose	14. Air pump for A.I.S.
3. Air relief valve	9. Check valve	15. Air pump air cleaner
4. A.B. valve	10. 3-way connector (M/T only)	16. Canister
5. B.C.D.D. solenoid valve	11. Thermal vacuum valve	
6. B.C.D.D.	12. B.P.T. valve	

1978 510 emission controls system—others similar

for an extended period of time, promoting the formation of sludge in the engine.

The above explanation and the trouble-shooting procedure which follows applies to all engines with PCV systems.

TESTING

Check the PCV system hoses and connections, to see that there are no leaks; then replace or tighten, as necessary.

To check the valve, remove it and blow through both of its ends. When blowing from the side which goes toward the intake manifold, very little air should pass through it. When blowing from the crankcase (valve cover) side, air should pass through freely.

Replace the valve with a new one, if the valve fails to function as outlined.

NOTE: *Do not attempt to clean or adjust the valve; replace it with a new one.*

REMOVAL AND INSTALLATION

To remove the PCV valve, simply loosen the hose clamp and remove the valve from the manifold-to-crankcase hose and intake manifold. Install the PCV valve in the reverse order of removal.

Evaporative Emission Control System

When raw fuel evaporates, the vapors contain hydrocarbons. To prevent these nasties from escaping into the atmosphere, the fuel evaporative emission control system was developed.

There are two different evaporative emission control systems used on Datsuns.

The system used through 1974 consists of a sealed fuel tank, a vapor-liquid separator, a flow guide (check) valve, and all of the hoses connecting these components, in the above order, leading from the fuel tank to the PCV hose, which connects the crankcase to the PCV valve.

In operation, the vapor formed in the fuel tank passes through the vapor separator, onto the flow guide valve and the crankcase. When the engine is not running, if the fuel vapor pressure in the vapor separator goes above 0.4 in. Hg, the flow guide valve opens and allows the vapor to enter the engine crankcase. Otherwise the flow guide valve is closed to the vapor separator while the engine is not running. When the engine is running, and a vacuum is developed in the fuel tank or in the engine crankcase and the difference of pressure between the relief side and the fuel tank or crankcase becomes 2 in.

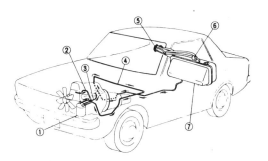

1. Carbon canister
2. Vacuum signal line
3. Canister vent line
4. Vapor vent line
5. Fuel filler cap with vacuum relief valve
6. Fuel check valve
7. Fuel tank

Evaporative emission control system schematic

Hg, the relief valve opens and allows ambient air from the air cleaner into the fuel tank or the engine crankcase. This ambient air replaces the vapor within the fuel tank or crankcase, bringing the fuel tank or crankcase back into a neutral or positive pressure range.

The system used on 1975 and later models consists of sealed fuel tank, vapor-liquid separator (certain models only), vapor vent line, carbon canister, vacuum signal line and a canister purge line.

In operation, fuel vapors and/or liquid are routed to the liquid/vapor separator or check valve where liquid fuel is directed back into the fuel tank as fuel vapors flow into the charcoal filled canister. The charcoal absorbs and stores the fuel vapors when the engine is not running or is at idle. When the throttle valves in the carburetor (or air intakes for fuel injection) are opened, vacuum from above the throttle valves is routed through a vacuum signal line to the purge control valve on the canister. The control valve opens and allows the fuel vapors to be drawn from the canister through a purge line and into the intake manifold and the combustion chambers.

INSPECTION AND SERVICE

Check the hoses for proper connections and damage. Replace as necessary. Check the vapor separator tank for fuel leaks, distortion and dents, and replace as necessary.

Flow Guide Valve—Through 1974

Remove the flow guide valve and inspect it for leakage by blowing air into the ports in the valve. When air is applied from the fuel tank side, the flow guide valve is normal if the air passes into the check side (crankcase side), but not into the relief side (air cleaner side). When air is applied from the check side, the valve is normal if the passage of air is restricted. When air is applied from the relief side (air cleaner side), the valve is normal if air passes into the fuel tank side or into the check side.

Carbon Canister and Purge Control Valve—1975 and Later

To check the operation of the carbon canister purge control valve, disconnect the rubber hose between the canister control valve and the T-fitting, at the T-fitting. Apply vacuum to the hose leading to the control valve. The vaccum condition should be maintained indefinitely. If the control valve leaks, remove the top cover of the valve and check for a dislocated or cracked diaphragm. If the diaphragm is damaged, a repair kit containing a new diaphragm, retainer, and spring is available and should be installed.

The carbon canister has an air filter in the bottom of the canister. The filter element should be checked once a year or every 12,000 miles; more frequently if the car is operated in dusty areas. Replace the filter by pulling it out of the bottom of the canister and installing a new one.

REMOVAL AND INSTALLATION

Removal and installation of the various evaporative emission control system components consists of disconnecting the hoses, loosening retaining screws, and removing the part which is to be replaced or checked. Install in the reverse order. When replacing hose, make sure that it is fuel and vapor resistant.

Spark Timing Control System Dual Point Distributor

The 1973 510 and 610 are equipped with this system. The dual point distributor has two sets of breaker points which operate independently of each other and are positioned with a relative phase angle of 7° apart. This makes one set the advanced points and the other set the retarded points.

The two sets of points, which mechanically operate continuously, are connected in parallel to the primary side of the ignition circuit. One set of points controls the firing of the spark plugs and hence, the ignition timing, depending on whether or not the retarded set of points is energized.

When both sets of points are electrically energized, the first set to open (the advanced set, 7° sooner) has no control over breaking the ignition coil primary circuit because the retarded set is still closed and maintaining a complete circuit to ground. When the retarded set of points opens, the advanced set is still open, and the primary circuit is broken causing the electromagnetic field in the coil to collapse and the ignition spark is produced.

When the retarded set of points is removed from the primary ignition circuit through the operation of a distributor relay inserted into the retarded points circuit, the advanced set of points controls the primary circuit. The retarded set of points is activated as follows:

The retarded set of points is activated only while the throttle is partially open, the tem-

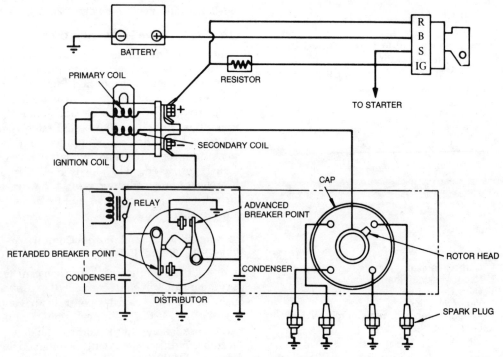

Dual point ignition system schematic

perature is above 50° F and the transmission is in any gear but Fourth gear.

NOTE: *When the ambient temperature is below 30° F, the retarded set of points is removed from the ignition circuit no matter what switch is ON.*

In the case of an automatic transmission, the retarded set of points is activated at all times except under heavy acceleration and high-speed cruising (wide open throttle) with the ambient temperature above 50° F.

There are three switches which control the operation of the distributor relay. All of the switches must be ON in order to energize the distributor relay, thus energizing the retarded set of points.

The switches and their operation are as follows:

A transmission switch located in the transmission closes an electrical circuit when the transmission is in all gears except Fourth gear.

A throttle switch located on the throttle linkage at the carburetor is ON when the throttle valve is moved within a 45° angle.

The temperature sensing switch is located near the hood release lever inside the passenger compartment. The temperature sensing switch comes on between 41° F and 55° F when the temperature is rising and goes OFF above 34° F when the temperature falls.

The distributor vacuum advance mechanism produces a spark advance based on the amount of vacuum in the intake manifold. With a high vacuum, less air/fuel mixture enters the engine cylinders and the mixture is therefore less highly compressed. Consequently, this mixture burns more slowly and the advance mechanism gives it more time to burn. This longer burning time results in higher combustion temperatures at peak pressure and hence, more time for nitrogen to react with oxygen and form nitrogen oxides (NO_x). At the same time, this advance timing results in less complete combustion due to the greater area of cylinder wall (quench area) exposed at the instant of ignition. This "cooled" fuel will not burn as readily and hence, results in higher unburned hydrocarbons (HC). The production of NO_x and HC resulting from vacuum advance is highest during idle and moderate acceleration in lower gears.

Retardation of the ignition timing is necessary to reduce NO_x and HC emissions. Various ways of retarding the ignition spark

have been used in automobiles, all of which remove vacuum to the distributor vacuum advance mechanism at different times under certain conditions. Another way of accomplishing the same goal is the dual point distributor system.

INSPECTION AND ADJUSTMENTS
Phase Difference

1. Disconnect the wiring harness of the distributor from the engine harness.

2. Connect the black wire of the engine harness to the black wire of the distributor harness with a jumper wire. This connects the advanced set of points.

3. With the engine idling, adjust the ignition timing by rotating the distributor.

4. Disconnect the jumper wire from the black wire of the distributor harness and connect it to the yellow wire of the distributor harness. The retarded set of points is now activated.

5. With the engine idling, check the ignition timing. The timing should be retarded from the advanced setting 7°.

6. To adjust the out-of-phase angle of the ignition timing, loosen the adjuster plate set screws on the same side as the retarded set of points.

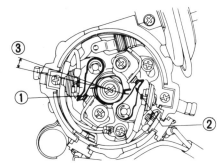

(1) Advance point set (2) Retarded point set (3) Phase difference

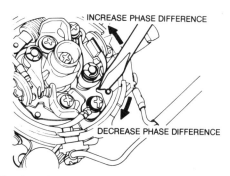

Adjusting phase difference

7. Place the blade of a screwdriver in the adjusting notch of the adjuster plate and turn the adjuster plate as required to obtain the correct retarded ignition timing specification. The ignition timing is retarded when the adjuster plate is turned counterclockwise. There are graduations on the adjuster plate to make the adjustment easier; one graduation is equal to 4° of crankshaft rotation.

8. Replace the distributor cap, start the engine and check the ignition timing with the retarded set of points activated (yellow wire of the distributor wiring harness connected to the black wire of the engine wiring harness).

9. Repeat the steps above as necessary to gain the proper retarded ignition timing.

Transmission Switch

Disconnect the electrical leads at the switch and connect a self-powered test light to the electrical leads. The switch should conduct electricity only when the gearshift is moved to Fourth gear.

If the switch fails to perform in the above manner, replace it with a new one..

Throttle Switch

The throttle switch located on the throttle linkage at the carburetor is checked with a self-powered test light. Disconnect the electrical leads of the switch and connect the test light. The switch should not conduct current when the throttle valve is closed or opened, up to 45°. When the throttle is fully opened, the switch should conduct current.

Temperature Sensing Switch

The temperature sensing switch mounted in the passenger compartment near the hood release lever should not conduct current when the temperature is above 55° F when connected to a self-powered test light as previously outlined for the throttle switch.

Dual Spark Plug Ignition System—Z20E, Z20S

The California model Z-series engine has two spark plugs per cylinder. This arrangement allows the engine to burn large amounts of recirculated exhaust gases without effecting performance. In fact, the system works so well it improves gas mileage under most circumstances.

Both spark plugs fire simultaneously, which substantially shortens the time required to burn the air/fuel mixture when exhaust gases (EGR) are not being recirculated. When gases are being recirculated, the dual spark plug system brings the ignition level up to that of a single plug system which is not recirculating exhaust gases.

ADJUSTMENT

The only adjustments necessary are the tune-up and maintenance procedures outlined in chapters one and two.

Spark Timing Control System

The spark timing control system has been used in different forms on Datsuns since 1972. The first system, Transmission Controlled Spark System (TCS) was used on most Datsuns through 1979. This system consists of a thermal vacuum valve, a vacuum switching valve, a high gear detecting switch, and a number of vacuum hoses. Basically, the system is designed to retard full spark advance except when the car is in high gear and the engine is at normal operating temperature. At all other times, the spark advance is retarded to one degree or another.

The 1980 Spark Timing Control System replaces the TCS system. The major difference is that it works solely from engine water temperature changes rather than a transmission-mounted switch. The system includes a thermal vacuum valve, a vacuum delay valve, and attendant hoses. It performs the same function as the earlier TCS system; to retard full spark advance at times when high levels of pollutants would otherwise be given off.

INSPECTION AND ADJUSTMENTS

Normally the TCS and Spark Timing Control systems should be trouble-free. However, if you suspect a problem in the system, first check to make sure all wiring (if so equipped) and hoses are connected and free from dirt. Also check to make sure the distributor vacuum advance is working properly. If everything appears all right, connect a timing light to the engine and make sure the initial timing is correct. On vehicles with the TCS system, run the engine until it reaches normal operating temperature, and then have an assistant sit in the car and shift the transmission through all the gears slowly. If the system is functioning properly, the timing will be 10 to 15 degrees advanced in high gear (compared

Adjusting BCDD pressure. TOCS similar

to the other gear positions). If the system is still not operating correctly, you will have to check for continuity at all the connections with a test light.

To test the Spark Timing Control System, connect a timing light and check the ignition timing while the temperature gauge is in the "cold" position. Write down the reading. Allow the engine to run with the timing light attached until the temperature needle reaches the center of the gauge. As the engine is warming up, check with the timing light to make sure the ignition timing retards. When the temperature needle is in the middle of the gauge, the ignition timing should advance from its previous position. If the ignition timing does not change, replace the thermal vacuum valve.

Early Fuel Evaporation System

The Early Fuel Evaporation System is used on the A-series and some L-series engines. The system's purpose is to heat the air/fuel mixture when the engine is below normal operating temperature. The 1973–79 A-series and all L-series engines use a system much akin to the old style exhaust manifold heat riser. The only adjustment necessary is to occasionally lubricate the counterweight. Other than that, the system should be trouble-free.

The 1980 carbureted engines use coolant water heat instead of exhaust gas heat to pre-warm the fuel mixture. This system should be trouble-free.

Boost Control Deceleration Device (BCDD) / Throttle Opener Control System (TOCS)

The Boost Control Deceleration Device (BCDD) used on the L-series and non-fuel injected Z-series engines, and the Throttle Opener Control System (TOCS) used on A-series engines (except 1980 California) both accomplish the same purpose: to reduce hydrocarbon emissions during coasting conditions.

High manifold vacuum during coasting prevents the complete combustion of the air/fuel mixture because of the reduced amount of air. This condition will result in a large amount of HC emission. Enriching the air/fuel mixture for a short time (during the high vacuum condition) will reduce the emission of the HC.

However, enriching the air/fuel mixture with only the mixture adjusting screw will cause poor engine idle or invite an increase in the carbon monoxide (CO) content of the exhaust gases. The BCDD consists of an independent system that kicks in when the engine is coasting and enriches the air/fuel mixture, which reduces the hydrocarbon content of the exhaust gases. This is accomplished without adversely affecting engine idle and the carbon monoxide content of the exhaust gases.

The TOCS system used on 1980 A-series non-California models achieves the same end as the BCDD system but uses a slightly different method. The system consists of a servo diaphragm, vacuum control valve, throttle opener solenoid valve, speed detecting switch and amplifier on manual transmission models. Automatic transmission models use an inhibitor and inhibitor relay in the place of the speed detecting switch and amplifier. At the moment when the manifold vacuum increases, as during deceleration, the vacuum control valve opens to transfer the manifold vacuum to the servo diaphragm chamber, and the carburetor throttle valve opens slightly. Under this condition, the proper amount of fresh air is sucked into the combustion chamber. As a result, a more thorough ignition takes place, burning much of the HC in the exhaust gases.

1980 Z20E ENGINE (200SX)

This engine uses a simplified version of the boost control system. In place of the BCDD (see above) is a vacuum control valve which works on manifold vacuum. Service is restricted to replacing the valve.

ADJUSTMENT

Normally, the BCDD never needs adjustment. However, if the need should arise because of suspected malfunction of the system, proceed as follows:

ON: CAR SPEED—BELOW 16 KM/H (10 MPH)
OFF: CAR SPEED—ABOVE 16 KM/H (10 MPH)

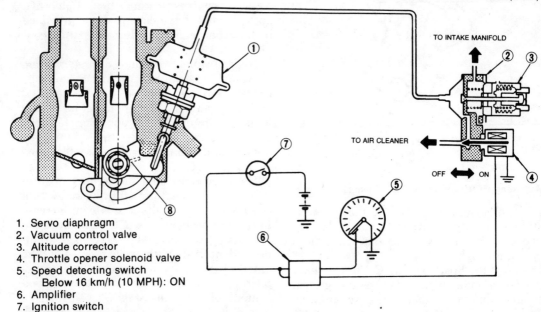

TO INTAKE MANIFOLD

TO AIR CLEANER

OFF ⟷ ON

1. Servo diaphragm
2. Vacuum control valve
3. Altitude corrector
4. Throttle opener solenoid valve
5. Speed detecting switch
   Below 16 km/h (10 MPH): ON
6. Amplifier
7. Ignition switch
8. Primary throttle valve

TOCS system—1980 310

1. Connect a tachometer to the engine.

2. Connect a quick-response vacuum gauge to the intake manifold.

3. Disconnect the solenoid valve electrical leads.

4. Start and warm up the engine until it reaches normal operating temperature.

5. Adjust the idle speed to the proper specification.

6. Raise the engine speed to 3,000–3,500 rpm under no-load (transmission in Neutral or Park), then allow the throttle to close quickly. Take notice as to whether or not the engine rpm returns to idle speed and if it does, how long the fall in rpm is interrupted before it reaches idle speed.

At the moment the throttle is snapped closed at high engine rpm the vacuum in the intake manifold reaches between −23 to −27.7 in. Hg and then gradually falls to about −16.5 in. Hg at idle speed. The process of the fall of the intake manifold vacuum and the engine rpm will take one of the following three forms:

a. When the operating pressure of the BCDD is too high, the system remains inoperative, and the vacuum in the intake manifold decreases without interruption just like that of an engine without a BCDD;

b. When the operating pressure is lower than that of the case given above, but still higher than the proper set pressure, the fall of vacuum in the intake manifold is interrupted and kept constant at a certain level (operating pressure) for about one second and then gradually falls down to the normal vacuum at idle speed;

c. When the set of operating pressure of the BCDD is lower than the intake manifold vacuum when the throttle is suddenly released, the engine speed will not lower to idle speed.

To adjust the set operating pressure of the BCDD, remove the adjusting screw cover from the BCDD mechanism mounted on the side of the carburetor. On 810 models, the BCDD system is installed under the throttle chamber.

The adjusting screw is a left-hand threaded screw. Late models may have an adjusting nut instead of a screw. Turning the screw ⅛ of a turn in either direction will change the operation pressure about 0.79 in. Hg. Turning the screw counterclockwise will increase

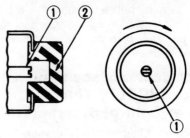

(1) BCDD adjusting screw (2) cover

the amount of vacuum needed to operate the mechanism. Turning the screw clockwise will decrease the amount of vacuum needed to operate the mechanism.

The operating pressure for the BCDD on most models should be between −19.9 to −22.05 in. Hg. The decrease in intake manifold vacuum should be interrupted at these levels for about one second when the BCDD is operating correctly.

Don't forget to install the adjusting screw cover after the system is adjusted.

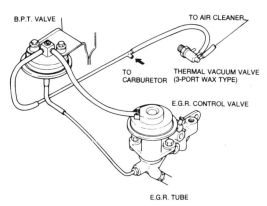

Non-California 1980 210 Thermal Vacuum Valve

Adjustment—TOCS

Adjustment procedures for TOCS are the same as those for BCDD. Observe the following pressures.

When snapping the throttle closed as described in step 6 for BCDD, the vacuum in the intake manifold should reach −23.6 in. Hg or above and then gradually decreases to idle lever.

The operating pressure of the TOCS should be −22.05± 0.79 in. Hg.

Turning the adjusting screw clockwise raises the vacuum level. Turning the screw counterclockwise lowers the vacuum level.

NOTE: *When adjusting the TOCS, turn the adjusting nut in or out with the lock spring in place. Always set the lock spring properly to prevent changes in the set pressure.*

Automatic Temperature Controlled Air Cleaner

This system is used on all Datsun models covered in this guide except the 810 and the 200SX.

The rate of fuel atomization varies with the temperature of the air that the fuel is being mixed with. The air/fuel ratio cannot be held constant for efficient fuel combustion with a wide range of air temperatures. Cold air being drawn into the engine causes a denser and richer air/fuel mixture, inefficient fuel atomization, and thus, more hydrocarbons in the exhaust gas. Hot air being drawn into the engine causes a leaner air/fuel mixture and more efficient atomization and combustion for less hydrocarbons in the exhaust gases.

The automatic temperature controlled air cleaner is designed so that the temperature of the ambient air being drawn into the engine is automatically controlled, to hold the temperature of the air and, consequently, the fuel/air ratio at a constant rate for efficient fuel combustion.

A temperature sensing vacuum switch controls vacuum applied to a vacuum motor operating a valve in the intake snorkle of the air cleaner. When the engine is cold or the air being drawn into the engine is cold, the vacuum motor opens the valve, allowing air heated by the exhaust manifold to be drawn into the engine. As the engine warms up, the temperature sensing unit shuts off the vacuum applied to the vacuum motor which allows the valve to close, shutting off the heated air and allowing cooler, outside (under hood) air to be drawn into the engine.

TESTING

When the air around the temperature sensor of the unit mounted inside the air cleaner housing reaches 100° F, the sensor should block the flow of vacuum to the air control valve vacuum motor. When the temperature around the temperature sensor is below 100° F, the sensor should allow vacuum to pass onto the air valve vacuum motor thus blocking off the air cleaner snorkle to under hood (unheated) air.

When the temperature around the sensor is above 118° F, the air control valve should be completely open to under hood air.

If the air cleaner fails to operate correctly, check for loose or broken vacuum hoses. If the hoses are not the cause, replace the vacuum motor in the air cleaner.

Exhaust Gas Recirculation (EGR)

This system is used on all 1974 and later models. Exhaust gas recirculation is used to

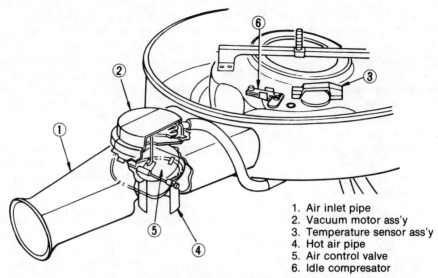

1. Air inlet pipe
2. Vacuum motor ass'y
3. Temperature sensor ass'y
4. Hot air pipe
5. Air control valve
6. Idle compresator

Automatic temperature controlled air cleaner

reduce combustion temperatures in the engine, thereby reducing the oxides of nitrogen emissions.

An EGR valve is mounted on the center of the intake manifold. The recycled exhaust gas is drawn into the bottom of the intake manifold riser portion through the exhaust manifold heat stove and EGR valve. A vacuum diaphragm is connected to a timed signal port at the carburetor flange.

As the throttle valve is opened, vacuum is applied to the EGR valve vacuum diaphragm. When the vacuum reaches about 2

in. Hg, the diaphragm moves against spring pressure and is in a fully up position at 8 in. Hg of vacuum. As the diaphragm moves up, it opens the exhaust gas metering valve which allows exhaust gas to be pulled into the engine intake manifold. The system does not operate when the engine is idling because the exhaust gas recirculation would cause a rough idle.

On 1975 and later models, a thermal vacuum valve inserted in the engine thermostat housing controls the application of the vacuum to the EGR valve. When the engine coolant reaches a predetermined temperature, the thermal vacuum valve opens and allows vacuum to be routed to the EGR valve. Below the predetermined temperature, the thermal vacuum valve closes and blocks vacuum to the EGR valve.

All 1978–79 models and the 1980 210, 510(Canadian), 200SX(Canadian), 310 and 810 have a B.P.T. valve installed between the EGR valve and the thermal vacuum valve. The B.P.T. valve has a diaphragm which is raised or lowered by exhaust back pressure. The diaphragm opens or closes an air bleed, which is connected into the EGR vacuum line. High pressure results in higher levels of EGR, because the diaphragm is raised, closing off the air bleed, which allows more vacuum to reach and open the EGR valve. Thus, the amount of recirculated exhaust gas varies with exhaust pressure.

The 1980 510(USA), 200SX(USA), 310(California), and 210(California) use a V.V.T. valve (venturi vacuum transducer valve) in-

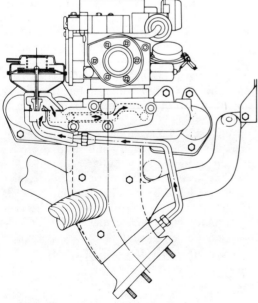

EGR system—carbureted models

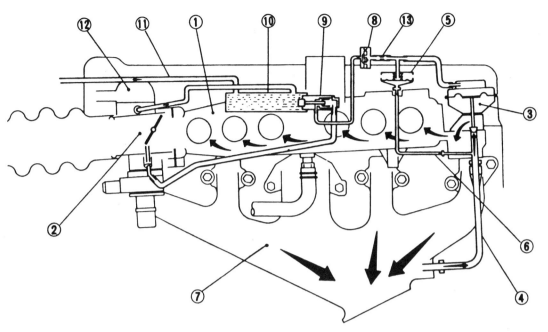

1. Intake manifold
2. Throttle chamber
3. E.G.R. control valve
4. E.G.R. tube
5. B.P.T. valve

6. B.P.T. valve control tube
7. Exhaust manifold
8. Vacuum delay valve
   (California automatic
   transmission models only)

9. Thermal vacuum vlave
10. Heater housing
11. Water return tube
12. Thermostat housing
13. Vacuum orifice

810 EGR system schematic

stead of the B.P.T. valve. The V.V.T. valve monitors exhaust pressure and carburetor vacuum in order to activate the diaphragm which controls the throttle vacuum applied to the EGR control valve. This system expands the operating range of the EGR unit, as well as increasing the EGR flow rate as compared to the B.P.T. unit.

Many 1975 and later Datsuns are equipped with an EGR warning system which signals via a light in the dashboard that the EGR system may need service. The EGR warning light should come on every time the starter is engaged as a test to make sure the bulb is not blown. The system uses a counter which works in conjunction with the odometer, and lights the warning signal after the vehicle has traveled a pre-determined number of miles.

To reset the counter, which is mounted in the engine compartment, remove the grommet installed in the side of the counter and insert the tip of a small screwdriver into the hole. Press down on the knob inside the hole. Reinstall the grommet.

TESTING—PRE-1975

Check the operation of the EGR system as follows:

1. Visually inspect the entire EGR control system. Clean the mechanism free of oil and dirt. Replace any rubber hoses found to be cracked or broken.

2. Make sure that the EGR solenoid valve is properly wired.

3. Increase the engine speed from idling to 2,000–3,500 rpm. The plate of the EGR control valve diaphragm and the valve shaft should move upward as the engine speed is increased.

4. Disconnect the EGR solenoid valve electrical leads and connect them directly to the vehicle's 12-volt electrical supply (battery). Race the engine again with the EGR solenoid valve connected to a 12-volt power

EGR valve removal

source. The EGR control valve should remain stationary.

5. With the engine running at idle, push up on the EGR control valve diaphragm with your finger. When this is done, the engine idle should become rough and uneven.

Inspect the two components of the EGR system as necessary in the following manner:

a. Remove the EGR control valve from the intake manifold;

b. Apply 4.7–5.1 in. Hg of vacuum to the EGR control valve by sucking on a tube attached to the outlet on top of the valve. The valve should move to the full up position. The valve should remain open for more than 30 seconds after the application of vacuum is discontinued and the vacuum hose is blocked;

c. Inspect the EGR valve for any signs of warpage or damage;

d. Clean the EGR valve seat with a brush and compressed air to prevent clogging;

e. Connect the EGR solenoid valve to a 12-volt DC power source and notice if the valve clicks when intermittently electrified. If the valve clicks, it is considered to be working properly;

f. Check the EGR temperature sensing switch by removing it from the engine and placing it in a container of water together with a thermometer. Connect a self-powered test light to the two electrical leads of the switch;

g. Heat the container of water;

h. The switch should conduct current when the water temperature is below 77° F and stop conducting current when the water reaches a temperature somewhere between 88°–106° F. Replace the switch if it functions otherwise.

1975 AND LATER

1. Remove the EGR valve and apply enough vacuum to the diaphragm to open the valve.

2. The valve should remain open for over 30 seconds after the vacuum is removed.

3. Check the valve for damage, such as warpage, cracks, and excessive wear around the valve and seat.

4. Clean the seat with a brush and compressed air and remove any deposits from around the valve and port (seat).

5. To check the operation of the thermal vacuum valve, remove the valve from the engine and apply vacuum to the ports of the

valve. The valve should not allow vacuum to pass.

6. Place the valve in a container of water with a thermometer and heat the water. When the temperature of the water reaches 134°–145° F, remove the valve and apply vacuum to the ports; the valve should allow vacuum to pass through it.

7. To test the B.P.T. valve installed on 1978 and later models, disconnect the two vacuum hoses from the valve. Plug one of the ports. While applying pressure to the bottom of the valve, apply vacuum to the unplugged port and check for leakage. If any exists, replace the valve.

8. To test the check valve installed in some 1978 and later models, remove the valve and blow into the side which connects to the EGR valve. Air should flow. When air is applied to the other side, air flow resistance should be greater. If not, replace the valve.

9. To check the V.V.T. valve which replaces the B.T.P. valve on some 1980 models, disconnect the top and bottom center hoses and apply a vacuum to the top hose. Check for leaks. If a leak is present, replace the valve.

Mixture Ratio Rich-Lean and EGR Large-Small Exchange System (1980 California A-series Engines)

This system controls the air-fuel mixture ratio and the amount of recirculated exhaust gas (manual transmission models only) in accordance with the engine coolant temperature and car speed. The system consists of a vacuum switching valve, a power valve, a speed detecting switch located in the speedometer, a speed detecting switch amplifier and a water temperature switch.

When the coolant temperature is above 122° F and the car is traveling at least 40 miles per hour, the vacuum switching valve is on and acts to lean down the fuel mixture. It also allows a small amount of EGR to be burned on manual transmission cars. When the coolant temperature is above 122° F but the vehicle is traveling less than 40 miles per hour, the vacuum switching valve is off and allows the mixture to richen. It also allows a large amount of EGR to be burned in manual transmission models. When coolant temperature is below 122° F the vacuum switching valve is always on and acts to lean down the fuel mixture.

TESTING

Warm up the engine and jack up the drive wheels of the vehicle. Support the raised end of the car on jack stands and chock the wheels still on the ground. Start the engine and shift the transmission into TOP speed and maintain a speedometer speed higher than 50 MPH. Pinch the hose running from the vacuum switching valve to the air cleaner and see if the engine speed decreases and operates erratically. Shift the transmission into 3RD speed and run the car at a speed lower than 30 MPH. Disconnect the vacuum hose running between the vacuum switching valve and the power valve, by detaching it at the power valve and blocking its open end with your finger. The engine should operate erratically. If the expected engine reaction in both of these tests does not happen, check all wiring connections and hoses for breaks and blockage.

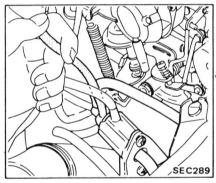

Checking the vacuum switching valve 1980 310 (California)

Air Injection Reactor System

This system is used on 1974 and later models. In gasoline engines, it is difficult to completely burn the air/fuel mixture through normal combustion in the combustion chambers. Under certain operating conditions, unburned fuel is exhausted into the atmosphere.

The air injection reactor system is designed so that ambient air, pressurized by the air pump, is injected through the injection nozzles into the exhaust ports near each exhaust valve. The exhaust gases are at high temperatures and ignite when brought into contact with the oxygen. Unburned fuel is then burned in the exhaust ports and manifold.

In 1976 California models utilized a secondary system consisting of an air control valve which limits injection of secondary air and an emergency relief valve which controls the supply of secondary air. This system protects the catalytic converter from overheating. In 1977 the function of these two valves was taken by a single combined air control (C.A.C.) valve.

All engines with the air pump system have a series of minor alterations to accommodate the system. These are:

1. Special close-tolerance carburetor. Most engines, except the L16, require a slightly rich idle mixture adjustment.

2. Distributor with special advance curve. Ignition timing is retarded about 10° at idle in most cases.

3. Cooling system changes such as larger fan, higher fan speed, and thermostatic fan clutch. This is required to offset the increase in temperature caused by retarded timing at idle.

4. Faster idle speed.

5. Heated air intake on some engines.

The only periodic maintenance required on the air pump system is replacement of the air filter element and adjustment of the drive belt.

TESTING

Air Pump

If the air pump makes an abnormal noise and cannot be corrected without removing the pump from the vehicle, check the following in sequence:

1. Turn the pulley ¾ of a turn in the clockwise direction and ¼ of a turn in the counterclockwise direction. If the pulley is binding and if rotation is not smooth, a defective bearing is indicated.

2. Check the inner wall of the pump body, vanes and rotor for wear. If the rotor has abnormal wear, replace the air pump.

3. Check the needle roller bearing for wear and damage. If the bearings are defective, the air pump should be replaced.

4. Check and replace the rear side seal if abnormal wear or damage is noticed.

5. Check and replace the carbon shoes holding the vanes if they are found to be worn or damaged.

6. A deposit of carbon particles on the inner wall of the pump body and vanes is normal, but should be removed with com-

Air pump (arrow)

pressed air before reassembling the air pump.

Check Valve

Remove the check valve from the air pump discharge line. Test it for leakage by blowing air into the valve from the air pump side and from the air manifold side. Air should only pass through the valve from the air pump side if the valve is functioning normally. A small amount of air leakage from the manifold side can be overlooked. Replace the check valve if it is found to be defective.

Anti-Backfire Valve

Disconnect the rubber hose connecting the mixture control valve with the intake manifold and plug the hose. If the mixture control

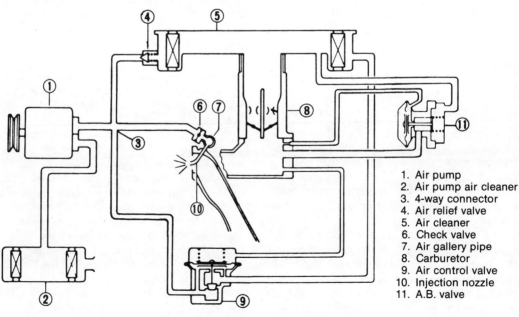

1. Air pump
2. Air pump air cleaner
3. 4-way connector
4. Air relief valve
5. Air cleaner
6. Check valve
7. Air gallery pipe
8. Carburetor
9. Air control valve
10. Injection nozzle
11. A.B. valve

Air injection system schematic—typical

valve is operating correctly, air will continue to blow out the mixture control valve for a few seconds after the accelerator pedal is fully depressed (engine running) and released quickly. If air continues to blow out for more than five seconds, replace the mixture control valve.

Air Pump Relief Valve

Disconnect the air pump discharge hose leading to the exhaust manifold. With the engine running, restrict the air-flow coming from the pump. The air pump relief valve should vent the pressurized air to the atmosphere if it is working properly.

NOTE: *When performing this test do not completely block the discharge line of the air pump as damage may result if the relief valve fails to function properly.*

Air Injection Nozzles

Check around the air manifold for air leakage with the engine running at 2,000 rpm. If air is leaking from the eye joint bolt, retighten or replace the gasket. Check the air nozzles for restrictions by blowing air into the nozzles.

Hoses

Check and replace hoses if they are found to be weakened or cracked. Check all hose connections and clips. Be sure that the hoses are not in contact with other parts of the engine.

Emergency Air Relief Valve

1. Warm up the engine.
2. Check all hoses for leaks, kinks, improper connections, etc.
3. Run the engine up to 2000 rpm under no load. No air should be discharged from the valve.
4. Disconnect the vacuum hose from the valve. This is the hose which runs to the intake manifold. Run the engine up to 2000 rpm. Air should be discharged from the valve. If not, replace it.

Combined Air Control Valve

1. Check all hoses for leaks, kinks, and improper connections.
2. Thoroughly warm up the engine.
3. With the engine idling, check for air discharge from the relief opening in the air cleaner case.
4. Disconnect and plug the vacuum hose from the valve. Air should be discharged from the valve with the engine idling. If the disconnected vacuum hose is not plugged, the engine will stumble.
5. Connect a hand-operated vacuum pump to the vacuum fitting on the valve and apply 7.8–9.8 in. Hg. of vacuum. Run the engine speed up to 3000 rpm. No air should be discharged from the valve.
6. Disconnect and plug the air hose at the check valve, with the conditions as in the preceding step. This should cause the valve to discharge air. If not, or if any of the conditions in this procedure are not met, replace the valve.

Electric Choke

The purpose of the electric choke, used on all models, except the 810, and Z20E (200SX) covered in this guide is to shorten the time the choke is in operation after the engine is started, thus shortening the time of high HC output.

An electric heater warms the bimetal spring which controls the opening and closing of the choke valve. The heater starts to heat as soon as the engine starts.

Electric choke (arrow)

Catalytic Converter

This system is used on all 1975 and later models delivered in California in addition to the air injection system, EGR and the engine modifications, the catalyst further reduces pollutants. Through catalytic action, it changes residual hydrocarbons and carbon monoxide in the exhaust gas into carbon dioxide and water before the exhaust gas is discharged into the atmosphere.

NOTE: *Only unleaded fuel must be used with catalytic converters; lead in fuel will quickly pollute the catalyst and render it useless.*

The emergency air relief valve is used as a catalyst protection device. When the temperature of the catalyst goes above maximum operating temperature, the temperature sensor signals the switching module to activate the emergency air relief valve. This stops air injection into the exhaust manifold and lowers the temperature of the catalyst.

Certain late 1970's catalyst-equipped models have a floor temperature warning system which emits a warning if the catalytic converter or engine becomes overly hot or malfunctions, causing floor temperature to rise.

FUEL SYSTEM

Fuel Pump—All Except 810, 200SX

The fuel pump is a mechanically-operated, diaphragm-type driven by the fuel pump eccentric on the camshaft.

Design of the fuel pump permits disassembly, cleaning, and repair or replacement of defective parts.

TESTING

1. Disconnect the line between the carburetor and the pump at the carburetor.

2. Connect a fuel pump pressure gauge into the line.

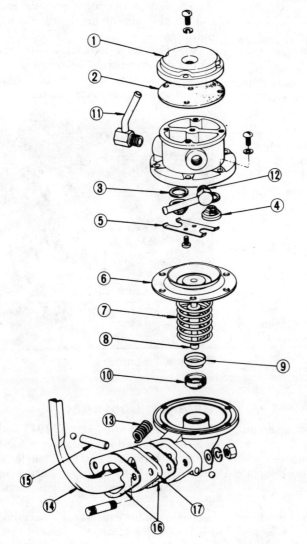

1. Fuel pump cap
2. Cap gasket
3. Valve packing assembly
4. Fuel pump valve assembly
5. Valve retainer
6. Diaphragm assembly
7. Diaphragm spring
8. Pull rod
9. Lower body seal washer
10. Lower body seal
11. Inlet connector
12. Outlet connector
13. Rocker arm spring
14. Rocker arm
15. Rocker arm side pin
16. Fuel pump packing
17. Spacer-fuel pump to cylinder block

L-series engine fuel pump

Fuel pump location—1980 510, L-series fours

3. Start the engine. The pressure should be between 3.0 and 3.9 psi. There is usually enough gas in the float bowl to perform this test.

4. If the pressure is ok, perform a capacity test. Remove the gauge from the line. Use a graduated container to catch the gas from the fuel line. Fill the carburetor float bowl with gas. Run the engine for one minute at about 1,000 rpm. The pump for A-series engines should deliver 600cc in one minute or less and for L and Z-series engines, the pump should deliver 1,000cc in a minute or less.

REMOVAL AND INSTALLATION

1. Disconnect the two fuel lines from the fuel pump. Be sure to keep the line leading from the fuel tank up high to prevent the excess loss of fuel.

2. Remove the two fuel pump mounting nuts and remove the fuel pump assembly from the side of the engine.

3. Install the fuel pump in the reverse order of removal, using a new gasket and sealer on the mating surface.

Fuel Pump—810, 200SX

The fuel injected 810 and 200SX use an electric fuel pump mounted near the fuel tank on

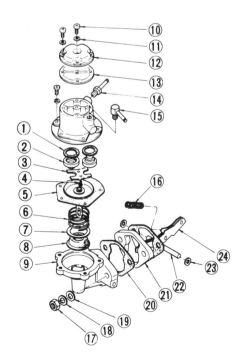

1. Packing
2. Valve assembly
3. Retainer
4. Screw
5. Diaphragm assembly
6. Diaphragm spring
7. Retainer
8. Diaphragm assembly
9. Complete-body lower
10. Screw
11. Washer-spring
12. Fuel pump cap
13. Cap gasket
14. Connector-inlet
15. Connector-outlet
16. Rocker arm spring
17. Nut
18. Washer-spring
19. Washer-plain
20. Gasket
21. Spacer
22. Rocker pin
23. Spacer
24. Rocker arm

A-series engine fuel pump

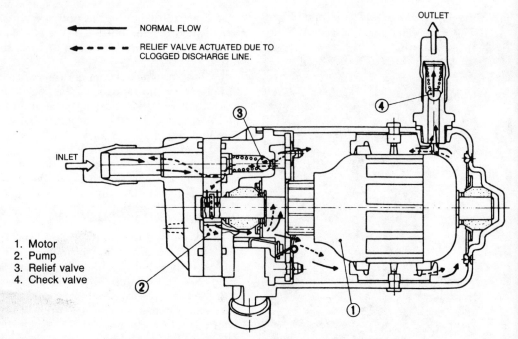

1. Motor
2. Pump
3. Relief valve
4. Check valve

NORMAL FLOW

RELIEF VALVE ACTUATED DUE TO
CLOGGED DISCHARGE LINE.

INLET

OUTLET

Cross section of 810 electric fuel pump. 1980 200SX similar

the 810 and near the center of the car on the 200SX. The pump is of wet type construction. A vane pump and roller are directly coupled to a motor filled with fuel. A relief valve in the pump is designed to open when the pressure in the fuel line rises over 64 psi. Normal operating pressure is 36–43 psi. The pump is automatically activated when the ignition switch is turned to the "start" position. If the engine stalls for some reason, the fuel pump is cut off even though the ignition switch remains in the "on" position.

TESTING

Fuel pressure must be reduced to zero before tests are made.

On 1977–79 810's, disconnect the ground

cable from the battery. Disconnect the cold start valve wiring harness at the connector. Connect two jumper wires to the terminals of the cold start valve. Touch the other ends of the jumpers to the positive and negative terminals of the battery for a few seconds to release the pressure.

For 1980 810's and 200SX', start the engine, disconnect the harness connector of fuel pump relay-2 while the engine is running. After the engine stalls, crank it over two or three times to make sure all of the fuel pressure is released.

NOTE: *If the engine will not start, remove the fuel pump relay-2 harness connector and crank the engine for about 5 seconds.*

To test pressure:

1. Connect a fuel pressure gauge between

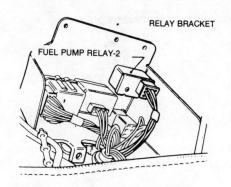

Releasing pressure at the cold-start valve—810　　　**Unplug harness connector—1980 200SX**

the fuel feed pipe and the fuel filter outlet.

2. Start the engine and read the pressure. It should be 30 psi at idle, and 37 psi at the moment the accelerator pedal is fully depressed.

3. If pressure is not as specified, replace the pressure regulator and repeat the test. If the pressure is still incorrect, check for clogged or deformed fuel lines, then replace the fuel pump.

FUEL PUMP REMOVAL AND INSTALLATION—810, 200SX

1. Reduce the fuel pressure to zero. See procedures under the "Testing" section, above.

2. Disconnect the electrical harness connector at the pump. The 810 pump is located near the fuel tank. The 200SX pump is located near the center of the car.

3. Clamp the hose between the fuel tank and the pump to prevent gas from spewing out from the tank.

4. Remove the inlet and outlet hoses at the pump. Unclamp the inlet hose and allow the fuel lines to drain into a suitable container.

5. Unbolt and remove the pump. The 200SX pump and fuel damper can be removed at the same time.

6. Installation is the reverse of removal. Use new clamps and be sure all hoses are properly seated on the fuel pump body.

Carburetor

The carburetor used is a two-barrel downdraft type with a low-speed (primary) side and a high-speed (secondary) side.

All models have an electrically-operated anti-dieseling solenoid. As the ignition switch is turned off, the valve is energized and shuts off the supply of fuel to the idle circuit of the carburetor.

REMOVAL AND INSTALLATION

1. Remove the air cleaner.

2. Disconnect the fuel and vacuum lines from the carburetor.

3. Remove the throttle lever.

4. Remove the four nuts and washers retaining the carburetor to the manifold.

5. Lift the carburetor from the manifold.

6. Remove and discard the gasket used between the carburetor and the manifold.

7. Install the carburetor in the reverse

order of removal, using a new carburetor base gasket.

THROTTLE LINKAGE ADJUSTMENT

On all models, make sure the throttle is wide open when the accelerator pedal is floored. Some models have an adjustable accelerator pedal stop to prevent strain on the linkage.

DASHPOT ADJUSTMENT

A dashpot is used on carburetors of all cars with automatic transmissions and many late model manual transmission models. The dashpot slowly closes the throttle on automatic transmissions to prevent stalling and serves as an emission control device on all late model vehicles.

The dashpot should be adjusted to contact the throttle lever on deceleration at approximately 1,900–2,100 rpm for manual transmissions or 1,600–1,800 rpm for automatic transmissions with the L-series engines, or 2,000–2,300 rpm for all models of the A-series engines. The 1980 Z20S engine's dashpot contact point should be between 1,400–1,600 rpm for automatic transmissions.

NOTE: *Before attempting to adjust the dashpot, make sure the idle speed, timing and mixture adjustments are correct.*

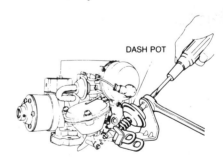

DASH POT

L-series dashpot adjustment

SECONDARY THROTTLE LINKAGE ADJUSTMENT

All Datsun carburetors discussed in this book are two stage type carburetors. On this type of carburetor, the engine runs on the primary barrel most of the time, with the secondary barrel being used for acceleration purposes. When the throttle valve on the primary side opens to an angle of approximately 50 degrees (from its fully closed position), the secondary throttle valve is pulled open by the connecting linkage. The fifty degree angle of throttle valve opening works out to a clear-

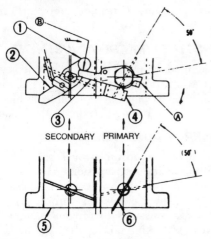

1. Roller
2. Connecting lever
3. Return plate
4. Adjust plate
5. Throttle chamber
6. Throttle valve

Secondary throttle linkage adjustment

Carburetor used on L-series engines

Close-up of float level sight window

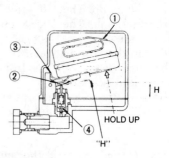

1. Float
2. Float seat
3. Float stopper
4. Needle valve

1200 and B210 float level adjustment

ance measurement of somewhere between 0.26–0.32 in. between the throttle valve and the carburetor body. The easiest way to measure this is to use a drill bit. Drill bits from size H to size P (standard letter size drill bits) should fit. Check the appendix in the back of the book for the exact size of the various drill bits. If an adjustment is necessary, bend the connecting link between the two linkage assemblies.

FLOAT LEVEL ADJUSTMENT

The fuel level is normal if it is within the lines on the window glass of the float chamber (or the sight glass) when the vehicle is resting on level ground and the engine is off.

If the fuel level is outside the lines, remove the float housing cover. Have an absor-

bent cloth under the cover to catch the fuel from the fuel bowl. Adjust the float level by bending the needle seat on the float.

The needle valve should have an effective stroke of about 0.0591 in. When necessary, the needle valve stroke can be adjusted by bending the float stopper.

NOTE: *Be careful not to bend the needle valve rod when installing the float and baffle plate, if removed.*

FAST IDLE ADJUSTMENT

1. With the carburetor removed from the vehicle, place the upper side of the fast idle screw on the second step (first step for 1977–80 L and Z engines) of the fast idle cam and measure the clearance between the throttle valve and the wall of the throttle valve chamber at the center of the throttle valve. Check it against the following specifications:

1973 1200, 1974–76 B210:
• 0.0315–0.0346 in. M/T
• 0.0421–0.0461 in. A/T

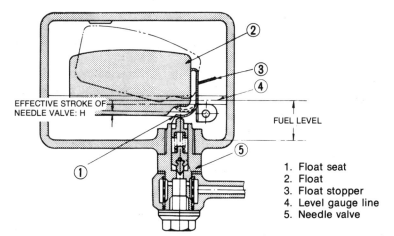

EFFECTIVE STROKE OF
NEEDLE VALVE: H

FUEL LEVEL

1. Float seat
2. Float
3. Float stopper
4. Level gauge line
5. Needle valve

Z20S, and L-series float level adjustment

1973 510, 1973–74 610, 1974 710:
- 0.035–0.039 in. M/T
- 0.044–0.048 in. A/T

1975–76 610, 710:
- 0.040–0.048 in. M/T
- 0.049–0.052 in. A/T

1977–78 B210, F10:
- 0.0287–0.0343 in. M/T
- 0.0394–0.0449 in. A/T

1977 710, 1978–79 510, 200SX:
- 0.0370–0.0465 in. M/T
- 0.0457–0.0551 in. A/T

1980 310:
- 0.0283–0.0350 in.

1980 510:
- 0.0299–0.0354 in. M/T
- 0.0378–0.0433 in. M/T

1980 210, A12A engine:
- 0.0248–0.0315 in. M/T

A14 engine:
- 0.0283–0.0350 in. M/T

A15 engine:
- 0.0386–0.0461 in. A/T

"M/T" means manual transmission. "A/T" means automatic transmission.

NOTE: *The first step of the fast idle adjustment procedure is not absolutely necessary.*

2. Install the carburetor on the engine.

3. Start the engine and measure the fast idle rpm with the engine at operating temperature. The cam should be at the 2nd step.

1974 B210, 1973 1200:
- M/T 1,720–2,050 rpm
- A/T 2,650–2,950 rpm

1974–76 710, 610, 1973 510:
- M/T 1,900–2,100 rpm
- A/T 2,300–2,500 rpm

1975–76 B210:
- M/T 2,450–2,650 rpm
- A/T 2,700–2,900 rpm

1977–78 B210, F10:
- M/T 1,900–2,700 rpm
- A/T 2,400–3,200 rpm

1977 710, 1978–79 510, 200SX:
- M/T 1,900–2,800 rpm
- A/T 2,200–3,200 rpm

1980 310:
- 49 states, 2,400–3,200 rpm
- California, 2,300–3,100 rpm

1980 210, A12A, A14 engines:
- 49 states M/T 2,400–3,200 rpm
- California M/T 2,300–3,100 rpm

A15 engine:
- A/T 2,700–3,500 rpm

4. To adjust the fast idle speed, turn the fast idle adjusting screw counterclockwise to increase the fast idle speed and clockwise to decrease the fast idle speed.

AUTOMATIC CHOKE ADJUSTMENT

1. With the engine cold, make sure the choke is fully closed (press the gas pedal all the way to the floor and release).

2. Check the choke linkage for binding. The choke plate should be easily opened and closed with your finger. If the choke sticks or binds, it can usually be freed with a liberal application of a carburetor cleaner made for the purpose. A couple of quick squirts of the right stuff normally does the trick.

If not, the carburetor will have to be disassembled for repairs.

3. The choke is correctly adjusted when the index mark on the choke housing (notch) aligns with the center mark on the carburetor body. If the setting is incorrect, loosen the

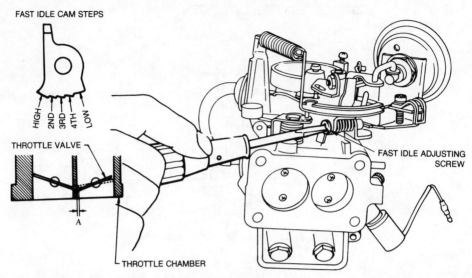

Fast idle adjustment

three screws clamping the choke body in place and rotate the choke cover left or right until the marks align. Tighten the screws carefully to avoid cracking the housing.

CHOKE UNLOADER ADJUSTMENT

1. Close the choke valve completely.
2. Hold the choke valve closed by stretching a rubber band between the choke piston lever and a stationary part of the carburetor.
3. Open the throttle lever fully.
4. Adjust the gap between the choke plate and the carburetor body to:
A-series engines:
• 1973–77: 0.0791 in.
• 1978–80: 0.0929 in. except:
• 1978–80: Non-Cal. 5 speed hatchback
• 210, B210 and 1980 Canada manual trans. A12A: 0.0854 in.
L-series engines, 1980 Z20S engine:
•1973–74: 0.173 in.
• 1975–77: 0.096 in., except:
• 1977 710: 0.0807–0.1122 in.
• 1978–80: 0.0807–0.1122 in.

OVERHAUL

Efficient carburetion depends greatly on careful cleaning and inspection during overhaul, since dirt, gum, water, or varnish in or on the carburetor parts are often responsible for poor performance.

Overhaul your carburetor in a clean, dust-free area. Carefully disassemble the carburetor, referring often to the exploded views. Keep all similar and look-alike parts segregated during disassembly and cleaning

to avoid accidental interchange during assembly. Make a note of all jet sizes.

When the carburetor is disassembled, wash all parts (except diaphragms, electric choke units, pump plunger, and any other plastic, leather, fiber, or rubber parts) in clean carburetor solvent. Do not leave parts in the solvent any longer than is necessary to sufficiently loosen the deposits. Excessive cleaning may remove the special finish from the float bowl and choke valve bodies, leaving these parts unfit for service. Rinse all parts in clean solvent and blow them dry with compressed air to allow them to air dry. Wipe clean all cork, plastic, leather, and fiber parts with a clean, lint-free cloth.

Blow out all passages and jets with compressed air and be sure that there are no restrictions or blockages. Never use wire or similar tools to clean jets, fuel passages, or air bleeds. Clean all jets and valves separately to avoid accidental interchange.

Check all parts for wear or damage. If wear or damage is found, replace the defective parts. Especially check the following:
1. Check the float needle and seat for wear. If wear is found, replace the complete assembly.
2. Check the float hinge pin for wear and the float(s) for dents or distortion. Replace the float if fuel has leaked into it.
3. Check the throttle and choke shaft bores for wear or an out-of-round condition. Damage or wear to the throttle arm, shaft, or shaft bore will often require replacement of the throttle body. These parts require a close

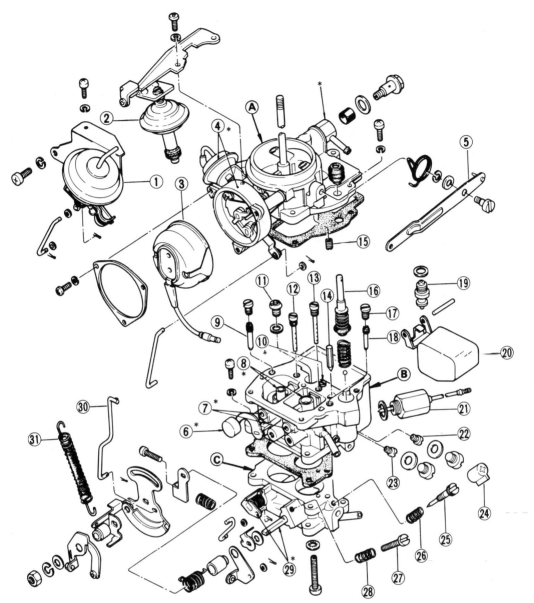

Ⓐ Choke chamber
Ⓑ Center body
Ⓒ Throttle chamber

1. Servo diaphragm of throttle
    opener
2. Dash pot
3. Automatic choke cover
4.* Automatic choke body and
    diaphragm chamber
5. Accelerating pump lever
6.* Auxiliary valve
7.* Venturi stopper screw
8.* Primary and secondary small
    venturi

9. Secondary slow jet
10.* Safe orifice
11. Power valve
12. Secondary main air bleed
13. Primary main air bleed
14. Injector weight
15. Primary slow air bleed
16. Accelerating pump
17. Plug
18. Primary slow jet
19. Needle valve
20. Float
21. Anti-dieseling solenoid valve

22. Primary main jet
23. Secondary main jet
24. Idle limiter cap
25. Idle adjust screw
26. Spring
27. Throttle adjust screw
28. Spring
29.* Primary and secondary throttle
    valve
30. Accelerating pump rod
31. Throttle return spring

Note: Do not remove the parts
    marked with an asterisk

Exploded view of 1975 B210 carburetor—other A-series similar

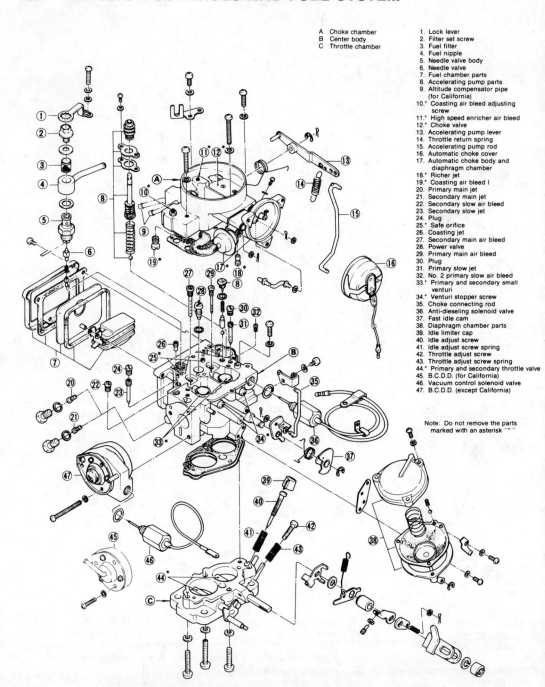

A Choke chamber
B Center body
C Throttle chamber

1. Lock lever
2. Filter set screw
3. Fuel filter
4. Fuel nipple
5. Needle valve body
6. Needle valve
7. Fuel chamber parts
8. Accelerating pump parts
9. Altitude compensator pipe
   (for California)
10.* Coasting air bleed adjusting
    screw
11.* High speed enricher air bleed
12.* Choke valve
13. Accelerating pump lever
14. Throttle return spring
15. Accelerating pump rod
16. Automatic choke cover
17. Automatic choke body and
    diaphragm chamber
18.* Richer jet
19.* Coasting air bleed I
20. Primary main jet
21. Secondary main jet
22. Secondary slow air bleed
23. Secondary slow jet
24. Plug
25.* Safe orifice
26. Coasting jet
27. Secondary main air bleed
28. Power valve
29. Primary main air bleed
30. Plug
31. Primary slow jet
32. No. 2 primary slow air bleed
33.* Primary and secondary small
    venturi
34.* Venturi stopper screw
35. Choke connecting rod
36. Anti-dieseling solenoid valve
37. Fast idle cam
38. Diaphragm chamber parts
39. Idle limiter cap
40. Idle adjust screw
41. Idle adjust screw spring
42. Throttle adjust screw
43. Throttle adjust screw spring
44.* Primary and secondary throttle valve
45. B.C.D.D. (for California)
46. Vacuum control solenoid valve
47. B.C.D.D. (except California)

Note: Do not remove the parts
marked with an asterisk "*"

Exploded view of 1975 710 carburetor—other L-series similar

tolerance of fit; wear may allow air leakage, which could affect starting and idling.

NOTE: *Throttle shafts and bushings are not included in overhaul kits. They can be purchased separately.*

4. Inspect the idle mixture adjusting needles for burrs or grooves. Any such condition requires replacement of the needle,

since you will not be able to obtain a satisfactory idle.

5. Test the accelerator pump check valves. They should pass air one way but not the other. Test for proper seating by blowing and sucking on the valve. Replace the valve if necessary. If the valve is satisfactory, wash the valve again to remove breath moisture.

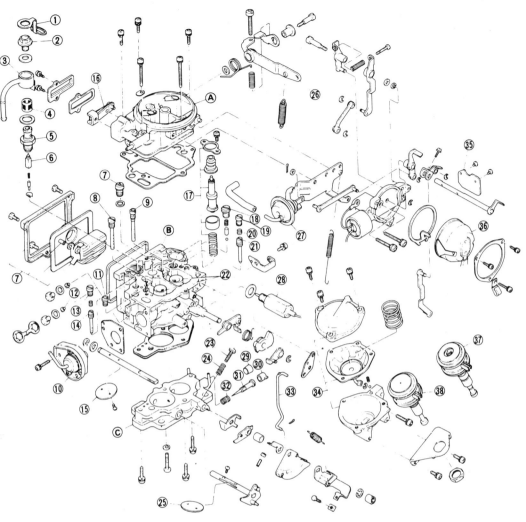

1. Lock lever
2. Filter set screw
3. Fuel nipple
4. Fuel filter
5. Needle valve body
6. Needle valve
7. Power valve
8. Secondary main air bleed
9. Primary main air bleed
10. B.C.D.D.
11. Secondary slow air bleed
12. Secondary main jet
13. Plug
14. Secondary slow jet
15. Primary throttle valve
16. Idle compensator
17. Accelerating pump parts
18. Plug for accelerating mechanism
19. Plug
20. Spring
21. Primary slow jet
22. Primary and secondary small venturi
23. Throttle adjusting screw
24. Throttle adjusting screw spring
25. Secondary throttle valve
26. Accelerating pump lever
27. Vacuum break diaphragm
28. Anti-dieseling solenoid valve
29. Blind plug (California)
30. Idle limiter cap (Except California)
31. Idle adjusting screw
32. Idle adjusting screw spring
33. Choke connecting rod
34. Diaphragm chamber parts
35. Choke valve
36. Automatic choke cover
37. F.I. pot (A/T)
38. F.I.C.D. actuator (M/T air conditioner equipped models only)

Exploded view of 1980 510 (Z20S) engine carburetor

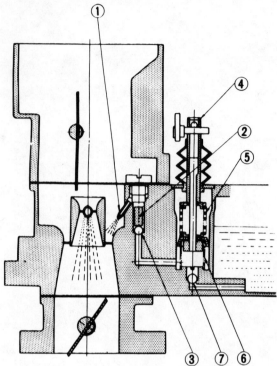

1. Pump injector
2. Weight
3. Outlet valve
4. Piston
5. Damper spring
6. Piston return spring
7. Inlet valve

L-series carburetor acceleration circuit

6. Check the bowl cover for warped surfaces with a straightedge.

7. Closely inspect the valves and seats for wear and damage, replacing as necessary.

8. After the carburetor is assembled, check the choke valve for freedom of operation.

Carburetor overhaul kits are recommended for each overhaul. These kits contain all gaskets and new parts to replace those that deteriorate most rapidly. Failure to replace all parts supplied with the kit (especially gaskets) can result in poor performance later.

Some carburetor manufactures supply overhaul kits of three basic types: minor repair; major repair; and gasket kits. Basically, they contain the following:

Minor Repair Kits:
- All gaskets
- Float needle valve
- Volume control screw
- All diaphragms
- Spring for the pump diaphragm

Major Repair Kits:
- All jets and gaskets
- All diaphragms
- Float needle valve
- Volume control screw
- Pump ball valve

- Main jet carrier
- Float

Gasket Kits:
- All gaskets

After cleaning and checking all components, reassemble the carburetor, using new parts and referring to the exploded view. When reassembling, make sure that all screws and jets are tight in their seats, but do not overtighten as the tips will be distorted. Tighten all screws gradually in rotation. Do not tighten needle valves into their seats; uneven jetting will result. Always use new gaskets. Be sure to adjust the float level when reassembling.

Electronic Fuel Injection System (EFI)

The electronic fuel injection system used on the L24 engine in the 810 and with slight alteration on the Z20E engine in the 1980 200SX is a Bosch L-Jetronic unit built under license in Japan.

The electric fuel pump pumps fuel through a damper and filter to the pressure regulator. The fuel injectors are electric solenoid valves which open and close by signals from the Electronic Control Unit.

Carburetor Specifications

Year	Engine	Vehicle Model	Carb Model	Main Jet #		Main Air Bleed #		Slow Jet #		Float Level (in.)	Power Jet #
				Primary	Secondary	Primary	Secondary	Primary	Secondary		
1973	L16	510	DCH340-7 ① / DCH340-6 ②	97.5	170	65	60	48 ③	90 ③	0.906	53
	L18	610	DCH340-2 ① / DCH340-1 ②	97.5	170	65	60	48 ③	90 ③	0.906	53
	A12	1200	DCH306-4 ① / DCH306-5 ②	95	140	80	80	43 ④	50 ④	0.709–0.748	60
1974	L18	710	DCH340-10 ① / DCH340-11 ②	100	170	60	60	45 ③	90 ③	0.906	41
	A13	B210	DCH306-6 ① / DCH306-7 ②	140	145	65	80	43 ⑤	50 ⑤	0.709–0.748	55
	L20B	610	DCH340-15 ① / DCH340-14 ②	102	170	60	60	46 ③	160 ③	0.906	50
1975	L20B (California)	710	DCH340-41 ① / DCH340-42 ②	99	160	70	60	48	80	0.906	43
	L20B (Federal)	710	DCH340-43 ① / DCH340-44 ②	97	160	70	60	48	100	0.906	48
	A14 (California)	B210	DCH306-11 ① / DCH306-15 ②	104	150	95	80	45	50	0.75	43
	A14 (Federal)	B210	DCH306-10 ① / DCH306-14 ②	102	150	95	80	45	50	0.75	45
1976	A14 (California)	B210	DCH306-11A ① / DCH306-15A ②	104	145	95	80	45	50	0.75	43

Carburetor Specifications (cont.)

Year	Engine	Vehicle Model	Carb Model	Main Jet #		Main Air Bleed #		Slow Jet #		Float Level (in.)	Power Jet #
				Primary	Secondary	Primary	Secondary	Primary	Secondary		
1976	A14 (Federal)	B210	DCH306-10A ① DCH306-14A ②	102	145	95	80	45	50	0.75	45
	L20B (California)	710,610	DCH340-41A ① DCH340-42B ②	101	160	70	60	48	80	0.906	40
	L20B (Federal)	710,610	DCH340-43A ① DCH340-44A ②	99	160	70	60	48	100	0.906	43
	A14 (California)	F10	DCH306-17	105	145	95	80	45	50	0.75	40
	A14 (Federal)	F10	DCH306-16	103	145	95	80	45	50	0.75	40
1977	L20B (California)	710	DCH340-41B ① DCH340-42C ②	101	160	70	60	48	80	0.91	40
	L20B (Federal)	710	DCH340-51A ① DCH340-52A ②	105	165	60	60	48	100	0.91	43
	A14 (California)	F10	DCH306-17A	106	145	95	80	45	50	0.75	40
	A14 (Federal)	F10	DCH306-16A	105	145	95	80	45	50	0.75	40
	L20B (California)	200SX	DCH340-49A ① DCH340-50A ②	101	160	70	60	48	80	0.91	43
	L20B (Federal)	200SX	DCH340-53B ① DCH340-54B ②	105	165	60	60	48	100	0.91	43

Year			Carburetor								
1978	A14 (California)	B210	DCH306-11 ① / DCH306-15 ②	105 / 104	145	95	80	45	50	0.75	40 / 48
	A14 (Federal)	B210	DCH306-60 ① / DCH306-14 ②	104	145	110 / 95	80	45	50	0.75	48 / 40
	A14 (FU Model)	B210	DCH306-37	107	145	65	60	46	50	0.75	48
	A14 (California)	F10	DCH306-65	106	145	95	80	45	50	0.75	40
	A14 (Federal)	F10	DCH306-64	105	145	95	80	45	50	0.75	40
	L20B (California)	200SX	DCH340-91A ① / DCH340-92A ②	102	158	70	60	48	70	0.91	40
	L20B (Federal)	200SX	DCH340-93A ① / DCH340-94A ②	104	160	60	60	48	70	0.91	43
	L20B (California)	510	DCH340-99 ① / DCH340-92A ②	103 / 102	158	70	60	48	70	0.91	35 / 40
	L20B (Federal)	510	DCH340-93A ① / DCH340-94A ②	104	160	60	60	48	70	0.91	43
1979	L20B (California)	200SX	DCH340-91C ① / DCH340-92C ②	102	158	70	60	48	70	0.91	40
	L20B (Federal)	200SX	DCH340-69 ① / DCH340-94B ②	104	160	60	60	48	70	0.91	35 / 43
	L20B (California)	510	DCH340-99C ① / DCH340-92C ②	103 / 102	158	70	60	48	70	0.91	35 / 40
	L20B (Federal)	510	DCH340-69 ① / DCH340-94B ②	104	160	60	60	48	70	0.91	35 / 43

Carburetor Specifications (cont.)

Year	Engine	Vehicle Model	Carb Model	Main Jet # Primary	Main Jet # Secondary	Main Air Bleed # Primary	Main Air Bleed # Secondary	Slow Jet # Primary	Slow Jet # Secondary	Float Level (in.)	Power Jet #
1979	A14, A15 (California)	210	DCH306-61① DCH306-63②	107	145	95	80	45	50	0.75	43
	A14, A15 (Federal)	210	DCH306-60E① DCH306-68②	106 105	145	110 95	80	45	50	0.75	40 38
	A14 (FU Model)	210	DCH306-67	107	145	65	60	46	50	0.75	48
	A14 (California)	310	DCH306-75	107	145	95	80	45	50	0.75	43
	A14 (Federal)	310	DCH306-76	105	145	110	80	45	50	0.75	40
1980	A14 (California)	310	DCH306-112	107	145	80	80	45	50	0.75	38
	A14 (Federal)	310	DCH306-102	107	143	65	60	45	50	0.75	43
	A12A (California)	210	DCH306-115	94	145	95	80	45	50	0.75	38
	A14, A15 (California)	210	DCH306-110① DCH306-111②	107	145	80	80	45	50	0.75	38
	A12A (Federal)	210	DCH306-105	95	138	65	60	45	50	0.75	35
	A14, A15 (Federal)	210	DCH306-100① DCH306-101②	107	143	65	60	45	50	0.75	43

CHILTON'S
FUEL ECONOMY
& TUNE-UP TIPS

Tune-Up • Spark Plug Diagnosis • Emission Controls

Fuel System • Cooling System • Tires and Wheels

General Maintenance

CHILTON'S FUEL ECONOMY & TUNE-UP TIPS

Fuel economy is important to everyone, no matter what kind of vehicle you drive. The maintenance-minded motorist can save both money and fuel using these tips and the periodic maintenance and tune-up procedures in this Repair and Tune-Up Guide.

There are more than 130,000,000 cars and trucks registered for private use in the United States. Each travels an average of 10-12,000 miles per year, and, in total they consume close to 70 billion gallons of fuel each year. This represents nearly ⅔ of the oil imported by the United States each year. The Federal government's goal is to reduce consumption 10% by 1985. A variety of methods are either already in use or under serious consideration, and they all affect your driving and the cars you will drive. In addition to "down-sizing", the auto industry is using or investigating the use of electronic fuel delivery, electronic engine controls and alternative engines for use in smaller and lighter vehicles, among other alternatives to meet the federally mandated Corporate Average Fuel Economy (CAFE) of 27.5 mpg by 1985. The government, for its part, is considering rationing, mandatory driving curtailments and tax increases on motor vehicle fuel in an effort to reduce consumption. The government's goal of a 10% reduction could be realized — and further government regulation avoided — if every private vehicle could use just 1 less gallon of fuel per week.

How Much Can You Save?

Tests have proven that almost anyone can make at least a 10% reduction in fuel consumption through regular maintenance and tune-ups. When a major manufacturer of spark plugs sur-

TUNE-UP

1. Check the cylinder compression to be sure the engine will really benefit from a tune-up and that it is capable of producing good fuel economy. A tune-up will be wasted on an engine in poor mechanical condition.

2. Replace spark plugs regularly. New spark plugs alone can increase fuel economy 3%.

3. Be sure the spark plugs are the correct type (heat range) for your vehicle. See the Tune-Up Specifications.

Heat range refers to the spark plug's ability to conduct heat away from the firing end. It must conduct the heat away in an even pattern to avoid becoming a source of pre-ignition, yet it must also operate hot enough to burn off conductive deposits that could cause misfiring.

The heat range is usually indicated by a number on the spark plug, part of the manufacturer's designation for each individual spark plug. The numbers in bold-face indicate the heat range in each manufacturer's identification system.

Periodically, check the spark plugs to be sure they are firing efficiently. They are excellent indicators of the internal condition of your engine.

Manufacturer	Typical Designation
AC	R **45** TS
Bosch (old)	WA **145** T30
Bosch (new)	HR **8** Y
Champion	RBL **15** Y
Fram/Autolite	**4**15
Mopar	P-**62** PR
Motorcraft	B**R**F-42
NGK	BP **5** ES-15
Nippondenso	W **16** EP
Prestolite	14GR **5** 2A

On AC, Bosch (new), Champion, Fram/Autolite, Mopar, Motorcraft and Prestolite, a higher number indicates a hotter plug. On Bosch (old), NGK and Nippondenso, a higher number indicates a colder plug.

4. Make sure the spark plugs are properly gapped. See the Tune-Up Specifications in this book.

5. Be sure the spark plugs are firing efficiently. The illustrations on the next 2 pages show you how to "read" the firing end of the spark plug.

6. Check the ignition timing and set it to specifications. Tests show that almost all cars

veyed over 6,000 cars nationwide, they found that a tune-up, on cars that needed one, increased fuel economy over 11%. Replacing worn plugs alone, accounted for a 3% increase. The same test also revealed that 8 out of every 10 vehicles will have some maintenance deficiency that will directly affect fuel economy, emissions or performance. Most of this mileage-robbing neglect could be prevented with regular maintenance.

Modern engines require that all of the functioning systems operate properly for maximum efficiency. A malfunction anywhere wastes fuel. You can keep your vehicle running as efficiently and economically as possible, by being aware of your vehicles operating and performance characteristics. If your vehicle suddenly develops performance or fuel economy problems it could be due to one or more of the following:

PROBLEM	POSSIBLE CAUSE
Engine Idles Rough	Ignition timing, idle mixture, vacuum leak or something amiss in the emission control system.
Hesitates on Acceleration	Dirty carburetor or fuel filter, improper accelerator pump setting, ignition timing or fouled spark plugs.
Starts Hard or Fails to Start	Worn spark plugs, improperly set automatic choke, ice (or water) in fuel system.
Stalls Frequently	Automatic choke improperly adjusted and possible dirty air filter or fuel filter.
Performs Sluggishly	Worn spark plugs, dirty fuel or air filter, ignition timing or automatic choke out of adjustment.

Check spark plug wires on conventional point type ignition for cracks by bending them in a loop around your finger.

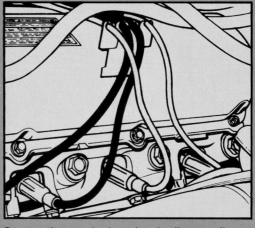

Be sure that spark plug wires leading to adjacent cylinders do not run too close together. (Photo courtesy Champion Spark Plug Co.)

have incorrect ignition timing by more than 2°.

7. If your vehicle does not have electronic ignition, check the points, rotor and cap as specified.

8. Check the spark plug wires (used with conventional point-type ignitions) for cracks and burned or broken insulation by bending them in a loop around your finger. Cracked wires decrease fuel efficiency by failing to deliver full voltage to the spark plugs. One misfiring spark plug can cost you as much as 2 mpg.

9. Check the routing of the plug wires. Misfiring can be the result of spark plug leads to adjacent cylinders running parallel to each other and too close together. One wire tends to pick up voltage from the other causing it to fire "out of time".

10. Check all electrical and ignition circuits for voltage drop and resistance.

11. Check the distributor mechanical and/or vacuum advance mechanisms for proper functioning. The vacuum advance can be checked by twisting the distributor plate in the opposite direction of rotation. It should spring back when released.

12. Check and adjust the valve clearance on engines with mechanical lifters. The clearance should be slightly loose rather than too tight.

SPARK PLUG DIAGNOSIS

Normal

APPEARANCE: This plug is typical of one operating normally. The insulator nose varies from a light tan to grayish color with slight electrode wear. The presence of slight deposits is normal on used plugs and will have no adverse effect on engine performance. The spark plug heat range is correct for the engine and the engine is running normally.

CAUSE: Properly running engine.

RECOMMENDATION: Before reinstalling this plug, the electrodes should be cleaned and filed square. Set the gap to specifications. If the plug has been in service for more than 10-12,000 miles, the entire set should probably be replaced with a fresh set of the same heat range.

Oil Deposits

APPEARANCE: The firing end of the plug is covered with a wet, oily coating.

CAUSE: The problem is poor oil control. On high mileage engines, oil is leaking past the rings or valve guides into the combustion chamber. A common cause is also a plugged PCV valve, and a ruptured fuel pump diaphragm can also cause this condition. Oil fouled plugs such as these are often found in new or recently overhauled engines, before normal oil control is achieved, and can be cleaned and reinstalled.

RECOMMENDATION: A hotter spark plug may temporarily relieve the problem, but the engine is probably in need of work.

Incorrect Heat Range

APPEARANCE: The effects of high temperature on a spark plug are indicated by clean white, often blistered insulator. This can also be accompanied by excessive wear of the electrode, and the absence of deposits.

CAUSE: Check for the correct spark plug heat range. A plug which is too hot for the engine can result in overheating. A car operated mostly at high speeds can require a colder plug. Also check ignition timing, cooling system level, fuel mixture and leaking intake manifold.

RECOMMENDATION: If all ignition and engine adjustments are known to be correct, and no other malfunction exists, install spark plugs one heat range colder.

Photos Courtesy Champion Spark Plug Co.

Carbon Deposits

APPEARANCE: Carbon fouling is easily identified by the presence of dry, soft, black, sooty deposits.

CAUSE: Changing the heat range can often lead to carbon fouling, as can prolonged slow, stop-and-start driving. If the heat range is correct, carbon fouling can be attributed to a rich fuel mixture, sticking choke, clogged air cleaner, worn breaker points, retarded timing or low compression. If only one or two plugs are carbon fouled, check for corroded or cracked wires on the affected plugs. Also look for cracks in the distributor cap between the towers of affected cylinders.

RECOMMENDATION: After the problem is corrected, these plugs can be cleaned and reinstalled if not worn severely.

MMT Fouled

APPEARANCE: Spark plugs fouled by MMT (Methycyclopentadienyl Maganese Tricarbonyl) have reddish, rusty appearance on the insulator and side electrode.

CAUSE: MMT is an anti-knock additive in gasoline used to replace lead. During the combustion process, the MMT leaves a reddish deposit on the insulator and side electrode.

RECOMMENDATION: No engine malfunction is indicated and the deposits will not affect plug performance any more than lead deposits (see Ash Deposits). MMT fouled plugs can be cleaned, regapped and reinstalled.

High Speed Glazing

APPEARANCE: Glazing appears as shiny coating on the plug, either yellow or tan in color.

CAUSE: During hard, fast acceleration, plug temperatures rise suddenly. Deposits from normal combustion have no chance to fluff-off; instead, they melt on the insulator forming an electrically conductive coating which causes misfiring.

RECOMMENDATION: Glazed plugs are not easily cleaned. They should be replaced with a fresh set of plugs of the correct heat range. If the condition recurs, using plugs with a heat range one step colder may cure the problem.

Ash (Lead) Deposits

APPEARANCE: Ash deposits are characterized by light brown or white colored deposits crusted on the side or center electrodes. In some cases it may give the plug a rusty appearance.

CAUSE: Ash deposits are normally derived from oil or fuel additives burned during normal combustion. Normally they are harmless, though excessive amounts can cause misfiring. If deposits are excessive in short mileage, the valve guides may be worn.

RECOMMENDATION: Ash-fouled plugs can be cleaned, gapped and reinstalled.

Detonation

APPEARANCE: Detonation is usually characterized by a broken plug insulator.

CAUSE: A portion of the fuel charge will begin to burn spontaneously, from the increased heat following ignition. The explosion that results applies extreme pressure to engine components, frequently damaging spark plugs and pistons.

Detonation can result by over-advanced ignition timing, inferior gasoline (low octane) lean air/fuel mixture, poor carburetion, engine lugging or an increase in compression ratio due to combustion chamber deposits or engine modification.

RECOMMENDATION: Replace the plugs after correcting the problem.

Photos Courtesy Fram Corporation

EMISSION CONTROLS

13. Be aware of the general condition of the emission control system. It contributes to reduced pollution and should be serviced regularly to maintain efficient engine operation.

14. Check all vacuum lines for dried, cracked or brittle conditions. Something as simple as a leaking vacuum hose can cause poor performance and loss of economy.

15. Avoid tampering with the emission control system. Attempting to improve fuel econ-

FUEL SYSTEM

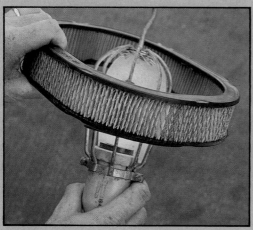

Check the air filter with a light behind it. If you can see light through the filter it can be reused.

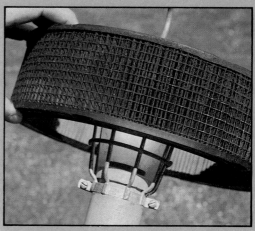

Extremely clogged filters should be discarded and replaced with a new one.

18. Replace the air filter regularly. A dirty air filter richens the air/fuel mixture and can increase fuel consumption as much as 10%. Tests show that ⅓ of all vehicles have air filters in need of replacement.

19. Replace the fuel filter at least as often as recommended.

20. Set the idle speed and carburetor mixture to specifications.

21. Check the automatic choke. A sticking or malfunctioning choke wastes gas.

22. During the summer months, adjust the automatic choke for a leaner mixture which will produce faster engine warm-ups.

COOLING SYSTEM

29. Be sure all accessory drive belts are in good condition. Check for cracks or wear.

30. Adjust all accessory drive belts to proper tension.

31. Check all hoses for swollen areas, worn spots, or loose clamps.

32. Check coolant level in the radiator or expansion tank.

33. Be sure the thermostat is operating properly. A stuck thermostat delays engine warm-up and a cold engine uses nearly twice as much fuel as a warm engine.

34. Drain and replace the engine coolant at least as often as recommended. Rust and scale

TIRES & WHEELS

38. Check the tire pressure often with a pencil type gauge. Tests by a major tire manufacturer show that 90% of all vehicles have at least 1 tire improperly inflated. Better mileage can be achieved by over-inflating tires, but never exceed the maximum inflation pressure on the side of the tire.

39. If possible, install radial tires. Radial tires deliver as much as ½ mpg more than bias belted tires.

40. Avoid installing super-wide tires. They only create extra rolling resistance and decrease fuel mileage. Stick to the manufacturer's recommendations.

41. Have the wheels properly balanced.

omy by tampering with emission controls is more likely to worsen fuel economy than improve it. Emission control changes on modern engines are not readily reversible.

16. Clean (or replace) the EGR valve and lines as recommended.

17. Be sure that all vacuum lines and hoses are reconnected properly after working under the hood. An unconnected or misrouted vacuum line can wreak havoc with engine performance.

---

23. Check for fuel leaks at the carburetor, fuel pump, fuel lines and fuel tank. Be sure all lines and connections are tight.

24. Periodically check the tightness of the carburetor and intake manifold attaching nuts and bolts. These are a common place for vacuum leaks to occur.

25. Clean the carburetor periodically and lubricate the linkage.

26. The condition of the tailpipe can be an excellent indicator of proper engine combustion. After a long drive at highway speeds, the inside of the tailpipe should be a light grey in color. Black or soot on the insides indicates an overly rich mixture.

27. Check the fuel pump pressure. The fuel pump may be supplying more fuel than the engine needs.

28. Use the proper grade of gasoline for your engine. Don't try to compensate for knocking or "pinging" by advancing the ignition timing. This practice will only increase plug temperature and the chances of detonation or pre-ignition with relatively little performance gain.

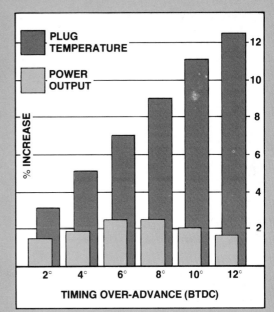

Increasing ignition timing past the specified setting results in a drastic increase in spark plug temperature with increased chance of detonation or preignition. Performance increase is considerably less. (Photo courtesy Champion Spark Plug Co.)

---

that form in the engine should be flushed out to allow the engine to operate at peak efficiency.

35. Clean the radiator of debris that can decrease cooling efficiency.

36. Install a flex-type or electric cooling fan, if you don't have a clutch type fan. Flex fans use curved plastic blades to push more air at low speeds when more cooling is needed; at high speeds the blades flatten out for less resistance. Electric fans only run when the engine temperature reaches a predetermined level.

37. Check the radiator cap for a worn or cracked gasket. If the cap does not seal properly, the cooling system will not function properly.

---

42. Be sure the front end is correctly aligned. A misaligned front end actually has wheels going in different directions. The increased drag can reduce fuel economy by .3 mpg.

43. Correctly adjust the wheel bearings. Wheel bearings that are adjusted too tight increase rolling resistance.

Check tire pressures regularly with a reliable pocket type gauge. Be sure to check the pressure on a cold tire.

GENERAL MAINTENANCE

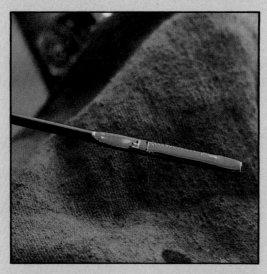

Check the fluid levels (particularly engine oil) on a regular basis. Be sure to check the oil for grit, water or other contamination.

A vacuum gauge is another excellent indicator of internal engine condition and can also be installed in the dash as a mileage indicator.

44. Periodically check the fluid levels in the engine, power steering pump, master cylinder, automatic transmission and drive axle.

45. Change the oil at the recommended interval and change the filter at every oil change. Dirty oil is thick and causes extra friction between moving parts, cutting efficiency and increasing wear. A worn engine requires more frequent tune-ups and gets progressively worse fuel economy. In general, use the lightest viscosity oil for the driving conditions you will encounter.

46. Use the recommended viscosity fluids in the transmission and axle.

47. Be sure the battery is fully charged for fast starts. A slow starting engine wastes fuel.

48. Be sure battery terminals are clean and tight.

49. Check the battery electrolyte level and add distilled water if necessary.

50. Check the exhaust system for crushed pipes, blockages and leaks.

51. Adjust the brakes. Dragging brakes or brakes that are not releasing create increased drag on the engine.

52. Install a vacuum gauge or miles-per-gallon gauge. These gauges visually indicate engine vacuum in the intake manifold. High vacuum = good mileage and low vacuum = poorer mileage. The gauge can also be an excellent indicator of internal engine conditions.

53. Be sure the clutch is properly adjusted. A slipping clutch wastes fuel.

54. Check and periodically lubricate the heat control valve in the exhaust manifold. A sticking or inoperative valve prevents engine warm-up and wastes gas.

55. Keep accurate records to check fuel economy over a period of time. A sudden drop in fuel economy may signal a need for tune-up or other maintenance.

Z20S (California)	510	All	107	170	110	60	47	100	0.91	35
Z20S (Federal)	510	All	99	166	90	60	47	100	0.91	40

① Manual Transmission
② Automatic Transmission
③ Slow jet air bleed: Primary #145, Secondary #100
④ Slow jet air bleed: Primary #215, Secondary #100
⑤ Slow jet air bleed: Primary #240, Secondary #100
FU models are 5-speed Hatchbacks sold in the United States except California.

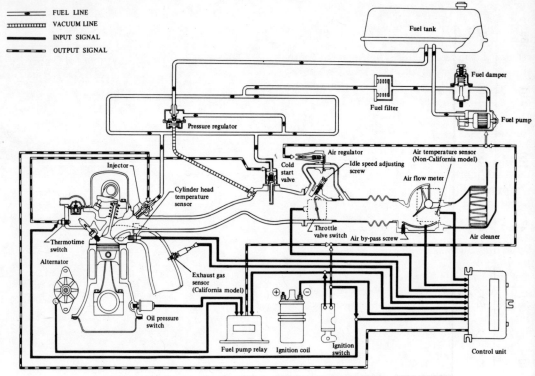

FUEL LINE
VACUUM LINE
INPUT SIGNAL
OUTPUT SIGNAL

1980 810 fuel injection system. Many components similar to 1980 200SX

EFI connector numbering

NOTE: *The 1979–80 Electronic Control Unit must not be installed on 1978 or earlier models. Damage to the ECU will result. A special adapter harness must be used with the factory EFI analyzer when testing the 1979–80 ECU.*

CHECKING FUNCTIONAL PARTS

For the following tests you will need a small testing light and an ohmmeter. Be sure the car's battery is fully charged before making the tests.

ELECTRONIC CONTROL UNIT TEST

1. Connect the testing lamp to the harness-side connector of the injector.

2. Crank the engine. If the light flashes due to the pulse voltage applied to the injector, the control unit is operating.

Because two different transistors are used in the system, you will have to test both the No. 1 and 4 cylinders.

NOTE: *The engine must be turning over at a speed of more than 80 rpm to complete the test.*

To further test 1977–79 810's, remove the connector on the coolant sensor. The installed testing lamp should flash more brightly.

TESTING THE POTENTIOMETER

The Potentiometer monitors the amount of air passing into the intake manifold and sends an appropriate signal to the control unit which in turn adjusts the fuel/air mixture for best efficiency. It is also referred to as the air flow meter.

CAUTION: *Before checking the air flow meter, or the potentiometer, remove the ground cable from the battery.*

1. Remove the air flow meter.

2. Measure the resistance between terminals 8 and 6, through 1978, or 33 and 34 for 1979–80 models. It should be 180 ohms through 1978 and 100–400 ohms thereafter.

3. Measure the resistance between terminals 8 and 9 through 1978, or 34 and 35 for 1979–80. Resistance should be 100 ohms through 1978, 200–500 ohms for 1979–80.

4. For models through 1978: connect a 12-volt battery to terminal 9 (positive) and terminal 6 (negative).

Connect the positive lead of a voltmeter to terminal 8 and the negative lead to terminal 7.

Reaching into the air flow meter, slowly open the flap so that the volt flow slowly decreases. If the indicator varies suddenly, the problem may be in the potentiometer.

5. For 1979–80 models: slide the flap open and measure the resistance between terminals 32 and 34. Resistance other than zero or infinity is correct.

AIR FLOW METER INSULATION CHECK

Connect an ohmmeter to any one terminal on the flow meter. Touch the flow meter body with the other connector. If any continuity is indicated, the unit out of order.

CHECKING THE AIR FLAP

Reach into the air flow meter with your fingers. If the flap opens and closes smoothly, without binding, the mechanical portion of the unit is working.

AIR TEMPERATURE SENSOR-EXCEPT 1980 CALIFORNIA 810

Checking Continuity

1. Disconnect the battery ground cable.

2. Remove the air flow meter.

3. Check the temperature of your surroundings and make note of it.

4. Connect an ohmmeter to terminals 27 and 6 for models through 1978, or 25 and 34 for 1979–80 on the air flow meter connector and check the resistance indicated. Make a note of it.

The resistance values should be as indicated in the chart. Should the test results vary a great deal from the ranges provided, replace the air temperature sensor and the air flow meter as a unit.

Insulation Resistance

Connect an ohmmeter to terminal 27 of the air flow meter for models through 1978, or

Air Flow Meter Resistance Specifications

Air temperature °C (°F)	Resistance (kΩ)
−30 (−22)	20.3 to 33.0
−10 (−14)	7.6 to 10.8
10 (50)	3.25 to 4.15
20 (68)	2.25 to 2.75
50 (122)	0.74 to 0.94
80 (176)	0.29 to 0.36

terminal 25 for 1979–80 models, and touch the body of the unit with the other connector. Should continuity be indicated, replace the unit.

WATER TEMPERATURE SENSOR

This test may be done either on or off the vehicle. The test should be done with the coolant both hot and cold.

NOTE: *1980 810's are equipped with cylinder head temperature sensors rather than water temperature sensors. However, the test is the same for both units.*

1. Disconnect the battery ground cable.

2. Disconnect the water temperature sensor harness.

3. Place a thermometer in the coolant when the engine is cold. Make note of the indication.

4. Read the resistance indicated on the meter and compare it with the chart for temperature/resistance values.

To measure the coolant temperature and resistance values when hot:

1. Connect the water temperature sensor harness.

2. Connect the battery ground cable.

3. Warm the engine and disconnect the harness and battery cable.

4. Read the sensor resistance as described in the cold process.

Sensor Check-Off The Engine

1. Remove the sensor and dip the unit into water maintained at 68° F. Read the resistance.

Water Temperature Sensor Resistance Specifications

Cooling water temperature °C (°F)	Resistance (kΩ)
−30 (−22)	20.3 to 33.0
−10 (−14)	7.6 to 10.8
10 (50)	3.25 to 4.15
20 (68)	2.25 to 2.75
50 (122)	0.74 to 0.94
80 (176)	0.29 to 0.36

2. Heat the water to 176° F and check the resistance.

In either type of check, should the resistance be far outside the ranges provided, replace the sensor unit.

Sensor Insulation Check

This check is done on the engine.
1. Disconnect the battery ground cable.
2. Disconnect the sensor harness connector.
3. Connect an ohmmeter to one of the terminals on the sensor and touch the engine block with the other. Any indication of continuity indicates need to replace the unit.

THERMOTIME SWITCH—810

1. Disconnect the ground cable from the battery.
2. Disconnect the electric connector of the thermotime switch and measure the resistance between output terminal and the switch body.

The resistance should be zero with water temperatures less than 57° F.

The resistance should be zero or infinite with temperatures of 57° to 72° F.

The resistance should be infinite with a temperature of 72° F.

3. Measure the resistance between input terminal and the switch body.

70–86 ohms through 1977 . . . . OK
51–62 ohms, 1978 . . . . OK
40–70 ohms, 1979–80 . . . . OK

Any different reading than shown indicates replacement.

COLD START VALVE—810

Steps 1 and 2 are for models through 1978 only.
1. Disconnect the lead wire from the "S" terminal of the starter motor.
2. Turn the ignition switch to START and make sure the fuel pump is working. You should be able to hear it.
3. Disconnect the ground cable from the battery.
4. Remove the screws holding the cold start valve to the intake manifold and remove the valve.
5. Disconnect the start valve electrical connector.
6. Put the start valve into a large glass container and plug the neck of the jar.
7. For models through 1978, connect the ground cable of the battery and turn the ignition switch to START. The valve should not inject fuel.

For 1979 models, disconnect the connector at the oil pressure switch, or the connector at the alternator "L" terminal; turn the ignition switch to ON. The valve should not inject fuel.

8. Turn the switch to OFF and connect jumper wires between the valve and the battery terminals. Leave the valve in the jar.

At this point, the valve should inject fuel. If not, proceed to the next step for models through 1977 only. For 1978 and later models, replace the valve.

9. With the ignition switch in the START position, and the jumper wire installed as described, check for fuel flow. If the fuel is injected to the jar, the unit is operating. If not, replace.

FUEL INJECTION AND FUEL PUMP RELAYS

The fuel injection system is equipped with one relay and the fuel pump has two. Testing and service should be left to your Datsun dealer.

NOTE: *A faulty relay could disrupt fuel pump operation and injection performance. Be sure to have the relays checked before simply replacing them, as they are rather expensive.*

FUEL INJECTOR TEST

For continuity, remove the ground cable from the battery and disconnect the electric connectors from the injectors.

Check for continuity readings between the

two terminals. If there is not an indication, the injector is faulty and must be replaced.

Check the injectors for sound as follows:

If the engine is running, run it at idle and place screwdriver tip against each injector and put your ear to the handle to check for operating sounds. You should hear a click sound at regular intervals. Note, however, that as the engine speed increases, the click intervals shorten. If no click is heard, check the Electronic Control Unit as described at the beginning of this section. If one injector sounds different from the rest, it is probably faulty: replace it.

If the engine is not running, disconnect the connector of the cold start valve (810 only) and crank the engine. Check for the same sounds described in the above paragraph.

NOTE: *If none of the injectors is working, make sure the wiring harnesses are connected and check the fuel injection fusible link near the battery for damage. See chapter 5 on electrical systems, below.*

AIR REGULATOR TEST

1. Start the engine and pinch the rubber hose between the throttle chamber and the air regulator. On a cold engine, the engine speed should decrease. On a warm engine the engine speed should not be affected.

To test the air regulator continuity, disconnect the electric connector and check for continuity between the terminals. If none is found, the regulator is faulty.

To open the valve, pry with a screwdriver

and then close. If the operation is smooth, the valve is operating correctly. Any binding indicates replacement.

RELIEVING FUEL PRESSURE

See section under Electric Fuel Pump, Testing, for procedure.

THROTTLE CHAMBER

The 810 has a single barrel throttle chamber while the 200SX is equipped with a two barrel chamber. Check the throttle for smooth operation and make sure the by-pass port is free from obstacles and is clean. Check to make sure the idle speed adjusting screw moves smoothly.

Do not touch the EGR vacuum port screw or, on some later models, the throttle valve stopper screw, as they are factory adjusted.

Because of the sensitivity of the air flow meter, there cannot be any air leaks in the fuel system. Even the smallest leak could unbalance the system and affect the performance of the automobile.

During every check, pay attention to hose connections, dipstick and oil filler cap for evidence of air leaks. Should you encounter any, take steps to correct the problem.

Fuel Tank
REMOVAL AND INSTALLATION
1973 510

1. Remove the rear seat, seat back, and back trim. Disconnect the battery.

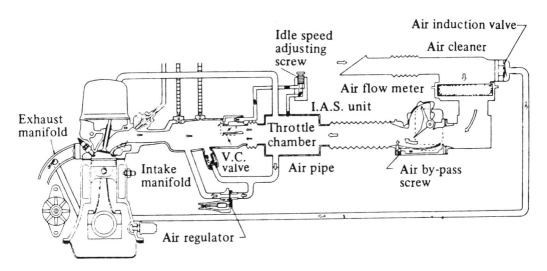

1980 200SX fuel injection system

2. Remove the trunk finishing panel from within the trunk.

3. Disconnect the gauge unit lead wire and drain the tank.

4. Remove the filler tube.

5. Remove the retaining bolts and disconnect the rubber lines for fuel outlet and return from the tank.

6. Remove the tank.

1200

1. Disconnect the battery. Remove the drain plug from the tank bottom and completely drain the tank.

2. Remove the fuel lines.

3. Remove the trunk finishing panel.

4. Remove the four bolts retaining the tank.

5. Disconnect the hose clamp and gauge wire.

6. Remove the fuel tank.

B210 Sedan, 610, and 710 Sedan and Hardtop

1. Disconnect the battery ground cable.

2. Remove the front trunk panel.

3. Remove the spare tire and the plug from the spare housing.

4. Place a pan under the drain plug and remove the plug.

5. Disconnect the filler hose, ventilation lines, and fuel line from the tank.

6. Disconnect the fuel gauge wires from the tank.

7. Remove the rear seat cushion and back. Remove the front mounting bolts.

8. Remove the other two retaining bolts and lift out the tank.

9. Installation is the reverse of removal.

B210 Coupe

1. Disconnect the battery ground cable.

2. Remove the finish panel from the right-side of the trunk.

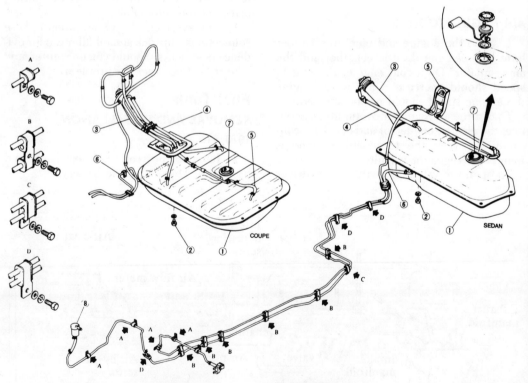

1. Fuel tank
2. Drain plug
3. Filler hose
4. Ventilation tube
5. Evaporation tube
6. Fuel outlet hose
7. Fuel tank unit gauge
8. Fuel strainer

B210 fuel tank and lines

3. Place a pan under the drain plug and remove the plug.

4. Disconnect the filler hose, ventilation lines, and fuel line from the tank.

5. Disconnect the evaporative lines from the reservoir tank.

6. Remove the spare tire and then the inspection plate from the rear floor.

7. Disconnect the sending unit wires.

8. Remove the fuel tank mounting bolts and lift the tank out of the car.

9. Installation is the reverse of removal.

610 and 710 Station Wagon

1. Disconnect the battery ground cable.

2. Remove the inspection plate from the rear floor. Disconnect the gauge wiring.

3. Remove the spare tire.

4. Place a pan under the drain plug and remove the plug.

5. Disconnect the filler hose, ventilation lines, and the fuel line from the tank.

6. Remove the retaining bolts and remove the tank.

7. Installation is the reverse of removal.

F10 Sedan and Hatchback

1. Disconnect the battery ground cable.

2. Drain the fuel into a suitable container.

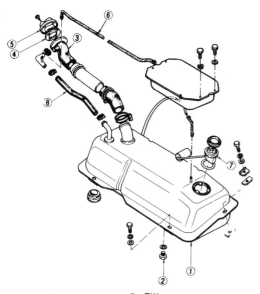

1. Fuel tank	5. Filler cap
2. Drain plug	6. Breather tube
3. Filler hose	7. Fuel gauge unit
4. Filler neck	8. Ventilation hose

710 fuel tank

3. Disconnect the filler hose, the air vent hose, fuel return hose, and fuel outlet hose.

4. Disconnect the wires from the sending unit.

5. Remove the bolts securing the fuel tank and remove the tank.

6. Installation is in the reverse order of removal.

F10 Wagon

The removal procedure is the same as that for the sedan and hatchback. However, when removing the fuel tank bolts, it is easier if you start at the three bolts at the front of the tank.

1977–79 200SX

1. Disconnect the battery ground cable.

2. Remove the rubber plug located on the floor panel above the left side rear axle.

3. Remove the drain plug and drain the tank.

4. Detach the rear seat cushion, seat back, and rear seat backboard.

5. Disconnect the fuel hose.

6. Remove the two bolts which secure the fuel tank in the front.

7. Open the trunk, remove the trim in front of the tank, and remove all the hoses and lines.

8. Remove the two bolts which hold the fuel tank in the back and remove the tank.

9. Installation is in the reverse order of removal.

810 Sedan

1. Disconnect the battery ground cable.

2. Remove the mat and the spare tire from the trunk.

3. Place a suitable container under the fuel tank and drain the tank. There is a drain plug in the bottom of the tank.

4. Disconnect the filler hose, the vent tube, and the outlet hose.

5. Disconnect the wires from the sending unit.

6. Remove the four bolts securing the fuel tank and remove the tank.

7. Installation is in the reverse order of removal.

810 Station Wagon

1. Disconnect the battery ground cable.

2. Loosen the tire hanger and take out the spare tire.

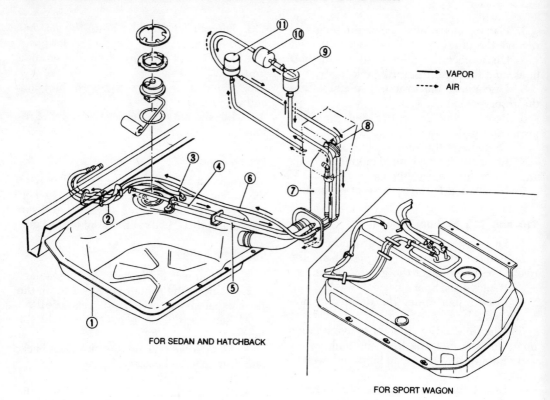

VAPOR

AIR

FOR SEDAN AND HATCHBACK

FOR SPORT WAGON

1. Fuel tank
2. Fuel outlet hose
3. Fuel return hose
4. Evaporation hose to fuel tank
5. Air vent line
6. Evaporation hose to engine
7. Filler hose
8. Filler cap
9. Separator
10. Limit valve
11. Vent cleaner

F10 fuel tank

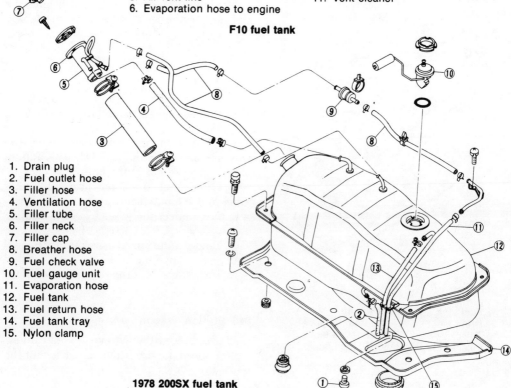

1. Drain plug
2. Fuel outlet hose
3. Filler hose
4. Ventilation hose
5. Filler tube
6. Filler neck
7. Filler cap
8. Breather hose
9. Fuel check valve
10. Fuel gauge unit
11. Evaporation hose
12. Fuel tank
13. Fuel return hose
14. Fuel tank tray
15. Nylon clamp

1978 200SX fuel tank

SEDAN

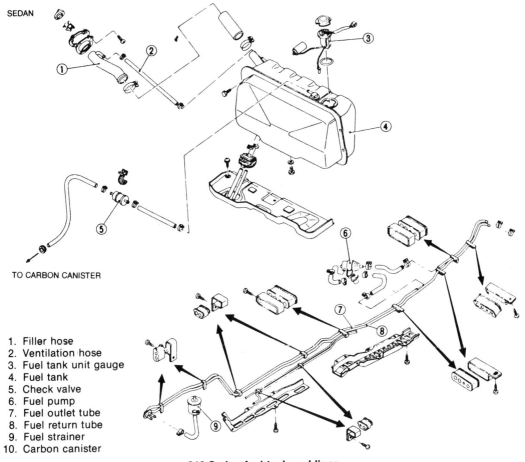

TO CARBON CANISTER

1. Filler hose
2. Ventilation hose
3. Fuel tank unit gauge
4. Fuel tank
5. Check valve
6. Fuel pump
7. Fuel outlet tube
8. Fuel return tube
9. Fuel strainer
10. Carbon canister

810 Sedan fuel tank and lines

3. Loosen the drain plug and drain the tank.

4. Disconnect the filler hose, ventilation hose, evaporation hose, and outlet hose.

5. Remove the tire stopper. Disconnect the wiring from the gauge.

6. Remove the four bolts securing the fuel tank and remove the tank.

7. Installation is in the reverse order of removal.

1978–80 510 Sedan

1. Disconnect the battery ground cable.

2. Remove the back seat trim in the luggage compartment.

3. Drain the fuel in the fuel tank.

4. Disconnect all the hoses and wires from the tank.

5. Remove the bolts securing the tank and remove the tank.

6. Installation is in the reverse order of removal.

1978–80 510 Hatchback

1. Disconnect the battery ground cable.

2. Drain the fuel from the tank, then disconnect the fuel hose.

3. Remove the luggage carpet, luggage board, and fuel filler hose protector.

4. Disconnect all the hoses and wires to the tank.

5. Unbolt the fuel tank and remove it.

6. Installation is in the reverse order of removal.

1978–80 510 Station Wagon

1. Disconnect the battery ground cable.

2. Drain the fuel from the tank. Disconnect all the hoses and lines.

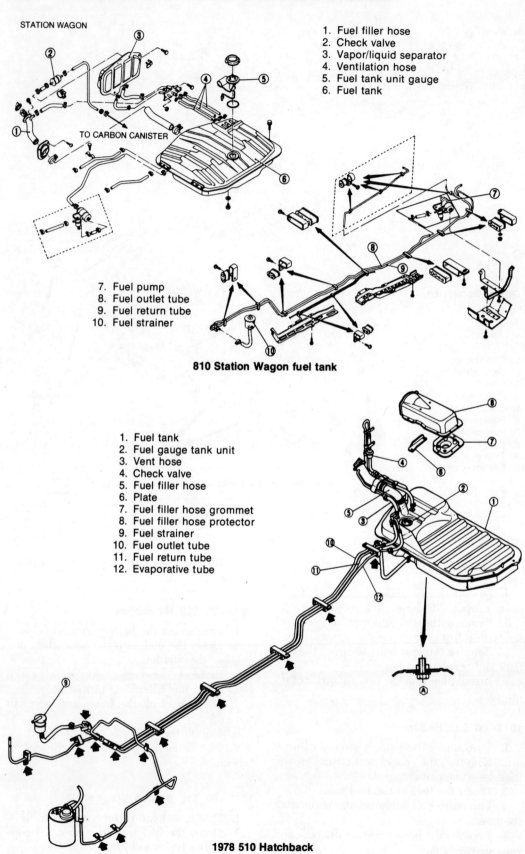

STATION WAGON

TO CARBON CANISTER

1. Fuel filler hose
2. Check valve
3. Vapor/liquid separator
4. Ventilation hose
5. Fuel tank unit gauge
6. Fuel tank

7. Fuel pump
8. Fuel outlet tube
9. Fuel return tube
10. Fuel strainer

810 Station Wagon fuel tank

1. Fuel tank
2. Fuel gauge tank unit
3. Vent hose
4. Check valve
5. Fuel filler hose
6. Plate
7. Fuel filler hose grommet
8. Fuel filler hose protector
9. Fuel strainer
10. Fuel outlet tube
11. Fuel return tube
12. Evaporative tube

1978 510 Hatchback

1. Fuel tank
2. Fuel gauge tank unit
3. Vent hose
4. Check valve
5. Fuel filler hose grommet
6. Fuel filler hose
7. Fuel strainer
8. Fuel outlet tube
9. Fuel return tube
10. Evaporative tube

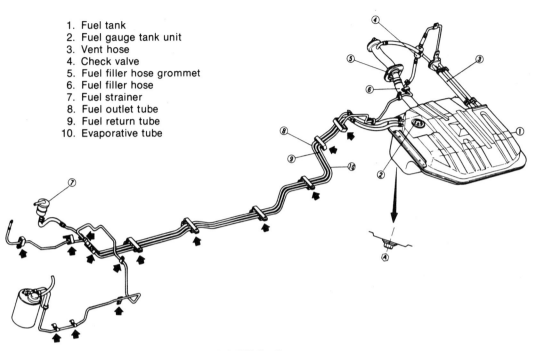

1978 510 Station wagon

3. Remove the spare tire and fuel tank support.
4. Unbolt and remove the tank.
5. Installation is in the reverse order of removal.

1979-80 310

1. Disconnect the battery ground cable.
2. Remove the drain plug and drain the fuel.
3. Disconnect the filler tube and filler hose from the fuel tank.
4. Disconnect the hoses attached to the fuel tank near the filler hose and at the bottom front of the tank.
5. Loosen the tension on the parking brake and disconnect the wire on the fuel tank gauge unit.
6. Remove the retaining bolts and remove the tank by sliding it forward and down.
Installation is the reverse of removal.

1979-80 210 Sedan

1. Disconnect the battery ground cable.
2. Drain the fuel from the fuel tank, then disconnect the fuel hose.
3. Remove the filler hose protector and inspection cover in the luggage compartment.
4. Disconnect the fuel filler hose, vent hoses and the fuel tank gauge unit wire connector.
5. Remove the fuel tank protector.
6. Remove the fuel tank.
Installation is the reverse of removal.

1979-80 210 Hatchback and Station Wagon

1. Disconnect the battery ground cable.
2. Drain the fuel from the fuel tank, then disconnect the fuel hose.
3. Remove the luggage carpet, luggage board, inspection cover and side finisher.
4. Disconnect the fuel filler hose, vent hoses and the fuel tank gauge unit wire connector.
5. Remove the fuel tank protector.
6. Remove the fuel tank.
Installation is the reverse of removal.

1980 200SX

1. Remove the battery ground cable.
2. Drain the fuel from the fuel tank.
3. Remove the protector from the luggage compartment, and then remove the following parts:
   a. Harness connector for the fuel tank gauge unit
   b. Ventilation hose
   c. Evaporation hoses
   d. Fuel filler hose (Hatchback)

1. Fuel tank
2. Fuel suction hose
3. Fuel return hose
4. Evaporation hose
5. Vent tube
6. Filler hose
7. Filler tube
8. Filler cap

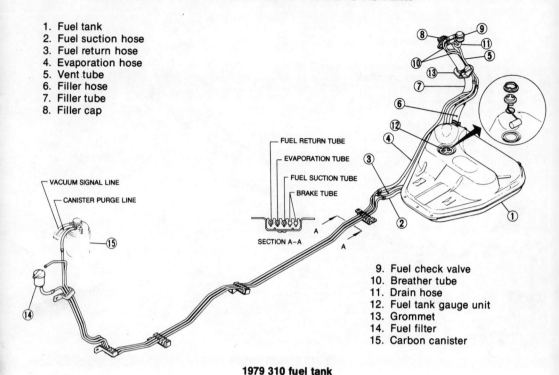

9. Fuel check valve
10. Breather tube
11. Drain hose
12. Fuel tank gauge unit
13. Grommet
14. Fuel filter
15. Carbon canister

1979 310 fuel tank

4. Remove the following parts from beneath the floor:
  a. Fuel outlet hose
  b. Fuel return hose
  c. Evaporation hose
  d. Fuel filler hose (Hardtop)
5. Remove the bolts which secure the fuel tank and remove the tank.

Installation is the reverse of removal.

To remove the Reservoir tank from the Hatchback:
1. Remove the battery cable.
2. Remove the protector from the luggage compartment. Also remove the right hand speaker and side lower finisher.
3. Remove the evaporation hoses and then remove the reservoir tank.

Installation is the reverse of removal.

Chassis Electrical

HEATER

Heater Assembly

REMOVAL AND INSTALLATION

1973 510

1. Drain the coolant.
2. Disconnect the water pipes to the engine.
3. Disconnect the blower motor electrical connector.
4. Remove the three heater control wires at the heater unit.
5. Remove the two bolts and ventilator.
6. Remove the four bolts and detach the heater unit.
7. Reverse the procedure for installation.

1973 1200

1. Remove the package tray and ashtray.
2. Drain coolant. Disconnect the two hoses between the heater and engine.
3. Disconnect the cables from the heater unit and heater controls. Disconnect the wiring.
4. Disconnect the two control wires from the water cock and interior valve, and the control rod from the shut valve. Set the heater control upper lever to DEF and lower lever to OFF.

5. Pull off the right and left defroster hoses.
6. Remove the four screws holding the heater unit to the firewall. Remove the control knob and remove the screws holding the control unit to the instrument panel. Remove the heater unit.
7. Reverse the procedure for installation.

610, 710, and B210

1. Disconnect the battery ground cable.
2. Drain the coolant.
3. Detach the coolant inlet and outlet hoses.
4. On the 610, remove the center ventilator grille from the bottom of the instrument panel.
5. Remove the heater duct hose from both sides of the heater unit. Remove the defroster hose or hoses on the 610 and the B210. On the 710, remove the intake duct and defroster duct from both sides of the heater unit. Remove the console box on the 710 if so equipped.
6. Disconnect the electrical wires of the heater unit (and air conditioner, if so equipped) at their connections.
7. Disconnect and remove the heater control cables.
8. On 710 and 1974–76 610, remove the two bolts on each side of the unit and one on

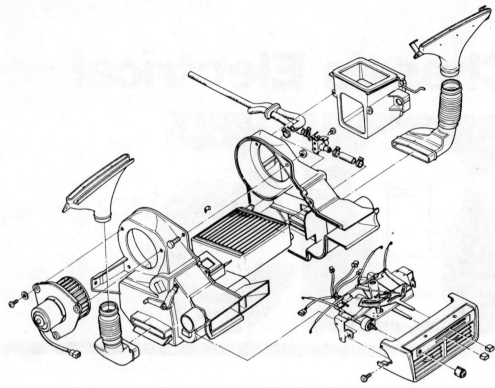

Heater assembly—1977–79 200SX

the top. For 1973 610 and all B210's, remove one attaching bolt from each side and one from the top center of the unit.

9. Remove the unit.

10. Installation is the reverse of removal. Run the engine for a few minutes with the heater to make sure the system if filled with coolant.

1977–79 200SX

1. Disconnect the battery cable.

2. Drain the engine coolant and remove the heater hoses from the engine side.

3. Inside the passenger compartment, disconnect the lead wires from the heater unit to the instrument harness.

4. At this point, the instrument panel must be removed in order to remove the heater assembly. To remove the panel, proceed as follows:

5. Remove the steering wheel cover.

6. Disconnect the speedometer cable and the radio antenna cable.

7. After noting their position, disconnect the following connectors: instrument harness to body, harness to engine room, transistor ignition unit, and the wiring to the console.

8. Remove the bolts securing column clamp and lower the steering column.

9. Remove the package tray.

10. Remove the bolts which attach the instrument panel to the mounting brackets on the left and right-hand sides.

11. Remove the trim on the right side windshield pillar, and remove the bolt attaching the instrument panel to the pillar.

12. Remove the trim on the top of the instrument panel. It is referred to as instrument garnish in the illustration (page 178).

13. Remove the bolts attaching the instrument panel.

14. Move the instrument panel to the right to remove it.

15. Remove the defroster hoses on both sides of the heater unit.

16. If the car is air-conditioned, disconnect the wires to the air-conditioner.

17. Remove the three heater retaining bolts and remove the heater assembly.

18. Installation is in the reverse order of removal.

1980 200SX

1. Set the TEMP lever to the HOT position and drain the coolant.

2. Disconnect the heater hoses from the driver's side of the heater unit.

3. At this point the manufacturer

suggests you remove the front seats. To do this, remove the plastic covers over the ends of the seat runners, both front and back, to expose the seat mounting bolts. Remove the bolts and remove the seats.

4. Remove the console box and the floor carpets.

5. Remove the instrument panel lower covers from both the driver's and passenger's sides of the car. Remove the lower cluster lids.

6. Remove the left hand side ventilator duct.

7. Remove the radio, sound balancer and stereo cassette deck. (See below for procedures).

8. Remove the instrument panel-to-transmission tunnel stay.

9. Remove the rear heater duct from the floor of the vehicle.

10. Remove the center ventilator duct.

11. Remove the left and right-hand side air guides from the lower heater outlets.

12. Disconnect the wire harness connections.

13. Remove the two screws at the bottom sides of the heater unit and the one screw and the top of the unit and remove the unit together with the heater control assembly. Installation is the reverse of removal.

NOTE: *You may be able to skip several of* *the above steps if only certain components of the heater unit need service.*

810

1. Disconnect the battery ground cable.
2. Drain the engine coolant.
3. Remove the console box and the console box bracket. Remove the front floor mat.
4. Loosen the screws and remove the rear heater duct.
5. Remove the hose clamps and remove the inlet and outlet hoses.
6. Remove the heater duct and remove the defroster hoses from the assembly.
7. Remove the air intake door control cable.
8. Disconnect the wiring harness to the heater.
9. Remove the retaining bolts and remove the heater unit.
10. Installation is in the reverse order of removal.

F10

1. Disconnect the battery ground cable.
2. Drain the engine coolant and remove the heater hoses.
3. Remove the defroster hoses from each side of the heater assembly.
4. Remove the cable retaining clamps and remove the cables for the intake and floor doors.

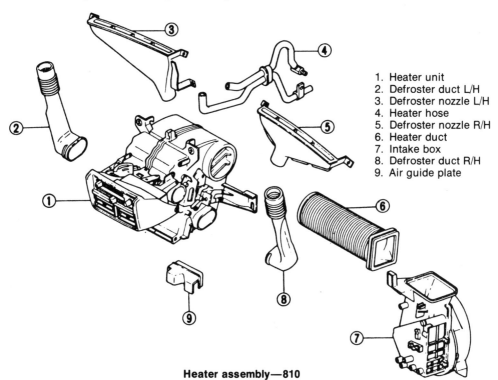

1. Heater unit
2. Defroster duct L/H
3. Defroster nozzle L/H
4. Heater hose
5. Defroster nozzle R/H
6. Heater duct
7. Intake box
8. Defroster duct R/H
9. Air guide plate

Heater assembly—810

5. Disconnect the three pole connector.

6. Remove the four heater retaining screws. Remove the heater.

7. Installation is in the reverse order of removal.

1978–80 510, 210

1. Disconnect the ground cable at the battery. Drain the coolant.

2. Remove the console box on the 510 and package tray on the 210, if so equipped.

3. Remove the driver's side of the instrument panel. See the section below for instructions.

4. Remove the heater control assembly: remove the defroster ducts, vent door cables at the doors, harness connector and the control assembly.

5. Remove the radio.

6. Disconnect the heater ducts, side defrosters and the center vent duct.

7. Remove the screws attaching the defroster nozzle to the unit. Disconnect the blower wiring harness and the heater hoses.

8. Remove the retaining bolts and the heater unit.

9. Installation is the reverse of removal.

310

1. Disconnect the battery ground cable.

2. Set the temperature lever to the HOT position and drain the engine coolant.

3. Remove the instrument panel assembly. See the following section for instructions.

4. Disconnect the control cables and rod from the heater unit. Disconnect the heater motor harness.

5. Disconnect the inlet and the outlet heater hoses from the engine compartment.

6. Remove the two lower and three upper bolts attaching the heater and blower units to the vehicle. The air conditioning unit is on the passenger's side of the vehicle. It does not have to be removed to remove the heater and blower units.

7. Remove the heater and blower units.

8. Installation is the reverse of removal.

Heater Blower

REMOVAL AND INSTALLATION

1973 510

1. Remove the heater unit as described above.

2. Remove the four clips and separate the case halves. The blower is in one of the halves.

3. To remove the motor, remove the fan and remove the four retaining bolts.

B210, F10, 610, 710, 1977–79 200SX

1. Remove the heater unit as described above.

NOTE: *You may be able to remove the blower on some models without removing the heater unit from the vehicle.*

2. Remove the three or four screws holding the blower motor in the case and remove the motor with the fan attached.

3. Installation is the reverse of removal.

1980 200SX

1. Remove the instrument panel lower cover and cluster lid on the right-hand side.

2. Disconnect the negative battery cable.

3. Disconnect the control cable and harness connector from the blower unit.

4. Remove the three bolts and remove the blower unit.

5. Remove the three screws holding the blower motor in the case, unplug the hose running from the rear of the motor into the case and pull the motor together with the fan out of the case.

Installation is the reverse of removal.

810

1. Disconnect the negative battery cable.

2. Remove the heater duct running from the blower case to the heater unit.

3. Disconnect the control cable from the blower case.

4. Disconnect the harness connector.

5. Remove the screws holding the blower case in place and remove the blower case.

6. Remove the three bolts holding the blower motor in place and remove the blower motor.

7. Installation is the reverse of removal.

210

1. Disconnect the battery ground cable.

2. Disconnect the heater blower harness connector.

3. Remove the three outer bolts holding the blower motor assembly in place and remove the motor with the fan attached.

NOTE: *Make sure you remove the outer bolts and not the bolts holding the motor to the backing plate.*

4. Installation is the reverse of removal.

310

1. Disconnect the battery ground cable.

2. Remove the instrument panel lower cover on the driver's side.

3. Disconnect the wiring harness at the

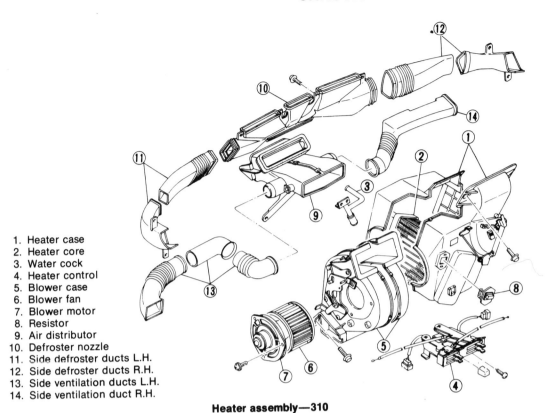

1. Heater case
2. Heater core
3. Water cock
4. Heater control
5. Blower case
6. Blower fan
7. Blower motor
8. Resistor
9. Air distributor
10. Defroster nozzle
11. Side defroster ducts L.H.
12. Side defroster ducts R.H.
13. Side ventilation ducts L.H.
14. Side ventilation duct R.H.

Heater assembly—310

blower and wherever else it constricts removal of the blower motor.

4. Remove the control wire and rod from in front of the motor.

5. Remove the three screws holding the control assembly in front of the blower motor and move the assembly out of the way.

6. Remove the three blower motor at-

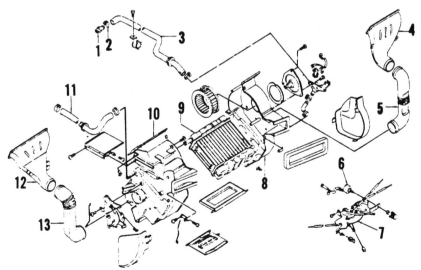

1. Connector	6. Heater switch	11. Heater hose (outlet)
2. Clip	7. Heater control	12. Defroster nozzle (L.H.)
3. Heater hose (inlet)	8. Heater case (R.H.)	13. Defroster duct (L.H.)
4. Defroster nozzle (R.H.)	9. Heater core	
5. Defroster duct (R.H.)	10. Heater case (L.H.)	

Heater assembly—F10

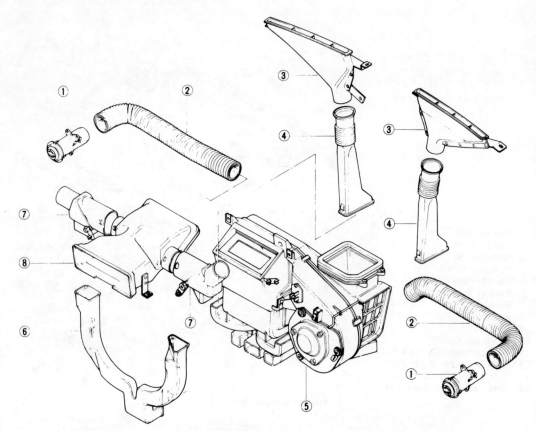

1. Side outlet
2. Cooler duct
3. Defroster nozzle
4. Defroster duct
5. Heater unit
6. Side defroster center duct
7. Side defroster connector
8. Center ventilation duct

Heater assembly—1978 510

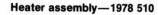
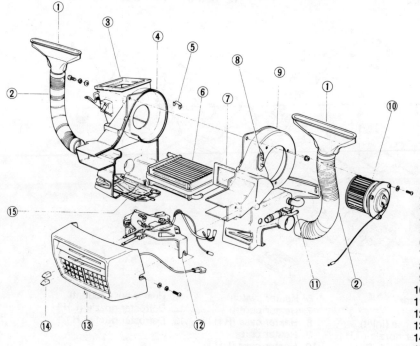

1. Defroster nozzle
2. Defroster hose
3. Air intake box
4. Heater box (L.H.)
5. Clip
6. Heater core
7. Ventilator valve
8. Resistor
9. Heater box (R.H.)
10. Fan and fan motor
11. Heater cock
12. Heater control
13. Center ventilator
14. Knob
15. Heat valve

B210 heater

taching screws and then remove the blower motor with the fan attached.

7. Installation is the reverse of removal.

1978-80 510

1. Disconnect the battery ground cable.
2. Disconnect the blower motor harness connector.
3. Remove the blower motor by removing the three outer retaining screws and pulling the motor with the fan out of the case.

NOTE: *Make sure you remove the three outer screws and not the three screws holding the motor to the backing plate.*

4. Installation is the reverse of removal.

Heater Core
REMOVAL AND INSTALLATION
1973 510

1. Remove the four clips and separate the lower cover.
2. Unbolt and remove the heater core.
3. Installation is the reverse of removal.

610, 710

The heater unit need not be removed to remove the heater core. It must be removed to remove the blower motor.

1. Drain the coolant.
2. Detach the coolant hoses.
3. Disconnect the control cables on the sides of the heater unit.
4. Remove the clips and the cover from the front of the heater unit.
5. Pull out the core.
6. Reverse the procedure for installation. Run the engine with the heater on for a few minutes to make sure that the system fills with coolant.

F10

1. Remove the heater assembly as described earlier.
2. Remove the sealing sponges. Unfasten the seven clips that hold the heater case together.
3. Remove the heater core from the cases.
4. Installation is the reverse of removal.

1200, B210

1. Remove the heater from the car.
2. Remove the clip and slide the hose from the heater core cock.
3. Remove the clips and separate the left and right sides of the heater case.
4. Lift out the heater core.

1977-79 200SX

1. Remove the heater assembly as described earlier.
2. Remove the control lever assembly. Remove the knobs, disconnect the lamp wire, remove the center vent (4 screws), disconnect the fan wires, remove the clips and cables, remove the retaining screws and the unit.
3. Disconnect the hose from the heater cock.
4. Remove the connection rod (with bracket) from the air door.
5. Remove the clips on each side of the box, split the box, and remove the core.
6. Installation is the reverse of removal.

1980 200SX

1. Remove the heater unit as described earlier.
2. Remove the hoses from the heater core and remove the core.
3. Installation is the reverse of removal.

810

1. Remove the heater assembly as outlined earlier.
2. Loosen the clips and screws and remove the center ventilation cover and heater control assembly.
3. Remove the screws securing the door shafts.
4. Remove the clips securing the left and right heater cases, and then separate the cases.
5. Remove the heater core.
6. Installation is in the reverse order of removal.

1978-80 510, 210

1. Remove the heater unit as outlined earlier.
2. Loosen the hose clamps and disconnect the inlet and outlet hoses.
3. Remove the clips securing the case halves and separate the cases.
4. Remove the heater core.
5. Installation is in the reverse order of removal.

310

1. Remove the heater unit from the vehicle.
2. Disconnect the inlet and outlet hoses from the core if you have not done so already.
3. Remove the clips securing the case halves and separate the halves.

4. Remove the heater core.

5. Installation is the reverse of removal.

RADIO

REMOVAL AND INSTALLATION

1973 510

1. Detach all electrical connections.

2. Remove the radio knobs and retaining nuts.

3. Remove the mounting screws, tip the radio down at the rear, and remove.

4. Reverse the procedure for installation.

1200, B210, 610, 710, F10

1. Remove the instrument cluster.

2. Detach all electrical connections.

3. Remove the radio knobs and retaining nuts.

4. Remove the rear support bracket.

5. Remove the radio.

6. Reverse the procedure for installation.

1977-79 200SX

1. The instrument panel must be removed in order to remove the radio. The instrument panel is referred to as the cluster lid in the illustrations.

2. Pull out the radio switch knobs.

3. In order to remove the instrument panel, first remove the steering wheel and cover.

4. Remove the control knobs on the instrument panel by pushing in on them and turning them counterclockwise. Once the knobs are removed, remove the nuts.

5. Remove the instrument panel screws. See the illustration for their location.

6. Disconnect the switch wires (after noting their location) and remove the panel.

7. Loosen the screws and remove the radio from its bracket. Disconnect the wires and pull the radio free.

8. Installation is in the reverse order of removal.

1980 200SX

1. Disconnect the battery. Before removing the radio (audio assembly), you must remove the center instrument cluster which holds the heater controls, etc. Remove the two side screws in the cluster. Remove the heater control and the control panel. Remove the two bolts behind the heater control panel and the two bolts at the base of the cluster. Pull the cluster out of the way after disconnecting the lighter wiring and any other control cables.

2. Remove the radio knobs and fronting panel.

3. Remove the five screws holding the radio assembly in place.

4. Remove the radio after unplugging all connections.

5. Installation is the reverse of removal.

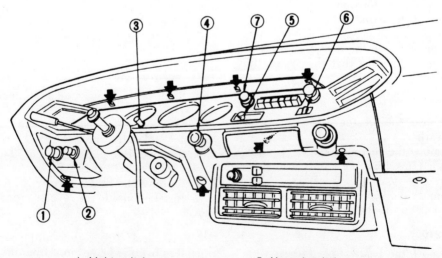

1. Light switch
2. Illumination control knob
3. Trip meter knob
4. Windshield wiper and washer
   switch knob
5. Hazard switch
6. Rear defogger switch
7. Radio knob

Instrument panel removal points—1977-79 200SX

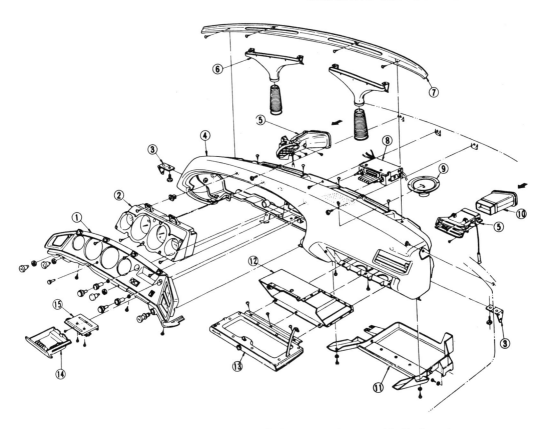

1. Cluster lid
2. Meter assembly
3. Instrument mounting lower
    bracket
4. Instrument pad
5. Ventilation grille

6. Defroster nozzle
7. Instrument garnish
8. Radio
9. Speaker
10. Ventilation duct

11. Package tray
12. Glove box
13. Glove box lid
14. Ash tray
15. Outer case

1977-79 200SX instrument panel

810

1. Disconnect the battery ground cable.
2. Remove the knobs and nuts on the radio and the choke control wire. Remove the ash tray.
3. Remove the steering column cover, and disconnect the main harness connectors.
4. Remove the retaining screws and remove the instrument panel cover.
5. Disconnect the wires from the radio and remove the radio from the bracket.
6. Installation is in the reverse order of removal.

1978-80 510

1. Disconnect the battery ground cable.
2. Remove the steering column covers and disconnect the hazard warning switch connector.
3. Loosen the wiper switch attaching screws and remove the wiper switch.

4. Pull out the ash tray and the heater control knobs.
5. Remove the heater control finisher. See the illustration. Insert a screwdriver into the FAN lever slit to remove the finisher. Remove finisher A. (See the illustration.)
6. Remove the radio knobs, nuts and washers.
7. Remove the manual choke knob and the defroster control knob.
8. Disconnect the following connectors:
    a. center illumination light
    b. cigarette lighter
    c. clock
    d. turn signal switch
9. Remove the screws from the instrument panel (referred to as cluster lid A in the illustration). The black arrows mark the screws locations.
10. Remove the instrument panel cover. Remove the connections from the radio and remove the radio from its bracket.

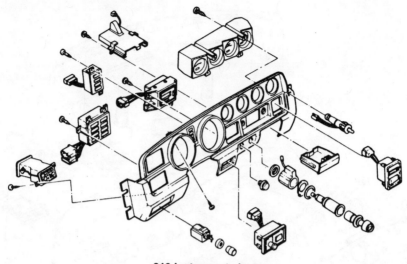

810 instrument cluster

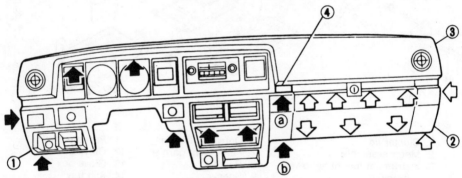

1. Cluster lid A
2. Cluster lid B
3. Instrument panel
4. Finisher A
◀ Cluster lid A securing screw positions
◇ Cluster lid B securing screw positions

1978 510 instrument panel removal points

Wiper motor—1978 510

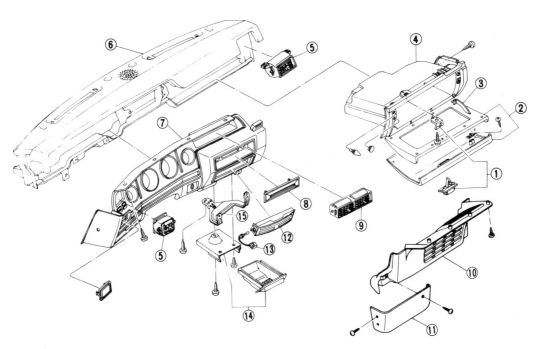

1. Lock and striker
2. Lid finisher
3. Lid stopper
4. Cluster lid B compartment
5. Side vent grille
6. Instrument panel assembly
7. Cluster lid A
8. Radio mask
9. Center vent grille
10. Instrument lower assist cover
11. Instrument lower center cover
12. Heater control finisher
13. Illumination lamp
14. Ash tray
15. Heater control lever bracket

1980 210 instrument panel

11. Installation is in the reverse order of removal.

210

NOTE: *The dashboard must be removed to gain access to the radio.*

1. Disconnect the battery ground cable.
2. Remove the steering column cover.
3. Remove the lighting control rheostat.
4. Pull out the heater control knob and remove the heater control panel facing.
5. Remove the screws attaching the heater control assembly to the dash panel, or cluster lid "A".
6. Pull out the radio knobs and remove the nuts and washers.
7. Pull out the ash tray and remove the screws holding the ash tray holder in place.
8. Remove the eight screws holding the dashboard in place: three along the bottom, one on the driver's door side and four along the windshield. Remove the dashboard.
9. Remove the radio bracket by loosening the retaining screws.
10. Disconnect the harness connector and the antenna feeder cable.
11. Remove the radio.
12. Installation is the reverse of removal.

310

1. Disconnect the battery ground cable.
2. Remove the center bezel.
3. Loosen and remove the screws retaining the radio in place.
4. Remove the radio and disconnect the antenna feeder cable, power lines and speaker connections.
5. Installation is the reverse of removal.

WINDSHIELD WIPER MOTOR AND LINKAGE

REMOVAL AND INSTALLATION
1200, B210

The wiper motor is on the firewall under the hood. The operating linkage is on the firewall inside the car.

1. Detach the motor wiring plug.
2. Inside the car, remove the nut connecting the linkage to the wiper shaft.
3. Unbolt and remove the wiper motor from the firewall.
4. Reverse the procedure for installation.

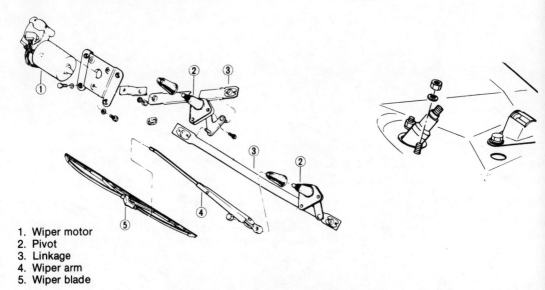

1. Wiper motor
2. Pivot
3. Linkage
4. Wiper arm
5. Wiper blade

Windshield wiper motor and linkage—B210

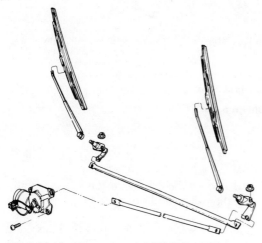

Windshield wiper motor and linkage—710

1973 510, 610, 710, 810, 1977–79 200SX

1. Disconnect the battery ground cable.

2. The wiper motor and linkage are accessible from under the hood. Raise the wiper blade from the windshield and remove the retaining nut. Remove the wiper blades and arms.

3. Remove the nuts holding the wiper pivots to the body.

4. Remove the screws holding the wiper motor to the firewall.

5. Disconnect the wiper motor wiring connector.

6. Remove the cowl air intake grille.

7. Disconnect the wiper motor from the linkage.

8. Remove the linkage assembly through the cowl top.

9. Installation is the reverse of removal.

NOTE: *If the wipers do not park correctly, adjust the position of the automatic stop cover of the wiper motor, if so equipped.*

F10

1. Disconnect the battery ground cable.

2. Lift the wiper arms, remove their attaching nuts and remove them.

3. Remove the meter cover.

4. Remove the glove box.

5. Remove the wiper motor attaching bolts.

6. Remove the ball joint connecting the motor shaft to the wiper link.

7. Remove the wiper motor from the cowl dash panel after disconnecting its wiring.

8. Remove the wiper pivot bolts from under the dashboard and remove the linkage.

9. Installation is the reverse of removal.

NOTE: *Make sure you install the wiper arms in the correct positions by running the system without the arms on, stopping it, then attaching the arms.*

1978–80 510

1. Disconnect the battery ground cable.

2. Remove the wiper motor.

3. Remove the wiper link inspection cover under the hood.

4. Remove the wiper arms from the pivot shafts by lifting the arms then removing the attaching nuts.

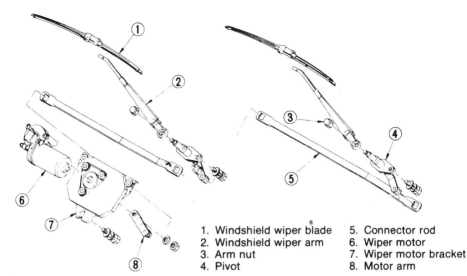

1. Windshield wiper blade
2. Windshield wiper arm
3. Arm nut
4. Pivot
5. Connector rod
6. Wiper motor
7. Wiper motor bracket
8. Motor arm

F10 wiper motor linkage

5. Loosen and remove the large nuts securing the pivot shafts to the body.

6. Remove the linkage through the inspection hole.

7. Installation is the reverse of removal.

NOTE: *Make sure you install the wiper arms in the correct positions by running the system without the arms on, stopping it, then attaching the arms.*

210, 310, 1980 200SX

1. Disconnect the battery ground cable.

2. Open the hood and disconnect the motor wiring connection.

3. Unbolt the motor from the body.

4. Disconnect the wiper linkage from the motor and remove the motor.

5. Installation is the reverse of removal.

1200

1. Disconnect the battery negative lead.

2. Depress the wiper, light switch, and choke knobs, turning them counterclockwise to remove.

3. From the rear, disconnect the lighter wire. Turn and remove the lighter outer case.

4. Remove the radio and heater knobs.

5. Remove the shell cover from the steering column.

6. Remove the screws which hold the instrument cluster to the instrument panel. Pull out the cluster.

7. Disconnect the wiring connector. Disconnect the speedometer cable by unscrewing the nut at the back of the speedometer.

8. Individual instruments may be removed from the rear of the cluster.

INSTRUMENT CLUSTER

REMOVAL AND INSTALLATION

1973 510

1. Disconnect the speedometer cable by unscrewing the nut at the back of the speedometer.

2. Remove the screws holding the instrument cluster to the instrument panel.

3. Pull out the instrument cluster enough to detach the wiring.

4. Remove the cluster. Individual instrument units can be removed from the rear of the cluster.

1200 instrument cluster removal

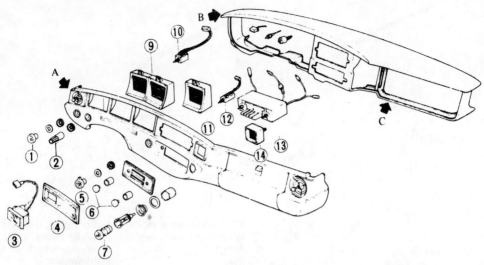

A. Cluster cover
B. Instrument pad
C. Instrument panel
1. Light switch knob
2. Light control knob
3. Rear window defogger switch

4. Escutcheon
5. Wiper switch knob
6. Radio knob
7. Cigarette lighter
8. Gauges

9. Light switch
10. Tachometer
11. Wiper switch
12. Radio
13. Clock

B210 instrument cluster removal

610, 710, and B210

1. Disconnect the battery ground cable.
2. Remove the four screws and the steering column cover.
3. Remove the screws which attach the cluster face. Two are just above the steering column, and there is one inside each of the outer instrument recesses.
4. Pull the cluster lid forward.
5. Disconnect the multiple connector.
6. Disconnect the speedometer cable.
7. Disconnect any other wiring.
8. Remove the cluster face.
9. Remove the odometer knob if the vehicle has one.
10. Remove the six screws and the cluster.
11. Instruments may now be readily replaced.
12. Reverse the procedure for installation.
NOTE: *It may be necessary to drop the steering column to aid removal.*

F10

1. Disconnect the battery ground cable.
2. Disconnect the speedometer cable from the back of the speedometer.
3. Remove the package tray and disconnect the heater control cables from the heater.
4. Disconnect all wire harness connec-

tors from the back of the instrument panel after noting their locations and tagging them.
5. Remove the choke knob and nut.
6. Remove the steering column bracket installation bolts.
7. Loosen the instrument panel upper attaching screws.
8. Remove the bolts securing the sides of the instrument panel.
9. Remove the bolts attaching the instrument panel to the pedal bracket.
10. Remove the instrument panel.
11. Installation is in the reverse order of removal.

810

1. Disconnect the battery ground cable.
2. Remove the knobs and nuts on the radio and the knob on the choke control wire. Remove the ash tray.
3. Remove the steering column covers.
4. Disconnect the harness connectors after noting their location and marking them.
5. Remove the retaining screws and remove the instrument panel.
6. Installation is in the reverse order of removal.

1977–79 200SX

1. Disconnect the battery ground cable.
2. Remove the steering column covers.

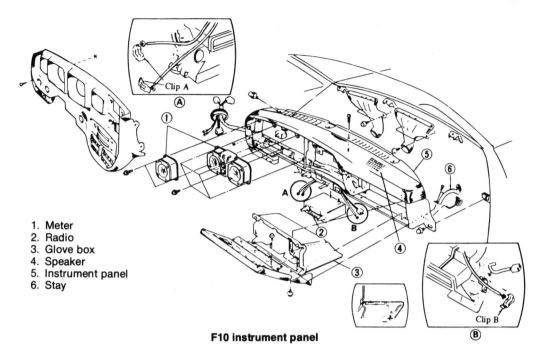

1. Meter
2. Radio
3. Glove box
4. Speaker
5. Instrument panel
6. Stay

F10 instrument panel

3. Disconnect the speedometer cable and the radio antenna.

4. Disconnect all the wires from the back of the panel after noting their location and marking them.

5. Remove the bolts which secure the steering column clamp. Remove the package tray.

6. Unbolt the panel from the brackets on the left and right-hand sides.

7. Remove the right-side windshield pillar trim and remove the bolt which attaches the panel to the pillar.

8. Remove the instrument garnish (see the illustration).

9. Remove the retaining bolts and remove the panel.

10. Installation is in the reverse order of removal.

1980 200SX

1. Disconnect the battery ground terminal.

2. It may be necessary to remove the steering wheel and covers to remove the instrument cluster.

3. Remove the screws holding the cluster lid in place and remove the lid.

4. Remove the five bolts holding the cluster in place and pull the cluster out, then remove all connections from its back. Make sure you mark the wiring to avoid confusion during reassembly.

5. Remove the instrument cluster.

6. Installation is the reverse of removal.

1978 510

1. Disconnect the battery ground cable.

2. Remove the instrument panel cover (see the radio removal procedure).

3. Disconnect the speedometer cable from the back of the speedometer. Remove the antenna.

4. Mark their location and remove the wiring connectors.

5. Disconnect the heater control cables. Disconnect the heater ground harness connector.

6. Remove the screws and remove the instrument panel.

7. Installation is in the reverse order of removal.

210

See 210 Radio Removal and Installation section for instrument cluster removal and installation procedure.

310

1. Disconnect the battery terminals.

2. Remove the steering wheel and the steering column covers.

3. Remove the instrument cluster lid by removing its screws.

4. Remove the instrument cluster screws, pull the unit out and disconnect all wiring

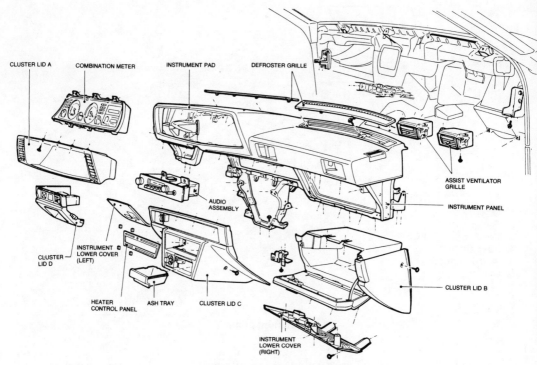

CLUSTER LID A   COMBINATION METER   INSTRUMENT PAD   DEFROSTER GRILLE

ASSIST VENTILATOR GRILLE

INSTRUMENT PANEL

AUDIO ASSEMBLY

CLUSTER LID D

INSTRUMENT LOWER COVER (LEFT)

HEATER CONTROL PANEL   ASH TRAY   CLUSTER LID C

CLUSTER LID B

INSTRUMENT LOWER COVER (RIGHT)

1980 200SX instrument panel

and cables from its rear. Mark the wires to avoid confusion during assembly. Be careful not to damage the printed circuit.

5. Remove the cluster.

6. Installation is the reverse of removal.

SPEEDOMETER CABLE REPLACEMENT

1. Remove any lower dash covers that may be in the way and disconnect the speedometer cable from the back of the speedometer.

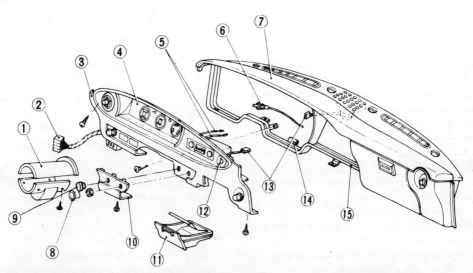

1. Steering column covers	6. Speedometer cable	11. Ash tray
2. Instrument harness	7. Upper instrument pad	12. Clock
3. Cluster cover	8. Wiper/washer switch knob	13. Speaker harness
4. Gauges	9. Light control switch	14. Illumination bulb
5. Light monitor	10. Cluster cover	15. Instrument panel

710 instrument cluster removal

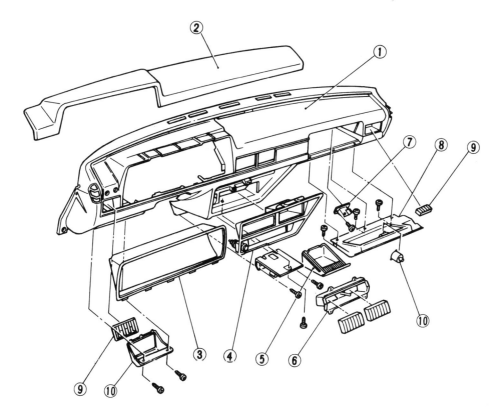

1. Instrument panel
2. Instrument pad
3. Cluster lid
4. Center bezel
5. Ash tray
6. Center ventilator
7. Striker
8. Glove lid
9. Side ventilator case
10. Key lock
11. Coin pocket

310 instrument panel

NOTE: *On some models it may be easier to remove the instrument cluster to gain access to the cable.*

2. Pull the cable from the cable housing. If the cable is broken, the other half of the cable will have to be removed from the transmission end. Unscrew the retaining knob at the transmission and remove the cable from the transmission extension housing.

3. Lubricate the cable with graphite power (sold as speedometer cable lubricant) and feed the cable into the housing. It is best to start at the speedometer end and feed the cable down towards the transmission. It is also usually necessary to unscrew the transmission connection and install the cable end to the gear, then reconnect the housing to the transmission. Slip the cable end into the speedometer and reconnect the cable housing.

Ignition Switch

Ignition switch removal and installation procedures are covered in Chapter 8; Suspension and Steering.

SEATBELT SYSTEM

Warning Buzzer and Light
1973 510, 1200, 610

Beginning in 1972, all cars are required to have a warning system which operates a buzzer and warning light if either of the front seat belts are not fastened when the seats are occupied and the car is in a forward gear.

A light with the words "Seat Belts", or "Fasten Seat Belts" is located on the dash board while a buzzer is located under the dash. They are controlled by pressure-sensitive switches hidden in the front bench or bucket seats. A switch in each of the front seat belt retractors turns off the warning system only when the belt or belts are pulled a specified distance out of their retractors.

Two different types of switches are used to control the system, depending upon the type of transmission used:

On manual transmission-equipped cars, the transmission neutral switch is used to activate the seat belt warning circuit.

Automatic transmissions use the inhibitor switch to activate the seat belt warning circuit.

When removing the seats, be sure to unplug the pressure-sensitive switches at their connections.

Seat Belt/Starter Interlock System

1974—75

As required by law, all 1974 and most 1975 Datsun passenger cars cannot be started until the front seat occupants are seated and have fastened their seat belts. If the proper sequence is not followed, e.g., the occupants fasten the seat belts and *then* sit on them, the engine cannot be started.

The shoulder harness and lap belt are permanently fastened together, so that they both must be worn. The shoulder harness uses an inertia-lock reel to allow freedom of movement under normal driving conditions. NOTE: *This type of reel locks up when the car decelerates rapidly, as during a crash.*

The switches for the interlock system have been removed from the lap belt retractors and placed in the belt buckles. The seat sensors remain the same as those used in 1973.

For ease of service, the car may be started from outside, by reaching in and turning the key, but without depressing the seat sensors.

In case of system failure, an override switch is located under the hood. This is a "one start" switch and it must be reset each time it is used.

LIGHTING

Headlights

REMOVAL AND INSTALLATION

NOTE: *Many Datsuns have radiator grilles which are unit-constructed to also*

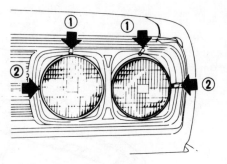

1. Vertical adjustment
2. Horizontal adjustment

1979 510 headlight adjusting screws—do not disturb when removing light

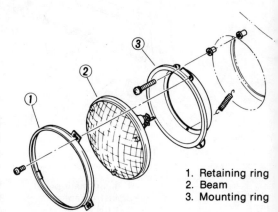

1. Retaining ring
2. Beam
3. Mounting ring

Exploded view of standard headlight

serve as headlight frames. In this case, it will be necessary to remove the grille to gain access to the headlights.

1. Remove the grille, if necessary.
2. Remove the headlight retaining ring screws. These are the three or four short screws in the assembly. There are also two longer screws at the top and side of the headlight which are used to aim the headlight. Do not tamper with these or the headlight will have to be re-aimed.
3. Remove the ring on round headlights by turning it clockwise.
4. Pull the headlight bulb from its socket and disconnect the electrical plug.
5. Connect the plug to the new bulb.
6. Position the headlight in the shell. Make sure that the word "TOP" is, indeed, at the top and that the knobs in the headlight lens engage the slots in the mounting shell.
7. Place the retaining ring over the bulb and install the screws.
8. Install the grille, if removed.

CIRCUIT PROTECTION

Fusible Links

A fusible link is a protective device used in an electrical circuit. When current increases beyond a certain amperage, the fusible metal wire of the link melts, thus breaking the electrical circuit and preventing further damage to the other components and wiring. Whenever a fusible link is melted because of a short circuit, correct the cause before installing a new link.

Use the following chart to locate the fusible link(s) on your Datsun.

All Datsun fusible links are the plug in kind. To replace them, simply unplug the bad link and insert the new one.

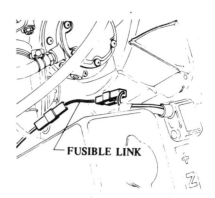

Most fusible links are found beside the battery

Fusible Links

Year	Model	Number	Color/Protects	Location
1973	1200	1	Green/Charging system	At positive battery terminal
1973–74	610	2	Brown/Charging system Red/Lights and Misc.	At positive battery terminal
1976 1974–77	610 710	4	2 Brown/Headlights, ignition, misc. 1 Green (or Brown)/Charging system, misc. 1 Red/Lights, accessories	On relay bracket, front right side of engine compartment
1974–78	B210	1	Green/Fuse block, electrical systems	At positive battery terminal
1976–78	F10	2	Red/N.A. Green/N.A.	At positive battery terminal
1977–80	810	6①	1 Red/Charging system, fuse block 3 Brown/Headlights, ignition, fuel pump 2 Green/Fuel injection harness	On relay bracket, in engine compartment ①
1977–79	200SX	2	Green/N.A.	At positive battery terminal
1980	200SX	4	2 Green/Ignition, fuel injection 1 Red/Charging system, fuse block 1 Brown/Fuel injection, starting	At positive battery terminal
1978–80	510,210	2	Green/Starting, ignition, charging, headlights	At positive battery terminal
1979–80	310	4	1 Red/Fuse block 3 Green/Ignition, lights, fan	Mounted on fender well beside battery

① The fuel injection links are at the positive battery terminal

Fuse Box and Flasher Location

Year	Model	Fuse Box Location	Flasher Location
1973	510	Engine compartment, right rear	N/A
1973	1200	Under instrument panel, right of steering wheel	N/A
1973–77	610,710	Under instrument panel	Top of pedal assembly ①
1974–78	B210	Below hood release knob	Turn signal: Behind radio Hazard: Under driver's side of dashboard
1976–78	F10	Below hood release knob	Under driver's side of dashboard ①
1977–80	810	Right side kick panel	Under driver's side of dashboard ①
1977–79	200SX	Underneath glove box	Turn signal: Behind radio Hazard: Behind glove box
1980	200SX	Underneath glove box	Under driver's side dashboard ①
1978–80	510	Under instrument panel	Under driver's side dashboard ①
1979–80	210	Below hood release knob	Under driver's side dashboard ①
1979–80	310	Below hood release knob	Turn signal: Passenger side kick board Hazard: Driver's side at hood release

① Both the turn signal and the hazard flashers are side by side
NOTE: The original turn signal flasher unit is pink, and larger than the original hazard flasher unit, which is gold.

WIRING DIAGRAMS

Wiring diagrams have been left out of this book. As cars have become more complex, and available with longer and longer option lists, wiring diagrams have grown in size and complexity also. It has become virtually impossible to provide a readable reproduction in a reasonable number of pages.

Clutch and Transmission

MANUAL TRANSMISSION

Various four speed transmissions are standard equipment on all models covered in this guide, with the exception of the 200SX, which comes standard with a five speed transmission. Five speed transmissions are also available on the F10, B210, 210, 310, the 1978–80 510, and the 1979–80 810. With the exception of the F10 and the 310, both front wheel drive vehicles, all models feature intergral shift linkage, which requires no adjustment. Some 1973 510 and 1200 cars are equipped with model R3W56L (1200), and model R3W65L (1973 510) three speed transmissions.

The four speed transmission used in the 510 and 710 is model F4W63L. The 610 uses model F4W63. These transmissions are identified by their bottom covers, either a cast, ribbed cover or a stamped steel one. The 810 four speed transmission is model F4W71B. It is constructed in three sections: clutch housing, transmission housing and extension housing. It has no cover plates. There is a cast iron adapter between the transmission and extension housing. The 1973 1200, 1974 B210 and some 1980 210's use the model F4W56 four speed transmission, which is constructed in two sections: a combined clutch and transmission housing and an ex-

tension housing. There is a cast iron adapter plate between the housings. There are no case cover plates. 1975–78 B210's, 1979 and some 1980 210's use a revised version of the four speed used in the 1200 and the early B210. On this transmission, model F4W60(L), the adapter plate is aluminum instead of cast iron.

The F10 and the 310 both use the same transaxle model, F4WF60A (four speed), and F5WF60A (five speed).

The 1977–78 B210, 1978–80 510 and the 1977–79 200SX all use the model FS5W63A five speed transmission. The 1979 210 has a model FS5W60L five speed transmission while the 1980 210 is equipped with a model FS5W60A five speed. The 1979–80 810 and the 1980 200SX use the model FS5W71B five speed transmission.

F10 LINKAGE ADJUSTMENT
Four-Speed Models

1. The adjustment is made at the shift rods on the transmission. Loosen the adjusting nuts marked 1 and 2 in the illustration.

2. Measure the clearance between the shift lever marked 3 in the illustration and the transmission case. Make sure the shift lever is pushed completely into the transmis-

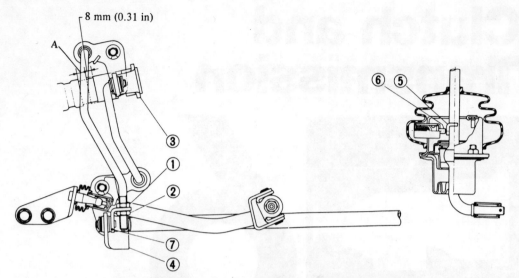

Four speed F10 linkage is adjusted at the numbered points

sion case. The clearance is marked "A" in the illustration.

3. Place the transmission in fourth gear. Shift lever 3 should now be fully downward.

4. Increase the initial clearance "A" by 8 mm (0.31 in.).

5. Push lever 4 fully upward. Now tighten nut 1 until it makes contact with trunnion 7. Then back the nut off one full turn and tighten it with nut 2.

Five Speed Models

1. Loosen locknuts 1, 2, 3, and 4.

2. Make sure shift lever 5 is pushed completely into the transmission case, then move it back 8 mm (0.31 in.).

3. Place the car in third gear.

4. Push select lever 6 fully down. Turn nut 3 until it comes into contact with trunnion 9. Back the nut off one or two turns, and

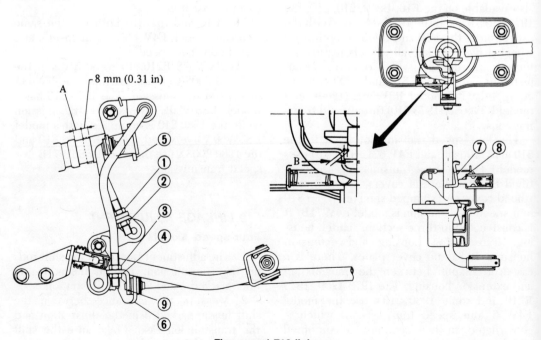

Five speed F10 linkage

then tighten nut 3 with nut 4. Tighten nuts 1 and 2.

310 LINKAGE ADJUSTMENT

Four and Five-Speed Models

Adjustment can be made by adjusting the select lever.

1. Loosen the adjusting nuts at each end of the control rod lever near the bottom of the linkage.

2. Set the shift control lever in the Neutral position.

3. Fully push the shift lever (transmission side) in the direction Pl, as shown in the illustration. On the four speed transmission, pull the lever back about 8 mm (0.31 in.). On the five speed, pull the shift lever back 11.5 mm (0.453 in.). With the select lever held in the above position, move the shift lever in direction P2, which engages third gear on four speed transmissions and second gear on five speed transmissions.

4. Push the control rod select lever as far as it will go in direction P3, then turn the upper adjusting nut until it touches the trunnion. Turn the nut a quarter turn more, and lock the select lever with the other adjusting nut.

5. Operate the shift control lever in the car to see if it shifts smoothly through the gears.

REMOVAL AND INSTALLATION

All Models Except F10, 310

1. Raise and support the vehicle. Disconnect the battery. On the 1973 510 disconnect

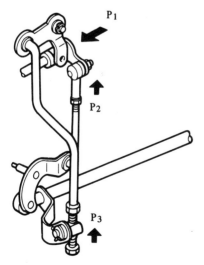

Four speed 310 linkage

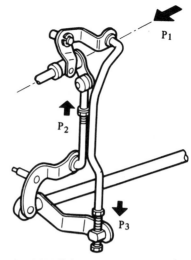

Five speed 310 linkage

the handbrake cable at the equalizer pivot. Disconnect the backup lightswitch, neutral switch and any other switches on the transmission after noting their positions for reassembly.

2. On the 1973 510, loosen the muffler clamps and turn the muffler to one side to allow room for driveshaft removal. On models with the A12, A12A, A13, A14, A15, L18, L20B and Z20 engine, disconnect the exhaust pipe from the manifold and bracket. On the 1980 200SX disconnect the accelerator linkage.

3. Unbolt the driveshaft at the rear and remove. If there is a center bearing, unbolt it from the crossmember. Seal the end of the transmission extension housing to prevent leakage of transmission oil.

4. Disconnect the speedometer drive cable from the transmission.

5. Remove the shift lever.

6. Remove the clutch operating cylinder from the clutch housing.

7. Support the engine with a large wood block and a jack under the oil pan.

610, 710 shift lever removal

8. Unbolt the transmission from the crossmember. Support the transmission with a jack and remove the crossmember.

9. Lower the rear of the engine to allow clearance.

10. Remove the starter.

11. Unbolt the transmission. Lower and remove it to the rear.

12. Installation is the reverse of removal. Check the clutch linkage adjustment.

F10, 310

You must remove the engine/transmission unit as a whole. Refer to chapter 3 for procedures.

After removal, remove the bolts holding the transmission to the engine and separate by pulling the transmission towards the clutch housing.

NOTE: *The clutch assembly will remain attached to the engine.*

Installation is the reverse of removal.

CAUTION: *If the clutch has been removed, it will have to be re-aligned, and when connecting drive shafts, insert O-rings between the differential side flanges and the drive shafts.*

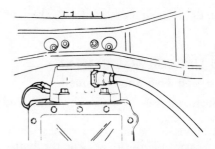

Disconnect speedometer and back-up light switch

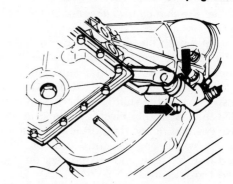

Remove the clutch slave cylinder

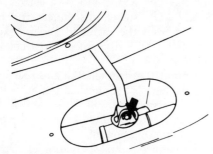

1200 and B210 shift lever removal

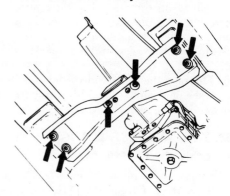

610, 710 crossmember bolts

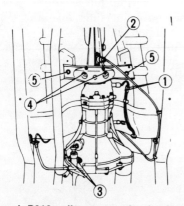

1200 and B210—disconnect the back-up light switch (1), speedometer cable (2), clutch slave cylinder (3), rear engine mount bolts (4), crossmember bolts (5)

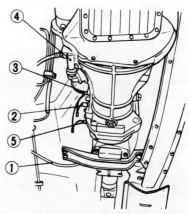

810 transmission—disconnect speedometer cable (1), top detecting switch (2), back-up lamp switch (3), clutch slave cylinder (4), and overdrive detecting switch (5)

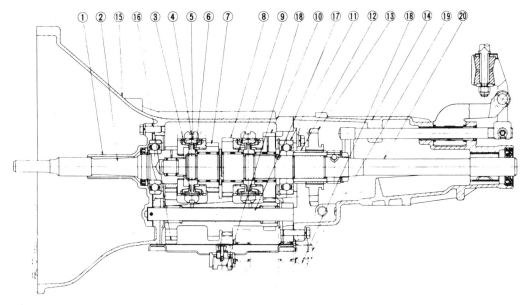

1. Front cover
2. Main drive shaft
3. Baulk ring
4. Coupling sleeve
5. Shifting insert
6. Synchronizer hub
7. 3rd speed gear, mainshaft

8. 2nd speed gear, mainshaft
9. Needle bearing
10. 1st speed gear, mainshaft
11. Mainshaft bearing
12. Reverse hub
13. Reverse gear
14. Rear extension housing

15. Transmission case
16. Counter gear
17. Countershaft
18. Reverse idler gear
19. Reverse idler shaft
20. Mainshaft

Cutaway of four-speed transmission used in the 710

CLUTCH

The purpose of the clutch is to disconnect and connect engine power from the transmission. A car at rest requires a lot of engine torque to get all that weight moving. An internal-combustion engine does not develop a high starting torque (unlike steam engines), so it must be allowed to operate without any load until it builds up enough torque to move the car. Torque increases with engine rpm. The clutch allows the engine to build up torque by physically disconnecting the engine from the transmission, relieving the engine of any load or resistance. The transfer of engine power to the transmission (the load) must be smooth and gradual; if it wasn't driveline components would wear out or break quickly. This gradual power transfer is made possible by gradually releasing the clutch pedal. The clutch disc and pressure plate are the connecting link between the engine and transmission. When the clutch pedal is released, the disc and plate contact each other (clutch engagement), physically joining the engine and transmission. When the pedal is pushed in, the disc and plate separate (the clutch is disengaged), discon-necting the engine from the transmission.

The clutch assembly consists of the flywheel, the clutch disc, the clutch pressure plate, the throwout bearing and fork, the clutch master cylinder, slave cylinder and connecting line, and the pedal. The flywheel and clutch pressure plate (driving members) are connected to the engine crankshaft and rotate with it. The clutch disc is located between the flywheel and pressure plate, and splined to the transmission shaft. A driving member is one that is attached to the engine and transfers engine power to a driven member (clutch disc) on the transmission shaft. A driving member (pressure plate) rotates (drives) a driven member (clutch disc) on contact and, in so doing, turns the transmission shaft. There is a circular diaphragm spring within the pressure plate cover (transmission side). In a relaxed state (when the clutch pedal is fully released), this spring is convex; that is, it is dished outward toward the transmission. Pushing in the clutch pedal actuates the slave cylinder. Connected to the other end of the slave cylinder rod is the throwout bearing fork. The throwout bearing is attached to the fork. When the clutch pedal is depressed, the slave cylinder pushes

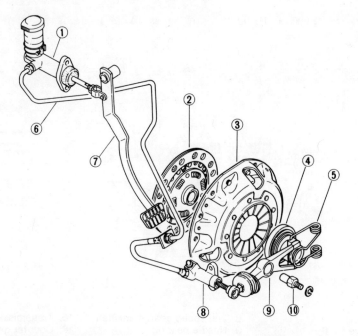

1. Clutch master cylinder
2. Clutch disc assembly
3. Clutch cover assembly
4. Release bearing and sleeve assembly
5. Return spring
6. Clutch line
7. Clutch pedal
8. Operating cylinder
9. Withdrawal lever
10. Withdrawal lever ball pin

1200 and B210 clutch control system

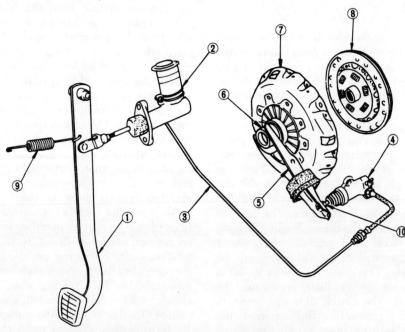

1. Clutch pedal
2. Clutch master cylinder
3. Clutch piping
4. Operating cylinder
5. Withdrawal lever
6. Release bearing
7. Clutch cover
8. Clutch disc
9. Return spring
10. Push rod

510, 610 and 710 clutch control system

the fork and bearing forward to contact the diaphragm spring of the pressure plate. The outer edges of the spring are secured to the pressure plate and are pivoted on rings so that when the center of the spring is compressed by the throwout bearing, the outer edges bow outward, and, by so doing, pull the pressure plate in the same direction—away from the clutch disc. This action separates the disc from the plate, disengaging the clutch and allowing the transmission to be shifted into another gear. Releasing the pedal allows the throwout bearing to pull away from the diaphragm spring resulting in a reversal of spring position. As bearing pressure is gradually released from the spring center, the outer edges of the spring bow inward, pushing the pressure plate into closer contact with the clutch disc. As the disc and plate move closer together, friction between the two increases and slippage is reduced until, when full spring pressure is applied (by fully releasing the pedal), the speed of the disc and plate arc the same. This stops all slipping, creating a direct connection between the plate and disc which results in the transfer of power from the engine to the transmission. The clutch disc is now rotating with the pressure plate at engine speed and, because it is splined to the transmission shaft, the shaft now turns at the same engine speed.

All Datsun models included in this guide are equipped with hydraulic clutch control. This system consists of the clutch pedal and return spring, master cylinder, connecting hydraulic line, and slave (operating) cylinder.

ADJUSTMENT

Refer to the Clutch Specifications Chart for clutch pedal height above floor and pedal free play.

All models have a hydraulically operated clutch. Pedal height is usually adjusted with

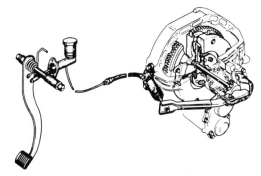

F10 clutch control system. 310 similar

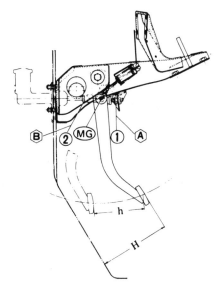

1. Adjust pedal height here
2. Adjust pedal free-play here
MG. Lubricate with multipurpose grease here
H. is pedal height
h. is free-play

Clutch adjusting points

Clutch Specifications

Model	Pedal Height Above Floor (in.)	Pedal Free-Play (in.)
510	5.3	0.10
1200	5.6	0.12
610	6.9	0.04−0.12
B210	6.02	0.04−0.12
710	7.09	0.04−0.20
F10	6.9	0.23−0.55
1977−79 200SX	7.60	0.04−0.12
810	6.9	0.04−0.20
1978−80 510	6.5	0.04−0.20
210	5.75	0.04−0.20
310	7.15	0.04−0.20
1980 200SX	6.70	0.04−0.20

a stopper limiting the upward travel of the pedal. Pedal free-play is adjusted at the master cylinder pushrod. If the pushrod is non-adjustable, free-play is adjusted by placing shims between the master cylinder and the firewall. On a few models, pedal free play can also be adjusted at the operating (slave) cylinder pushrod. Pushrods are available in three lengths for the F10 and the 310.

REMOVAL AND INSTALLATION

All Models except F10, 310

Some 1973 510s are equipped with a coil spring pressure plate. All other models in all years use diaphragm spring pressure plates. Replacements for the 1973 510 may be of either type.

Models With Coil Spring Clutch

1. Remove the transmission from the engine.
2. Temporarily lock the release lever.
3. Loosen the retaining bolts in sequence, a turn at a time. Remove the bolts.
4. Remove the pressure plate and disc.
5. Inspect the pressure plate for scoring, wear, grooves, etc. The surface must be perfectly smooth for proper clutch operation. Reface or replace as necessary. Check the release bearing for wear and replace as necessary. Apply a small amount of grease to the disc splines before installation. Do not allow any grease to get onto the pressure plate or disc.
6. Replace the disc with the longer chamfered splined end of the hub toward the transmission.
7. Align the disc to the flywheel with a splined dummy shaft.
8. Install the pressure plate. Most models have two pressure plate locating dowels in the flywheel. Tighten the pressure plate bolts in sequence, a turn at a time. Torque to 11–16 ft lbs.
9. Remove the dummy shaft. Unlock the release lever.
10. Replace the release bearing and transmission.

Models With Diaphragm Spring Clutch

1. Remove the transmission from the engine.
2. Loosen the bolts in sequence, a turn at a time. Remove the bolts.
3. Remove the pressure plate and clutch disc.

4. Remove the release mechanism. Apply multi-purpose grease to the bearing sleeve inside groove, the contact point of the withdrawal lever and bearing sleeve, the contact surface of the lever ball pin and lever. Replace the release mechanism.
5. Inspect the pressure plate for wear, scoring, etc., and reface or replace as necessary. Inspect the release bearing and replace as necessary. Apply a small amount of grease to the transmission splines. Install the disc on the splines and slide back and forth a few times. Remove the disc and remove excess grease on hub. Be sure no grease contacts the disc or pressure plate.
6. Install the disc, aligning it with a splined dummy shaft.
7. Install the pressure plate and torque the bolts to 11–16 ft lbs.
8. Remove the dummy shaft.
9. Replace the transmission.

F10, 310 TRANSAXLE CLUTCH

Because of the unique configuration of the F10 and 310 transmission/drive shaft system (transaxle), the transmission is impossible to remove from the car without removing the engine.

Due to this problem, Datsun has made provisions for clutch service through an access plate (cover) on the top of the housing. The engine and transmission need not be removed to permit repair or replacement.

NOTE: *The clutch cover and pressure plate are balanced as a unit. If replacement is necessary, replace both parts.*

1. Disconnect the following cables, wires and hoses:

> Battery ground cable
> Fresh air duct
> Engine harness connectors on the clutch housing
> Ignition wire between the coil and the distributor
> Carbon canister hoses

2. Remove the inspection plate from the top of the clutch housing and remove the six bolts holding the clutch cover.

NOTE: *In order to reach all six bolts, you are going to have to jack up the car and, as you loosen the bolts, rotate the right front wheel with the car in top gear. This will rotate the clutch cover.*

CAUTION: *Be sure to loosen the bolts evenly in order.*

3. Rotate the steering wheel all the way to

the right and remove the inspection plate inside the right wheel well.

4. Disconnect the withdrawal lever and remove the six bolts on the bearing house. Reaching through the wheel well inspection hole, pull out the primary drive gear assembly.

NOTE: *To remove the withdrawal lever pin you must first remove the E-ring that holds it to the bearing housing.*

5. After removing the drive gear, go back to the engine compartment and lift the clutch cover and disc assembly out through the open section of the clutch housing. You may also remove the diaphragm at the same time.

6. Remove the strap holding the pressure plate to the clutch cover and remove the clutch from the center.

NOTE: *The strap must be replaced in the same position it had before removal. Mark the relative position before removal. Installing it out of position will cause an imbalance.*

Installation is the reverse of removal. But, you must observe the following:

1. Paying particular attention to the alignment marks, reassemble the disc and cover to the pressure plate. Tighten the strap bolts to 5–6 ft lbs. (F10), 7–9 ft lbs. (310).

2. Put the diaphragm spring and cover assembly onto the flywheel and screw the bolts in with your fingers.

NOTE: *These bolts should remain loose*

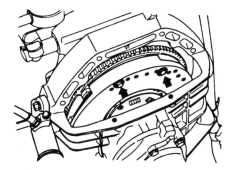

Removing clutch cover bolts—F10, 310

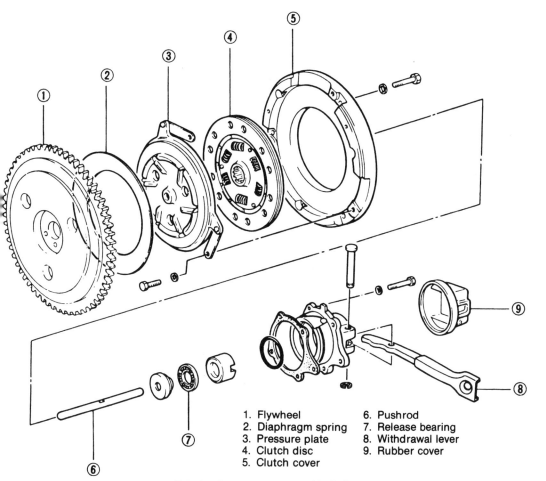

1. Flywheel
2. Diaphragm spring
3. Pressure plate
4. Clutch disc
5. Clutch cover
6. Pushrod
7. Release bearing
8. Withdrawal lever
9. Rubber cover

F10 clutch components—310 similar

enough to shift the assembly when installing the drive gear. There are a pair of aligning pins on the flywheel.

3. Install the drive gear assembly by aligning the disc hub with the gear spline. After alignment, tighten the cover bolts to 5–7.2 ft lbs.

NOTE: *There are two aligning pins on the flywheel.*

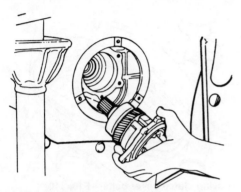

Removing the primary drive gear

Clutch Master Cylinder
REMOVAL AND INSTALLATION

1. Disconnect the clutch pedal arm from the pushrod.

2. Disconnect the clutch hydraulic line from the master cylinder.

NOTE: *Take precautions to keep brake fluid from coming in contact with any painted surfaces.*

3. Remove the nuts attaching the master cylinder and remove the master cylinder and pushrod toward the engine compartment side.

4. Install the master cylinder in the reverse order of removal and bleed the clutch hydraulic system.

OVERHAUL

1. Remove the master cylinder from the vehicle.

2. Drain the clutch fluid from the master cylinder reservoir.

3. Remove the boot and circlip and remove the pushrod.

4. Remove the stopper, piston, cup and return spring.

5. Clean all of the parts in clean brake fluid.

6. Check the master cylinder and piston for wear, corrosion and scores and replace the parts as necessary. Light scoring and

glaze can be removed with crocus cloth soaked in brake fluid.

7. Generally, the cup seal should be replaced each time the master cylinder is disassembled. Check the cup and replace it if it is worn, fatigued, or damaged.

8. Check the clutch fluid reservoir, filler cap, dust cover and the pipe for distortion and damage and replace the parts as necessary.

9. Lubricate all new parts with clean brake fluid.

10. Reassemble the master cylinder parts in the reverse order of disassembly, taking note of the following:

    a. Reinstall the cup seal carefully to prevent damaging the lipped portions;

    b. Adjust the height of the clutch pedal after installing the master cylinder in position on the vehicle;

    c. Fill the master cylinder and clutch fluid reservoir and then bleed the clutch hydraulic system.

Clutch Slave Cylinder
REMOVAL AND INSTALLATION

1. Remove the slave cylinder attaching bolts and the pushrod from the shift fork.

2. Disconnect the flexible fluid hose from the slave cylinder and remove the unit from the vehicle.

3. Install the slave cylinder in the reverse order of removal and bleed the clutch hydraulic system.

OVERHAUL

1. Remove the slave cylinder from the vehicle.

2. Remove the pushrod and boot.

3. Force out the piston by blowing compressed air into the slave cylinder at the hose connection.

NOTE: *Be careful not to apply excess air pressure to avoid possible injury.*

4. Clean all of the parts in clean brake fluid.

5. Check and replace the slave cylinder bore and piston if wear or severe scoring exists. Light scoring and glaze can be removed with crocus cloth soaked in brake fluid.

6. Normally the piston cup should be replaced when the slave cylinder is disassembled. Check the piston cup and replace it if it is found to be worn, fatigued or scored.

7. Replace the rubber boot if it is cracked or broken.

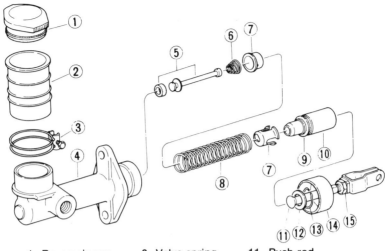

1. Reservoir cap
2. Reservoir
3. Reservoir band
4. Cylinder body
5. Valve assembly

6. Valve spring
7. Spring seat
8. Return spring
9. Piston cup
10. Piston

11. Push rod
12. Stopper
13. Stopper ring
14. Dust cover
15. Nut

Exploded view of typical master cylinder

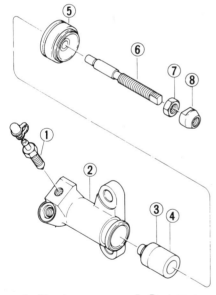

1. Bleeder screw
2. Cylinder body
3. Piston cup
4. Piston

5. Dust cover
6. Push rod
7. Lock nut
8. Push nut

Exploded view of 510, 610 and 710 slave cylinder

8. Lubricate all of the new parts in clean brake fluid and reassemble in the reverse order of disassembly, taking note of the following:

a. Use care when reassembling the piston cup to prevent damaging the lipped portion of the piston cup;

b. Fill the master cylinder with brake fluid and bleed the clutch hydraulic system;

c. Adjust the clearance between the pushrod and the shift fork to $5/64$ in.

Bleeding the Clutch Hydraulic System

1. Check and fill the clutch fluid reservoir to the specified level as necessary. During the bleeding process, continue to check and replenish the reservoir to prevent the fluid level from getting lower than ½ the specified level.

2. Remove the dust cap from the bleeder screw on the clutch slave cylinder and connect a tube to the bleeder screw and insert the other end of the tube into a clean glass or metal container.

NOTE: *Take precautionary measures to prevent the brake fluid from getting on any painted surfaces.*

3. Pump the clutch pedal several times, hold it down and loosen the bleeder screw slowly.

4. Tighten the bleeder screw and release the clutch pedal gradually. Repeat this operation until air bubbles disappear from the brake fluid being expelled out through the bleeder screw.

5. Repeat until all evidence of air bubbles

completely disappears from the brake fluid being pumped out through the tube.

6. When the air is completely removed, securely tighten the bleeder screw and replace the dust cap.

7. Check and refill the master cylinder reservoir as necessary.

8. Depress the clutch pedal several times to check the operation of the clutch and check for leaks.

AUTOMATIC TRANSMISSION

All Datsuns, except the F10 and 310, covered in this book can be optionally equipped with an automatic three-speed transmission. Except for the procedures outlined here, it is recommended that automatic transmission service be left to an authorized Datsun dealer who has the special tools and expertise to work on these units.

PAN REMOVAL

1. Jack up the front of the car and support it safely on stands.

2. Slide a drain pan under the transmission. Loosen the rear oil pan bolts first, to allow most of the fluid to drain off without making a mess on your garage floor.

3. Remove the remaining bolts and drop the pan.

4. Discard the old gasket, clean the pan, and reinstall the pan with a new gasket.

5. Tighten the retaining bolts in a crisscross pattern starting at the center.

CAUTION: *The transmission case is aluminum, so don't exert too much force on the bolts.*

6. Refill the transmission through the dipstick tube. Check the fluid level as described in Chapter 1.

SHIFT LINKAGE ADJUSTMENT

1. Loosen the trunnion locknuts at the lower end of the control lever. Remove the selector lever knob and console.

2. Place the selector lever in Neutral.

3. Place the transmission shift lever in the Neutral position by pushing it all the way back, then pulling it forward two stops.

4. Check the vertical clearance between the top of the shift lever pin and transmission control bracket. The clearance, should be 0.020–0.059 in. Adjust by turning the nut at the lower end of the selector lever compression rod.

5. Check the horizontal clearance, of the shift lever pin and transmission control bracket. This should be 0.020 in. Adjust with the trunnion locknuts.

6. Replace the console, making sure that the shift pointer is correctly aligned. Install the knob.

DOWNSHIFT SOLENOID CHECK

This solenoid is controlled by a downshift switch on the accelerator linkage inside the car. To test the switch and solenoid operation:

1. Turn the ignition on.

2. Push the accelerator all the way down to actuate the switch.

3. The solenoid should click when actuated. The transmission solenoid is screwed into the outside of the case. If there is no click, check the switch, wiring, and solenoid.

To remove the solenoid, first drain 2–3 pints of fluid, then unscrew the unit.

NEUTRAL SAFETY AND BACKUP LIGHT SWITCH ADJUSTMENT

The switch unit is bolted to the left-side of the transmission case, behind the transmission shift lever. The switch prevents the engine from being started in any transmission position except Park or Neutral. It also controls the backup lights.

1. Remove the transmission shift lever retaining nut and the lever.

2. Remove the switch.

3. Remove the machine screw in the case under the switch.

4. Align the switch to the case by inserting a 0.059 in. (1.5 mm) diameter pin through the hole in the switch into the screw hole. Mark the switch location.

5. Remove the pin, replace the machine screw, install the switch as marked, and replace the transmission shift lever and retaining nut.

6. Make sure while holding the brakes on, that the engine will start only in Park or Neutral. Check that the backup lights go on only in Reverse.

REMOVAL AND INSTALLATION

1. Disconnect the battery cable.

2. Remove the accelerator linkage.

3. Detach the shift linkage.

4. Disconnect the neutral safety switch and downshift solenoid wiring.

5. Remove the drain plug and drain the torque converter. If there is no converter

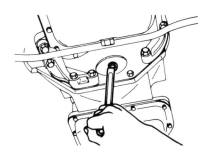

Disconnecting the torque converter bolts through access hole

drain plug, drain the transmission. If there is no transmission drain plug, remove the pan to drain. Replace the pan to keep out dirt.

6. Remove the front exhaust pipe.

7. Remove the vacuum tube and speedometer cable.

8. Disconnect the fluid cooler tubes.

9. Remove the driveshaft and starter.

10. Support the transmission with a jack under the oil pan. Support the engine also.

11. Remove the rear crossmember.

12. Mark the relationship between the torque converter and the drive plate. Remove the four bolts holding the converter to the drive plate through the hole at the front, under the engine. Unbolt the transmission from the engine.

13. Reverse the procedure for installation. Make sure that the drive plate is warped no more than 0.020 in. Torque the drive plate-to-torque converter and converter housing-to-engine bolts to 29–36 ft lbs. Drive plate-to-crankshaft bolt torque is 101–116 ft lbs.

14. Refill the transmission and check the fluid level.

Drive Train

7

DRIVELINE

Driveshaft and Universal Joints

The driveshaft transfers power from the engine and transmission to the differential and rear axles and then to the rear wheels to drive the car. All of the models covered in this book utilize a conventional driveshaft except for the F10 and the 310 front wheel drive models. Except on the 610 wagon, the 810, and the 200SX manual transmission models, the driveshaft assembly has two universal joints—one at each end—and a slip yoke at the front of the assembly which fits into the back of the transmission. The 610, 810, and 200SX incorporate an additional universal joint at the center of the driveshaft with a support bearing. The F10 and 310 do not use a driveshaft in the conventional sense. Instead, power is transmitted to the

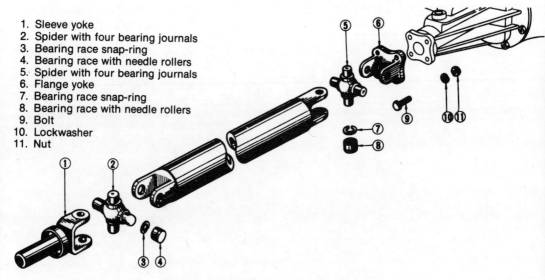

1. Sleeve yoke
2. Spider with four bearing journals
3. Bearing race snap-ring
4. Bearing race with needle rollers
5. Spider with four bearing journals
6. Flange yoke
7. Bearing race snap-ring
8. Bearing race with needle rollers
9. Bolt
10. Lockwasher
11. Nut

Exploded view of 1200 and B210 driveshaft

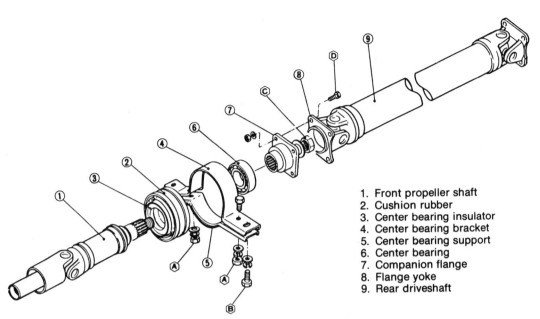

1. Front propeller shaft
2. Cushion rubber
3. Center bearing insulator
4. Center bearing bracket
5. Center bearing support
6. Center bearing
7. Companion flange
8. Flange yoke
9. Rear driveshaft

Exploded view of 810 driveshaft

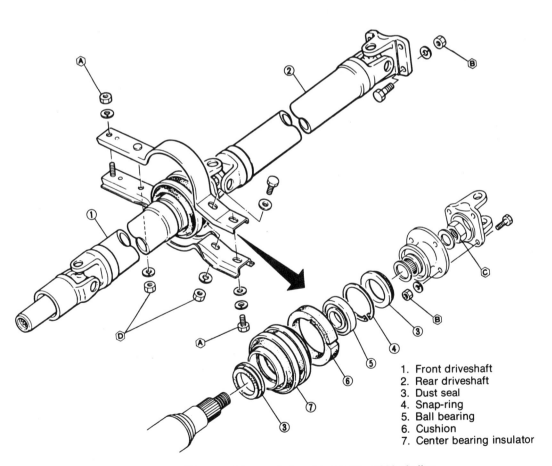

1. Front driveshaft
2. Rear driveshaft
3. Dust seal
4. Snap-ring
5. Ball bearing
6. Cushion
7. Center bearing insulator

1977–79 200SX manual transmission driveshaft—1980 similar

front wheels through a pair of axle shafts which are connected to the transaxle assembly. These driveshafts (or axle shafts) do not use universal joints, but rather constant velocity joints. The shafts are equipped with a CV joint at either end for a total of four.

REMOVAL AND INSTALLATION

1200, B210, 210

These driveshafts are all one-piece units with a U-joint and flange at the rear, and a U-joint and a splined sleeve yoke which fits into the rear of the transmission, at the front. Early models generally have U-joints with grease fittings. U-joints without grease fittings must be disassembled for lubrication, usually at 24,000 mile intervals. The splines are lubricated by transmission oil.

1. Be ready to catch oil coming from the rear of the transmission and to plug the extension housing.
2. Unbolt the rear flange.
3. Pull the driveshaft down and back.
4. Plug the transmission extension housing.
5. Reverse the procedure to install, oiling the splines. Flange bolt torque is 15–20 ft lbs (1200), 17–24 ft lbs (B210-210).

510, 610 (except Station Wagon), 710, 200SX (with Automatic Trans.)

These driveshafts are the one-piece type with a U-joint and flange at the rear, and a U-joint and a splined sleeve yoke which fits into the rear of the transmission, at the front. The U-joints must be disassembled for lubrication at 24,000 mile intervals. The splines are lubricated by transmission oil.

1. Release the handbrake.
2. Loosen the 510 muffler and rotate it out of the way.
3. On the 510, remove the handbrake rear

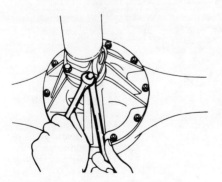

Disconnecting the rear driveshaft flange

cable adjusting nut and disconnect the left handbrake cable from the adjuster.
4. Unbolt the rear flange.
5. Pull the driveshaft down and back.
6. Plug the transmission extension housing.
7. Reverse the procedure to install, oiling the splines. Flange bolt torque is 15–24 ft lbs.

610 Station Wagon, 810, 200SX (Manual Trans.)

These models use a driveshaft with three U-joints and a center support bearing. The driveshaft is balanced as an assembly.

1. Mark the relationship of the driveshaft flange to the differential flange.
2. Unbolt the center bearing bracket.
3. Unbolt the driveshaft flange from the differential flange.
4. Pull the driveshaft back under the rear axle. Plug the rear of the transmission to prevent oil or fluid loss.
5. On installation, align the marks made in Step 1. Torque the flange bolts to 15–24 ft lbs.

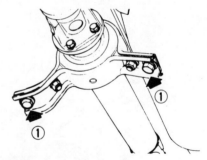

610 station wagon center bearing bracket

U-JOINT OVERHAUL

Disassembly

1. Mark the relationship of all components for reassembly.
2. Remove the snap-rings. On early units, the snap-rings are seated in the yokes. On later units, the snap-rings seat in the needle bearing races.
3. Tap the yoke with brass or rubber mallet to release one bearing cap. Be careful not to lose the needle rollers.
4. Remove the other bearing caps. Remove the U-joint spiders from the yokes.

Inspection

1. Spline backlash should not exceed 0.0197 in. (0.5 mm).

2. Driveshaft run-out should not exceed 0.015 in. (0.4 mm).

3. On later models with snap-rings seated in the needle bearing races, different thicknesses of snap-rings are available for U-joint adjustment. Play should not exceed 0.0008 in. (0.02 mm).

4. U-joint spiders must be replaced if their bearing journals are worn more than 0.0059 in. (0.15 mm) from their original diameter.

Assembly

1. Place the needle rollers in the races and hold them in place with grease.

2. Put the spider into place in its yokes.

3. Replace all seals.

4. Tap the races into position and secure them with snap-rings.

CENTER BEARING REPLACEMENT

The center bearing is a sealed unit which must be replaced as an assembly if defective.

1. Remove the driveshaft.

2. Paint a matchmark across where the flanges behind the center yoke are joined. This is for assembly purposes. If you don't paint or somehow mark the relationship between the two shafts, they may be out of balance when you put them back together.

3. Remove the bolts and separate the shafts. Make a matchmark on the front driveshaft half which lines up with the mark you made on the flange half.

4. You must devise a way to hold the driveshaft while unbolting the companion flange from the front driveshaft. Do not place the front driveshaft tube in a vise, because the chances are it will get crushed. The best way is to grip the flange somehow while loosening the nut. It is going to require some strength to remove.

5. Press the companion flange off the front driveshaft and press the center bearing from its mount.

6. The new bearing is already lubricated. Install it into the mount, making sure that the seals and so on are facing the same way as when removed.

7. Slide the companion flange on to the front driveshaft, aligning the marks made during removal. Install the washer and lock nut. If the washer and locknut are separate pieces, tighten them to 145–175 ft-lbs. If they are a unit, tighten it to 180–217 ft-lbs. Check that the bearing rotates freely around the driveshaft. Stake the nut.

8. Connect the companion flange to the other half of the driveshaft, aligning the marks made during removal. Tighten the bolts securely.

9. Install the driveshaft.

F-10, 310 DRIVESHAFT REMOVAL AND INSTALLATION

The drive axles are variously called driveshafts or axles, or drive axles. Strictly speaking, they are not driveshafts, but drive axles. A special puller is necessary to remove the axles. The tool is illustrated here.

1. Jack up the car and support it with safety stands.

2. Remove the wheel and tire.

3. Pull out the cotter pin and then remove the wheel bearing nut. You'll have to hold

310, F10 axle shaft removal tool

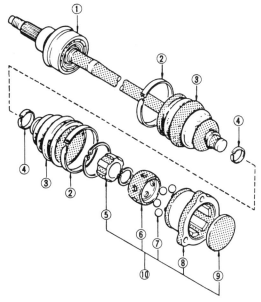

1. Outside joint assembly (Birfield joint)
2. Band
3. Dust cover
4. Band
5. Inner ring
6. Cage
7. Ball
8. Outer ring
9. Plug
10. Inside joint assembly (Double offset joint)

F10, 310 drive axle components

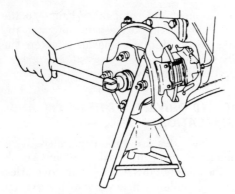

Hub nut removal

the wheel hub still somehow while you do this.

4. Remove the bolts which secure the drive axle to the transaxle assembly. The drive axle is splined into the hub assembly and is removed from underneath the car.

5. Install the puller on the hub and remove the drive axle by screwing the tool inward. This will force the drive axle out the back of the hub assembly.

6. The drive axle is installed by lightly hammering it back into place in the hub assembly. Quite often, this is a difficult job since the splines are a tight fit. Unfortunately, there is no other way to do it unless you want to remove the steering knuckle and then press the shaft on. Light persistent tapping should get the job done.

7. The rest of the procedure is the reverse of removal. Be careful not to damage the grease seal. Torque the wheel bearing nut to 90–145 ft lbs.

NOTE: *If you are going to remove the steering knuckle assembly along with the drive axle, see chapter 8, Suspension and Steering, for procedures.*

REAR AXLE

There are several different types of rear axles used on the cars covered in this guide. A solid rear axle is used on 1200, B210, 210, 200SX, 710, and all station wagon models. The 1978–80 510 uses a solid rear axle with either coil springs or leaf springs, depending on whether it is a sedan or a wagon. Independent rear suspension is used on the 1973 510, the 610 sedans, and the 810 sedan. In this design, separate axle driveshafts are used to transmit power from the differential to the wheels. The F10, being a front wheel drive

car, utilizes a simple beam axle in the rear on wagon models, and trailing arms on the sedans. The 310 is equipped with coil springs and trailing arms.

Axle Shaft

REMOVAL AND INSTALLATION

Solid Rear Axle Models

NOTE: *Bearings must be pressed on and off the shaft with an arbor press. Unless you have access to one, it is inadvisable to attempt any repair work on the axle shaft and bearing assemblies.*

1. Remove the hub cap or wheel cover. Loosen the lug nuts.

2. Raise the rear of the car and support it safely on stands.

3. Remove the rear wheel. Remove the four brake backing plate retaining nuts. Detach the parking brake linkage from the brake backing plate.

4. Attach a slide hammer to the axle shaft and remove it. Use the slide hammer and a two-pronged puller to remove the oil seal from the housing.

NOTE: *If a slide hammer is not available, the axle can sometimes be pried out using pry bars on opposing sides of the hub.*

If end-play is found to be excessive, the bearing should be replaced. Shimming the bearing is not recommended as this ignores end-play of the bearing itself and could result in improper seating of the bearing.

5. Using a chisel, carefully nick the bearing retainer in three or four places. The retainer does not have to be cut, only collapsed enough to allow the bearing retainer to be slid off the shaft.

6. Pull or press the old bearing off and install the new one by pressing it into position.

7. Install the outer bearing retainer with its raised surface facing the wheel hub, and then install the bearing and the inner bearing retainer in that order on the axle shaft.

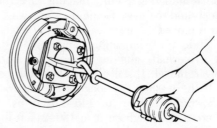

Removing axle on solid rear axle models using a slide hammer

8. With the smaller chamfered side of the inner bearing retainer facing the bearing, press on the retainer. The edge of the retainer should fully touch the bearing.

9. Clean the oil seal seat in the rear axle housing. Apply a thin coat of chassis grease.

10. Using a seal installation tool, drive the oil seal into the rear axle housing. Wipe a thin coat of bearing grease on the lips of the seal.

11. Determine the number of retainer gaskets which will give the correct bearing-to-outer retainer clearance of 0.01 in.

12. Insert the axle shaft assembly into the axle housing, being careful not to damage the seal. Ensure that the shaft splines engage those of the differential pinion. Align the vent holes of the gasket and the outer bearing retainer. Install the retaining bolts.

13. Install the nuts on the bolts and tighten them evenly, and in a criss-cross pattern, to 20 ft lbs.

Independent Rear Suspension Models

1. Jack up and support the rear of the car.

2. Remove the wheel and brake drum or disc.

3. Disconnect the axle driveshaft from the axle shaft at the flange.

4. Remove the wheel bearing locknut while holding the axle shaft outer flange from turning.

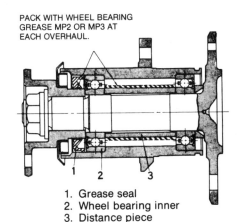

PACK WITH WHEEL BEARING GREASE MP2 OR MP3 AT EACH OVERHAUL.

1. Grease seal
2. Wheel bearing inner
3. Distance piece

Cutaway of wheel bearing

5. Pull out the axle shaft with a slide hammer. Remove the distance piece and inner flange.

6. Drive the inner wheel bearing and oil seal out toward the center of the car.

7. Press or pull the outer wheel bearing from the axle shaft.

8. Pack the wheel bearings with grease. Coat the seal lip also.

9. Reinstall the wheel bearings. Install the outer bearing on the axle shaft so that the side with the seal will be toward the wheel. Always press or drive on the inner bearing race.

10. The distance piece may be reused if it is not collapsed or deformed. The distance

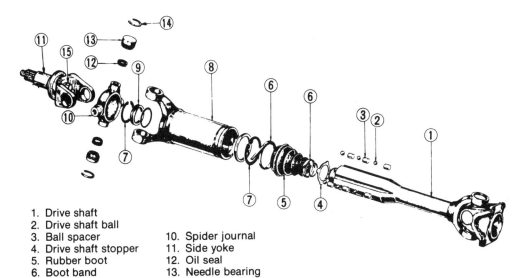

1. Drive shaft
2. Drive shaft ball
3. Ball spacer
4. Drive shaft stopper
5. Rubber boot
6. Boot band
7. Snap ring
8. Sleeve yoke
9. Sleeve yoke plug
10. Spider journal
11. Side yoke
12. Oil seal
13. Needle bearing
14. Snap ring
15. Side yoke fitting bolt

Exploded view of axle driveshaft—1973 510. 610 models similar

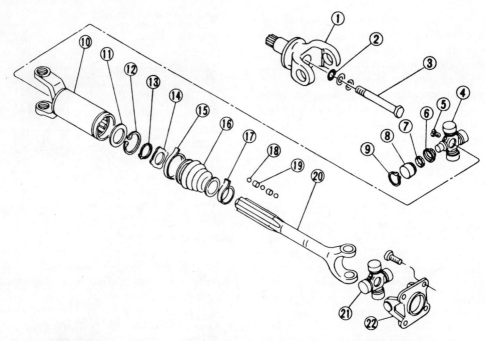

1. Side yoke
2. O-ring
3. Side yoke bolt
4. Spider journal
5. Filler plug
6. Dust cover
7. Oil seal
8. Bearing race assembly

9. Bearing race snap ring
10. Sleeve yoke
11. Sleeve yoke stopper
12. Snap ring
13. Drive shaft snap ring
14. Drive shaft stopper
15. Boot band (long)
16. Rubber boot

17. Boot band (short)
18. Ball
19. Ball spacer
20. Driveshaft
21. Spider assembly
22. Flange yoke

810 axle shaft—exploded view

piece must always carry the same mark, A, B, or C, as the bearing housing.

11. Fill the area illustrated with grease.

12. Replace the axle shaft and flange. Tighten the bearing locknut to the specified torque.

13. The torque required to start the axle shaft turning should be 3.9 in. lbs or less. This is a 28.7 oz or less pull at the hub bolt. Axle shaft end-play, checked with a dial indicator, should be 0–0.006 in.

14. If the turning torque or axle shaft play is incorrect, disassemble the unit and install a new distance piece.

The axle shafts must be removed and disassembled to lubricate the ball splines every 30,000 miles. Handle the shaft carefully; it is easily damaged. No repair parts for the shafts are available. If a shaft is defective in any way, it must be replaced as an assembly.

To disassemble:

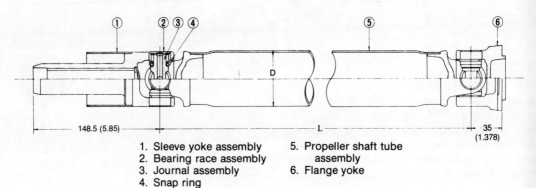

1. Sleeve yoke assembly
2. Bearing race assembly
3. Journal assembly
4. Snap ring

5. Propeller shaft tube assembly
6. Flange yoke

Cutaway of 710 driveshaft

1. Remove the U-joint spider from the differential end of the shaft.

2. Remove the snap-ring and sleeve yoke plug.

3. Compress the driveshaft and remove the snap-ring and stopper.

4. Disconnect the boot and separate the driveshaft carefully so as not to lose the balls and spacer.

5. Pack about 10 grams (0.35 oz) of grease into the ball grooves. Also pack about 35 grams (1.23 oz) of grease into the other area.

6. Twisting play between the two shaft halves should not exceed 0.004 in. Check play with the driveshaft completely compressed.

7. While reassembling, adjust the U-joint side play to 0.001 in. or less by selecting suitable snap-rings. Four different thicknesses are available for adjustment. Axle driveshaft flange nut torque is 36–43 ft lbs.

DIFFERENTIAL

NOTE: *Differential service is one place where the amateur mechanic should give way to the skill of the professional. A great many special tools are required as well as a good deal of experience.*

Introduction

The rear axle must transmit power through a 90° bend. To accomplish this, straight cut bevel gears or spiral bevel gears were originally used. This type of gear is satisfactory for differential side gears, but since the centerline of the gears must intersect, they are not suitable for ring and pinion gears. The lowering of the driveshaft brought about a variation of bevel gears called the hypoid gear. This type of gear does not require a meeting of the gear centerlines and can therefore be underslung, relative to the centerline of the ring gear.

Operation

The differential is an arrangement of gears which permits the rear wheels to turn at different speeds when cornering and divides the torque between the axle shafts. The differential gears are mounted on a pinion shaft and the gears are free to rotate on this shaft. The pinion shaft is fitted in a bore in the differential case and is at right angles to the axle shafts.

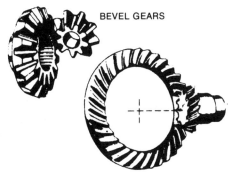

BEVEL GEARS

SPIRAL BEVEL GEARS

Bevel gears

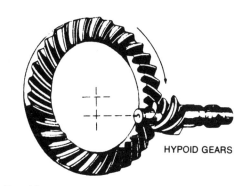

HYPOID GEARS

Hypoid gears

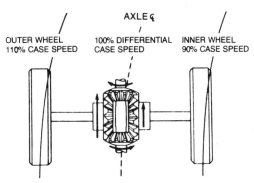

AXLE ₵

OUTER WHEEL
110% CASE SPEED

100% DIFFERENTIAL
CASE SPEED

INNER WHEEL
90% CASE SPEED

Differential action during cornering

Power flow through the differential is as follows. The drive pinion, which is turned by the driveshaft, turns the ring gear. The ring gear, which is bolted to the differential case, rotates the case. The differential pinion forces the pinion gears against the side gears. In cases where both wheels have equal traction, the pinion gears do not rotate on the pinion shaft, because the input force of the pinion gear is divided equally between the two side gears. Consequently the pinion gears revolve with the pinion shaft, although they do not rotate on the pinion shaft itself. The side gears, which are splined to the axle shafts, and meshed with the pinion gears, rotate the axle shafts.

When it becomes necessary to turn a corner, the differential becomes effective and allows the axle shafts to rotate at different speeds. As the inner wheel slows down, the side gear splined to the inner wheel axle shaft also slows down. The pinion gears act as balancing levers by maintaining equal tooth loads to both gears while allowing unequal speeds of rotation at the axle shafts. If the vehicle speed remains constant, and the inner wheel slows down to 90 percent of vehicle speed, the outer wheel will speed up to 110 percent.

Determining Gear Ratio

Determining the axle ratio of any given axle is an esoteric subject, relatively useless until you have to know. But, as a "junkyard art," it is invaluable.

The rear axle ratio is said to have a certain ratio, say, 4.11. It is called a 4.11 rear al-though the 4.11 actually means 4.11:1. This means that the driveshaft will turn 4.11 times for every turn of the rear wheel. The number 4.11 is determined by dividing the number of teeth on the pinion gear into the number of teeth on the ring gear. In the case of a 4.11, there could be 9 teeth on the pinion and 37 teeth on the ring gear $(37 \div 9 = 4.11)$. This provides a sure way (although troublesome—except to those who are really interested) of determining your rear axle ratio. You must drain the rear axle and remove the rear cover, if it has one, and count the teeth on the ring and pinion.

An easier method is to jack and support the vehicle so that BOTH rear wheels are off the ground. Make a chalk mark on the rear wheel and the driveshaft. Block the front wheels, set the parking brake and put the transmission in Neutral. Turn the rear wheel one complete revolution and count the number of turns that the driveshaft makes. The number of turns that the driveshaft makes in one complete revolution of the rear wheel is an *approximation* of the rear axle ratio.

Suspension and Steering

FRONT SUSPENSION

All models covered in this book use Mac-Pherson strut front suspension. In this type of suspension, each strut combines the function of coil spring and shock absorber. The spindle is mounted to the lower part of the strut through a single ball joint. No upper suspension arm is required in this design. The lower suspension arm is bolted to the front subframe assembly. Except on the F10 and 310, the spindle and lower control arm are located fore and aft by tension rods which attach to the chassis.

Springs and Shock Absorbers
TESTING SHOCK ABSORBER ACTION

Shock absorbers require replacement if the vehicle fails to recover quickly after a large bump is encountered, if there is a tendency for the vehicle to sway or nose dive excessively, or, sometimes, if the suspension is overly susceptible to vibration.

A good way to test the shocks is to intermittently apply downward pressure to one corner of the vehicle until it is moving up and down for almost the full suspension travel, then release it and watch the recovery. If the vehicle bounces slightly about one more time and then comes to rest, the shock absorbers

are serviceable. If the vehicle goes on bouncing, the shocks require replacement.

Strut
REMOVAL AND INSTALLATION

1. Jack up the car and support it safely. Remove the wheel.

2. Disconnect and plug the brake hose. Remove the brake caliper as outlined in Chapter 9. Remove the disc and hub as described in this chapter.

3. Disconnect the tension rod and stabilizer bar from the transverse link.

Strut mounting points (top)—1978–80 510 shown, others similar

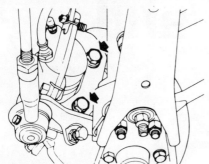

Brake caliper-to-strut mounting bolts

4. Unbolt the steering arm. Pry the control arm down to detach it from the strut.

5. Place a jack under the bottom of the strut.

6. Open the hood and remove the nuts holding the top of the strut.

7. Lower the jack slowly and cautiously until the strut assembly can be removed.

8. Reverse the procedure to install. The self-locking nuts holding the top of the strut must be replaced. Bleed the brakes.

Coil Spring and Shock Absorber
REMOVAL AND INSTALLATION

CAUTION: *The coil springs are under considerable tension, and can exert enough force to cause serious injury. Disassemble the struts only if the proper tools are available, and use extreme caution.*

Coil springs on all models must be removed with the aid of a coil spring compressor. If you don't have one, don't try to improvise by using something else: you could risk injury. The Datsun coil spring compressor is Special Tool ST3565S001 or variations of that number. Basically, they are all the same tool, except for the 1980 200SX spring compressor, Special Tool HT71730000, which is a totally different unit. These are the recommended compressors, although they are probably not the only spring compressors which will work. Always follow manufacturer's instructions when operating a spring compressor. You can now buy cartridge type shock absorbers for many Datsuns: installation procedures are not the same as those

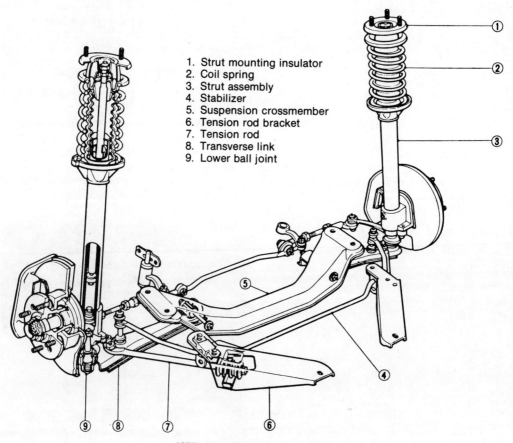

1. Strut mounting insulator
2. Coil spring
3. Strut assembly
4. Stabilizer
5. Suspension crossmember
6. Tension rod bracket
7. Tension rod
8. Transverse link
9. Lower ball joint

1977–79 200SX front suspension

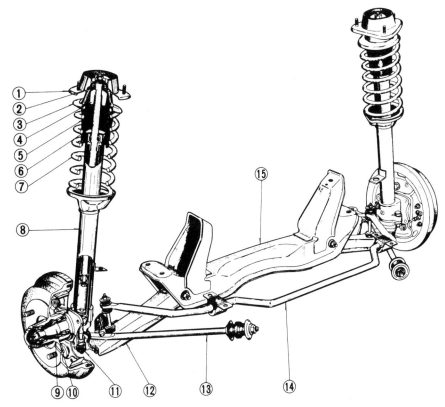

1. Strut mounting insulator
2. Strut mounting bearing
3. Upper spring seat
4. Bumper rubber
5. Dust cover
6. Piston rod
7. Front spring
8. Strut assembly
9. Hub assembly
10. Spindle
11. Ball joint
12. Transverse link
13. Tension rod
14. Stabilizer
15. Suspension member

1200 and B210 front suspension

given here. In this case, follow the instructions that come with the shock absorbers.

To remove the coil spring, you must first remove the strut assembly from the vehicle. See above for procedures.

1. Secure the strut assembly in a vise.

2. Attach the spring compressor to the spring, leaving the top few coils free.

3. Remove the dust cap from the top of the strut to expose the center nut, if a dust cap is provided.

4. Compress the spring just far enough to permit the strut insulator to be turned by hand. Remove the self-locking center nut.

5. Take out the strut insulator, strut bearing, oil seal, upper spring seat and bound bumper rubber from the top of the strut. Note their sequence of removal and be sure to assemble them in the same order.

6. Remove the spring with the spring compressor still attached.

Assembly is the reverse of disassembly.

Observe the following. Make sure you assemble the unit with the shock absorber piston rod fully extended. When assembling, take care that the rubber spring seats, both top and bottom, and the spring are positioned in their grooves before releasing the spring.

7. To remove the shock absorber: Remove the dust cap, if so equipped, and push the piston rod down until it bottoms. With the piston in this position, loosen and remove the gland packing shock absorber retainer. This calls for Datsun Special Tool ST35500001, but you should be able to loosen it either with a pipe wrench or by tapping it around with a drift.

NOTE: *If the gland tube is dirty, clean it before removing it to prevent dirt from contaminating the fluid inside the strut tube.*

8. Remove the O-ring from the top of the piston rod guide and lift out the piston rod

1. Transverse link bushing
2. Transverse link
3. Connecting bolt
4. Stabilizer bracket
5. Stabilizer
6. Stabilizer bushing

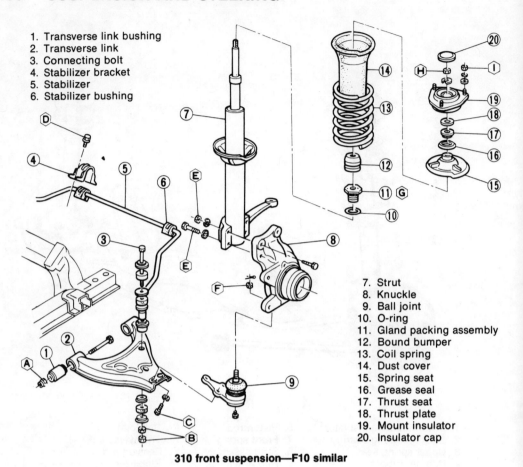

7. Strut
8. Knuckle
9. Ball joint
10. O-ring
11. Gland packing assembly
12. Bound bumper
13. Coil spring
14. Dust cover
15. Spring seat
16. Grease seal
17. Thrust seat
18. Thrust plate
19. Mount insulator
20. Insulator cap

310 front suspension—F10 similar

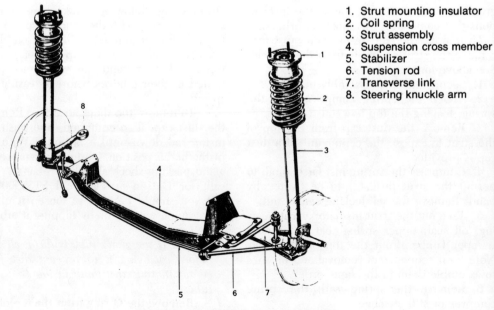

1. Strut mounting insulator
2. Coil spring
3. Strut assembly
4. Suspension cross member
5. Stabilizer
6. Tension rod
7. Transverse link
8. Steering knuckle arm

610, 710, and 1973 510 front suspension

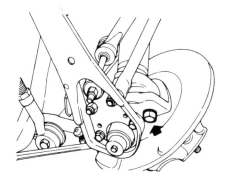

1200 and B210 strut-to-control arm/steering knuckle bolts

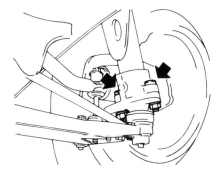

610, 710 and 1973 510 strut-to-control arm/steering knuckle bolts

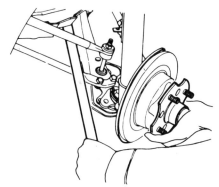

Pry the control arm down to separate the strut from the knuckle

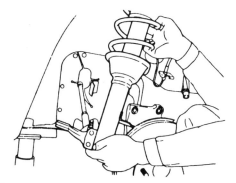

Removing the strut and spring—F10. 310 similar

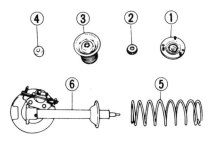

1. Strut mounting insulator
2. Bearing
3. Spring upper seat and dust cover
4. Damper rubber
5. Coil spring
6. Strut assembly

Exploded view of 1200 and B210 strut, others similar

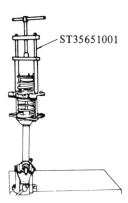

ST35651001

Datsun spring compressor correctly mounted on coil spring

Removing the shock absorber from the gland tube

together with the cylinder. Drain all of the fluid from the strut and shock components into a suitable container. Clean all parts.

NOTE: *The piston rod, piston rod guide and cylinder are a matched set: single parts of this shock assembly should not be exchanged with parts of other assemblies.*

Assembly is the reverse of disassembly with the following notes.

After installing the cylinder and piston rod assembly (the shock absorber kit) in the outer

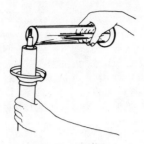

Filling the shock assembly with oil

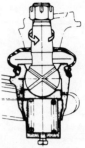

Cross section of a ball joint. Note plug at the bottom for grease nipple

casing, remove the piston rod guide, if so equipped, from the cylinder and pour the correct amount of new fluid into the cylinder and strut outer casing. To find this amount consult the instructions with your shock absorber kit. The amount of oil should be listed. Use only Nissan Genuine Strut Oil or its equivalent.

NOTE: *It is important that the correct amount of fluid be poured into the strut to assure correct shock absorber damping force.*

Install the O-ring, fluid and any other cylinder components. Fit the gland packing and tighten it after greasing the gland packing-to-piston rod mating surfaces.

NOTE: *When tightening the gland packing, extend the piston rod about 3 to 5 inches from the end of the outer casing to expel most of the air from the strut.*

After the kit is installed, bleed the air from the system in the following manner: hold the strut with its bottom end facing down. Pull the piston rod out as far as it will go. Turn the

strut upside down and push the piston in as far as it will go. Repeat this procedure several times until an equal pressure is felt on both the pull out and the push in strokes of the piston rods. The remaining assembly is the reverse of disassembly.

Ball Joint
INSPECTION

The lower ball joint should be replaced when play becomes excessive. Datsun does not publish specifications on just what constitutes excessive play, relying instead on a method of determining the force (in inch pounds) required to keep the ball joint turning. This method is not very helpful to the backyard mechanic since it involves removing the ball joint, which is what we are trying to avoid in the first place. An effective way to determine ball joint play is to jack up the car until the wheel is just a couple of inches off

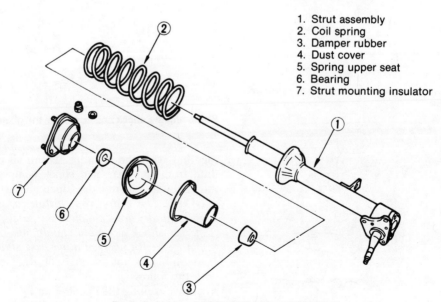

1. Strut assembly
2. Coil spring
3. Damper rubber
4. Dust cover
5. Spring upper seat
6. Bearing
7. Strut mounting insulator

Exploded view of 1973 510, 610 and 710 strut

he ground and the ball joint is unloaded meaning you can't jack directly underneath he ball joint). Place a long bar under the tire and move the wheel and tire assembly up and down. Keep one hand on top of the tire while you are doing this. If there is over ¼ inch of play at the top of the tire, the ball joint is probably bad. This is assuming that the wheel bearings are in good shape and properly adjusted. As a double check on this, have someone watch the ball joint while you move the tire up and down with the bar. If you can see considerable play, besides feeling play at the top of the wheel, the ball joint needs replacing.

REMOVAL AND INSTALLATION

All Models Except F10, 310

The ball joint should be greased every 30,000 miles. There is a plugged hole in the bottom of the joint for the installation of grease fitting.

1. Raise and support the car so that the wheels hang free. Remove the wheel.
2. Unbolt the tension rod and stabilizer bar from transverse link.
3. Unbolt the strut from the steering arm.

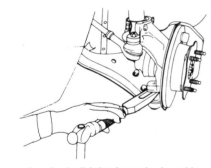

eparating the ball joint from the knuckle

emoving the ball joint

4. Remove the cotter pin and ball joint stud nut. Separate the ball joint and steering arm.
5. Unbolt the ball joint from the transverse link.
6. Reverse the procedure to install a new ball joint. Grease the joint after installation.

F10 Ball Joint Removal and Installation

1. Raise the car and support it on jack stands. Remove the wheel.
2. Remove the nut holding the ball stud to the knuckle and force out the stud with a ball joint fork, being careful not to damage the ball joint dust cover.
3. Remove the ball joint bolts and the ball joint.

Install the ball joint in the reverse order of removal. Tighten the ball stud attaching nut to 22–29 ft-lbs, and the ball joint to transverse link attaching bolts to 40–47 ft-lbs.

310 Ball Joint Removal and Installation

1. Jack up the car and support it on stands.
2. Remove the wheel.
3. Remove the drive shaft. Refer to chapter 7 for procedures.
4. Separate the ball joint from the steering knuckle with a ball joint remover, being careful not to damage the ball joint dust cover if the ball joint is to be used again.
5. Remove the other ball joint bolts from the transverse link and remove the ball joint.

Installation is the reverse of removal. Tighten the ball stud attaching nut (from ball joint to steering knuckle) to 22–29 ft lbs, and the Ball joint to transverse link bolts to 40–47 ft lbs.

Lower Control Arm (Transverse Link) and Ball Joint

REMOVAL AND INSTALLATION

You'll need a ball joint remover for this operation.

1. Jack up the vehicle and support it with jack stands; remove the wheel.
2. Remove the splash board, if so equipped.
3. Remove the cotter pin and castle nut from the side rod (steering arm) ball joint and separate the ball joint from the side rod. You'll need either a fork type or puller type ball joint remover.
4. Separate the steering knuckle arm from the MacPherson strut.
5. Remove the tension rod and stabilizer

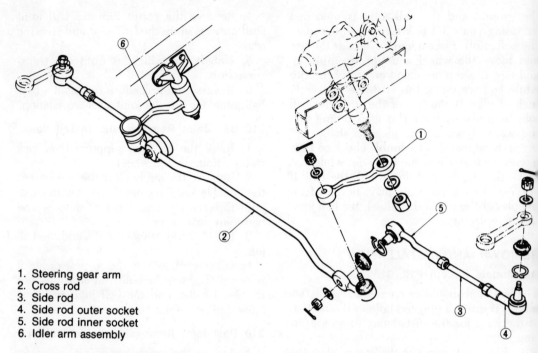

1. Steering gear arm
2. Cross rod
3. Side rod
4. Side rod outer socket
5. Side rod inner socket
6. Idler arm assembly

Steering linkage—toe-in adjustment is made at the side rod (tie rod)

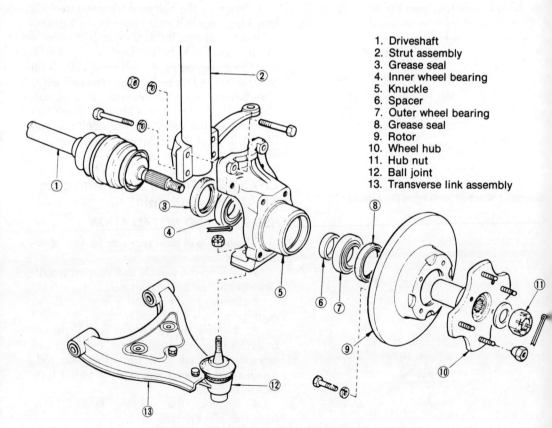

1. Driveshaft
2. Strut assembly
3. Grease seal
4. Inner wheel bearing
5. Knuckle
6. Spacer
7. Outer wheel bearing
8. Grease seal
9. Rotor
10. Wheel hub
11. Hub nut
12. Ball joint
13. Transverse link assembly

F10 hub and knuckle and suspension parts. 310 similar

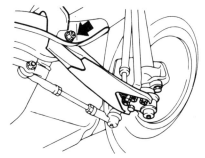

Removing bolt connecting control arm to crossmember—210

bar from the lower arm. The F10 and the 310 do not have tension rods.

6. Remove the nuts or bolts connecting the lower control arm (transverse link) to the suspension crossmember on all models.

7. On the 810, to remove the transverse link (control arm) on the steering gear side, separate the gear arm from the sector shaft and lower steering linkage; to remove the transverse link on the idler arm side, detach the idler arm assembly from the body frame and lower steering linkage.

8. Remove the lower control arm (transverse link) with the suspension ball joint and knuckle arm still attached.

Installation is the reverse of removal with the following notes.

9. When installing the control arm, temporarily tighten the nuts and/or bolts securing the control arm to the suspension crossmember. Tighten them fully only after the car is sitting on its wheels.

10. Lubricate the ball joints after assembly.

Front End Alignment
CASTER AND CAMBER

Caster is the forward or rearward tilt of the upper end of the kingpin, or the upper ball joint, which results in a slight tilt of the steering axis forward or backward. Rearward tilt is referred to as a positive caster, while forward tilt is referred to as negative caster.

Camber is the inward or outward tilt from the vertical, measured in degrees, of the front wheels at the top. An outward tilt gives the wheel positive camber. Proper camber is critical to assure even tire wear.

Since caster and camber are adjusted traditionally by adding or subtracting shims behind the upper control arms, and the Dat-

suns covered in this guide have replaced the upper control arm with the MacPherson strut, the only way to adjust caster and camber is to replace bent or worn parts of the front suspension.

TOE

Toe is the amount, measured in a fraction of an inch, that the wheels are closer together at one end than the other. Toe-in means that the front wheels are closer together at the front than the rear; toe-out means the rears are closer than the front. Datsuns are adjusted to have a slight amount of toe-in. Toe-in is adjusted by turning the tie-rod, which has a right-hand thread on one end and a left-hand thread on the other.

You can check your vehicle's toe-in yourself without special equipment if you make careful measurements. The wheels must be straight ahead.

1. Toe-in can be determined by measuring the distance between the center of the tire treads, at the front of the tire and at the rear. If the tread pattern of your car's tires makes this impossible, you can measure between the edges of the wheel rims, but make sure to move the car forward and measure in a couple of places to void errors caused by bent rims or wheel runout.

2. If the measurement is not within specifications, loosen the locknuts at both ends of the tie-rod (the driver's side locknut is left-hand threaded).

3. Turn the top of the tie-rod toward the front of the car to reduce toe-in, or toward the rear to increase it. When the correct dimension is reached, tighten the locknuts and check the adjustment.

NOTE: *The length of the tie-rods must always be equal to each other.*

STEERING ANGLE ADJUSTMENT

The maximum steering angle is adjusted by stopper bolts on the steering arms. Loosen the locknut on the stopper bolt, turn the stopped bolt in or out as required to obtain the proper maximum steering angle and retighten the locknut.

SUSPENSION HEIGHT

Suspension height is adjusted by replacing the springs. Various springs are available for adjustment.

Wheel Alignment Specifications

Year	Model	Caster Range (deg)	Caster Preferred Setting (deg)	Camber Range (deg)	Camber Preferred Setting (deg)	Toe-In (in.)	Steering Axis Inclination (deg)	Wheel Pivot Ratio (deg) Inner Wheel	Wheel Pivot Ratio (deg) Outer Wheel
1973	510	—	1°40'	—	1	0.35–0.47	8	38–39	22°30'–33°30'
	1200	40'–1°40'	1°10'	35'–1°35'	1°05'	0.16–0.24	7°55'	42–44	35–37
	610	0°45'–2°15'	—	1°–2°30'	—	0.24–0.35	7°05'	37–38	30°40'–32°40'
	610 Station Wagon	0°55'–2°25'	—	1°10'–2°40'	—	0.32–0.43	6°55'	37–38	30°40'–32°40'
1974	B210	1°15'–2°15'	—	40'–1°40'	—	0.079–0.157	7°47'–8°47'	37°–39°	31°–33°
	610	1°15'–2°45'	—	1°15'–2°45' 1°30'–3°	—	0.430–0.550	5°55'–7°25'	37°	30°42'–32°42'
	710	1°10'–2°40'	—	1°25'–2°55'	—	0.550–0.670	6°25'	37°–38°	30°42'–32°42'
1975	610	1°15'–2°15'	1°50'	1°15'–2°45'	2°	0.43–0.55	5°55'–7°25'	32–33	29°30'–31°30'
	610 Station Wagon	1°15'–2°15'	1°50'	1°30'–3°00'	2°15'	0.43–0.55	5°45'–7°15'	32–33	29°30'–31°30'
	710	1°10'–2°40'	1°55'	1°25'–2°55'	2°10'	0.32–0.43	6°25'	32–33	29°30'–31°30'
1975–78	B210	1°00'–2°30'	1°45'	0°25'–1°55'	1°10'	0.08–0.16	7°32'–9°02'	37–39	31–33
1976–77	610,710	1°–2°35'	1°45'	1°15'–2°45'	2°	①	6°15'–7°45'	32°–33°	29°30'–31°30'
1976–78	F10	20'–1°50'	—	50'–2°20'	—	②	9°15'–10°45'	36°30'–39°30'	31°–34°
1977–79	200SX	1°05'–2°35'	—	20'–1°50'	—	0.08–0.16	7°20'–8°20'	34°–36°	29°–31°

Year	Model							
1977–80	810	1°10'–2°40'	—	0°–1°30'	—	0.0–0.08	7°10'–8°40'	36°–40°	29°–33°
1978–80	510 Sedan, Hatchback	1°05'–2°35'	—	–15' to 1°15'	—	0.04–0.12	8°05'–9°35'	40°–42°	32°30'–36°30'
	510 Station Wagon	55'–2°25'	—	5'–1°35'	—	0.04–0.12	7°45'–9°15'	40°–42°	32°30'–36°30'
1979–80	210 Sedan, Hatchback	1°40'–3°10'	—	0°–1°30'	—	0.04–0.12	7°50'–9°20'	38°–42°	31°30'–35°30'
	210 Station Wagon	1°55'–3°25'	—	0°–1°30'	—	0.04–0.12	7°50'–9°20'	38°–42°	31°30'–35°30'
	310	25'–1°55'	—	15'–1°45'	—	0.0–0.08	11°10'–12°30'	36°30'–39°30'	29°30'–32°30'
1980	200SX	1°45'–3°15'	—	–40'–50'	—	0.0–0.08	7°25'–8°55'	33°–35°	27°–29°

—Information not applicable
① 0.16–0.24 Radial tires
  0.24–0.31 Bias tires
② 0–0.79 Radial tires
  0.20–0.28 Bias tires

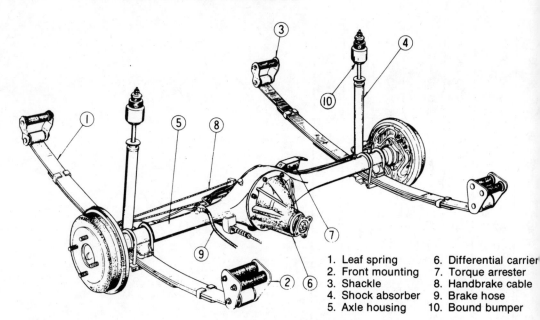

1. Leaf spring
2. Front mounting
3. Shackle
4. Shock absorber
5. Axle housing
6. Differential carrier
7. Torque arrester
8. Handbrake cable
9. Brake hose
10. Bound bumper

1200 and B210 rear suspension

REAR SUSPENSION

There are several different types of rear suspensions used on the Datsuns covered in this guide. All 1200, B210, 710 and 1977–79 200SX models are equipped with solid rear axles suspended by leaf springs. The 1973 510, the 610 sedan and the 810 sedan have independent rear suspensions which incorporate semi-trailing arms and coil springs.

The 1978–80 510 sedans and hatchbacks, 1979–80 210's, and the 1980 200SX' are equipped with four-link type solid rear axles with coil springs. The F10 sedan and hatchback and the 310 have trailing arms and coil springs. All station wagons except the 210 models use a solid rear axle supported by leaf springs.

CAUTION: *Before doing any rear suspension work, block the front wheels of the*

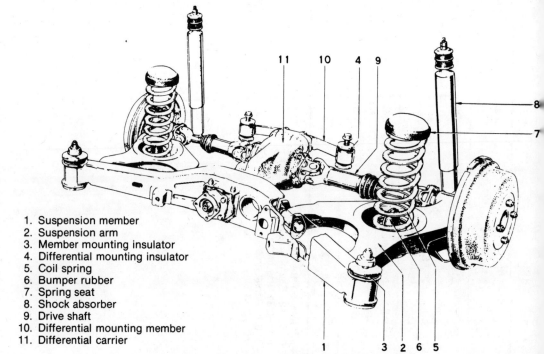

1. Suspension member
2. Suspension arm
3. Member mounting insulator
4. Differential mounting insulator
5. Coil spring
6. Bumper rubber
7. Spring seat
8. Shock absorber
9. Drive shaft
10. Differential mounting member
11. Differential carrier

610, 1973 510 rear suspension (except station wagon)

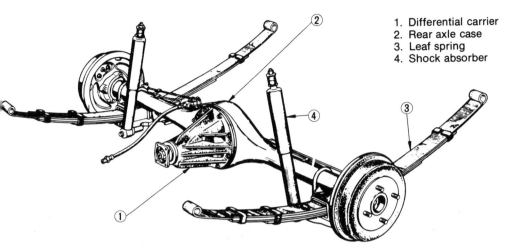

1. Differential carrier
2. Rear axle case
3. Leaf spring
4. Shock absorber

Rear suspension—610 station wagon and all 710 models

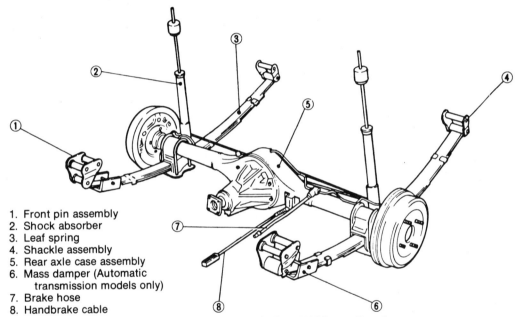

1. Front pin assembly
2. Shock absorber
3. Leaf spring
4. Shackle assembly
5. Rear axle case assembly
6. Mass damper (Automatic
   transmission models only)
7. Brake hose
8. Handbrake cable

1977–79 200SX rear suspension. 1980 has coil springs

vehicle to insure that it won't move or shift while you are under it. Remember, you are dealing with spring steel that has enough force to physically damage you if you don't follow the removal and installation procedures exactly.

Springs

REMOVAL AND INSTALLATION

Leaf Spring Type

1200 AND B210

1. Raise the rear axle until the wheels hang free. Support the car on stands. Support the rear axle with a jack.

2. Unbolt the bottom end of shock absorber.

3. Unbolt the axle from the spring leaves. Unbolt and remove the front spring bracket. Lower the front of the spring to the floor.

4. Unbolt and remove the spring rear shackle.

5. Before reinstallation, coat the front bracket pin, bushing, shackle pin, and shackle bushing with a soap solution.

6. Reverse the procedure to install. The front pin nut and the shock absorber mounting should be tightened before the vehicle is lowered to the floor.

610 STATION WAGON AND ALL 710 AND 1977–79 200SX MODELS

1. Raise the rear axle until the wheels hang free. Support the car on stands. Support the rear axle with floor jack.

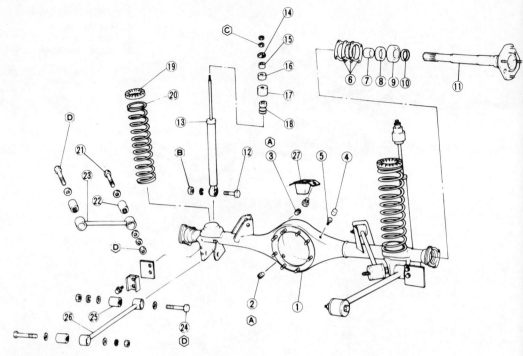

1. Rear axle case
2. Drain plug
3. Filler plug
4. Breather cap
5. Breather
6. Rear axle case end shim
7. Bearing collar
8. Oil seal
9. Rear axle bearing
10. Bearing spacer
11. Rear axle shaft
12. Shock absorber lower end bolt
13. Shock absorber assembly
14. Special washer
15. Shock absorber mounting bushing A
16. Shock absorber mounting bushing B
17. Bound bumper cover
18. Bound bumper rubber
19. Shock absorber mounting insulato
20. Coil spring
21. Upper link bushing bolt
22. Upper link bushing

1978–80 510 sedan rear suspension. 1980 200SX, 210 similar

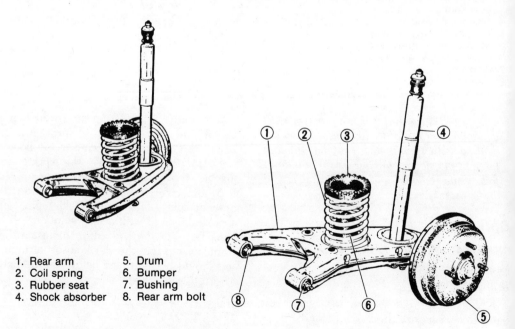

1. Rear arm
2. Coil spring
3. Rubber seat
4. Shock absorber
5. Drum
6. Bumper
7. Bushing
8. Rear arm bolt

F10 sedan and hatchback rear suspension, 310 similar

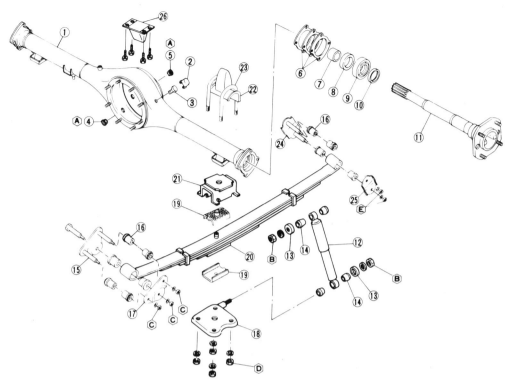

1. Rear axle case
2. Breather cap
3. Breather
4. Drain plug
5. Filler plug
6. Rear axle case end shim
7. Bearing collar
8. Oil seal
9. Rear axle bearing
10. Bearing spacer
11. Rear axle shaft
12. Shock absorber assembly
13. Special washer
14. Shock absorber bushing
15. Front pin assembly
16. Spring bushing
17. Front pin outer plate
18. Lower spring seat
19. Spring seating pad
20. Rear spring assembly
21. Location plate
22. Rear axle bumper
23. U-bolt (Spring clip)
24. Shackle pin assembly
25. Shackle
26. Torque arrester

1978–80 510 station wagon rear suspension—other wagons similar

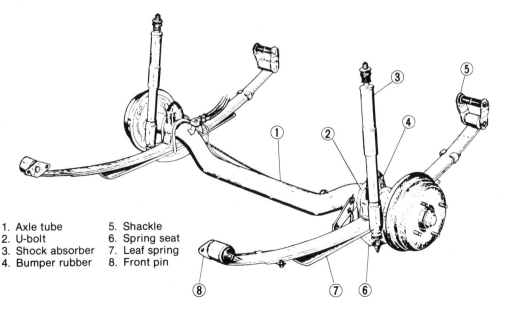

1. Axle tube
2. U-bolt
3. Shock absorber
4. Bumper rubber
5. Shackle
6. Spring seat
7. Leaf spring
8. Front pin

F10 station wagon rear suspension

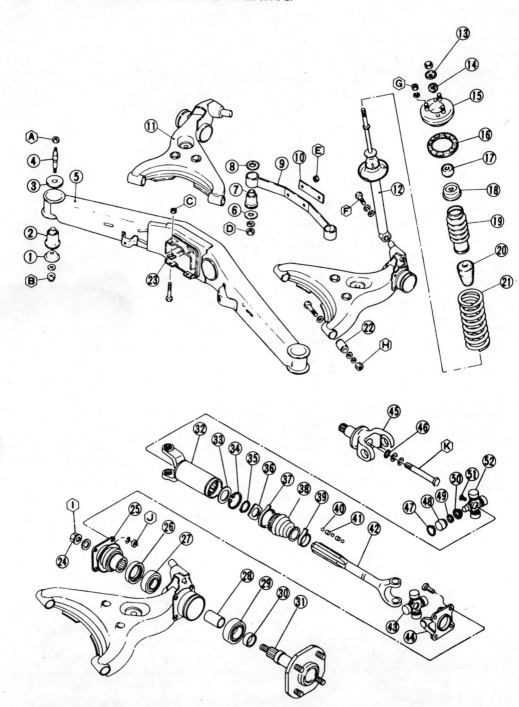

1. Member mounting lower stopper
2. Member mounting insulator
3. Member mounting upper stopper
4. Suspension mounting bolt
5. Suspension member assembly
6. Differential mounting lower stopper
7. Differential mounting insulator
8. Differential mounting upper stopper
9. Differential mounting member
10. Differential mounting plate
11. Suspension arm assembly
12. Shock absorber
13. Special washer
14. Shock absorber mounting bushing A
15. Shock absorber mounting
16. Spring seat rubber
17. Shock absorber mounting bushing B
18. Bumper cover
19. Dust cover
20. Bumper
21. Coil spring
22. Suspension arm bushing
23. Differential mounting spacer
24. Wheel bearing locknut
25. Companion flange
26. Grease seal
27. Inner wheel bearing
28. Spacer

Exploded view of 810 rear suspension (sedan)

29. Outer wheel bearing	37. Boot band (Long)	45. Side yoke
30. Bearing spacer	38. Rubber boot	46. O-ring
31. Rear axle shaft assembly	39. Boot band (Short)	47. Bearing race snap-ring
32. Sleeve yoke	40. Ball	48. Bearing race assembly
33. Sleeve yoke stopper	41. Ball spacer	49. Oil seal
34. Snap-ring	42. Driveshaft	50. Dust cover
35. Driveshaft snap-ring	43. Spider assembly	51. Filler plug
36. Driveshaft stopper	44. Flange yoke	52. Spider journal

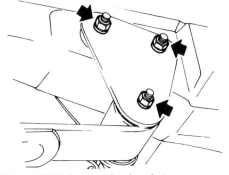

1200 and B210 front spring bracket

1200 and B210 rear spring shackle

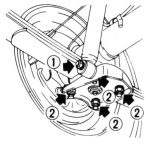

Detach lower shock absorber mount (1) and spring U-bolts (2)—1200 and B210 coupe shown

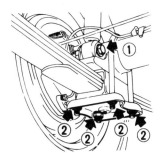

Detach lower shock absorber mount (1) and spring U-bolts (2)—1200 and B210 sedan shown

2. Remove the spare tire.

3. Unbolt the bottom end of the shock absorber.

4. Unbolt the axle from the spring leaves.

5. Unbolt the front spring bracket from the body. Lower the spring end and bracket to the floor.

6. Unbolt and remove the rear shackle.

7. Unbolt the bracket from the spring.

8. Before reinstallation, coat the front bracket pin and bushing, and the shackle pin and bushing with a soap solution.

9. Reverse the procedure to install. The front pin nut and the shock absorber mounting should be tightened after the vehicle is lowered to the floor. Make sure that the elongated flange of the rubber bumper is to the rear.

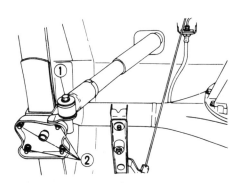

Detach lower shock absorber mount (1) and spring U-bolts (2)—610 station wagon and all 710 models

Remove the spring shackle

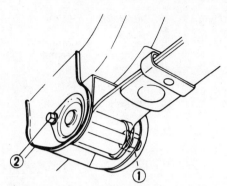

Remove the spring pin by removing nuts (1) and (2)—610 station wagon and all 710 models

510, AND 810 STATION WAGONS

1. Raise the rear of the car and support it with jackstands.

2. Remove the wheels and tires.

3. Disconnect the lower end of the shock absorber and remove the U-bolt nuts.

4. Place a jack under the rear axle.

5. Disconnect the spring shackle bolts at the front and rear of the spring.

6. Lower the jack slowly and remove the spring.

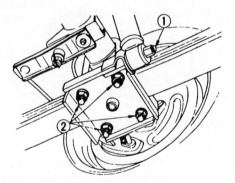

Removing shock absorber lower nut and U-bolts—810

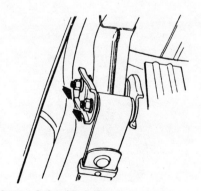

Spring and shackle bolts

7. Installation is in the reverse order of removal.

F10 STATION WAGON

1. Jack up the car and support it with safety stands.

2. Remove the wheel and tire.

3. Remove the nuts from the lower portion of the shock absorber.

4. Remove the nuts from the U-bolts, and detach the bumper rubbers and the spring seat.

5. Jack up the axle until it clears the leaf spring.

6. Remove the hand brake clamp from the leaf spring.

7. Remove the front pin and shackle, and detach the spring from the body.

8. Installation is in the reverse order of removal.

Coil Spring Type

1973 510 AND 610 MODELS (EXCEPT STATION WAGON)

1. Raise the rear of the vehicle and support it on stands.

2. Remove the wheels.

3. Disconnect the handbrake linkage and return spring.

4. Unbolt the axle driveshaft flange at the wheel end.

5. Unbolt the rubber bumper inside the bottom of the coil spring.

6. Jack up the suspension arm and unbolt the shock absorber lower mounting.

7. Lower the jack slowly and cautiously. Remove the coil spring, spring seat, and rubber bumper.

8. Reverse the procedure to install, making sure that the flat face of the spring is at the top.

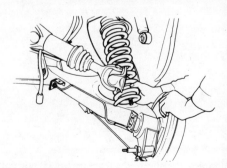

Coil spring removal

810 SEDAN MODELS

1. The coil spring and shock absorber are removed as a unit. Disassembly of the unit requires a spring compressor.

2. Raise the rear of the car and support it with jackstands.

3. Open the trunk and remove the three nuts which secure the top of the shock to the body.

4. Disconnect the shock absorber at the bottom by removing the bolt at the suspension arm.

5. Installation is in the reverse order of removal.

Top mounting point—810 rear shock

1978 510 SEDAN AND HATCHBACK MODELS, 210, 1980 200SX

1. Raise the car and support it with jackstands.

2. Support the center of the differential with a jack or other suitable tool.

3. Remove the rear wheels.

4. Remove the bolts securing the lower ends of the shock absorbers.

5. Lower the jack under the differential slowly and carefully and remove the coil springs after they are fully extended.

6. Installation is in the reverse order of removal.

F10, 310 SEDAN AND HATCHBACK

1. Jack up the rear of the car and support it with safety stands.

2. Remove the wheels and tires.

3. Support the trailing arm with a jack.

4. Remove the upper and lower shock absorber nuts.

5. Lower the jack slowly and carefully. Remove the coil spring.

6. Installation is in the reverse order of removal.

Shock Absorber
INSPECTION AND TESTING

Inspect and test the rear shock absorbers in the same manner as outlined for the front shock absorbers.

REMOVAL AND INSTALLATION
1200 and B210

1. Jack up the rear of the car and support the rear axle on two stands.

2. Disconnect the lower shock mounting bolt at the spring plate.

3. From inside the car, remove the rear seat back and disconnect the upper mounting nut.

4. Remove the shock absorber.

5. Install the replacement shock in the reverse of the removal procedure.

All Except 1200, B210, 810 and 510, 610, 710 Station Wagons

1. Open the trunk and remove the cover panel if necessary to expose the shock

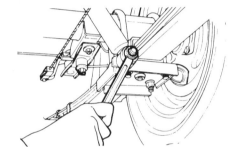

Removing the lower shock absorber nut

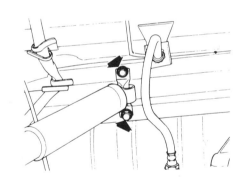

Upper shock absorber retaining bolts

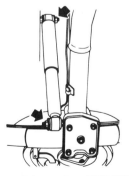

Rear shock retaining nuts—1978 510

mounts. Pry off the mount covers, if so equipped. On leaf spring models, jack up the rear of the vehicle and support the rear axle on stands.

2. Remove the two nuts holding the top of the shock absorber. Unbolt the bottom of the shock absorber.

3. Remove the shock absorber.

4. Installation is the reverse of removal.

1978–80 510, 610, 710, 810 Station Wagon

1. Jack up the rear of the car and support the axle on stands.

2. Remove the lower retaining nut on the shock absorber.

3. Remove the upper retaining bolt(s).

4. Remove the shock from under the car.

5. On the 610, remove the retaining strap from the old shock and install it on the replacement shock.

6. Installation is the reverse of removal.

810 Sedan Models

The shock absorber and the coil spring are removed as a unit on these models. See "Spring Removal" in this chapter. Disassembly of the spring/shock unit on the rear of this vehicle is similar to the disassembly procedures for the front shock absorbers. You will need a spring compressor. See the section above.

STEERING

Steering Wheel

REMOVAL AND INSTALLATION

1. Position the wheels in the straight-ahead direction. The steering wheel should be right-side up and level.

2. Disconnect the battery ground cable.

3. Look at the back of your steering wheel. If there are countersunk screws in the

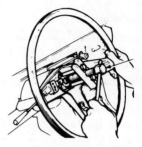
Using puller to remove the steering wheel

back of the spokes, remove the screws and pull off the horn pad. Some models have a horn wire running from the pad to the steering wheel. Disconnect it.

There are three other types of horn buttons or rings on Datsuns. The first simply pulls off. The second, which is usually a large, semi-triangular pad, must be pushed up, then pulled off. The third must be pushed in and turned clockwise.

4. Remove the rest of the horn switching mechanism, noting the relative location of the parts. Remove the mechanism only if it hinders subsequent wheel removal procedures.

5. Match-mark the top of the steering column shaft and the steering wheel flange.

6. Remove the attaching nut and remove the steering wheel with a puller.

CAUTION: *Do not strike the shaft with a hammer, which may cause the column to collapse.*

7. Install the steering wheel in the reverse order of removal, aligning the punch marks. Do not drive or hammer the wheel into place, or you may cause the collapsible steering column to collapse; in which case you'll have to buy a whole new steering column unit.

8. Tighten the steering wheel nut to 14–18 ft-lbs on the 1976–77 F10, 22–25 ft-lbs on the 1200, B210, 1978 F10, 310 and

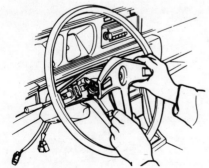
610 horn pad removal

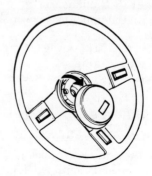
Removing horn pad—210

1977–79 200 SX. Tighten all other steering wheel nuts to 28–36 ft-lbs.

9. Reinstall the horn button, pad, or ring.

Turn Signal Switch
REMOVAL AND INSTALLATION

On some later model Datsuns, the turn signal switch is part of a combination switch. The whole unit is removed together.

1. Disconnect the battery ground cable.

2. Remove the steering wheel as previously outlined. Observe the "caution" on the collapsible steering column.

3. Remove the steering column covers.

4. Disconnect the electrical plugs from the switch.

5. Remove the retaining screws and remove the switch.

6. Installation is the reverse of removal. Many models have turn signal switches that have a tab which must fit into a hole in the steering shaft in order for the system to return the switch to the neutral position after the turn has been made. Be sure to align the tab and the hole when installing.

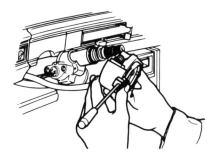

Removing the turn signal switch—610 shown

Steering Lock
REMOVAL AND INSTALLATION

The steering lock/ignition switch/warning buzzer assembly is attached to the steering column by special screws whose heads shear off on installation. The screws must be drilled out to remove the assembly. The ignition switch or warning switch can be replaced without removing the assembly. The ignition switch is on the back of the assembly, and the warning switch on the side. The warning buzzer, which sounds when the driver's door is opened with the steering unlocked, is located behind the instrument panel.

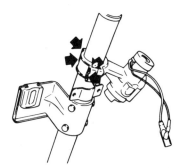

Steering lock securing screws—1977–79 200SX, others similar

Tie-Rod Ends (Steering Side Rods)
REMOVAL AND INSTALLATION

You will need a ball joint remover for this operation.

1. Jack up the front of the vehicle and support it on jack stands.

2. Locate the faulty tie-rod end. It will have a lot of play in it and the dust cover will probably be ripped.

3. Remove the cotter key and nut from the tie-rod stud. Note the position of the tie-rod end in relation to the rest of the steering linkage.

4. Loosen the locknut holding the tie-rod to the rest of the steering linkage.

5. Free the tie-rod ball joint from either the relay rod or steering knuckle by using a ball joint remover.

6. Unscrew and remove the tie-rod end, counting the number of turns it takes to completely free it.

7. Install the new tie-rod end, turning it in exactly as far as you screwed out the old one. Make sure it is correctly positioned in relation to the rest of the steering linkage.

8. Fit the ball joint and nut, tighten them and install a new cotter pin.

Before finally tightening the tie-rod lock nut or clamp, adjust the toe-in of the vehicle. See section under "Front Suspension."

Power Steering Pump
REMOVAL AND INSTALLATION

1. Remove the hoses at the pump and plug the openings shut to prevent contamination. Position the disconnected lines in a raised attitude to prevent leakage.

2. Remove the pump belt.

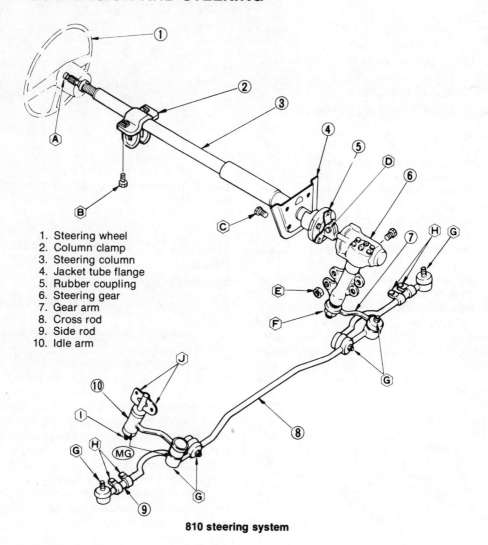

1. Steering wheel
2. Column clamp
3. Steering column
4. Jacket tube flange
5. Rubber coupling
6. Steering gear
7. Gear arm
8. Cross rod
9. Side rod
10. Idle arm

810 steering system

3. Loosen the retaining bolts and any braces, and remove the pump.

Installation is the reverse of removal. Adjust the belt tension by referring to the "Belts" section in chapter one, "General Information and Maintenance." Bleed the system.

BLEEDING THE POWER STEERING SYSTEM

1. Fill the pump reservoir and allow to remain undisturbed for a few minutes.

2. Raise the car until the front wheels are clear of the ground.

3. With the engine off, quickly turn the wheels right and left several times, lightly contacting the stops.

4. Add fluid if necessary.

5. Start the engine and let it idle.

6. Repeat Steps 3 and 4 with the engine idling.

7. With the steering wheel all the way to the left, open the bleeder screw on the steering gear to allow the air to bleed. Close the screw when fluid is expelled.

8. Stop the engine, lower the car until the wheels just touch the ground. Start the engine, allow it to idle, and turn the wheels back and forth several times. Check the fluid level and refill if necessary.

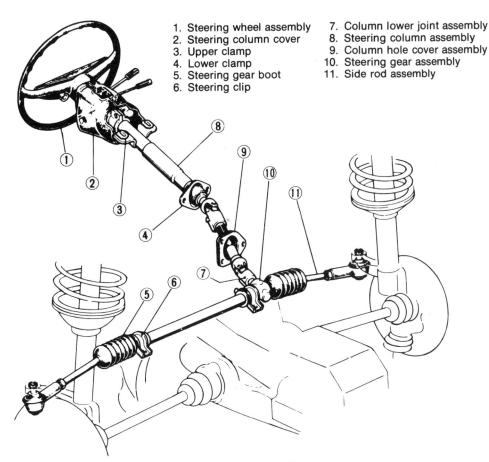

1. Steering wheel assembly
2. Steering column cover
3. Upper clamp
4. Lower clamp
5. Steering gear boot
6. Steering clip
7. Column lower joint assembly
8. Steering column assembly
9. Column hole cover assembly
10. Steering gear assembly
11. Side rod assembly

F10, 310 steering assembly

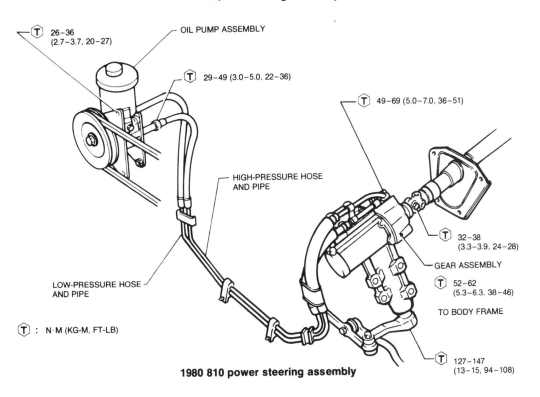

26–36
(2.7–3.7, 20–27)

OIL PUMP ASSEMBLY

29–49 (3.0–5.0, 22–36)

49–69 (5.0–7.0, 36–51)

HIGH-PRESSURE HOSE
AND PIPE

32–38
(3.3–3.9, 24–28)

GEAR ASSEMBLY

52–62
(5.3–6.3, 38–46)

TO BODY FRAME

LOW-PRESSURE HOSE
AND PIPE

T : N·M (KG-M, FT-LB)

127–147
(13–15, 94–108)

1980 810 power steering assembly

Brakes

BRAKE SYSTEM

Adjustment

Front disc brakes are used on all Datsuns covered in this manual except some 1200 and 1973 510 models. All models are equipped with independent front and rear hydraulic systems with a warning light to indicate loss of pressure in either system. All models except the 1980 200SX have rear drum brakes. The 1980 200SX is equipped with rear disc brakes with the parking brake system activating the main brake pads via a mechanical lever assembly. All models except the 1973 510 and the 1200 have a vacuum booster system to lessen the required pedal pressure. The parking brake on all models operates the rear brakes through a cable system.

> NOTE: *Only certain types of drum brakes require adjustment; some drum brakes are automatically adjusted when the parking brake is applied. No disc brakes need adjustment—they are self adjusting.*

To adjust the brakes, raise the wheels, disconnect the parking brake linkage from the rear wheels, apply the brakes hard a few times to center the drums, and proceed as follows:

BOLT-TYPE ADJUSTER

Turn the adjuster bolt on the backing plate

710 rear brake adjuster

until the wheel can no longer be turned, then back off until the wheel is free of drag. Repeat the procedure on the other adjuster bolt on the same wheel. Some models may have only one adjuster bolt per wheel.

Some models incorporate a "click" arrangement with the bolt adjuster. The adjustment proceeds in clicks or notches. The wheel will often be locked temporarily as the adjuster passes over the center for each click. Thus, the adjuster is alternately hard and easy to turn. When the wheel if fully locked, back off 1–3 clicks.

TOOTHED ADJUSTING NUT

Remove the rubber cover from the backing plate. Align the hole in the brake backing plate with the adjusting nut. To spread the brake shoes, turn the toothed adjusting nut with a conventional screwdriver. Stop turn-

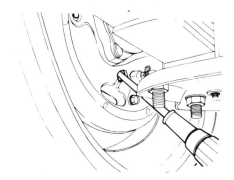

1978 B210 rear brake adjuster

ing when a considerable drag is felt. Back off the nut a few notches so that the correct clearance is reached between the brake drum and the brake shoes. Make sure that the wheel rotates freely.

AUTOMATIC ADJUSTERS

No manual adjustment is necessary. The self adjuster operates whenever the hand or foot brake brakes (on some models) are used.

After Adjustment—All Models

After adjusting the brakes, reconnect the handbrake linkage. Make sure that there is no rear wheel drag with the handbrake released. Loosen the handbrake adjustment if necessary.

BRAKE PEDAL ADJUSTMENT

Before adjusting the pedal, make sure that the wheelbrakes are correctly adjusted. Ad-

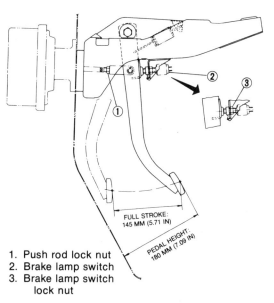

FULL STROKE: 145 MM (5.71 IN)

PEDAL HEIGHT: 180 MM (7.09 IN)

1. Push rod lock nut
2. Brake lamp switch
3. Brake lamp switch lock nut

Brake pedal adjustment—1978 810

just the pedal free play by means of the adjustable pushrod or by replacing shims between the master cylinder and the brake booster or firewall. Adjust the pedal height by means of the adjustable pedal arm stop pad in the driver's compartment. Free play should be approximately 0.04–0.20 in. on all models. Pedal height (floorboard to pedal pad) should be approximately 5½ in. on the 1200; 6 in. on manual transmission 1973 510, all B210, 1978–80 510, 1980 200SX, and all 210 models. Pedal height should be 7 in. on 1977–79 200SX, all 610, 710, 810, F10 and 310 models; and 8 in. for 1973 510 automatic transmission models.

HYDRAULIC SYSTEM

Master Cylinder
REMOVAL AND INSTALLATION

Clean the outside of the cylinder thoroughly, particularly around the cap and fluid lines. Disconnect the fluid lines and cap them to exclude dirt. Remove the clevis pin connecting the pushrod to the brake pedal arm inside the vehicle. This pin need not be removed with the vacuum booster. Unbolt the master cylinder from the firewall and remove. The adjustable pushrod is used to adjust brake pedal free-play. If the pushrod is not adjustable, there will be shims between the cylinder and the mount. These shims, or the adjustable pushrod, are used to adjust brake pedal free play. The 1980 200SX's pushrod is not adjustable, as the rod between the brake booster and the master cylinder is secured by adhesion. After installation, bleed the system and check the pedal free-play.

> NOTE: *Ordinary brake fluid will boil and cause brake failure under the high temperatures developed in disc brake systems. DOT 3 or 4 brake fluid for disc brake systems must be used.*

OVERHAUL

> CAUTION: *Master cylinders are supplied to Datsun by two manufacturers: Nabco and Tokico. Parts between these manufacturers are not interchangeable. Be sure you obtain the correct rebuilding kit for your master cylinder.*

The master cylinder can be disassembled using the illustrations as a guide. Clean all parts in clean brake fluid. Replace the cylinder or piston as necessary if clearance be-

Brake Identification Chart
Match the numbers on the chart with those below to identify your brake system

	1973	1974	1975	1976	1977	1978	1979	1980
1200	① ⑤ ⑧							
510	② ⑤ ⑧					③ ⑦	③ ⑦	③ ⑦
610	② ⑤	② ⑤	① ⑤	① ⑤				
710		② ⑤	② ⑤	③ ⑤	③ ⑤			
B210		① ⑤	① ⑤	① ⑤	① ⑥	① ⑥		
F10				① ⑥	① ⑥	① ⑥		
200SX					① ⑦	① ⑦	① ⑦	③ ④
810					③ ⑦	③ ⑦	③ ⑦	③ ⑦
210							① ⑦	① ⑦
310							① ⑦	① ⑦

① Annette Type front disc brakes
② SC front disc brakes
③ N20, N22, N22A, N32, N34L front disc brakes
④ AN12H rear disc brakes with parking brake assembly
⑤ Rear drum brakes with bolt-type adjuster
⑥ Rear drum brakes with internal, toothed adjusting nut
⑦ Rear drum brakes with automatic adjustment
⑧ Front drum brakes with top and bottom bolt type adjusters

tween the two exceeds 0.006 in. Lubricate all parts with clean brake fluid on assembly. Master cylinder rebuilding kits, containing all the wearing parts, are available to simplify overhaul.

BRAKE PROPORTIONING VALVE

All Datsuns covered in this guide are equipped with brake proportioning valves of several different types. The valves all do the same job, which is to separate the front and rear brake lines, allowing them to function independently, and preventing the rear brakes from locking before the front brakes. Damage, such as brake line leakage, in either the front or rear brake system will not affect the normal operation of the unaffected system. If, in the event of a panic stop, the rear brakes lock up before the front brakes, it could mean the proportioning valve is defective. In that case, replace the entire proportioning valve.

System Bleeding

Bleeding is required whenever air in the hydraulic fluid causes a spongy feeling pedal and sluggish response. This is almost always the case after some part of the hydraulic system has been repaired or replaced.

1. Fill the master cylinder reservoir with the proper fluid. Special fluid is required for disc brakes.

2. The usual procedure is to bleed at the points farthest from the master cylinder first.

3. Fit a rubber hose over the bleeder screw. Submerge the other end of the hose in clean brake fluid in a clear glass container. Loosen the bleeder screw.

4. Slowly pump the brake pedal several times until fluid free of bubbles is discharged. An assistant is required to pump the pedal.

5. On the last pumping stroke, hold the pedal down and tighten the bleeder screw. Check the fluid level periodically during the bleeding operation.

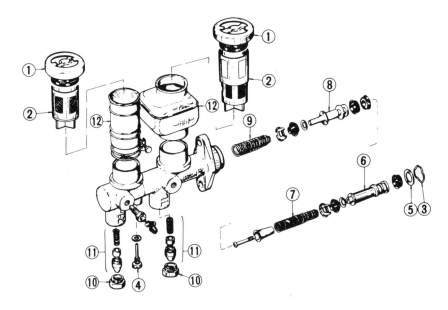

1. Reservoir cap
2. Filter
3. Stopper ring
4. Stopper screw
5. Stopper
6. Primary piston assembly
7. Primary piston return
   spring
8. Secondary piston assembly
9. Secondary piston return
   spring
10. Plug
11. Check valve
12. Reservoir

Exploded view of 610, 710, 1973 510 master cylinder—310 similar

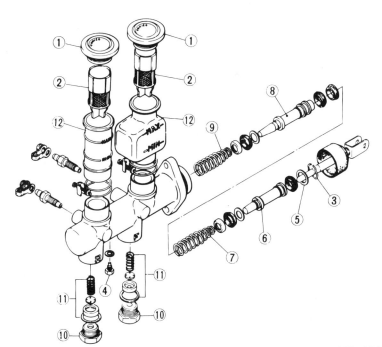

1. Reservoir cap
2. Filter
3. Stopper ring
4. Stopper screw
5. Stopper
6. Primary-piston assembly
7. Primary piston return
   spring
8. Secondary piston
   assembly
9. Secondary piston return
   spring
10. Plug
11. Check valve
12. Reservoir

Exploded view of 1200 and B210 master cylinder—210, 1978–80 510, 1980 200SX similar

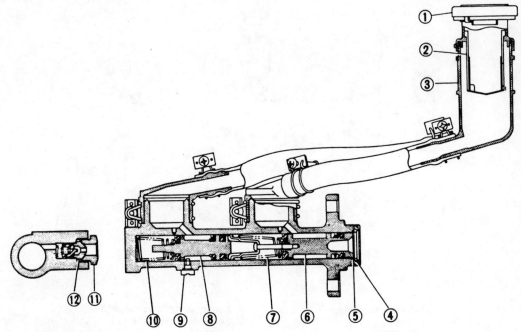

1. Reservoir cap
2. Filter
3. Reservoir tank assembly
4. Stopper ring
5. Stopper
6. Primary piston assembly
7. Primary return spring
8. Secondary piston assembly
9. Stopper screw
10. Secondary return spring
11. Plug
12. Check valve

F10 master cylinder

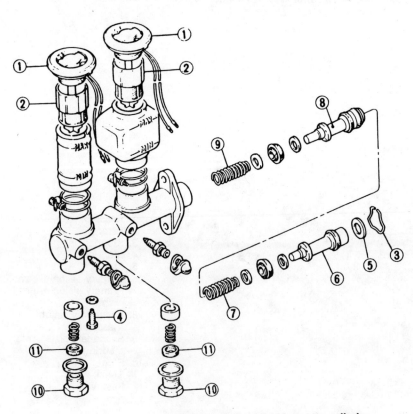

1. Reservoir cap
2. Strainer
3. Stopper ring
4. Stopper screw
5. Stopper
6. Primary piston
7. Spring
8. Secondary piston
9. Spring
10. Plug
11. Check valve

Exploded view of 810 master cylinder

6. Bleed the front brakes in the same way as the rear brakes. Note that some front drum brakes have two hydraulic cylinders and two bleeder screws. Both cylinders must be bled.

7. Check that the brake pedal is now firm. If not, repeat the bleeding operation.

FRONT DISC BRAKES

Disc Brake Pads

INSPECTION

You should be able to check the pad lining thickness without removing the pads. Check the Brake Specifications Chart at the end of this chapter to find the manufacturer's pad wear limit. However, this measurement may disagree with your state inspection laws. When replacing pads, always check the surface of the rotors for scoring or wear. The rotors should be removed for resurfacing if badly scored.

REMOVAL AND INSTALLATION

All four front brake pads must always be replaced as a set.

NOTE: *Use the Brake Identification Chart in this section to find the brake system your vehicle uses.*

TYPES N20, N22, N22A, N32, N34L

1. Raise and support the front of the car or truck. Remove the wheels.

2. Remove the retaining clip from the outboard pad.

3. Remove the pad pins retaining the anti-squeal springs.

4. Remove the pads.

5. To install, open the bleeder screw slightly and push the outer piston into the cylinder until the dust seal groove aligns with the end of the seal retaining ring, then close the bleed screw. Be careful because the piston can be pushed too far, requiring disassembly of the caliper to repair. Install the inner pad.

6. Pull the yoke to push the inner piston into place. Install the outer pad.

7. Lightly coat the areas where the pins touch the pads, and where the pads touch the caliper (at the top) with grease. Do not allow grease to get on the pad friction surfaces.

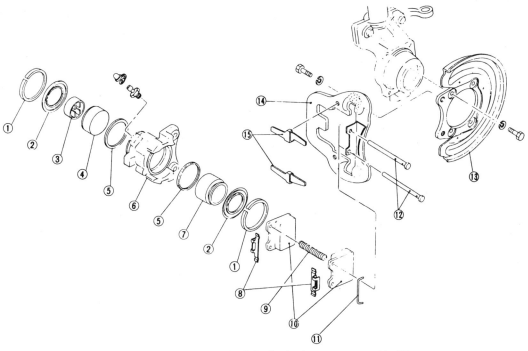

1. Retaining ring	6. Cylinder body	11. Clip
2. Boot	7. Piston B (outer piston)	12. Clevis pin
3. Bias ring	8. Hanger spring	13. Buffle plate
4. Piston A (inner piston)	9. Spring	14. Yoke
5. Piston seal	10. Pad	15. Yoke spring

Typical Annette disc brake

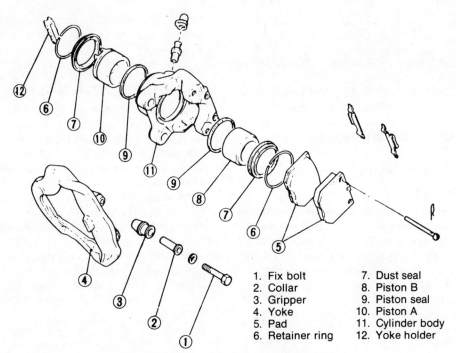

1. Fix bolt
2. Collar
3. Gripper
4. Yoke
5. Pad
6. Retainer ring
7. Dust seal
8. Piston B
9. Piston seal
10. Piston A
11. Cylinder body
12. Yoke holder

N22A disc brake—N20, N22, N32, N34L similar

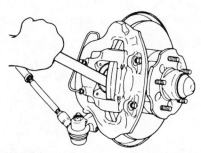

Pushing the inner piston in to install new brake pads (all calipers)

8. Install the anti-squeal springs and pad pins. Install the clip.

9. Apply the brakes a few times to seat the pads. Check the master cylinder level; add fluid if necessary. Bleed the brakes if necessary.

ANNETTE TYPE

1. Raise and support the front of the car. Remove the wheels.

2. Remove the clip, pull out the pins, and remove the pad springs.

3. Remove the pads by pulling them out with pliers.

4. To install, first lightly coat the yoke groove and end surface of the piston with grease. Do not allow grease to contact the pads or rotor.

5. Open the bleeder screw slightly and push the outer piston into the cylinder until its end aligns with the end of the boot retaining ring. Do not push too far, which will require caliper disassembly to correct. Install the inner pad.

6. Pull the yoke toward the outside of the car to push the inner piston into place. Install the outer pad.

7. Apply the brakes a few times to seat the pads. Check the master cylinder and add fluid if necessary. Bleed the brakes if necessary.

SC TYPE

1. Raise and support the front of the car. Remove the wheels.

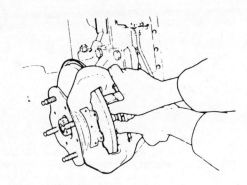

Don't push the piston in too far

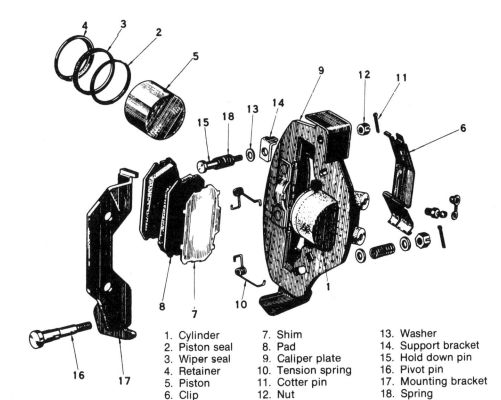

1. Cylinder
2. Piston seal
3. Wiper seal
4. Retainer
5. Piston
6. Clip
7. Shim
8. Pad
9. Caliper plate
10. Tension spring
11. Cotter pin
12. Nut
13. Washer
14. Support bracket
15. Hold down pin
16. Pivot pin
17. Mounting bracket
18. Spring

SC type disc brake

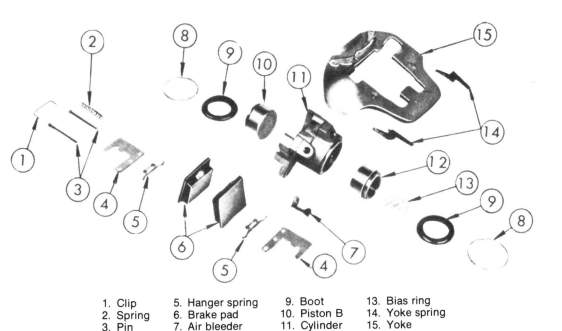

1. Clip
2. Spring
3. Pin
4. Shim
5. Hanger spring
6. Brake pad
7. Air bleeder
8. Retaining ring
9. Boot
10. Piston B
11. Cylinder
12. Piston A
13. Bias ring
14. Yoke spring
15. Yoke

1200 and B210 front brake caliper (Annette type)

2. Push up on the clip to remove.

3. Insert a screwdriver into the back of the pad opposite the piston and move the caliper all the way out.

4. Remove the pads.

5. Open the bleeder screw slightly and press the piston into the caliper.

6. Install the pads, shims, and clips.

7. Apply the brakes a few times to seat the pads. Check the master cylinder level and add fluid if necessary. Bleed the brakes as required.

Calipers and Brake Discs

NOTE: *Use the Brake Identification Chart in this section to find the brake system your vehicle uses.*

OVERHAUL

Types N20, N22, N22A, N32, N34L

1. With the vehicle supported safely and the front wheels off, remove the brake fluid tube from the caliper assembly.

2. Remove the caliper from the knuckle assembly by removing the mounting bolts, located at the rear of the caliper, and lifting the caliper from the rotor.

3. Remove the pads from the caliper (refer to the pad removal procedure).

4. Remove the gripper pin attaching nuts and separate the yoke from the cylinder body.

5. Remove the yoke holder from the piston and remove the retaining rings and dust seals from the ends of both pistons.

6. Apply air pressure *gradually* into the fluid chamber of the caliper, to force the pistons from the cylinders.

7. Remove the piston seals.

8. Inspect the components for damage or excessive wear. Replace or repair as needed.

9. To assemble, install the piston seals in the cylinder bore. Lubricate seals and pistons.

10. Slide the "A" piston into the cylinder, followed by the "B" piston so that its yoke groove coincides with the yoke groove of the cylinder.

11. Install the dust seal and clamp tightly with the retaining ring.

12. Install the yoke holder on the "A" piston and install the gripper to yoke.

NOTE: *The use of soapy water will aid in the installation of the gripper pins.*

13. Support the end of "B" piston and press the yoke into the yoke holder.

14. Install the pads, anti squeal springs, pad pins and retain with the clip.

15. Tighten the gripper pin attaching nuts to 12–15 ft lbs and install the caliper on the spindle knuckle. Torque the caliper mounting bolts to 53–72 ft lbs.

16. Bleed the system, check the fluid level, install the wheels and lower the vehicle.

Annette Type

1. Remove the pads.

2. Disconnect the brake tube.

3. Remove the two bottom strut assembly installation bolts to provide clearance.

4. Remove the caliper assembly mounting bolts.

5. Loosen the bleeder screw and press the pistons into their bores.

6. Clamp the yoke in a vise and tap the yoke head with a hammer to loosen the cylinder. Be careful that primary piston does not fall out.

7. Remove the bias ring from primary piston. Remove the retaining rings and boots from both pistons. Depress and remove the pistons from the cylinder. Remove the piston seal from the cylinder carefully with the fingers so as not to mar the cylinder wall.

8. Remove the yoke springs from the yoke.

9. Wash all parts with clean brake fluid.

PISTON A (INNER PISTON)   PISTON B (OUTER PISTON)

Piston comparison (inner and outer)

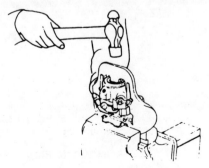

Tapping the yoke head with a hammer

10. If the piston or cylinder is badly worn or scored, replace both. The piston surface is plated and must not be polished with emery paper. Replace all seals. The rotor can be removed and machined if scored, but final thickness must be at least 0.331 in. Runout must not exceed 0.001 in.

11. Lubricate the cylinder bore with clean brake fluid and install the piston seal.

12. Insert the bias ring into primary piston so that the rounded ring portion comes to the bottom of the piston. Primary piston has a small depression inside, while secondary does not.

13. Lubricate the pistons with clean brake fluid and insert into the cylinder. Install the boot and retaining ring. The yoke groove of the bias ring of primary piston must align with the yoke groove of the cylinder.

14. Install the yoke springs to the yoke so the projecting portion faces to the disc (rotor).

15. Lubricate the sliding portion of the cylinder and yoke. Assemble the cylinder and yoke by tapping the yoke lightly.

16. Replace the caliper assembly and pads. Torque the mounting bolts to 33–41 ft lbs. Rotor bolt torque is 20–27 ft lbs. Strut bolt torque is 33–44 ft lbs. Bleed the system of air.

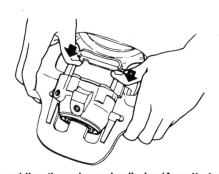

Assembling the yoke and cylinder (Annette type)

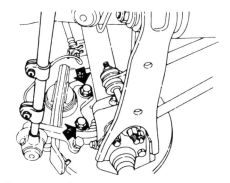

Caliper removal

SC Type

1. Remove the brake pads.

2. Disconnect the brake hose.

3. Remove the cotter pins from the hold down and pivot pins. Remove the retaining nuts.

4. Remove the caliper plate from its mounting bracket.

5. Remove the torsion spring and remove the cylinder assembly from the caliper plate.

6. Apply air into the fluid chamber of the caliper and force the piston from the cylinder.

7. Remove the wiper seal and piston seal retainer.

8. Inspect the components for abnormal wear or damage. Repair or replace as necessary.

9. Fit the seal into its groove in the cylinder. Lubricate the seal and piston. Install the piston into the cylinder.

10. Place the caliper plate over the cylinder assembly and install the torsion spring.

11. Install the caliper plate on the mounting bracket and install the nuts and cotter pins.

12. Bleed the system and check the reservoir level.

FRONT DRUM BRAKES

Some models of the 1200 and 1973 510 are equipped with front drum brakes.

Brake Drums
REMOVAL AND INSTALLATION

1. Jack up the front of the vehicle so that the wheel which is to be serviced is off the ground. Be sure to loosen the lug nuts before the wheel comes off the ground.

2. Remove the wheel and tire assembly.

3. Pull the brake drum off the hub. If the drum cannot be easily removed, back off on the brake adjustment.

NOTE: *Never depress the brake pedal while the brake drum is removed.*

4. Install the brake drum in the reverse order of removal and adjust the brakes.

Brake Shoes
REMOVAL AND INSTALLATION

1. Jack up the vehicle until the wheel which is to be serviced is off the ground. Remove the wheel and brake drum.

1973 1200 front brake drum

NOTE: *It is not absolutely essential to remove the hub assembly from the spindle, but it makes the job a great deal easier. If you can work with the hub in place, skip down to Step 7.*

2. Remove the hub dust cap.

3. Straighten the cotter pin and remove it from the spindle.

4. Unscrew the spindle nut and remove the adjusting cap, spindle nut, and spindle washer.

5. Wiggle the hub assembly until the outer bearing comes unseated and can be removed from the hub. Remove the outer bearing.

6. Pull the hub assembly off the spindle.

7. Unhook the return springs on the brake shoes and remove the fasteners holding the shoes in place on the 1973 510. Remove the shoes.

8. Apply brake grease to the adjuster assemblies and back the adjusters off the whole way using the bolts on the backing plate. Apply brake grease to the areas on the brake backing plate where the brake shoes make contact.

9. Install the brake shoes in the reverse order of removal.

10. Install the hub, brake drum and wheel in the reverse order of removal. Adjust the wheel bearings.

Wheel Cylinders

REMOVAL AND INSTALLATION

1. Jack up the wheel to be serviced.

2. Remove the wheel, brake drum, hub assembly, and brake shoes.

3. Disconnect the brake hose from the wheel cylinder.

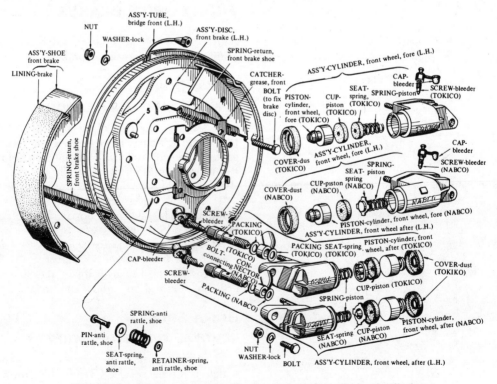

1973 510 front brake assembly showing both makes of wheel cylinders

4. Unscrew the wheel cylinder securing nut and remove the wheel cylinder from the brake backing plate.

5. Install the wheel cylinder in the reverse order of removal, assemble the remaining components, and bleed the brake hydraulic system.

OVERHAUL

NOTE: *Datsun obtains parts from two manufacturers: Nabco and Tokico. Parts are not interchangeable. The name of the manufacturer is usually on the wheel cylinder.*

1. Remove the wheel cylinder from the backing plate.

2. Remove the dust boot and take out the piston. Discard the piston cup. The dust boot can be reused, if necessary, but it is better to replace it.

3. Wash all of the components in clean brake fluid.

4. Inspect the piston and piston bore. Replace any components which are severely corroded, scored, or worn. The piston and piston bore can be polished lightly with crocus cloth. Move the crocus cloth around the piston bore; *not* in and out of the piston bore.

5. Wash the wheel cylinder and piston thoroughly in clean brake fluid, allowing them to remain lubricated for assembly.

6. Coat all of the new components to be installed in the wheel cylinder with clean brake fluid prior to assembly.

7. Assemble the wheel cylinder and install it in the reverse order of removal. Assemble the remaining components and bleed the brake hydraulic system.

FRONT WHEEL BEARINGS

Adjustment

ALL EXCEPT F10, 310

NOTE: *The F10 and 310, both front wheel drive vehicles, have pressed bearings which are not adjustable on the front wheels. However, their rear wheel bearings are adjustable. See the section under Rear Drum Brakes in this chapter for procedures.*

The factory procedures for wheel bearing adjustment is of little use to the backyard mechanic, since it involves the use of a spring scale, an inch pound torque wrench, and a ft-

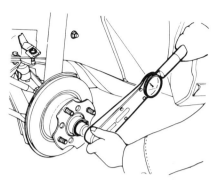
Tightening the hub nut with a torque wrench during wheel bearing adjustment

lb torque wrench. For the following procedure, you will only need a ft-lb torque wrench.

1. Jack up the car and remove the wheel.

2. Remove the bearing dust cap and the cotter pin.

3. Torque the spindle nut 16–18 ft-lbs on the 1200; 18–22 ft-lbs on the B210, 610, 710, 810, and 200SX; 22–25 ft-lbs on the 510 and 210.

4. Turn the hub a few times to seat the bearing and check the torque on the nut again.

5. Loosen the nut about 60° on all models except the 1978–80 510 and the 210. Loosen the nut about 90° on the 1978–80 510 and the 210.

6. Install the adjusting cap and a new cotter pin. It is permissible to loosen the nut 15° to allow the holes to align, on all models except the 1978–80 510 and the 210. On those models only, tighten the nut up to 15° to align the cotter pin holes.

7. Reinstall the tire and the wheel and rotate the whole assembly. There should be no roughness or binding. Grasp the top of the wheel and move it in and out. There should be negligible play. If there is excessive play,

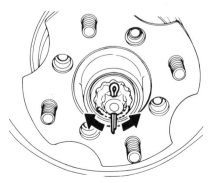
Split and spread the cotter pin

the wheel bearings must be retightened. If roughness persists, check the wheel bearing condition.

8. Install the cap and lower the car.

WHEEL BEARING PACKING AND REPLACEMENT

The most important thing to remember when working with the wheel bearings is that although they are basically durable, in some ways they are remarkably fragile. Mishandling, grit, misalignment, scratches, improper preload, etc. will quickly destroy any roller bearing, no matter how well hardened during manufacture.

1. Loosen the wheel nuts, raise the car, and remove the wheel and tire. Remove the brake drum or brake caliper, following the procedure in this chapter.

2. It is not necessary to remove the drum or disc from the hub. The outer wheel bearing will come off with the hub. Simply pull the hub and disc or drum assembly toward you off the spindle. Be sure to catch the bearing before it falls to the ground.

3. From the inner side of the hub, remove the inner grease seal, and lift the inner bearing from the hub. Discard the grease seal.

4. Clean the bearings in solvent and allow them to air dry. You risk leaving bits of lint in the races if you dry them with a rag. Clean the grease cap, nuts, spindle, and the races in the hub thoroughly, and allow the parts to dry.

5. Inspect the bearings carefully. If they are worn, cracked, brinelled, pitted, burned, scored, etc., they should be replaced, along with the bearing cups in which they run in the hub. Do not mix old and new parts.

6. If the cups are worn, remove them from the hub, by using a brass rod as a drift.

To install:

7. If the old cups were removed, install the new inner and outer cups into the hub, using either a tool made for the purpose, or a socket or piece of pipe of a large enough diameter to press on the outside rim of the cup only.

CAUTION: *Use care not to cock the bearing cups in the hub. If they are not fully seated, the bearings will be impossible to adjust properly.*

8. Pack the inside area of the hub and cups with grease. Pack the inside of the grease cap while you're at it, but do not install the cap into the hub.

9. Pack the inner bearing with grease. Place a large glob of grease into the palm of one hand and push the inner bearing through it with a sliding motion. The grease must be forced through the side of the bearing and in between each roller. Continue until the grease begins to ooze out the other side through the gaps between the rollers; the bearing must be completely packed with grease. Install the inner bearing into its cup in the hub, then press a new grease seal into place over it.

10. Install the hub and rotor or drum assembly onto the spindle. Pack the outer bearing with grease in the same manner as the inner bearing, then install the outer bearing into place in the hub.

11. Apply a thin coat of grease to the washer and the threaded portion of the spindle, then loosely install the washer and adjusting nut. Go on to the bearing preload adjustment.

REAR DISC BRAKES

The 1980 200SX has rear disc brakes of the Annette type, incorporating a cam-operated parking brake.

Brake Pads

REMOVAL AND INSTALLATION

1. Raise and support the rear of the car. Remove the wheels.

2. Remove the clip at the outside of the pad pins.

3. Remove the pad pins. Hold the anti-squeal springs in place with your finger.

4. Remove the pads.

5. To install, first clean the end of the piston with clean brake fluid.

6. Lightly coat the caliper-to-pad, the yoke-to-pad, retaining pin-to-pad, and retaining pin-to-bracket surfaces with grease. Do not allow grease to get on the rotor or pad surfaces.

7. Push the piston into place with a screwdriver by pushing in on the piston while at the same time turning it clockwise into the bore. Then, with a lever between the rotor and yoke, push the yoke over until the clearance to install the pads is equal.

8. Install the shims and pads, anti-squeal springs and pins. Install the clip. Note that the inner pad has a tab which must fit into the piston notch. Therefore, be sure that the

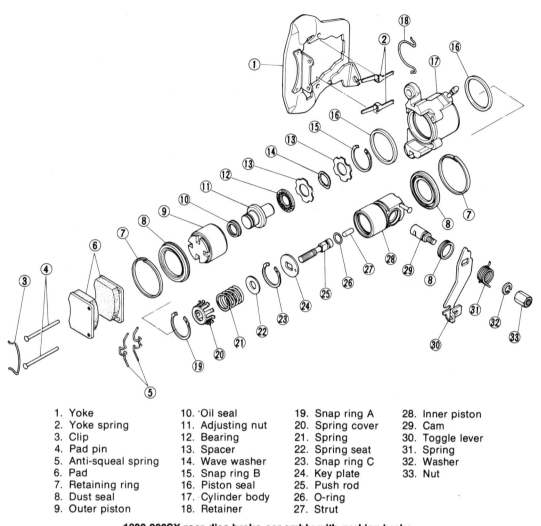

1. Yoke	10. Oil seal	19. Snap ring A	28. Inner piston
2. Yoke spring	11. Adjusting nut	20. Spring cover	29. Cam
3. Clip	12. Bearing	21. Spring	30. Toggle lever
4. Pad pin	13. Spacer	22. Spring seat	31. Spring
5. Anti-squeal spring	14. Wave washer	23. Snap ring C	32. Washer
6. Pad	15. Snap ring B	24. Key plate	33. Nut
7. Retaining ring	16. Piston seal	25. Push rod	
8. Dust seal	17. Cylinder body	26. O-ring	
9. Outer piston	18. Retainer	27. Strut	

1980 200SX rear disc brake assembly with parking brake

piston notch is centered to allow proper pad installation.

9. Apply the brakes a few times to center the pads. Check the master cylinder fluid level and add if necessary.

Caliper Overhaul

1. Disconnect the brake hose from the caliper. Plug the hose and caliper to prevent fluid loss.

2. Disconnect the parking brake cable.

3. Remove the mounting bolts and remove the caliper from the suspension arm.

4. Remove the pads.

5. Stand the caliper assembly on end, large end down, and push on the caliper to separate it from the yoke.

6. Remove the retaining rings and dust seals from both pistons.

7. Push in on the outer piston to force out the piston assembly. Remove the piston seals.

8. Remove the yoke spring from the yoke.

9. Disengage the piston assembly by turning the outer piston counterclockwise.

10. Disassemble the outer piston by removing the snap ring.

11. Disassemble the inner piston by removing the snap ring. This will allow the spring cover, spring, and spring seat to come out. Remove the inner snap ring to remove the key plate, push rod, and strut.

12. To install, assemble the pistons in reverse order of disassembly. Apply a thin coat of grease to the groove in the push rod, its O-ring, the strut ends, oil seal, piston seal, and the inside of the dust seal.

13. Install the piston seals. Apply a thin

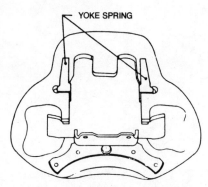

Yoke showing yoke springs (Annette type)

coat of grease to the sliding surfaces of the piston and caliper bore. Install the pistons into the caliper. Install the retainers onto the dust seals.

14. Install the yoke springs on the yoke.

15. Lightly coat the yoke and caliper body contact surfaces, and the pad pin hole, with silicone grease. Assemble the yoke to the caliper.

16. Install the pads.

17. Install the caliper to the suspension arm (28–38 ft lbs). Connect the parking brake cable. Connect the brake hose. Apply the brakes a few times to center the pads. Bleed the system.

REAR DRUM BRAKES

Brake Drums

REMOVAL AND INSTALLATION

1. Raise the rear of the vehicle and support it on jack stands.

2. Remove the wheels.

3. Release the parking brake.

4. Pull off the brake drums. On some models there are two threaded service holes in each brake drum. If the drum will not come off, fit two correct size bolts in the service holes and screw them in: this will force the drum away from the axle.

5. If the drum cannot be easily removed, back off the brake adjustment.

NOTE: *Never depress the brake pedal while the brake drum is removed.*

6. Installation is the reverse of removal.

INSPECTION

After removing the brake drum, wipe out the accumulated dust with a damp cloth.

CAUTION: *Do not blow the brake dust out of the drums with compressed air or lung power. Brake linings contain asbes-*

tos, *a known cancer causing substance. Dispose of the cloth after use.*

Inspect the drum for cracks, deep grooves, roughness, scoring, or out-of-roundness. Replace any brake drum which is cracked.

Smooth any slight scores by polishing the friction surface with the fine emery cloth. Heavy or extensive scoring will cause excessive brake lining wear and should be removed from the brake drum through resurfacing.

Brake Shoes

REMOVAL AND INSTALLATION

510, 610, 710, 810, and 1977–79 200SX

1. Raise the vehicle and remove the wheels.

2. Release the parking brake. Disconnect the cross rod from the lever of the brake cylinder. Remove the brake drum. Place a heavy rubber band around the cylinder to prevent the piston from coming out.

3. Remove the return springs and shoes.

4. Clean the backing plate and check the wheel cylinder for leaks. To remove the wheel cylinder, remove the brake line, dust cover, securing nuts or plates and adjusting shims. Clearance between the cylinder and the piston should not exceed 0.006 in.

5. The drums must be machined if scored or out of round more than 0.002 in. The drum inside diameter should not be machined beyond 9.04 in. Minimum safe lining thickness is 0.059 in.

6. Hook the return springs into the new shoes. The springs should be between the shoes and the backing plate. The longer return spring must be adjacent to the wheel cylinder. A very thin film of grease may be applied to the pivot points at the ends of the brake shoes. Grease the shoe locating buttons on the backing plate, also. Be careful not to get grease on the linings or drums.

7. Place one shoe in the adjuster and piston slots, and pry the other shoe into position.

8. Replace the drums and wheels. Adjust the brakes. Bleed the hydraulic system of air if the brake lines were disconnected.

9. Reconnect the handbrake, making sure that it does not cause the shoes to drag when it is released.

1200, B210, F10, 210, 310

1. Raise the vehicle and remove the wheels.

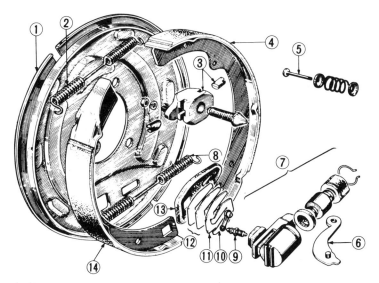

1. Brake disc
2. Return spring adjuster side
3. Brake shoe adjuster
4. Brake shoe assembly-fore
5. Anti-rattler pin
6. Lever
7. Rear wheel cylinder
8. Return spring cylinder side
9. Bleeder
10. Lock plate A
11. Lock plate B
12. Lock plate C and D
13. Dust cover
14. Brake shoe assembly-after

1973 510, 610 and 710 rear drum brake

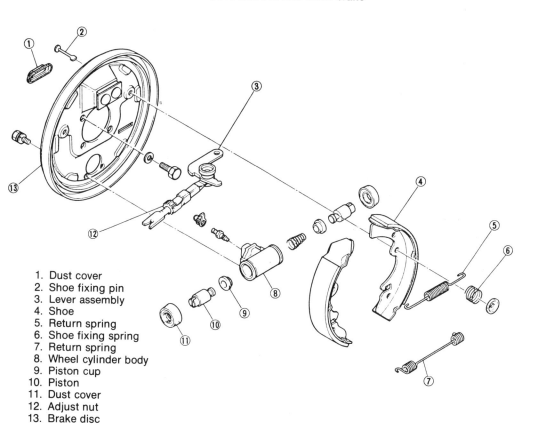

1. Dust cover
2. Shoe fixing pin
3. Lever assembly
4. Shoe
5. Return spring
6. Shoe fixing spring
7. Return spring
8. Wheel cylinder body
9. Piston cup
10. Piston
11. Dust cover
12. Adjust nut
13. Brake disc

F10 rear brake assembly—310 similar

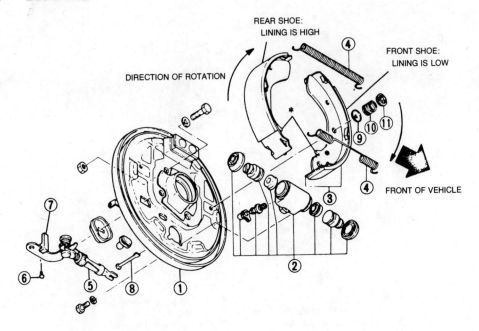

REAR SHOE:
LINING IS HIGH

DIRECTION OF ROTATION

FRONT SHOE:
LINING IS LOW

FRONT OF VEHICLE

*Both adjuster location
holes are at the bottom

1. Brake disc
2. Wheel cylinder assembly
3. Brake shoe assembly
4. Return spring
5. Adjuster assembly
6. Stopper pin
7. Stopper
8. Anti-rattle pin
9. Spring seat
10. Anti-rattle spring
11. Retainer

Exploded view of 1977–79 200SX rear drum brake

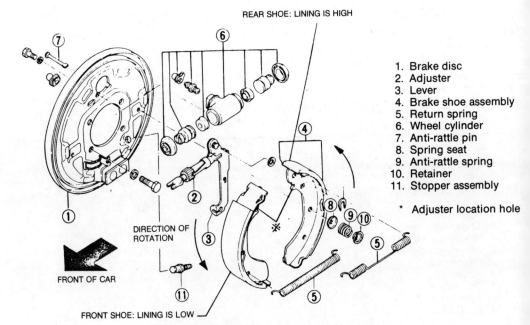

REAR SHOE: LINING IS HIGH

DIRECTION OF
ROTATION

FRONT OF CAR

FRONT SHOE: LINING IS LOW

1. Brake disc
2. Adjuster
3. Lever
4. Brake shoe assembly
5. Return spring
6. Wheel cylinder
7. Anti-rattle pin
8. Spring seat
9. Anti-rattle spring
10. Retainer
11. Stopper assembly

*   Adjuster location hole

Exploded view of 810 sedan rear drum brake

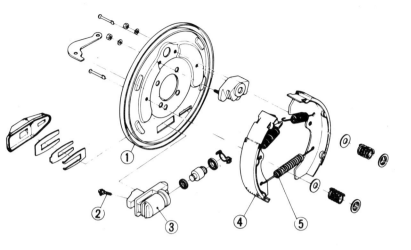

1. Brake disc
2. Bleeder
3. Wheel cylinder
4. Shoe assembly
5. Return spring

Exploded view of 1200 and B210 rear brake

2. Loosen the handbrake cable, remove the clevis pin from the wheel cylinder lever, disconnect the handbrake cable, and remove the return pull spring.

3. Remove the brake drum, shoe retainers, return springs, and brake shoes. Loosen the brake adjusters if the drums are difficult to remove. Place a heavy rubber band around the cylinder to prevent the piston from coming out.

4. Clean the backing plate and check the wheel cylinder for leaks. To remove the wheel cylinder, remove the brake line, dust cover, securing nuts or plates and adjusting shims. Clearance between cylinder and piston should not exceed 0.006 in.

5. The drums must be machined if scored or out-of-round more than 0.008 in. The drum inside diameter must not be machined beyond 8.04 in. Minimum safe lining thickness is 0.059 in. (0.039 in.-F10).

6. Follow Steps 6–9 for 510, 610, 710, and 810.

Wheel Cylinder

See correct section under "Brake Shoes Removal and Installation" for wheel cylinder removal and installation procedures. On models with a sliding wheel cylinder, it will be easier to rebuild the cylinder while it is still attached to the brake backing plate. See the "Front Drum Brake Wheel Cylinder Overhaul" for overhaul procedures for the rear drum brake cylinders. Observe the "NOTE" about different manufacturers of wheel cylinder components.

Rear Wheel Bearings
ADJUSTMENT
F10, 310

The rear wheel bearings on the F10 and the 310 are adjustable the same way as front wheel bearings on other Datsuns covered in this guide. For rear wheel bearing packing and replacement, see the section under front wheel bearings in this chapter.

1. Raise the rear of the vehicle and support it on jack stands.

2. Remove the wheel.

3. Remove the bearing dust cap. A pair of channel locks will usually do the trick.

4. Remove the cotter pin and nut cap if so equipped. Throw the cotter pin away.

5. Tighten the wheel bearing nut on the F10 to 18–22 ft-lbs, and on the 310 to 29–33 ft-lbs.

6. Rotate the drum back and forth a few revolutions to snug down the bearing.

7. On the F10, loosen the nut until it can be turned by hand, then tighten it with a hand held socket as far as it will go.

8. On the 310, after turning the wheel, recheck the torque of the nut, then loosen it 90° from its position.

9. Install the adjusting cap, if so equipped. Align the cotter pin holes in the nut or nut cap with the hole in the spindle by turning the nut clockwise on the F10. On the 310, tighten the nut no more than 15° to align the holes.

10. Install the cotter pin, bend up its ends, and install the dust cap.

Assemble the remaining parts.

PARKING BRAKE

ADJUSTMENT

Handbrake adjustments are generally not needed, unless the cables have stretched.

All Models

There is an adjusting nut on the cable under the car, usually at the end of the front cable and near the point at which the two cables from the rear wheels come together (the equalizer). Some models also have a turn-buckle in the rear cable to compensate for cable stretching.

To adjust, proceed as follows:

1. Adjust the rear brakes with the parking brake fully released.

2. Apply the hand brake lever so that it is approximately 3–3¼ in. from its fully released position.

3. Adjust the parking brake turnbuckle, locknuts, or equalizer so that the rear brakes are locked.

4. Release the parking brake. The wheels should turn freely. If not, loosen the parking brake adjuster until the wheels turn with no drag.

1. Hand brake lever
2. Cable
3. Clip
4. Lock plate
5. Turn-buckle (Hand brake adjuster)
6. Cable
7. Cable
8. Hanger strap
9. Return spring
10. Cable shank
11. Hand brake lever cover

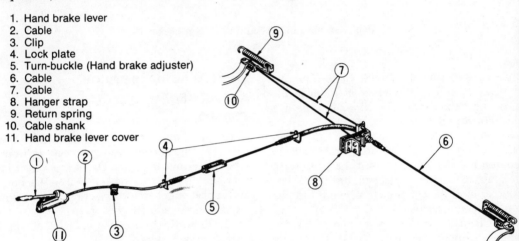

1200 and B210 parking brake assembly—210, 1978–80 510. 1977–79 200SX similar

1. Control stem
2. Control stem bracket
3. Front cable
4. Cable lock plate
5. Center lever
6. Return spring
7. Rear cable adjuster
8. Balance lever
9. Rear cable
10. Clevis

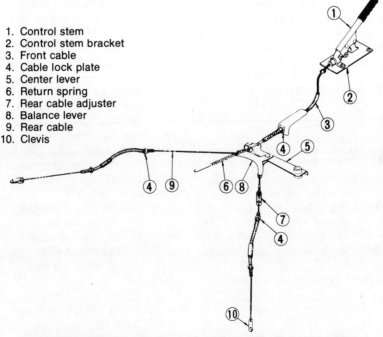

1973 510 and 610 (except station wagon) parking brake assembly

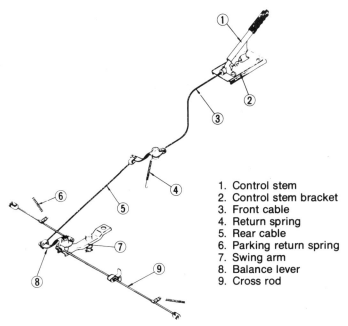

1. Control stem
2. Control stem bracket
3. Front cable
4. Return spring
5. Rear cable
6. Parking return spring
7. Swing arm
8. Balance lever
9. Cross rod

610 station wagon and all 710 models parking brake assembly

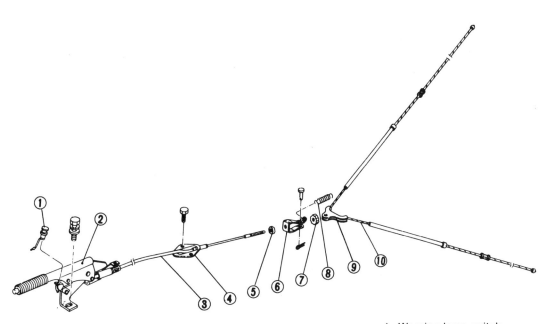

1. Warning lamp switch
2. Hand brake lever
3. Front cable
4. Cable supporter
5. Lock nut
6. Clevis
7. Adjuster
8. Return spring
9. Equalizer
10. Rear cable

F10 parking brake, sedan and hatchback—310 similar except has turnbuckle adjuster

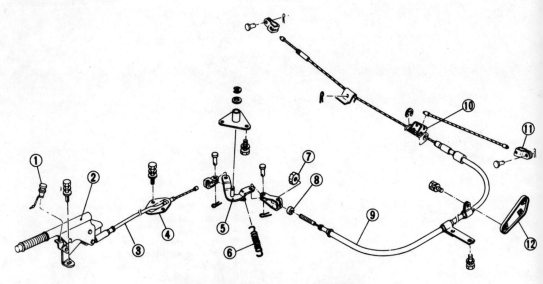

1. Warning lamp switch
2. Hand brake lever
3. Front cable
4. Cable supporter
5. Counter lever
6. Return spring
7. Adjuster
8. Lock nut
9. Rear cable
10. Equalizer
11. Clevis
12. Wire bracket

F10 station wagon parking brake

Brake Specifications

All measurements given are in inches unless noted

Model	Year	Lug Nut Torque (ft-lbs)	Master Cylinder Bore	Brake Disc		Drum		Minimum Lining Thickness	
				Minimum Thickness	Maximum Run-Out	Diameter	Max. Wear Limit	Front	Rear
510	1973	58–65	0.750	0.331	0.0048	9.000 ①	9.093	0.059 (drum) 0.040 (disc) 0.080	0.059
	1978–80	58–72	0.8125	0.331	0.0047	9.000	9.060		0.059
1200	1973	58–65	0.6875	0.3307	0.0012	8.000	8.051	0.0630 (disc) 0.0591 (drum)	0.0591
810	1977–80	58–72	0.8125	0.413	0.0059	9.000	9.060	0.080	0.059
B210	1974–78	58–65	0.750	0.331	0.0047	8.000	8.051	0.063	0.059
610	1973–74	58–65	0.750	0.331	0.0048	9.000	9.055	0.039	0.059
	1975	58–65	0.750	0.331	0.0048	9.000	9.055	0.063	0.059
	1976–77	58–65	0.750	0.331	0.0048	9.000	9.055	0.079	0.059
710	1974–75	58–65	0.750	0.331	0.0047	9.000	9.055	0.039	0.059
	1976–77	58–65	0.750	0.331	0.0047	9.000	9.055	0.079	0.059
200SX	1977–79	58–65	0.750	0.331	0.0047	9.000	9.060	0.059	0.059
F-10	1977–78	58–65	0.750	0.339	0.0059	8.000	8.050	0.063	0.039
210	1979–80	58–72	0.8125	0.331	0.0047	8.000	8.050	0.063	0.059
310	1979–80	58–72	0.8125	0.339	0.0047	8.000	8.050	0.079	0.059
200SX	1980	58–72	0.8750	0.413 ② 0.339 ③	0.0047 ② 0.0059 ③	—	—	0.079	0.079

— Not Applicable
① Uses front and rear brake drums
② Front brake disc
③ Rear brake disc
NOTE: Minimum lining thickness is as recommended by the manufacturer. Due to variation in state inspection regulations, the minimum allowable thickness may be different than recommended by the manufacturer.

Body

10

You can repair most minor auto body damage yourself. Minor damage usually falls into one of several categories: (1) small scratches and dings in the paint that can be repaired without the use of body filler, (2) deep scratches and dents that require body filler, but do not require pulling, or hammering metal back into shape and (3) rust-out repairs. The repair sequences illustrated in this chapter are typical of these types of repairs. If you want to get involved in more complicated repairs including pulling or hammering sheet metal back into shape, you will probably need more detailed instructions. Chilton's *Minor Auto Body Repair, 2nd Edition* is a comprehensive guide to repairing auto body damage yourself.

TOOLS AND SUPPLIES

The list of tools and equipment you may need to fix minor body damage ranges from very basic hand tools to a wide assortment of specialized body tools. Most minor scratches, dings and rust holes can be fixed using an electric drill, wire wheel or grinder attachment, half-round plastic file, sanding block, various grades of sandpaper (#36, which is coarse through #600, which is fine) in both wet and dry types, auto body plastic,

primer, touch-up paint, spreaders, newspaper and masking tape.

Most manufacturers of auto body repair products began supplying materials to professionals. Their knowledge of the best, most-used products has been translated into body repair kits for the do-it-yourselfer. Kits are available from a number of manufacturers and contain the necessary materials in the required amounts for the repair identified on the package.

Kits are available for a wide variety of uses, including:

- Rusted out metal
- All purpose kit for dents and holes
- Dents and deep scratches
- Fiberglass repair kit
- Epoxy kit for restyling.

Kits offer the advantage of buying what you need for the job. There is little waste and little chance of materials going bad from not being used. The same manufacturers also merchandise all of the individual products used—spreaders, dent pullers, fiberglass cloth, polyester resin, cream hardener, body filler, body files, sandpaper, sanding discs and holders, primer, spray paint, etc.

CAUTION: *Most of the products you will be using contain harmful chemicals, so be extremely careful. Always read the complete label before opening the containers. When* *you put them away for future use, be sure they are out of children's reach!*

Most auto body repair kits contain all the materials you need to do the job right in the kit. So, if you have a small rust spot or dent you want to fix, check the contents of the kit before you run out and buy any additional tools.

ALIGNING BODY PANELS

Doors

There are several methods of adjusting doors. Your vehicle will probably use one of those illustrated.

Whenever a door is removed and is to be reinstalled, you should matchmark the position of the hinges on the door pillars. The holes of the hinges and/or the hinge attaching points are usually oversize to permit alignment of doors. The striker plate is also moveable, through oversize holes, permitting up-and-down, in-and-out and fore-and-aft movement. Fore-and-aft movement is made by adding or subtracting shims from behind the striker and pillar post. The striker should be adjusted so that the door closes fully and remains closed, yet enters the lock freely.

DOOR HINGES

Don't try to cover up poor door adjustment with a striker plate adjustment. The gap on each side of the door should be equal and uniform and there should be no metal-to-metal contact as the door is opened or closed.

1. Determine which hinge bolts must be loosened to move the door in the desired direction.

2. Loosen the hinge bolt(s) just enough to allow the door to be moved with a padded pry bar.

3. Move the door a small amount and check the fit, after tightening the bolts. Be sure that there is no bind or interference with adjacent panels.

4. Repeat this until the door is properly positioned, and tighten all the bolts securely.

Hood, Trunk or Tailgate

As with doors, the outline of hinges should be scribed before removal. The hood and trunk can be aligned by loosening the hinge bolts in their slotted mounting holes and moving the hood or trunk lid as necessary.

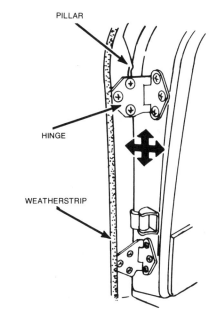
Door hinge adjustment

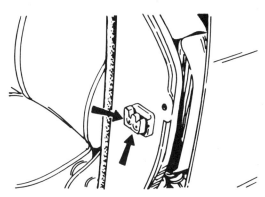
Move the door striker as indicated by arrows

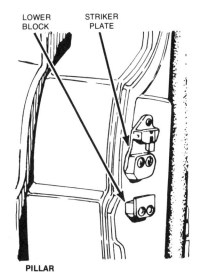
Striker plate and lower block

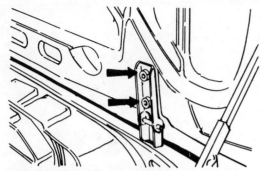

Loosen the hinge boots to permit fore-and-aft and horizontal adjustment

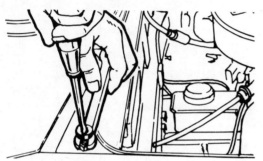

The hood is adjusted vertically by stop-screws at the front and/or rear

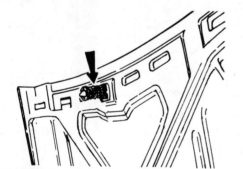

The hood pin can be adjusted for proper lock engagement

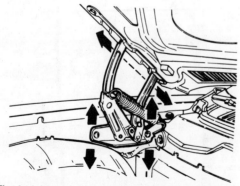

The height of the hood at the rear is adjusted by loosening the bolts that attach the hinge to the body and moving the hood up or down

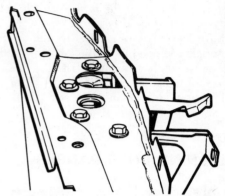

The base of the hood lock can also be re-positioned slightly to give more positive lock engagement

The hood and trunk have adjustable catch locations to regulate lock engagement. Bumpers at the front and/or rear of the hood provide a vertical adjustment and the hood lockpin can be adjusted for proper engagement.

The tailgate on the station wagon can be adjusted by loosening the hinge bolts in their slotted mounting holes and moving the tailgate on its hinges. The latchplate and latch striker at the bottom of the tailgate opening can be adjusted to stop rattle. An adjustable bumper is located on each side.

RUST, UNDERCOATING, AND RUSTPROOFING

Rust

Rust is an electrochemical process. It works on ferrous metals (iron and steel) from the inside out due to exposure of unprotected surfaces to air and moisture. The possibility of rust exists practically nationwide—anywhere humidity, industrial pollution or chemical salts are present, rust can form. In coastal areas, the problem is high humidity and salt air; in snowy areas, the problem is chemical salt (de-icer) used to keep the roads clear, and in industrial areas, sulphur dioxide is present in the air from industrial pollution and is changed to sulphuric acid when it rains. The rusting process is accelerated by high temperatures, especially in snowy areas, when vehicles are driven over slushy roads and then left overnight in a heated garage.

Automotive styling also can be a contributor to rust formation. Spot welding of panels creates small pockets that trap moisture and form an environment for rust formation. Fortunately, auto manufacturers have been working hard to increase the corrosion protection of their products. Galvanized sheet metal enjoys much wider use, along with the increased use of plastic and various rust retardant coatings. Manufacturers are also designing out areas in the body where rust-forming moisture can collect.

To prevent rust, you must stop it before it gets started. On new vehicles, there are two ways to accomplish this.

First, the car or truck should be treated with a commercial rustproofing compound. There are many different brands of franchised rustproofers, but most processes involve spraying a waxy "self-healing" compound under the chassis, inside rocker panels, inside doors and fender liners and similar places where rust is likely to form. Prices for a quality rustproofing job range from $100–$250, depending on the area, the brand name and the size of the vehicle.

Ideally, the vehicle should be rustproofed as soon as possible following the purchase. The surfaces of the car or truck have begun to oxidize and deteriorate during shipping. In addition, the car may have sat on a dealer's lot or on a lot at the factory, and once the rust has progressed past the stage of light, powdery surface oxidation rustproofing is not likely to be worthwhile. Professional rustproofers feel that once rust has formed, rustproofing will simply seal in moisture already present. Most franchised rustproofing operations offer a 3–5 year warranty against rust-through, but will not support that warranty if the rustproofing is not applied within three months of the date of manufacture.

Undercoating should not be mistaken for rustproofing. Undercoating is a black, tar-like substance that is applied to the underside of a vehicle. Its basic function is to deaden noises that are transmitted from under the car. It simply cannot get into the crevices and seams where moisture tends to collect. In fact, it may clog up drainage holes and ventilation passages. Some undercoatings also tend to crack or peel with age and only create more moisture and corrosion attracting pockets.

The second thing you should do immediately after purchasing the car is apply a paint sealant. A sealant is a petroleum based product marketed under a wide variety of brand names. It has the same protective properties as a good wax, but bonds to the paint with a chemically inert layer that seals it from the air. If air can't get at the surface, oxidation cannot start.

The paint sealant kit consists of a base coat and a conditioning coat that should be applied every 6–8 months, depending on the manufacturer. The base coat must be applied before waxing, or the wax must first be removed.

Third, keep a garden hose handy for your car in winter. Use it a few times on nice days during the winter for underneath areas, and it will pay big dividends when spring arrives. Spraying under the fenders and other areas which even car washes don't reach will help remove road salt, dirt and other build-ups which help breed rust. Adjust the nozzle to a high-force spray. An old brush will help break up residue, permitting it to be washed away more easily.

It's a somewhat messy job, but worth it in the long run because rust often starts in those hidden areas.

At the same time, wash grime off the door sills and, more importantly, the under portions of the doors, plus the tailgate if you have a station wagon or truck. Applying a coat of wax to those areas at least once before and once during winter will help fend off rust.

When applying the wax to the under parts of the doors, you will note small drain holes. These holes often are plugged with undercoating or dirt. Make sure they are cleaned out to prevent water build-up inside the doors. A small punch or penknife will do the job.

Water from the high-pressure sprays in car washes sometimes can get into the housings for parking and taillights, so take a close look. If they contain water merely loosen the retaining screws and the water should run out.

Repairing Scratches and Small Dents

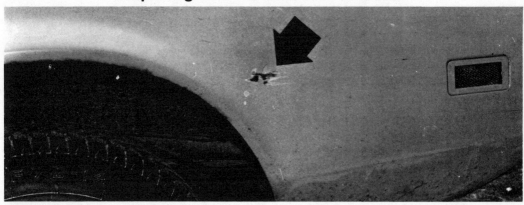

Step 1. This dent (arrow) is typical of a deep scratch or minor dent. If deep enough, the dent or scratch can be pulled out or hammered out from behind. In this case no straightening is necessary

Step 2. Using an 80-grit grinding disc on an electric drill grind the paint from the surrounding area down to bare metal. This will provide a rough surface for the body filler to grab

Step 3. The area should look like this when you're finished grinding

Step 4. Mix the body filler and cream hardener according to the directions

Step 5. Spread the body filler evenly over the entire area. Be sure to cover the area completely

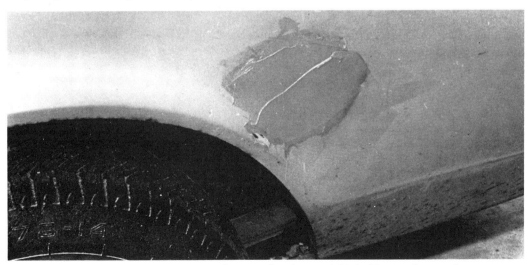

Step 6. Let the body filler dry until the surface can just be scratched with your fingernail

Step 7. Knock the high spots from the body filler with a body file

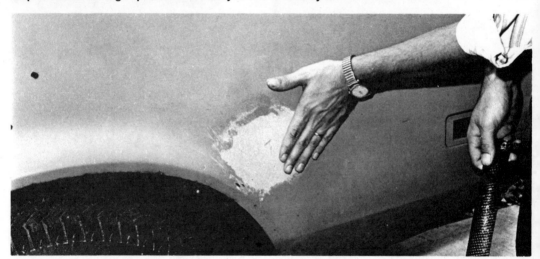

Step 8. Check frequently with the palm of your hand for high and low spots. If you wind up with low spots, you may have to apply another layer of filler

Step 9. Block sand the entire area with 320 grit paper

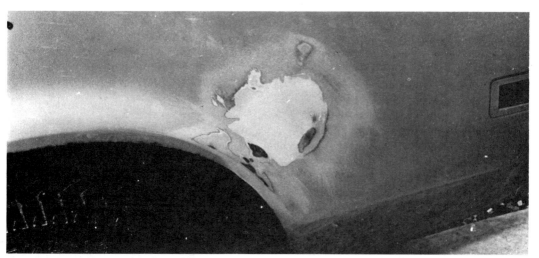

Step 10. When you're finished, the repair should look like this. Note the sand marks extending 2—3 inches out from the repaired area

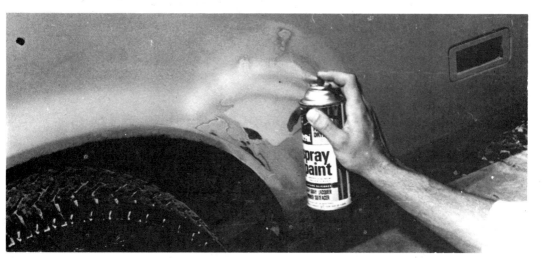

Step 11. Prime the entire area with automotive primer

Step 12. The finished repair ready for the final paint coat. Note that the primer has covered the sanding marks (see Step 10). A repair of this size should be able to be spotpainted with good results

REPAIRING RUST HOLES

One thing you have to remember about rust: even if you grind away all the rusted metal in a panel, and repair the area with any of the kits available, *eventually* the rust will return. There are two reasons for this. One, rust is a chemical reaction that causes pressure under the repair from the inside out. That's how the blisters form. Two, the back side of the panel (and the repair) is wide open to moisture, and unpainted body filler acts like a sponge. That's why the best solution to rust problems is to remove the rusted panel and install a new one or have the rusted area cut out and a new piece of sheet metal welded in its place. The trouble with welding is the expense; sometimes it will cost more than the car or truck is worth.

One of the better solutions to do-it-yourself rust repair is the process using a fiberglass cloth repair kit (shown here). This will give a strong repair that resists cracking and moisture and is relatively easy to use. It can be used on large or small holes and also can be applied over contoured surfaces.

Step 1. Rust areas such as this are common and are easily fixed

Step 2. Grind away all traces of rust with a 24-grit grinding disc. Be sure to grind back 3—4 inches from the edge of the hole down to bare metal and be sure all traces of rust are removed

Step 3. Be sure all rust is removed from the edges of the metal. The edges must be ground back to un-rusted metal

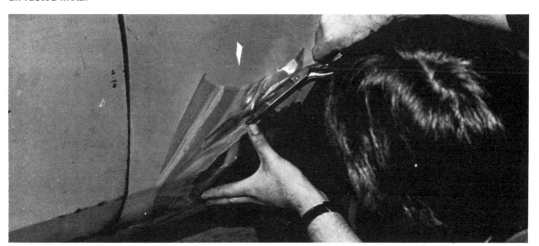

Step 4. If you are going to use release film, cut a piece about 2″ larger than the area you have sanded. Place the film over the repair and mark the sanded area on the film. Avoid any unnecessary wrinkling of the film

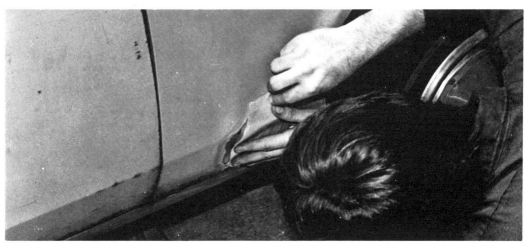

Step 5. Cut 2 pieces of fiberglass matte. One piece should be about 1″ smaller than the sanded area and the second piece should be 1″ smaller than the first. Use sharp scissors to avoid loose ends

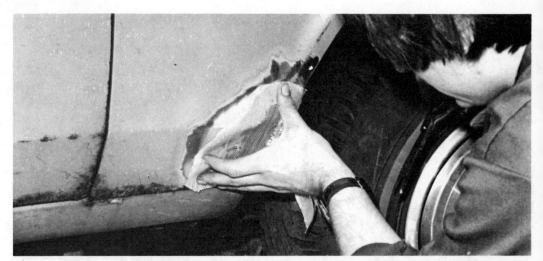

Step 6. Check the dimensions of the release film and cloth by holding them up to the repair area

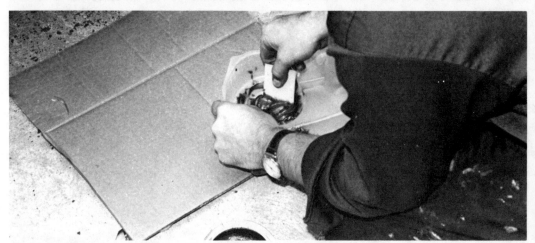

Step 7. Mix enough repair jelly and cream hardener in the mixing tray to saturate the fiberglass material or fill the repair area. Follow the directions on the container

Step 8. Lay the release sheet on a flat surface and spread an even layer of filler, large enough to cover the repair. Lay the smaller piece of fiberglass cloth in the center of the sheet and spread another layer of repair jelly over the fiberglass cloth. Repeat the operation for the larger piece of cloth. If the fiberglass cloth is not used, spread the repair jelly on the release film, concentrated in the middle of the repair

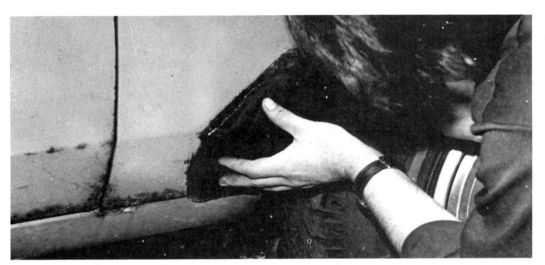

Step 9. Place the repair material over the repair area, with the release film facing outward

Step 10. Use a spreader and work from the center outward to smooth the material, following the body contours. Be sure to remove all air bubbles

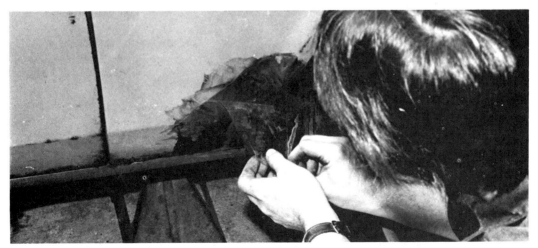

Step 11. Wait until the repair has dried tack-free and peel off the release sheet. The ideal working temperature is 65—90° F. Cooler or warmer temperatures or high humidity may require additional curing time

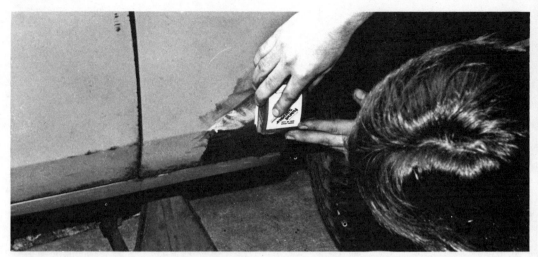

Step 12. Sand and feather-edge the entire area. The initial sanding can be done with a sanding disc on an electric drill if care is used. Finish the sanding with a block sander

Step 13. When the area is sanded smooth, mix some topcoat and hardener and apply it directly with a spreader. This will give a smooth finish and prevent the glass matte from showing through the paint

Step 14. Block sand the topcoat with finishing sandpaper

Step 15. To finish this repair, grind out the surface rust along the top edge of the rocker panel

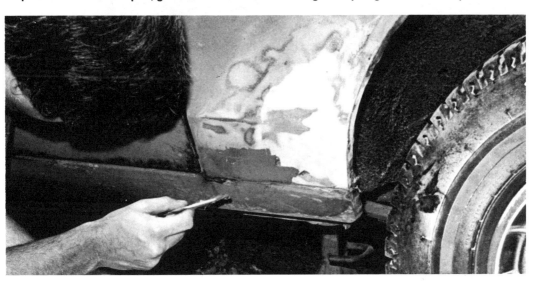

Step 16. Mix some more repair jelly and cream hardener and apply it directly over the surface

Step 17. When it dries tack-free, block sand the surface smooth

Step 18. If necessary, mask off adjacent panels and spray the entire repair with primer. You are now ready for a color coat

AUTO BODY CARE

There are hundreds—maybe thousands—of products on the market, all designed to protect or aid your car's finish in some manner. There are as many different products as there are ways to use them, but they all have one thing in common—the surface must be clean.

Washing

The primary ingredient for washing your car is water, preferably "soft" water. In many areas of the country, the local water supply is "hard" containing many minerals. The little rings or film that is left on your car's surface after it has dried is the result of "hard" water.

Since you usually can't change the local water supply, the next best thing is to dry the surface before it has a chance to dry itself.

Into the water you usually add soap. Don't use detergents or common, coarse soaps. Your car's paint never truly dries out, but is always evaporating residual oils into the air. Harsh detergents will remove these oils, causing the paint to dry faster than normal. Instead use warm water and a non-detergent soap made especially for waxed surfaces or a liquid soap made for waxed surfaces or a liquid soap made for washing dishes by hand.

Other products that can be used on painted surfaces include baking soda or plain soda water for stubborn dirt.

Wash the car completely, starting at the top, and rinse it completely clean. Abrasive grit should be loaded off under water pressure; scrubbing grit off will scratch the finish. The best washing tool is a sponge, cleaning mitt or soft towel. Whichever you choose, replace it often as each tends to absorb grease and dirt.

Other ways to get a better wash include:

• Don't wash your car in the sun or when the finish is hot.

• Use water pressure to remove caked-on dirt.

• Remove tree-sap and bird effluence immediately. Such substances will eat through wax, polish and paint.

One of the best implements to dry your car is a turkish towel or an old, soft bath towel. Anything with a deep nap will hold any dirt in suspension and not grind it into the paint.

Harder cloths will only grind the grit into the paint making more scratches. Always start drying at the top, followed by the hood and trunk and sides. You'll find there's always more dirt near the rocker panels and wheelwells which will wind up on the rest of the car if you dry these areas first.

Cleaners, Waxes and Polishes

Before going any farther you should know the function of various products.

Cleaners—remove the top layer of dead pigment or paint.

Rubbing or polishing compounds—used to remove stubborn dirt, get rid of minor scratches, smooth away imperfections and partially restore badly weathered paint.

Polishes—contain no abrasives or waxes; they shine the paint by adding oils to the paint.

Waxes—are a protective coating for the polish.

CLEANERS AND COMPOUNDS

Before you apply any wax, you'll have to remove oxidation, road film and other types of pollutants that washing alone will not remove.

The paint on your car never dries completely. There are always residual oils evaporating from the paint into the air. When enough oils are present in the paint, it has a healthy shine (gloss). When too many oils evaporate the paint takes on a whitish cast known as oxidation. The idea of polishing and waxing is to keep enough oil present in the painted surface to prevent oxidation; but when it occurs, the only recourse is to remove the top layer of "dead" paint, exposing the healthy paint underneath.

Products to remove oxidation and road film are sold under a variety of generic names—polishes, cleaner, rubbing compound, cleaner/polish, polish/cleaner, self-polishing wax, pre-wax cleaner, finish restorer and many more. Regardless of name there are two types of cleaners—abrasive cleaners (sometimes called polishing or rubbing compounds) that remove oxidation by grinding away the top layer of "dead" paint, or chemical cleaners that dissolve the "dead" pigment, allowing it to be wiped away.

Abrasive cleaners, by their nature, leave thousands of minute scratches in the finish, which must be polished out later. These should only be used in extreme cases, but are usually the only thing to use on badly oxidized paint finishes. Chemical cleaners are much milder but are not strong enough for severe cases of oxidation or weathered paint.

The most popular cleaners are liquid or paste abrasive polishing and rubbing compounds. Polishing compounds have a finer abrasive grit for medium duty work. Rubbing compounds are a coarser abrasive and for heavy duty work. Unless you are familiar with how to use compounds, be very careful. Excessive rubbing with any type of compound or cleaner can grind right through the paint to primer or bare metal. Follow the directions on the container—depending on type, the cleaner may or may not be OK for your paint. For example, some cleaners are not formulated for acrylic lacquer finishes.

When a small area needs compounding or heavy polishing, it's best to do the job by hand. Some people prefer a powered buffer for large areas. Avoid cutting through the paint along styling edges on the body. Small, hand operations where the compound is applied and rubbed using cloth folded into a thick ball allow you to work in straight lines along such edges.

To avoid cutting through on the edges when using a power buffer, try masking tape. Just cover the edge with tape while using power. Then finish the job by hand with the tape removed. Even then work carefully. The paint tends to be a lot thinner along the sharp ridges stamped into the panels.

Whether compounding by machine or by hand, only work on a small area and apply the compound sparingly. If the materials are spread too thin, or allowed to sit too long, they dry out. Once dry they lose the ability to deliver a smooth, clean finish. Also, dried out polish tends to cause the buffer to stick in one spot. This in turn can burn or cut through the finish.

WAXES AND POLISHES

Your car's finish can be protected in a number of ways. A cleaner/wax or polish/cleaner followed by wax or variations of each all provide good results. The two-step approach (polish followed by wax) is probably slightly better but consumes more time and effort. Properly fed with oils, your paint should never need cleaning, but despite the best polishing job, it won't last unless it's protected with wax. Without wax, polish must be renewed at least once a month to prevent oxidation. Years ago (some still swear by it today), the best wax was made from the Brazilian palm, the Carnuba, favored for its vegetable base and high melting point. However, modern synthetic waxes are harder, which means they protect against moisture better, and chemically inert silicone is used for a long lasting protection. The only problem with silicone wax is that it penetrates all layers of paint. To repaint or touch up a panel or car protected by silicone wax, you have to completely strip the finish to avoid "fish-eyes."

Under normal conditions, silicone waxes will last 4–6 months, but you have to be careful of wax build-up from too much waxing. Too thick a coat of wax is just as bad as no wax at all; it stops the paint from breathing.

Combination cleaners/waxes have become popular lately because they remove the old layer of wax plus light oxidation, while putting on a fresh coat of wax at the same time. Some cleaners/waxes contain abrasive cleaners which require caution, although many cleaner/waxes use a chemical cleaner.

Applying Wax or Polish

You may view polishing and waxing your car as a pleasant way to spend an afternoon, or as a boring chore, but it has to be done to keep the paint on your car. Caring for the paint doesn't require special tools, but you should follow a few rules.

1. Use a good quality wax.

2. Before applying any wax or polish, be sure the surface is completely clean. Just because the car looks clean, doesn't mean it's ready for polish or wax.

3. If the finish on your car is weathered, dull, or oxidized, it will probably have to be compounded to remove the old or oxidized paint. If the paint is simply dulled from lack of care, one of the non-abrasive cleaners known as polishing compounds will do the trick. If the paint is severely scratched or really dull, you'll probably have to use a rubbing compound to prepare the finish for waxing. If you're not sure which one to use, use the polishing compound, since you can easily ruin the finish by using too strong a compound.

4. Don't apply wax, polish or compound in direct sunlight, even if the directions on the can say you can. Most waxes will not cure properly in bright sunlight and you'll probably end up with a blotchy looking finish.

5. Don't rub the wax off too soon. The result will be a wet, dull looking finish. Let the wax dry thoroughly before buffing it off.

6. A constant debate among car enthusiasts is how wax should be applied. Some maintain pastes or liquids should be applied in a circular motion, but body shop experts have long thought that this approach results in barely detectable circular abrasions, especially on cars that are waxed frequently. They advise rubbing in straight lines, especially if any kind of cleaner is involved.

7. If an applicator is not supplied with the wax, use a piece of soft cheesecloth or very soft lint-free material. The same applies to buffing the surface.

SPECIAL SURFACES

One-step combination cleaner and wax formulas shouldn't be used on many of the special surfaces which abound on cars. The one-step materials contain abrasives to achieve a clean surface under the wax top coat. The abrasives are so mild that you could clean a car every week for a couple of years without fear of rubbing through the paint. But this same level of abrasiveness might, through repeated use, damage decals used for special trim effects. This includes wide stripes, wood-grain trim and other appliques.

Painted plastics must be cleaned with care. If a cleaner is too aggressive it will cut through the paint and expose the primer. If bright trim such as polished aluminum or chrome is painted, cleaning must be performed with even greater care. If rubbing compound is being used, it will cut faster than polish.

Abrasive cleaners will dull an acrylic finish. The best way to clean these newer finishes is with a non-abrasive liquid polish. Only dirt and oxidation, not paint, will be removed.

Taking a few minutes to read the instructions on the can of polish or wax will help prevent making serious mistakes. Not all preparations will work on all surfaces. And some are intended for power application while others will only work when applied by hand.

Don't get the idea that just pouring on some polish and then hitting it with a buffer will suffice. Power equipment speeds the operation. But it also adds a measure of risk. It's very easy to damage the finish if you use the wrong methods or materials.

Caring for Chrome

Read the label on the container. Many products are formulated specifically for chrome, but others contain abrasives that will scratch the chrome finish. If it isn't recommended for chrome, don't use it.

Never use steel wool or kitchen soap pads to clean chrome. Be careful not to get chrome cleaner on paint or interior vinyl surfaces. If you do, get it off immediately.

Troubleshooting

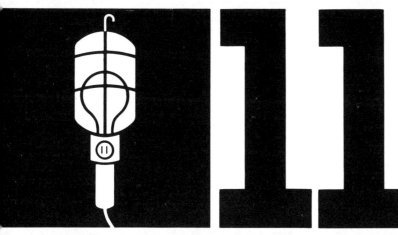

This section is designed to aid in the quick, accurate diagnosis of automotive problems. While automotive repairs can be made by many people, accurate troubleshooting is a rare skill for the amateur and professional alike.

In its simplest state, troubleshooting is an exercise in logic. It is essential to realize that an automobile is really composed of a series of systems. Some of these systems are interrelated; others are not. Automobiles operate within a framework of logical rules and physical laws, and the key to troubleshooting is a good understanding of all the automotive systems.

This section breaks the car or truck down into its component systems, allowing the problem to be isolated. The charts and diagnostic road maps list the most common problems and the most probable causes of trouble. Obviously it would be impossible to list every possible problem that could happen along with every possible cause, but it will locate MOST problems and eliminate a lot of unnecessary guesswork. The systematic format will locate problems within a given system, but, because many automotive systems are interrelated, the solution to your particular problem may be found in a number of systems on the car or truck.

USING THE TROUBLESHOOTING CHARTS

This book contains all of the specific information that the average do-it-yourself mechanic needs to repair and maintain his or her car or truck. The troubleshooting charts are designed to be used in conjunction with the specific procedures and information in the text. For instance, troubleshooting a point-type ignition system is fairly standard for all models, but you may be directed to the text to find procedures for troubleshooting an individual type of electronic ignition. You will also have to refer to the specification charts throughout the book for specifications applicable to your car or truck.

TOOLS AND EQUIPMENT

The tools illustrated in Chapter 1 (plus two more diagnostic pieces) will be adequate to troubleshoot most problems. The two other tools needed are a voltmeter and an ohmmeter. These can be purchased separately or in combination, known as a VOM meter.

In the event that other tools are required, they will be noted in the procedures.

256　TROUBLESHOOTING

Troubleshooting Engine Problems
See Chapters 2, 3, 4 for more information and service procedures.

Index to Systems

System	To Test	Group
Battery	Engine need not be running	1
Starting system	Engine need not be running	2
Primary electrical system	Engine need not be running	3
Secondary electrical system	Engine need not be running	4
Fuel system	Engine need not be running	5
Engine compression	Engine need not be running	6
Engine vacuum	Engine must be running	7
Secondary electrical system	Engine must be running	8
Valve train	Engine must be running	9
Exhaust system	Engine must be running	10
Cooling system	Engine must be running	11
Engine lubrication	Engine must be running	12

Index to Problems

Problem: Symptom	Begin at Specific Diagnosis, Number ____
Engine Won't Start:	
Starter doesn't turn	1.1, 2.1
Starter turns, engine doesn't	2.1
Starter turns engine very slowly	1.1, 2.4
Starter turns engine normally	3.1, 4.1
Starter turns engine very quickly	6.1
Engine fires intermittently	4.1
Engine fires consistently	5.1, 6.1
Engine Runs Poorly:	
Hard starting	3.1, 4.1, 5.1, 8.1
Rough idle	4.1, 5.1, 8.1
Stalling	3.1, 4.1, 5.1, 8.1
Engine dies at high speeds	4.1, 5.1
Hesitation (on acceleration from standing stop)	5.1, 8.1
Poor pickup	4.1, 5.1, 8.1
Lack of power	3.1, 4.1, 5.1, 8.1
Backfire through the carburetor	4.1, 8.1, 9.1
Backfire through the exhaust	4.1, 8.1, 9.1
Blue exhaust gases	6.1, 7.1
Black exhaust gases	5.1
Running on (after the ignition is shut off)	3.1, 8.1
Susceptible to moisture	4.1
Engine misfires under load	4.1, 7.1, 8.4, 9.1
Engine misfires at speed	4.1, 8.4
Engine misfires at idle	3.1, 4.1, 5.1, 7.1, 8.4

Sample Section

Test and Procedure	Results and Indications	Proceed to
4.1—Check for spark: Hold each spark plug wire approximately ¼" from ground with gloves or a heavy, dry rag. Crank the engine and observe the spark.	→ If no spark is evident:	→ **4.2**
	→ If spark is good in some cases:	→ **4.3**
	→ If spark is good in all cases:	→ **4.6**

Specific Diagnosis

This section is arranged so that following each test, instructions are given to proceed to another, until a problem is diagnosed.

Section 1—Battery

Test and Procedure	Results and Indications	Proceed to
1.1—Inspect the battery visually for case condition (corrosion, cracks) and water level.	If case is cracked, replace battery:	**1.4**
	If the case is intact, remove corrosion with a solution of baking soda and water (**CAUTION**: *do not get the solution into the battery*), and fill with water:	**1.2**

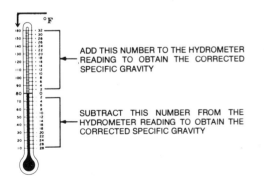

DIRT ON TOP OF BATTERY
PLUGGED VENT
CORROSION
LOOSE CABLE OR POSTS
CRACKS
LOW WATER LEVEL

Inspect the battery case

Test and Procedure	Results and Indications	Proceed to
1.2—Check the battery cable connections: Insert a screwdriver between the battery post and the cable clamp. Turn the headlights on high beam, and observe them as the screwdriver is gently twisted to ensure good metal to metal contact.	If the lights brighten, remove and clean the clamp and post; coat the post with petroleum jelly, install and tighten the clamp:	**1.4**
	If no improvement is noted:	**1.3**

TESTING BATTERY CABLE CONNECTIONS USING A SCREWDRIVER

Test and Procedure	Results and Indications	Proceed to
1.3—Test the state of charge of the battery using an individual cell tester or hydrometer.	If indicated, charge the battery. **NOTE**: *If no obvious reason exists for the low state of charge (i.e., battery age, prolonged storage), proceed to:*	**1.4**

°F

ADD THIS NUMBER TO THE HYDROMETER READING TO OBTAIN THE CORRECTED SPECIFIC GRAVITY

SUBTRACT THIS NUMBER FROM THE HYDROMETER READING TO OBTAIN THE CORRECTED SPECIFIC GRAVITY

Specific Gravity (@ 80° F.)

Minimum		Battery Charge
1.260	....	100% Charged
1.230	....	75% Charged
1.200	....	50% Charged
1.170	....	25% Charged
1.140	....	Very Little Power Left
1.110	....	Completely Discharged

The effects of temperature on battery specific gravity (left) and amount of battery charge in relation to specific gravity (right)

Test and Procedure	Results and Indications	Proceed to
1.4—Visually inspect battery cables for cracking, bad connection to ground, or bad connection to starter.	If necessary, tighten connections or replace the cables:	**2.1**

Section 2—Starting System
See Chapter 3 for service procedures

Test and Procedure	Results and Indications	Proceed to

Note: Tests in Group 2 are performed with coil high tension lead disconnected to prevent accidental starting.

2.1—Test the starter motor and solenoid: Connect a jumper from the battery post of the solenoid (or relay) to the starter post of the solenoid (or relay).

If starter turns the engine normally: — **2.2**

If the starter buzzes, or turns the engine very slowly: — **2.4**

If no response, replace the solenoid (or relay). — **3.1**

If the starter turns, but the engine doesn't, ensure that the flywheel ring gear is intact. If the gear is undamaged, replace the starter drive. — **3.1**

2.2—Determine whether ignition override switches are functioning properly (clutch start switch, neutral safety switch), by connecting a jumper across the switch(es), and turning the ignition switch to "start".

If starter operates, adjust or replace switch: — **3.1**

If the starter doesn't operate: — **2.3**

2.3—Check the ignition switch "start" position: Connect a 12V test lamp or voltmeter between the starter post of the solenoid (or relay) and ground. Turn the ignition switch to the "start" position, and jiggle the key.

If the lamp doesn't light or the meter needle doesn't move when the switch is turned, check the ignition switch for loose connections, cracked insulation, or broken wires. Repair or replace as necessary: — **3.1**

If the lamp flickers or needle moves when the key is jiggled, replace the ignition switch. — **3.3**

Checking the ignition switch "start" position

STARTER RELAY
(IF EQUIPPED)

2.4—Remove and bench test the starter, according to specifications in the engine electrical section.

If the starter does not meet specifications, repair or replace as needed: — **3.1**

If the starter is operating properly: — **2.5**

2.5—Determine whether the engine can turn freely: Remove the spark plugs, and check for water in the cylinders. Check for water on the dipstick, or oil in the radiator. Attempt to turn the engine using an 18″ flex drive and socket on the crankshaft pulley nut or bolt.

If the engine will turn freely only with the spark plugs out, and hydrostatic lock (water in the cylinders) is ruled out, check valve timing: — **9.2**

If engine will not turn freely, and it is known that the clutch and transmission are free, the engine must be disassembled for further evaluation: — **Chapter 3**

Section 3—Primary Electrical System

Test and Procedure	Results and Indications	Proceed to
3.1—Check the ignition switch "on" position: Connect a jumper wire between the distributor side of the coil and ground, and a 12V test lamp between the switch side of the coil and ground. Remove the high tension lead from the coil. Turn the ignition switch on and jiggle the key.	If the lamp lights:	**3.2**
	If the lamp flickers when the key is jiggled, replace the ignition switch:	**3.3**
	If the lamp doesn't light, check for loose or open connections. If none are found, remove the ignition switch and check for continuity. If the switch is faulty, replace it:	**3.3**

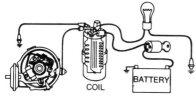

Checking the ignition switch "on" position

3.2—Check the ballast resistor or resistance wire for an open circuit, using an ohmmeter. See Chapter 3 for specific tests.	Replace the resistor or resistance wire if the resistance is zero. **NOTE:** *Some ignition systems have no ballast resistor.*	**3.3**

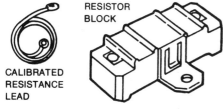

Two types of resistors

3.3—On point-type ignition systems, visually inspect the breaker points for burning, pitting or excessive wear. Gray coloring of the point contact surfaces is normal. Rotate the crankshaft until the contact heel rests on a high point of the distributor cam and adjust the point gap to specifications. On electronic ignition models, remove the distributor cap and visually inspect the armature. Ensure that the armature pin is in place, and that the armature is on tight and rotates when the engine is cranked. Make sure there are no cracks, chips or rounded edges on the armature.	If the breaker points are intact, clean the contact surfaces with fine emery cloth, and adjust the point gap to specifications. If the points are worn, replace them. On electronic systems, replace any parts which appear defective. If condition persists:	**3.4**

Test and Procedure	Results and Indications	Proceed to
3.4—On point-type ignition systems, connect a dwell-meter between the distributor primary lead and ground. Crank the engine and observe the point dwell angle. On electronic ignition systems, conduct a stator (magnetic pickup assembly) test. See Chapter 3.	On point-type systems, adjust the dwell angle if necessary. **NOTE:** *Increasing the point gap decreases the dwell angle and vice-versa.*	**3.6**
	If the dwell meter shows little or no reading;	**3.5**
	On electronic ignition systems, if the stator is bad, replace the stator. If the stator is good, proceed to the other tests in Chapter 3.	

CLOSE   OPEN
NORMAL DWELL

WIDE GAP
SMALL DWELL
INSUFFICIENT DWELL

NARROW GAP
LARGE DWELL
EXCESSIVE DWELL

Dwell is a function of point gap

3.5—On the point-type ignition systems, check the condenser for short: connect an ohmeter across the condenser body and the pigtail lead.	If any reading other than infinite is noted, replace the condenser	**3.6**

OHMMETER

Checking the condenser for short

3.6—Test the coil primary resistance: On point-type ignition systems, connect an ohmmeter across the coil primary terminals, and read the resistance on the low scale. Note whether an external ballast resistor or resistance wire is used. On electronic ignition systems, test the coil primary resistance as in Chapter 3.	Point-type ignition coils utilizing ballast resistors or resistance wires should have approximately 1.0 ohms resistance. Coils with internal resistors should have approximately 4.0 ohms resistance. If values far from the above are noted, replace the coil.	**4.1**

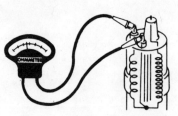

OHMMETER

Check the coil primary resistance

Section 4—Secondary Electrical System
See Chapters 2–3 for service procedures

Test and Procedure	Results and Indications	Proceed to
4.1—Check for spark: Hold each spark plug wire approximately ¼" from ground with gloves or a heavy, dry rag. Crank the engine, and observe the spark.	If no spark is evident:	**4.2**
	If spark is good in some cylinders:	**4.3**
	If spark is good in all cylinders:	**4.6**

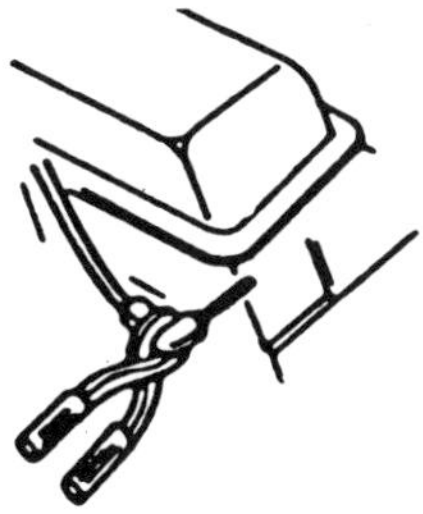

Check for spark at the plugs

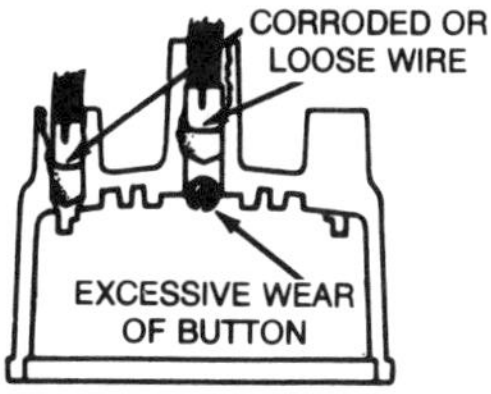

4.2—Check for spark at the coil high tension lead: Remove the coil high tension lead from the distributor and position it approximately ¼" from ground. Crank the engine and observe spark. **CAUTION:** *This test should not be performed on engines equipped with electronic ignition.*	If the spark is good and consistent:	**4.3**
	If the spark is good but intermittent, test the primary electrical system starting at 3.3:	**3.3**
	If the spark is weak or non-existent, replace the coil high tension lead, clean and tighten all connections and retest. If no improvement is noted:	**4.4**
4.3—Visually inspect the distributor cap and rotor for burned or corroded contacts, cracks, carbon tracks, or moisture. Also check the fit of the rotor on the distributor shaft (where applicable).	If moisture is present, dry thoroughly, and retest per 4.1:	**4.1**
	If burned or excessively corroded contacts, cracks, or carbon tracks are noted, replace the defective part(s) and retest per 4.1:	**4.1**
	If the rotor and cap appear intact, or are only slightly corroded, clean the contacts thoroughly (including the cap towers and spark plug wire ends) and retest per 4.1:	
	If the spark is good in all cases:	**4.6**
	If the spark is poor in all cases:	**4.5**

CORRODED OR LOOSE WIRE

EXCESSIVE WEAR OF BUTTON

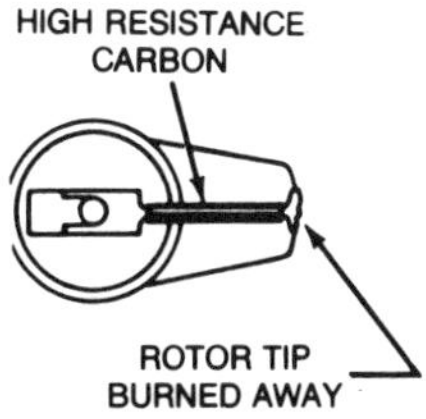

HIGH RESISTANCE CARBON

ROTOR TIP BURNED AWAY

Inspect the distributor cap and rotor

Test and Procedure	*Results and Indications*	*Proceed to*
4.4—Check the coil secondary resistance: On point-type systems connect an ohmmeter across the distributor side of the coil and the coil tower. Read the resistance on the high scale of the ohmmeter. On electronic ignition systems, see Chapter 3 for specific tests.	The resistance of a satisfactory coil should be between 4,000 and 10,000 ohms. If resistance is considerably higher (i.e., 40,000 ohms) replace the coil and retest per 4.1. **NOTE:** *This does not apply to high performance coils.*	

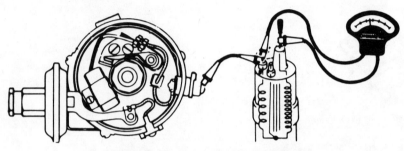

Testing the coil secondary resistance

4.5—Visually inspect the spark plug wires for cracking or brittleness. Ensure that no two wires are positioned so as to cause induction firing (adjacent and parallel). Remove each wire, one by one, and check resistance with an ohmmeter.	Replace any cracked or brittle wires. If any of the wires are defective, replace the entire set. Replace any wires with excessive resistance (over $8000\,\Omega$ per foot for suppression wire), and separate any wires that might cause induction firing.	4.6

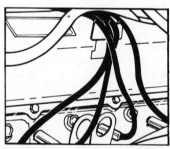

Misfiring can be the result of spark plug leads to adjacent, consecutively firing cylinders running parallel and too close together

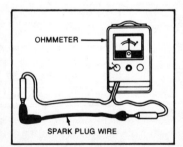

On point-type ignition systems, check the spark plug wires as shown. On electronic ignitions, do not remove the wire from the distributor cap terminal; instead, test through the cap

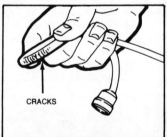

Spark plug wires can be checked visually by bending them in a loop over your finger. This will reveal any cracks, burned or broken insulation. Any wire with cracked insulation should be replaced

4.6—Remove the spark plugs, noting the cylinders from which they were removed, and evaluate according to the color photos in the middle of this book.	See following.	**See following.**

est and Procedure	Results and Indications	Proceed to

4.7—Examine the location of all the plugs.

The following diagrams illustrate some of the conditions that the location of plugs will reveal.

4.8

Two adjacent plugs are fouled in a 6-cylinder engine, 4-cylinder engine or either bank of a V-8. This is probably due to a blown head gasket between the two cylinders

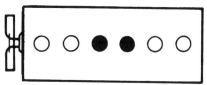

The two center plugs in a 6-cylinder engine are fouled. Raw fuel may be "boiled" out of the carburetor into the intake manifold after the engine is shut-off. Stop-start driving can also foul the center plugs, due to overly rich mixture. Proper float level, a new float needle and seat or use of an insulating spacer may help this problem

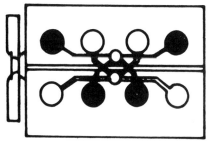

An unbalanced carburetor is indicated. Following the fuel flow on this particular design shows that the cylinders fed by the right-hand barrel are fouled from overly rich mixture, while the cylinders fed by the left-hand barrel are normal

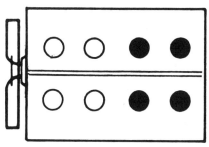

If the four rear plugs are overheated, a cooling system problem is suggested. A thorough cleaning of the cooling system may restore coolant circulation and cure the problem

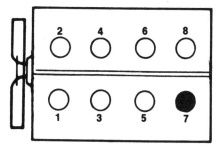

Finding one plug overheated may indicate an intake manifold leak near the affected cylinder. If the overheated plug is the second of two adjacent, consecutively firing plugs, it could be the result of ignition cross-firing. Separating the leads to these two plugs will eliminate cross-fire

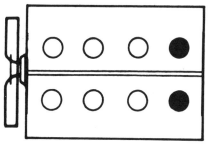

Occasionally, the two rear plugs in large, lightly used V-8's will become oil fouled. High oil consumption and smoky exhaust may also be noticed. It is probably due to plugged oil drain holes in the rear of the cylinder head, causing oil to be sucked in around the valve stems. This usually occurs in the rear cylinders first, because the engine slants that way

Test and Procedure	Results and Indications	Proceed to
4.8—Determine the static ignition timing. Using the crankshaft pulley timing marks as a guide, locate top dead center on the compression stroke of the number one cylinder.	The rotor should be pointing toward the No. 1 tower in the distributor cap, and, on electronic ignitions, the armature spoke for that cylinder should be lined up with the stator.	**4.8**
4.9—Check coil polarity: Connect a voltmeter negative lead to the coil high tension lead, and the positive lead to ground (**NOTE:** *Reverse the hook-up for positive ground systems*). Crank the engine momentarily. **Checking coil polarity**	If the voltmeter reads up-scale, the polarity is correct: If the voltmeter reads down-scale, reverse the coil polarity (switch the primary leads):	**5.1** **5.1**

Section 5—Fuel System
See Chapter 4 for service procedures

Test and Procedure	Results and Indications	Proceed to
5.1—Determine that the air filter is functioning efficiently: Hold paper elements up to a strong light, and attempt to see light through the filter.	Clean permanent air filters in solvent (or manufacturer's recommendation), and allow to dry. Replace paper elements through which light cannot be seen:	**5.2**
5.2—Determine whether a flooding condition exists: Flooding is identified by a strong gasoline odor, and excessive gasoline present in the throttle bore(s) of the carburetor.	If flooding is not evident: If flooding is evident, permit the gasoline to dry for a few moments and restart. If flooding doesn't recur: If flooding is persistent:	**5.3** **5.7** **5.5**

If the engine floods repeatedly, check the choke butterfly flap

Test and Procedure	Results and Indications	Proceed to
5.3—Check that fuel is reaching the carburetor: Detach the fuel line at the carburetor inlet. Hold the end of the line in a cup (not styrofoam), and crank the engine.	If fuel flows smoothly: If fuel doesn't flow (**NOTE:** *Make sure that there is fuel in the tank*), or flows erratically:	**5.7** **5.4**

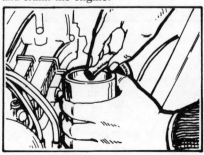

Check the fuel pump by disconnecting the output line (fuel pump-to-carburetor) at the carburetor and operating the starter briefly

Test and Procedure	Results and Indications	Proceed to
5.4—Test the fuel pump: Disconnect all fuel lines from the fuel pump. Hold a finger over the input fitting, crank the engine (with electric pump, turn the ignition or pump on); and feel for suction.	If suction is evident, blow out the fuel line to the tank with low pressure compressed air until bubbling is heard from the fuel filler neck. Also blow out the carburetor fuel line (both ends disconnected):	**5.7**
	If no suction is evident, replace or repair the fuel pump: **NOTE:** *Repeated oil fouling of the spark plugs, or a no-start condition, could be the result of a ruptured vacuum booster pump diaphragm, through which oil or gasoline is being drawn into the intake manifold (where applicable).*	**5.7**
5.5—Occasionally, small specks of dirt will clog the small jets and orifices in the carburetor. With the engine cold, hold a flat piece of wood or similar material over the carburetor, where possible, and crank the engine.	If the engine starts, but runs roughly the engine is probably not run enough. If the engine won't start:	**5.9**
5.6—Check the needle and seat: Tap the carburetor in the area of the needle and seat.	If flooding stops, a gasoline additive (e.g., Gumout) will often cure the problem:	**5.7**
	If flooding continues, check the fuel pump for excessive pressure at the carburetor (according to specifications). If the pressure is normal, the needle and seat must be removed and checked, and/or the float level adjusted:	**5.7**
5.7—Test the accelerator pump by looking into the throttle bores while operating the throttle.	If the accelerator pump appears to be operating normally:	**5.8**
	If the accelerator pump is not operating, the pump must be reconditioned. Where possible, service the pump with the carburetor(s) installed on the engine. If necessary, remove the carburetor. Prior to removal:	**5.8**

Check for gas at the carburetor by looking down the carburetor throat while someone moves the accelerator

Test and Procedure	Results and Indications	Proceed to
5.8—Determine whether the carburetor main fuel system is functioning: Spray a commercial starting fluid into the carburetor while attempting to start the engine.	If the engine starts, runs for a few seconds, and dies:	**5.9**
	If the engine doesn't start:	**6.1**

Test and Procedure	Results and Indications	Proceed to
5.9—Uncommon fuel system malfunctions: See below:	If the problem is solved:	**6.1**
	If the problem remains, remove and recondition the carburetor.	

Condition	Indication	Test	Prevailing Weather Conditions	Remedy
Vapor lock	Engine will not restart shortly after running.	Cool the components of the fuel system until the engine starts. Vapor lock can be cured faster by draping a wet cloth over a mechanical fuel pump.	Hot to very hot	Ensure that the exhaust manifold heat control valve is operating. Check with the vehicle manufacturer for the recommended solution to vapor lock on the model in question.
Carburetor icing	Engine will not idle, stalls at low speeds.	Visually inspect the throttle plate area of the throttle bores for frost.	High humidity, 32–40° F.	Ensure that the exhaust manifold heat control valve is operating, and that the intake manifold heat riser is not blocked.
Water in the fuel	Engine sputters and stalls; may not start.	Pump a small amount of fuel into a glass jar. Allow to stand, and inspect for droplets or a layer of water.	High humidity, extreme temperature changes.	For droplets, use one or two cans of commercial gas line anti-freeze. For a layer of water, the tank must be drained, and the fuel lines blown out with compressed air.

Section 6—Engine Compression
See Chapter 3 for service procedures

6.1—Test engine compression: Remove all spark plugs. Block the throttle wide open. Insert a compression gauge into a spark plug port, crank the engine to obtain the maximum reading, and record.	If compression is within limits on all cylinders:	**7.1**
	If gauge reading is extremely low on all cylinders:	**6.2**
	If gauge reading is low on one or two cylinders: (If gauge readings are identical and low on two or more adjacent cylinders, the head gasket must be replaced.)	**6.2**

Checking compression

6.2—Test engine compression (wet): Squirt approximately 30 cc. of engine oil into each cylinder, and retest per 6.1.	If the readings improve, worn or cracked rings or broken pistons are indicated:	**See Chapter 3**
	If the readings do not improve, burned or excessively carboned valves or a jumped timing chain are indicated: NOTE: *A jumped timing chain is often indicated by difficult cranking.*	**7.1**

Section 7—Engine Vacuum

See Chapter 3 for service procedures

Test and Procedure	Results and Indications	Proceed to
7.1—Attach a vacuum gauge to the intake manifold beyond the throttle plate. Start the engine, and observe the action of the needle over the range of engine speeds.	See below.	**See below**

INDICATION: normal engine in good condition

Proceed to: 8.1

Normal engine
Gauge reading: steady, from 17–22 in./Hg.

INDICATION: sticking valves or ignition miss

Proceed to: 9.1, 8.3

Sticking valves
Gauge reading: intermittent fluctuation at idle

INDICATION: late ignition or valve timing, low compression, stuck throttle valve, leaking carburetor or manifold gasket

Proceed to: 6.1

Incorrect valve timing
Gauge reading: low (10–15 in./Hg) but steady

INDICATION: improper carburetor adjustment or minor intake leak.

Proceed to: 7.2

Carburetor requires adjustment
Gauge reading: drifting needle

INDICATION: ignition miss, blown cylinder head gasket, leaking valve or weak valve spring

Proceed to: 8.3, 6.1

Blown head gasket
Gauge reading: needle fluctuates as engine speed increases

INDICATION: burnt valve or faulty valve clearance. Needle will fall when defective valve operates

Proceed to: 9.1

Burnt or leaking valves
Gauge reading: steady needle, but drops regularly

INDICATION: choked muffler, excessive back pressure in system

Proceed to: 10.1

Clogged exhaust system
Gauge reading: gradual drop in reading at idle

INDICATION: worn valve guides

Proceed to: 9.1

Worn valve guides
Gauge reading: needle vibrates excessively at idle, but steadies as engine speed increases

White pointer = steady gauge hand

Black pointer = fluctuating gauge hand

Test and Procedure	Results and Indications	Proceed to
7.2—Attach a vacuum gauge per 7.1, and test for an intake manifold leak. Squirt a small amount of oil around the intake manifold gaskets, carburetor gaskets, plugs and fittings. Observe the action of the vacuum gauge.	If the reading improves, replace the indicated gasket, or seal the indicated fitting or plug: If the reading remains low:	**8.1** **7.3**
7.3—Test all vacuum hoses and accessories for leaks as described in 7.2. Also check the carburetor body (dashpots, automatic choke mechanism, throttle shafts) for leaks in the same manner.	If the reading improves, service or replace the offending part(s): If the reading remains low:	**8.1** **6.1**

Section 8—Secondary Electrical System
See Chapter 2 for service procedures

Test and Procedure	Results and Indications	Proceed to
8.1—Remove the distributor cap and check to make sure that the rotor turns when the engine is cranked. Visually inspect the distributor components.	Clean, tighten or replace any components which appear defective.	**8.2**
8.2—Connect a timing light (per manufacturer's recommendation) and check the dynamic ignition timing. Disconnect and plug the vacuum hose(s) to the distributor if specified, start the engine, and observe the timing marks at the specified engine speed.	If the timing is not correct, adjust to specifications by rotating the distributor in the engine: (Advance timing by rotating distributor opposite normal direction of rotor rotation, retard timing by rotating distributor in same direction as rotor rotation.)	**8.3**
8.3—Check the operation of the distributor advance mechanism(s): To test the mechanical advance, disconnect the vacuum lines from the distributor advance unit and observe the timing marks with a timing light as the engine speed is increased from idle. If the mark moves smoothly, without hesitation, it may be assumed that the mechanical advance is functioning properly. To test vacuum advance and/or retard systems, alternately crimp and release the vacuum line, and observe the timing mark for movement. If movement is noted, the system is operating.	If the systems are functioning: If the systems are not functioning, remove the distributor, and test on a distributor tester:	**8.4** **8.4**
8.4—Locate an ignition miss: With the engine running, remove each spark plug wire, one at a time, until one is found that doesn't cause the engine to roughen and slow down.	When the missing cylinder is identified:	**4.1**

Section 9—Valve Train
See Chapter 3 for service procedures

Test and Procedure	Results and Indications	Proceed to
9.1—Evaluate the valve train: Remove the valve cover, and ensure that the valves are adjusted to specifications. A mechanic's stethoscope may be used to aid in the diagnosis of the valve train. By pushing the probe on or near push rods or rockers, valve noise often can be isolated. A timing light also may be used to diagnose valve problems. Connect the light according to manufacturer's recommendations, and start the engine. Vary the firing moment of the light by increasing the engine speed (and therefore the ignition advance), and moving the trigger from cylinder to cylinder. Observe the movement of each valve.	Sticking valves or erratic valve train motion can be observed with the timing light. The cylinder head must be disassembled for repairs.	**See Chapter 3**
9.2—Check the valve timing: Locate top dead center of the No. 1 piston, and install a degree wheel or tape on the crankshaft pulley or damper with zero corresponding to an index mark on the engine. Rotate the crankshaft in its direction of rotation, and observe the opening of the No. 1 cylinder intake valve. The opening should correspond with the correct mark on the degree wheel according to specifications.	If the timing is not correct, the timing cover must be removed for further investigation.	**See Chapter 3**

Section 10—Exhaust System

Test and Procedure	Results and Indications	Proceed to
10.1—Determine whether the exhaust manifold heat control valve is operating: Operate the valve by hand to determine whether it is free to move. If the valve is free, run the engine to operating temperature and observe the action of the valve, to ensure that it is opening.	If the valve sticks, spray it with a suitable solvent, open and close the valve to free it, and retest.	
	If the valve functions properly:	**10.2**
	If the valve does not free, or does not operate, replace the valve:	**10.2**
10.2—Ensure that there are no exhaust restrictions: Visually inspect the exhaust system for kinks, dents, or crushing. Also note that gases are flowing freely from the tailpipe at all engine speeds, indicating no restriction in the muffler or resonator.	Replace any damaged portion of the system:	**11.1**

Section 11—Cooling System
See Chapter 3 for service procedures

Test and Procedure	Results and Indications	Proceed to
11.1—Visually inspect the fan belt for glazing, cracks, and fraying, and replace if necessary. Tighten the belt so that the longest span has approximately ½″ play at its midpoint under thumb pressure (see Chapter 1).	Replace or tighten the fan belt as necessary:	**11.2**

Checking belt tension

11.2—Check the fluid level of the cooling system.	If full or slightly low, fill as necessary:	**11.5**
	If extremely low:	**11.3**
11.3—Visually inspect the external portions of the cooling system (radiator, radiator hoses, thermostat elbow, water pump seals, heater hoses, etc.) for leaks. If none are found, pressurize the cooling system to 14–15 psi.	If cooling system holds the pressure:	**11.5**
	If cooling system loses pressure rapidly, reinspect external parts of the system for leaks under pressure. If none are found, check dipstick for coolant in crankcase. If no coolant is present, but pressure loss continues:	**11.4**
	If coolant is evident in crankcase, remove cylinder head(s), and check gasket(s). If gaskets are intact, block and cylinder head(s) should be checked for cracks or holes. If the gasket(s) is blown, replace, and purge the crankcase of coolant:	**12.6**
	NOTE: *Occasionally, due to atmospheric and driving conditions, condensation of water can occur in the crankcase. This causes the oil to appear milky white. To remedy, run the engine until hot, and change the oil and oil filter.*	
11.4—Check for combustion leaks into the cooling system: Pressurize the cooling system as above. Start the engine, and observe the pressure gauge. If the needle fluctuates, remove each spark plug wire, one at a time, noting which cylinder(s) reduce or eliminate the fluctuation.	Cylinders which reduce or eliminate the fluctuation, when the spark plug wire is removed, are leaking into the cooling system. Replace the head gasket on the affected cylinder bank(s).	

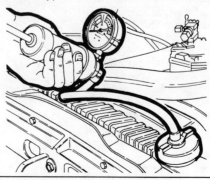

Pressurizing the cooling system

Test and Procedure	Results and Indications	Proceed to
11.5—Check the radiator pressure cap: Attach a radiator pressure tester to the radiator cap (wet the seal prior to installation). Quickly pump up the pressure, noting the point at which the cap releases.	If the cap releases within ± 1 psi of the specified rating, it is operating properly:	**11.6**
	If the cap releases at more than ± 1 psi of the specified rating, it should be replaced:	**11.6**

Checking radiator pressure cap

Test and Procedure	Results and Indications	Proceed to
11.6—Test the thermostat: Start the engine cold, remove the radiator cap, and insert a thermometer into the radiator. Allow the engine to idle. After a short while, there will be a sudden, rapid increase in coolant temperature. The temperature at which this sharp rise stops is the thermostat opening temperature.	If the thermostat opens at or about the specified temperature:	**11.7**
	If the temperature doesn't increase: (If the temperature increases slowly and gradually, replace the thermostat.)	**11.7**
11.7—Check the water pump: Remove the thermostat elbow and the thermostat, disconnect the coil high tension lead (to prevent starting), and crank the engine momentarily.	If coolant flows, replace the thermostat and retest per 11.6:	**11.6**
	If coolant doesn't flow, reverse flush the cooling system to alleviate any blockage that might exist. If system is not blocked, and coolant will not flow, replace the water pump.	

Section 12—Lubrication
See Chapter 3 for service procedures

Test and Procedure	Results and Indications	Proceed to
12.1—Check the oil pressure gauge or warning light: If the gauge shows low pressure, or the light is on for no obvious reason, remove the oil pressure sender. Install an accurate oil pressure gauge and run the engine momentarily.	If oil pressure builds normally, run engine for a few moments to determine that it is functioning normally, and replace the sender.	—
	If the pressure remains low:	**12.2**
	If the pressure surges:	**12.3**
	If the oil pressure is zero:	**12.3**
12.2—Visually inspect the oil: If the oil is watery or very thin, milky, or foamy, replace the oil and oil filter.	If the oil is normal:	**12.3**
	If after replacing oil the pressure remains low:	**12.3**
	If after replacing oil the pressure becomes normal:	—

Test and Procedure	Results and Indications	Proceed to
12.3—Inspect the oil pressure relief valve and spring, to ensure that it is not sticking or stuck. Remove and thoroughly clean the valve, spring, and the valve body.	If the oil pressure improves: If no improvement is noted:	— **12.4**
12.4—Check to ensure that the oil pump is not cavitating (sucking air instead of oil): See that the crankcase is neither over nor underfull, and that the pickup in the sump is in the proper position and free from sludge.	Fill or drain the crankcase to the proper capacity, and clean the pickup screen in solvent if necessary. If no improvement is noted:	**12.5**
12.5—Inspect the oil pump drive and the oil pump:	If the pump drive or the oil pump appear to be defective, service as necessary and retest per 12.1: If the pump drive and pump appear to be operating normally, the engine should be disassembled to determine where blockage exists:	**12.1** **See Chapter 3**
12.6—Purge the engine of ethylene glycol coolant: Completely drain the crankcase and the oil filter. Obtain a commercial butyl cellosolve base solvent, designated for this purpose, and follow the instructions precisely. Following this, install a new oil filter and refill the crankcase with the proper weight oil. The next oil and filter change should follow shortly thereafter (1000 miles).		

TROUBLESHOOTING EMISSION CONTROL SYSTEMS

See Chapter 4 for procedures applicable to individual emission control systems used on specific combinations of engine/transmission/model.

TROUBLESHOOTING THE CARBURETOR

See Chapter 4 for service procedures

Carburetor problems cannot be effectively isolated unless all other engine systems (particularly ignition and emission) are functioning properly and the engine is properly tuned.

Condition	Possible Cause
Engine cranks, but does not start	1. Improper starting procedure 2. No fuel in tank 3. Clogged fuel line or filter 4. Defective fuel pump 5. Choke valve not closing properly 6. Engine flooded 7. Choke valve not unloading 8. Throttle linkage not making full travel 9. Stuck needle or float 10. Leaking float needle or seat 11. Improper float adjustment
Engine stalls	1. Improperly adjusted idle speed or mixture **Engine hot** 2. Improperly adjusted dashpot 3. Defective or improperly adjusted solenoid 4. Incorrect fuel level in fuel bowl 5. Fuel pump pressure too high 6. Leaking float needle seat 7. Secondary throttle valve stuck open 8. Air or fuel leaks 9. Idle air bleeds plugged or missing 10. Idle passages plugged **Engine Cold** 11. Incorrectly adjusted choke 12. Improperly adjusted fast idle speed 13. Air leaks 14. Plugged idle or idle air passages 15. Stuck choke valve or binding linkage 16. Stuck secondary throttle valves 17. Engine flooding—high fuel level 18. Leaking or misaligned float
Engine hesitates on acceleration	1. Clogged fuel filter 2. Leaking fuel pump diaphragm 3. Low fuel pump pressure 4. Secondary throttle valves stuck, bent or misadjusted 5. Sticking or binding air valve 6. Defective accelerator pump 7. Vacuum leaks 8. Clogged air filter 9. Incorrect choke adjustment (engine cold)
Engine feels sluggish or flat on acceleration	1. Improperly adjusted idle speed or mixture 2. Clogged fuel filter 3. Defective accelerator pump 4. Dirty, plugged or incorrect main metering jets 5. Bent or sticking main metering rods 6. Sticking throttle valves 7. Stuck heat riser 8. Binding or stuck air valve 9. Dirty, plugged or incorrect secondary jets 10. Bent or sticking secondary metering rods. 11. Throttle body or manifold heat passages plugged 12. Improperly adjusted choke or choke vacuum break.
Carburetor floods	1. Defective fuel pump. Pressure too high. 2. Stuck choke valve 3. Dirty, worn or damaged float or needle valve/seat 4. Incorrect float/fuel level 5. Leaking float bowl

Condition	Possible Cause
Engine idles roughly and stalls	1. Incorrect idle speed 2. Clogged fuel filter 3. Dirt in fuel system or carburetor 4. Loose carburetor screws or attaching bolts 5. Broken carburetor gaskets 6. Air leaks 7. Dirty carburetor 8. Worn idle mixture needles 9. Throttle valves stuck open 10. Incorrectly adjusted float or fuel level 11. Clogged air filter
Engine runs unevenly or surges	1. Defective fuel pump 2. Dirty or clogged fuel filter 3. Plugged, loose or incorrect main metering jets or rods 4. Air leaks 5. Bent or sticking main metering rods 6. Stuck power piston 7. Incorrect float adjustment 8. Incorrect idle speed or mixture 9. Dirty or plugged idle system passages 10. Hard, brittle or broken gaskets 11. Loose attaching or mounting screws 12. Stuck or misaligned secondary throttle valves
Poor fuel economy	1. Poor driving habits 2. Stuck choke valve 3. Binding choke linkage 4. Stuck heat riser 5. Incorrect idle mixture 6. Defective accelerator pump 7. Air leaks 8. Plugged, loose or incorrect main metering jets 9. Improperly adjusted float or fuel level 10. Bent, misaligned or fuel-clogged float 11. Leaking float needle seat 12. Fuel leak 13. Accelerator pump discharge ball not seating properly 14. Incorrect main jets
Engine lacks high speed performance or power	1. Incorrect throttle linkage adjustment 2. Stuck or binding power piston 3. Defective accelerator pump 4. Air leaks 5. Incorrect float setting or fuel level 6. Dirty, plugged, worn or incorrect main metering jets or rods 7. Binding or sticking air valve 8. Brittle or cracked gaskets 9. Bent, incorrect or improperly adjusted secondary metering rods 10. Clogged fuel filter 11. Clogged air filter 12. Defective fuel pump

TROUBLESHOOTING FUEL INJECTION PROBLEMS

Each fuel injection system has its own unique components and test procedures, for which it is impossible to generalize. Refer to Chapter 4 of this Repair & Tune-Up Guide for specific test and repair procedures, if the vehicle is equipped with fuel injection.

TROUBLESHOOTING ELECTRICAL PROBLEMS

See Chapter 5 for service procedures

For any electrical system to operate, it must make a complete circuit. This simply means that the power flow from the battery must make a complete circle. When an electrical component is operating, power flows from the battery to the component, passes through the component causing it to perform its function (lighting a light bulb), and then returns to the battery through the ground of the circuit. This ground is usually (but not always) the metal part of the car or truck on which the electrical component is mounted.

Perhaps the easiest way to visualize this is to think of connecting a light bulb with two wires attached to it to the battery. If one of the two wires attached to the light bulb were attached to the negative post of the battery and the other were attached to the positive post of the battery, you would have a complete circuit. Current from the battery would flow to the light bulb, causing it to light, and return to the negative post of the battery.

The normal automotive circuit differs from this simple example in two ways. First, instead of having a return wire from the bulb to the battery, the light bulb returns the current to the battery through the chassis of the vehicle. Since the negative battery cable is attached to the chassis and the chassis is made of electrically conductive metal, the chassis of the vehicle can serve as a ground wire to complete the circuit. Secondly, most automotive circuits contain switches to turn components on and off as required.

Every complete circuit from a power source must include a component which is using the power from the power source. If you were to disconnect the light bulb from the wires and touch the two wires together (don't do this) the power supply wire to the component would be grounded before the normal ground connection for the circuit.

Because grounding a wire from a power source makes a complete circuit—less the required component to use the power—this phenomenon is called a short circuit. Common causes are: broken insulation (exposing the metal wire to a metal part of the car or truck), or a shorted switch.

Some electrical components which require a large amount of current to operate also have a relay in their circuit. Since these circuits carry a large amount of current, the thickness of the wire in the circuit (gauge size) is also greater. If this large wire were connected from the component to the control switch on the instrument panel, and then back to the component, a voltage drop would occur in the circuit. To prevent this potential drop in voltage, an electromagnetic switch (relay) is used. The large wires in the circuit are connected from the battery to one side of the relay, and from the opposite side of the relay to the component. The relay is normally open, preventing current from passing through the circuit. An additional, smaller, wire is connected from the relay to the control switch for the circuit. When the control switch is turned on, it grounds the smaller wire from the relay and completes the circuit. This closes the relay and allows current to flow from the battery to the component. The horn, headlight, and starter circuits are three which use relays.

It is possible for larger surges of current to pass through the electrical system of your car or truck. If this surge of current were to reach an electrical component, it could burn it out. To prevent this, fuses, circuit breakers or fusible links are connected into the current supply wires of most of the major electrical systems. When an electrical current of excessive power passes through the component's fuse, the fuse blows out and breaks the circuit, saving the component from destruction.

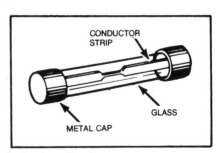

Typical automotive fuse

A circuit breaker is basically a self-repairing fuse. The circuit breaker opens the circuit the same way a fuse does. However, when either the short is removed from the circuit or the surge subsides, the circuit breaker resets itself and does not have to be replaced as a fuse does.

A fuse link is a wire that acts as a fuse. It is normally connected between the starter relay and the main wiring harness. This connection is usually under the hood. The fuse link (if installed) protects all the

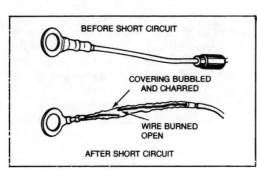

Most fusible links show a charred, melted insulation when they burn out

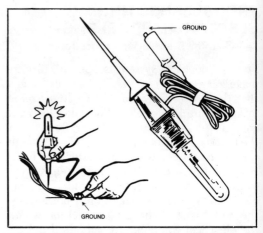

The test light will show the presence of current when touched to a hot wire and grounded at the other end

chassis electrical components, and is the probable cause of trouble when none of the electrical components function, unless the battery is disconnected or dead.

Electrical problems generally fall into one of three areas:

1. The component that is not functioning is not receiving current.

2. The component itself is not functioning.

3. The component is not properly grounded.

The electrical system can be checked with a test light and a jumper wire. A test light is a device that looks like a pointed screwdriver with a wire attached to it and has a light bulb in its handle. A jumper wire is a piece of insulated wire with an alligator clip attached to each end.

If a component is not working, you must follow a systematic plan to determine which of the three causes is the villain.

1. Turn on the switch that controls the inoperable component.

2. Disconnect the power supply wire from the component.

3. Attach the ground wire on the test light to a good metal ground.

4. Touch the probe end of the test light to the end of the power supply wire that was disconnected from the component. If the component is receiving current, the test light will go on.

NOTE: *Some components work only when the ignition switch is turned on.*

If the test light does not go on, then the problem is in the circuit between the battery and the component. This includes all the switches, fuses, and relays in the system. Follow the wire that runs back to the battery. The problem is an open circuit between the

battery and the component. If the fuse is blown and, when replaced, immediately blows again, there is a short circuit in the system which must be located and repaired. If there is a switch in the system, bypass it with a jumper wire. This is done by connecting one end of the jumper wire to the power supply wire into the switch and the other end of the jumper wire to the wire coming out of the switch. If the test light lights with the jumper wire installed, the switch or whatever was bypassed is defective.

NOTE: *Never substitute the jumper wire for the component, since it is required to use the power from the power source.*

5. If the bulb in the test light goes on, then the current is getting to the component that is not working. This eliminates the first of the three possible causes. Connect the power supply wire and connect a jumper wire from the component to a good metal ground. Do this with the switch which controls the component turned on, and also the ignition switch turned on if it is required for the component to work. If the component works with the jumper wire installed, then it has a bad ground. This is usually caused by the metal area on which the component mounts to the chassis being coated with some type of foreign matter.

6. If neither test located the source of the trouble, then the component itself is defective. Remember that for any electrical system to work, all connections must be clean and tight.

Troubleshooting Basic Turn Signal and Flasher Problems
See Chapter 5 for service procedures

Most problems in the turn signals or flasher system can be reduced to defective flashers or bulbs, which are easily replaced. Occasionally, the turn signal switch will prove defective.

F = Front   R = Rear   ● = Lights off   ○ = Lights on

Condition		Possible Cause
Turn signals light, but do not flash	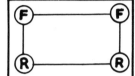	Defective flasher
No turn signals light on either side	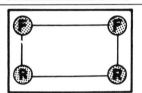	Blown fuse. Replace if defective. Defective flasher. Check by substitution. Open circuit, short circuit or poor ground.
Both turn signals on one side don't work	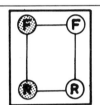	Bad bulbs. Bad ground in both (or either) housings.
One turn signal light on one side doesn't work	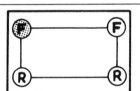	Defective bulb. Corrosion in socket. Clean contacts. Poor ground at socket.
Turn signal flashes too fast or too slowly	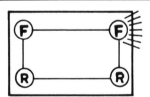	Check any bulb on the side flashing too fast. A heavy-duty bulb is probably installed in place of a regular bulb. Check the bulb flashing too slowly. A standard bulb was probably installed in place of a heavy-duty bulb. Loose connections or corrosion at the bulb socket.
Indicator lights don't work in either direction		Check if the turn signals are working. Check the dash indicator lights. Check the flasher by substitution.
One indicator light doesn't light		On systems with one dash indicator: See if the lights work on the same side. Often the filaments have been reversed in systems combining stoplights with taillights and turn signals. Check the flasher by substitution. On systems with two indicators: Check the bulbs on the same side. Check the indicator light bulb. Check the flasher by substitution.

Troubleshooting Lighting Problems
See Chapter 5 for service procedures

Condition	Possible Cause
One or more lights don't work, but others do	1. Defective bulb(s) 2. Blown fuse(s) 3. Dirty fuse clips or light sockets 4. Poor ground circuit
Lights burn out quickly	1. Incorrect voltage regulator setting or defective regulator 2. Poor battery/alternator connections
Lights go dim	1. Low/discharged battery 2. Alternator not charging 3. Corroded sockets or connections 4. Low voltage output
Lights flicker	1. Loose connection 2. Poor ground. (Run ground wire from light housing to frame) 3. Circuit breaker operating (short circuit)
Lights "flare"—Some flare is normal on acceleration—If excessive, see "Lights Burn Out Quickly"	High voltage setting
Lights glare—approaching drivers are blinded	1. Lights adjusted too high 2. Rear springs or shocks sagging 3. Rear tires soft

Troubleshooting Dash Gauge Problems
Most problems can be traced to a defective sending unit or faulty wiring. Occasionally, the gauge itself is at fault. See Chapter 5 for service procedures.

Condition	Possible Cause
COOLANT TEMPERATURE GAUGE	
Gauge reads erratically or not at all	1. Loose or dirty connections 2. Defective sending unit. 3. Defective gauge. To test a bi-metal gauge, remove the wire from the sending unit. Ground the wire for an instant. If the gauge registers, replace the sending unit. To test a magnetic gauge, disconnect the wire at the sending unit. With ignition ON gauge should register COLD. Ground the wire; gauge should register HOT.
AMMETER GAUGE—TURN HEADLIGHTS ON (DO NOT START ENGINE). NOTE REACTION	
Ammeter shows charge Ammeter shows discharge Ammeter does not move	1. Connections reversed on gauge 2. Ammeter is OK 3. Loose connections or faulty wiring 4. Defective gauge

Condition	Possible Cause

OIL PRESSURE GAUGE

Condition	Possible Cause
Gauge does not register or is inaccurate	1. On mechanical gauge, Bourdon tube may be bent or kinked.
	2. Low oil pressure. Remove sending unit. Idle the engine briefly. If no oil flows from sending unit hole, problem is in engine.
	3. Defective gauge. Remove the wire from the sending unit and ground it for an instant with the ignition ON. A good gauge will go to the top of the scale.
	4. Defective wiring. Check the wiring to the gauge. If it's OK and the gauge doesn't register when grounded, replace the gauge.
	5. Defective sending unit.

ALL GAUGES

Condition	Possible Cause
All gauges do not operate	1. Blown fuse
	2. Defective instrument regulator
All gauges read low or erratically	3. Defective or dirty instrument voltage regulator
All gauges pegged	4. Loss of ground between instrument voltage regulator and frame
	5. Defective instrument regulator

WARNING LIGHTS

Condition	Possible Cause
Light(s) do not come on when Ignition is ON, but engine is not started	1. Defective bulb
	2. Defective wire
	3. Defective sending unit. Disconnect the wire from the sending unit and ground it. Replace the sending unit if the light comes on with the ignition ON.
Light comes on with engine running	4. Problem in individual system
	5. Defective sending unit

Troubleshooting Clutch Problems

It is false economy to replace individual clutch components. The pressure plate, clutch plate and throwout bearing should be replaced as a set, and the flywheel face inspected, whenever the clutch is overhauled. See Chapter 6 for service procedures.

Condition	Possible Cause
Clutch chatter	1. Grease on driven plate (disc) facing
	2. Binding clutch linkage or cable
	3. Loose, damaged facings on driven plate (disc)
	4. Engine mounts loose
	5. Incorrect height adjustment of pressure plate release levers
	6. Clutch housing or housing to transmission adapter misalignment
	7. Loose driven plate hub
Clutch grabbing	1. Oil, grease on driven plate (disc) facing
	2. Broken pressure plate
	3. Warped or binding driven plate. Driven plate binding on clutch shaft
Clutch slips	1. Lack of lubrication in clutch linkage or cable (linkage or cable binds, causes incomplete engagement)
	2. Incorrect pedal, or linkage adjustment
	3. Broken pressure plate springs
	4. Weak pressure plate springs
	5. Grease on driven plate facings (disc)

Troubleshooting Clutch Problems (cont.)

Condition	Possible Cause
Incomplete clutch release	1. Incorrect pedal or linkage adjustment or linkage or cable binding 2. Incorrect height adjustment on pressure plate release levers 3. Loose, broken facings on driven plate (disc) 4. Bent, dished, warped driven plate caused by overheating
Grinding, whirring grating noise when pedal is depressed	1. Worn or defective throwout bearing 2. Starter drive teeth contacting flywheel ring gear teeth. Look for milled or polished teeth on ring gear.
Squeal, howl, trumpeting noise when pedal is being released (occurs during first inch to inch and one-half of pedal travel)	Pilot bushing worn or lack of lubricant. If bushing appears OK, polish bushing with emery cloth, soak lube wick in oil, lube bushing with oil, apply film of chassis grease to clutch shaft pilot hub, reassemble. NOTE: Bushing wear may be due to misalignment of clutch housing or housing to transmission adapter
Vibration or clutch pedal pulsation with clutch disengaged (pedal fully depressed)	1. Worn or defective engine transmission mounts 2. Flywheel run out. (Flywheel run out at face not to exceed 0.005") 3. Damaged or defective clutch components

Troubleshooting Manual Transmission Problems
See Chapter 6 for service procedures

Condition	Possible Cause
Transmission jumps out of gear	1. Misalignment of transmission case or clutch housing. 2. Worn pilot bearing in crankshaft. 3. Bent transmission shaft. 4. Worn high speed sliding gear. 5. Worn teeth or end-play in clutch shaft. 6. Insufficient spring tension on shifter rail plunger. 7. Bent or loose shifter fork. 8. Gears not engaging completely. 9. Loose or worn bearings on clutch shaft or mainshaft. 10. Worn gear teeth. 11. Worn or damaged detent balls.
Transmission sticks in gear	1. Clutch not releasing fully. 2. Burred or battered teeth on clutch shaft, or sliding sleeve. 3. Burred or battered transmission mainshaft. 4. Frozen synchronizing clutch. 5. Stuck shifter rail plunger. 6. Gearshift lever twisting and binding shifter rail. 7. Battered teeth on high speed sliding gear or on sleeve. 8. Improper lubrication, or lack of lubrication. 9. Corroded transmission parts. 10. Defective mainshaft pilot bearing. 11. Locked gear bearings will give same effect as stuck in gear.
Transmission gears will not synchronize	1. Binding pilot bearing on mainshaft, will synchronize in high gear only. 2. Clutch not releasing fully. 3. Detent spring weak or broken. 4. Weak or broken springs under balls in sliding gear sleeve. 5. Binding bearing on clutch shaft, or binding countershaft. 6. Binding pilot bearing in crankshaft. 7. Badly worn gear teeth. 8. Improper lubrication. 9. Constant mesh gear not turning freely on transmission mainshaft. Will synchronize in that gear only.

Condition	Possible Cause
Gears spinning when shifting into gear from neutral	1. Clutch not releasing fully. 2. In some cases an extremely light lubricant in transmission will cause gears to continue to spin for a short time after clutch is released. 3. Binding pilot bearing in crankshaft.
Transmission noisy in all gears	1. Insufficient lubricant, or improper lubricant. 2. Worn countergear bearings. 3. Worn or damaged main drive gear or countergear. 4. Damaged main drive gear or mainshaft bearings. 5. Worn or damaged countergear anti-lash plate.
Transmission noisy in neutral only	1. Damaged main drive gear bearing. 2. Damaged or loose mainshaft pilot bearing. 3. Worn or damaged countergear anti-lash plate. 4. Worn countergear bearings.
Transmission noisy in one gear only	1. Damaged or worn constant mesh gears. 2. Worn or damaged countergear bearings. 3. Damaged or worn synchronizer.
Transmission noisy in reverse only	1. Worn or damaged reverse idler gear or idler bushing. 2. Worn or damaged mainshaft reverse gear. 3. Worn or damaged reverse countergear. 4. Damaged shift mechanism.

TROUBLESHOOTING AUTOMATIC TRANSMISSION PROBLEMS

Keeping alert to changes in the operating characteristics of the transmission (changing shift points, noises, etc.) can prevent small problems from becoming large ones. If the problem cannot be traced to loose bolts, fluid level, misadjusted linkage, clogged filters or similar problems, you should probably seek professional service.

Transmission Fluid Indications

The appearance and odor of the transmission fluid can give valuable clues to the overall condition of the transmission. Always note the appearance of the fluid when you check the fluid level or change the fluid. Rub a small amount of fluid between your fingers to feel for grit and smell the fluid on the dipstick.

If the fluid appears:	It indicates:
Clear and red colored	Normal operation
Discolored (extremely dark red or brownish) or smells burned	Band or clutch pack failure, usually caused by an overheated transmission. Hauling very heavy loads with insufficient power or failure to change the fluid often result in overheating. Do not confuse this appearance with newer fluids that have a darker red color and a strong odor (though not a burned odor).
Foamy or aerated (light in color and full of bubbles)	1. The level is too high (gear train is churning oil) 2. An internal air leak (air is mixing with the fluid). Have the transmission checked professionally.
Solid residue in the fluid	Defective bands, clutch pack or bearings. Bits of band material or metal abrasives are clinging to the dipstick. Have the transmission checked professionally.
Varnish coating on the dipstick	The transmission fluid is overheating

TROUBLESHOOTING DRIVE AXLE PROBLEMS

First, determine when the noise is most noticeable.

Drive Noise: Produced under vehicle acceleration.

Coast Noise: Produced while coasting with a closed throttle.

Float Noise: Occurs while maintaining constant speed (just enough to keep speed constant) on a level road.

External Noise Elimination

It is advisable to make a thorough road test to determine whether the noise originates in the rear axle or whether it originates from the tires, engine, transmission, wheel bearings or road surface. Noise originating from other places cannot be corrected by servicing the rear axle.

ROAD NOISE

Brick or rough surfaced concrete roads produce noises that seem to come from the rear axle. Road noise is usually identical in Drive or Coast and driving on a different type of road will tell whether the road is the problem.

TIRE NOISE

Tire noise can be mistaken as rear axle noise, even though the tires on the front are at fault. Snow tread and mud tread tires or tires worn unevenly will frequently cause vibrations which seem to originate elsewhere; *temporarily, and for test purposes only,* inflate the tires to 40–50 lbs. This will significantly alter the noise produced by the tires,

but will not alter noise from the rear axle. Noises from the rear axle will normally cease at speeds below 30 mph on coast, while tire noise will continue at lower tone as speed is decreased. The rear axle noise will usually change from drive conditions to coast conditions, while tire noise will not. Do not forget to lower the tire pressure to normal after the test is complete.

ENGINE/TRANSMISSION NOISE

Determine at what speed the noise is most pronounced, then stop in a quiet place. With the transmission in Neutral, run the engine through speeds corresponding to road speeds where the noise was noticed. Noises produced with the vehicle standing still are coming from the engine or transmission.

FRONT WHEEL BEARINGS

Front wheel bearing noises, sometimes confused with rear axle noises, will not change when comparing drive and coast conditions. While holding the speed steady, lightly apply the footbrake. This will often cause wheel bearing noise to lessen, as some of the weight is taken off the bearing. Front wheel bearings are easily checked by jacking up the wheels and spinning the wheels. Shaking the wheels will also determine if the wheel bearings are excessively loose.

REAR AXLE NOISES

Eliminating other possible sources can narrow the cause to the rear axle, which normally produces noise from worn gears or bearings. Gear noises tend to peak in a narrow speed range, while bearing noises will usually vary in pitch with engine speeds.

Noise Diagnosis

The Noise Is:	Most Probably Produced By:
1. Identical under Drive or Coast	Road surface, tires or front wheel bearings
2. Different depending on road surface	Road surface or tires
3. Lower as speed is lowered	Tires
4. Similar when standing or moving	Engine or transmission
5. A vibration	Unbalanced tires, rear wheel bearing, unbalanced driveshaft or worn U-joint
6. A knock or click about every two tire revolutions	Rear wheel bearing
7. Most pronounced on turns	Damaged differential gears
8. A steady low-pitched whirring or scraping, starting at low speeds	Damaged or worn pinion bearing
9. A chattering vibration on turns	Wrong differential lubricant or worn clutch plates (limited slip rear axle)
10. Noticed only in Drive, Coast or Float conditions	Worn ring gear and/or pinion gear

Troubleshooting Steering & Suspension Problems

Condition	Possible Cause
Hard steering (wheel is hard to turn)	1. Improper tire pressure 2. Loose or glazed pump drive belt 3. Low or incorrect fluid 4. Loose, bent or poorly lubricated front end parts 5. Improper front end alignment (excessive caster) 6. Bind in steering column or linkage 7. Kinked hydraulic hose 8. Air in hydraulic system 9. Low pump output or leaks in system 10. Obstruction in lines 11. Pump valves sticking or out of adjustment 12. Incorrect wheel alignment
Loose steering (too much play in steering wheel)	1. Loose wheel bearings 2. Faulty shocks 3. Worn linkage or suspension components 4. Loose steering gear mounting or linkage points 5. Steering mechanism worn or improperly adjusted 6. Valve spool improperly adjusted 7. Worn ball joints, tie-rod ends, etc.
Veers or wanders (pulls to one side with hands off steering wheel)	1. Improper tire pressure 2. Improper front end alignment 3. Dragging or Improperly adjusted brakes 4. Bent frame 5. Improper rear end alignment 6. Faulty shocks or springs 7. Loose or bent front end components 8. Play in Pitman arm 9. Steering gear mountings loose 10. Loose wheel bearings 11. Binding Pitman arm 12. Spool valve sticking or improperly adjusted 13. Worn ball joints
Wheel oscillation or vibration transmitted through steering wheel	1. Low or uneven tire pressure 2. Loose wheel bearings 3. Improper front end alignment 4. Bent spindle 5. Worn, bent or broken front end components 6. Tires out of round or out of balance 7. Excessive lateral runout in disc brake rotor 8. Loose or bent shock absorber or strut
Noises (see also "Troubleshooting Drive Axle Problems")	1. Loose belts 2. Low fluid, air in system 3. Foreign matter in system 4. Improper lubrication 5. Interference or chafing in linkage 6. Steering gear mountings loose 7. Incorrect adjustment or wear in gear box 8. Faulty valves or wear in pump 9. Kinked hydraulic lines 10. Worn wheel bearings
Poor return of steering	1. Over-inflated tires 2. Improperly aligned front end (excessive caster) 3. Binding in steering column 4. No lubrication in front end 5. Steering gear adjusted too tight
Uneven tire wear (see "How To Read Tire Wear")	1. Incorrect tire pressure 2. Improperly aligned front end 3. Tires out-of-balance 4. Bent or worn suspension parts

HOW TO READ TIRE WEAR

The way your tires wear is a good indicator of other parts of the suspension. Abnormal wear patterns are often caused by the need for simple tire maintenance, or for front end alignment.

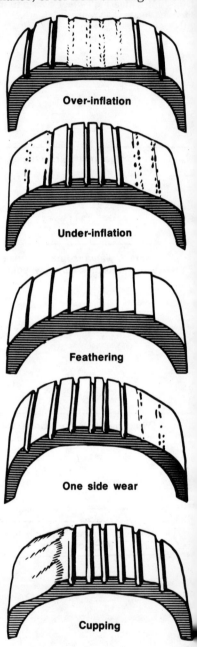

Excessive wear at the center of the tread indicates that the air pressure in the tire is consistently too high. The tire is riding on the center of the tread and wearing it prematurely. Occasionally, this wear pattern can result from outrageously wide tires on narrow rims. The cure for this is to replace either the tires or the wheels.

Over-inflation

This type of wear usually results from consistent under-inflation. When a tire is under-inflated, there is too much contact with the road by the outer treads, which wear prematurely. When this type of wear occurs, and the tire pressure is known to be consistently correct, a bent or worn steering component or the need for wheel alignment could be indicated.

Under-inflation

Feathering is a condition when the edge of each tread rib develops a slightly rounded edge on one side and a sharp edge on the other. By running your hand over the tire, you can usually feel the sharper edges before you'll be able to see them. The most common causes of feathering are incorrect toe-in setting or deteriorated bushings in the front suspension.

Feathering

When an inner or outer rib wears faster than the rest of the tire, the need for wheel alignment is indicated. There is excessive camber in the front suspension, causing the wheel to lean too much putting excessive load on one side of the tire. Misalignment could also be due to sagging springs, worn ball joints, or worn control arm bushings. Be sure the vehicle is loaded the way it's normally driven when you have the wheels aligned.

One side wear

Cups or scalloped dips appearing around the edge of the tread almost always indicate worn (sometimes bent) suspension parts. Adjustment of wheel alignment alone will seldom cure the problem. Any worn component that connects the wheel to the suspension can cause this type of wear. Occasionally, wheels that are out of balance will wear like this, but wheel imbalance usually shows up as bald spots between the outside edges and center of the tread.

Cupping

Second-rib wear is usually found only in radial tires, and appears where the steel belts end in relation to the tread. It can be kept to a minimum by paying careful attention to tire pressure and frequently rotating the tires. This is often considered normal wear but excessive amounts indicate that the tires are too wide for the wheels.

Second-rib wear

Troubleshooting Disc Brake Problems

Condition	Possible Cause
Noise—groan—brake noise emanating when slowly releasing brakes (creep-groan)	Not detrimental to function of disc brakes—no corrective action required. (This noise may be eliminated by slightly increasing or decreasing brake pedal efforts.)
Rattle—brake noise or rattle emanating at low speeds on rough roads, (front wheels only).	1. Shoe anti-rattle spring missing or not properly positioned. 2. Excessive clearance between shoe and caliper. 3. Soft or broken caliper seals. 4. Deformed or misaligned disc. 5. Loose caliper.
Scraping	1. Mounting bolts too long. 2. Loose wheel bearings. 3. Bent, loose, or misaligned splash shield.
Front brakes heat up during driving and fail to release	1. Operator riding brake pedal. 2. Stop light switch improperly adjusted. 3. Sticking pedal linkage. 4. Frozen or seized piston. 5. Residual pressure valve in master cylinder. 6. Power brake malfunction. 7. Proportioning valve malfunction.
Leaky brake caliper	1. Damaged or worn caliper piston seal. 2. Scores or corrosion on surface of cylinder bore.
Grabbing or uneven brake action—Brakes pull to one side	1. Causes listed under "Brakes Pull". 2. Power brake malfunction. 3. Low fluid level in master cylinder. 4. Air in hydraulic system. 5. Brake fluid, oil or grease on linings. 6. Unmatched linings. 7. Distorted brake pads. 8. Frozen or seized pistons. 9. Incorrect tire pressure. 10. Front end out of alignment. 11. Broken rear spring. 12. Brake caliper pistons sticking. 13. Restricted hose or line. 14. Caliper not in proper alignment to braking disc. 15. Stuck or malfunctioning metering valve. 16. Soft or broken caliper seals. 17. Loose caliper.
Brake pedal can be depressed without braking effect	1. Air in hydraulic system or improper bleeding procedure. 2. Leak past primary cup in master cylinder. 3. Leak in system. 4. Rear brakes out of adjustment. 5. Bleeder screw open.
Excessive pedal travel	1. Air, leak, or insufficient fluid in system or caliper. 2. Warped or excessively tapered shoe and lining assembly. 3. Excessive disc runout. 4. Rear brake adjustment required. 5. Loose wheel bearing adjustment. 6. Damaged caliper piston seal. 7. Improper brake fluid (boil). 8. Power brake malfunction. 9. Weak or soft hoses.

Troubleshooting Disc Brake Problems (cont.)

Condition	Possible Cause
Brake roughness or chatter (pedal pumping)	1. Excessive thickness variation of braking disc. 2. Excessive lateral runout of braking disc. 3. Rear brake drums out-of-round. 4. Excessive front bearing clearance.
Excessive pedal effort	1. Brake fluid, oil or grease on linings. 2. Incorrect lining. 3. Frozen or seized pistons. 4. Power brake malfunction. 5. Kinked or collapsed hose or line. 6. Stuck metering valve. 7. Scored caliper or master cylinder bore. 8. Seized caliper pistons.
Brake pedal fades (pedal travel increases with foot on brake)	1. Rough master cylinder or caliper bore. 2. Loose or broken hydraulic lines/connections. 3. Air in hydraulic system. 4. Fluid level low. 5. Weak or soft hoses. 6. Inferior quality brake shoes or fluid. 7. Worn master cylinder piston cups or seals.

Troubleshooting Drum Brakes

Condition	Possible Cause
Pedal goes to floor	1. Fluid low in reservoir. 2. Air in hydraulic system. 3. Improperly adjusted brake. 4. Leaking wheel cylinders. 5. Loose or broken brake lines. 6. Leaking or worn master cylinder. 7. Excessively worn brake lining.
Spongy brake pedal	1. Air in hydraulic system. 2. Improper brake fluid (low boiling point). 3. Excessively worn or cracked brake drums. 4. Broken pedal pivot bushing.
Brakes pulling	1. Contaminated lining. 2. Front end out of alignment. 3. Incorrect brake adjustment. 4. Unmatched brake lining. 5. Brake drums out of round. 6. Brake shoes distorted. 7. Restricted brake hose or line. 8. Broken rear spring. 9. Worn brake linings. 10. Uneven lining wear. 11. Glazed brake lining. 12. Excessive brake lining dust. 13. Heat spotted brake drums. 14. Weak brake return springs. 15. Faulty automatic adjusters. 16. Low or incorrect tire pressure.

Condition	Possible Cause
Squealing brakes	1. Glazed brake lining. 2. Saturated brake lining. 3. Weak or broken brake shoe retaining spring. 4. Broken or weak brake shoe return spring. 5. Incorrect brake lining. 6. Distorted brake shoes. 7. Bent support plate. 8. Dust in brakes or scored brake drums. 9. Linings worn below limit. 10. Uneven brake lining wear. 11. Heat spotted brake drums.
Chirping brakes	1. Out of round drum or eccentric axle flange pilot.
Dragging brakes	1. Incorrect wheel or parking brake adjustment. 2. Parking brakes engaged or improperly adjusted. 3. Weak or broken brake shoe return spring. 4. Brake pedal binding. 5. Master cylinder cup sticking. 6. Obstructed master cylinder relief port. 7. Saturated brake lining. 8. Bent or out of round brake drum. 9. Contaminated or improper brake fluid. 10. Sticking wheel cylinder pistons. 11. Driver riding brake pedal. 12. Defective proportioning valve. 13. Insufficient brake shoe lubricant.
Hard pedal	1. Brake booster inoperative. 2. Incorrect brake lining. 3. Restricted brake line or hose. 4. Frozen brake pedal linkage. 5. Stuck wheel cylinder. 6. Binding pedal linkage. 7. Faulty proportioning valve.
Wheel locks	1. Contaminated brake lining. 2. Loose or torn brake lining. 3. Wheel cylinder cups sticking. 4. Incorrect wheel bearing adjustment. 5. Faulty proportioning valve.
Brakes fade (high speed)	1. Incorrect lining. 2. Overheated brake drums. 3. Incorrect brake fluid (low boiling temperature). 4. Saturated brake lining. 5. Leak in hydraulic system. 6. Faulty automatic adjusters.
Pedal pulsates	1. Bent or out of round brake drum.
Brake chatter and shoe knock	1. Out of round brake drum. 2. Loose support plate. 3. Bent support plate. 4. Distorted brake shoes. 5. Machine grooves in contact face of brake drum (Shoe Knock). 6. Contaminated brake lining. 7. Missing or loose components. 8. Incorrect lining material. 9. Out-of-round brake drums. 10. Heat spotted or scored brake drums. 11. Out-of-balance wheels.

Troubleshooting Drum Brakes (cont.)

Condition	Possible Cause
Brakes do not self adjust	1. Adjuster screw frozen in thread. 2. Adjuster screw corroded at thrust washer. 3. Adjuster lever does not engage star wheel. 4. Adjuster installed on wrong wheel.
Brake light glows	1. Leak in the hydraulic system. 2. Air in the system. 3. Improperly adjusted master cylinder pushrod. 4. Uneven lining wear. 5. Failure to center combination valve or proportioning valve.

Appendix

General Conversion Table

Multiply by	To convert	To	
2.54	Inches	Centimeters	.3937
30.48	Feet	Centimeters	.0328
.914	Yards	Meters	1.094
1.609	Miles	Kilometers	.621
.645	Square inches	Square cm.	.155
.836	Square yards	Square meters	1.196
16.39	Cubic inches	Cubic cm.	.061
28.3	Cubic feet	Liters	.0353
.4536	Pounds	Kilograms	2.2045
4.226	Gallons	Liters	.264
.068	Lbs./sq. in. (psi)	Atmospheres	14.7
.138	Foot pounds	Kg. m.	7.23
1.014	H.P. (DIN)	H.P. (SAE)	.9861
—	To obtain	From	Multiply by

Note: 1 cm. equals 10 mm.; 1 mm. equals .0394".

Conversion—Common Fractions to Decimals and Millimeters

Common Fractions	Decimal Fractions	Millimeters (approx.)	Common Fractions	Decimal Fractions	Millimeters (approx.)	Common Fractions	Decimal Fractions	Millimeters (approx.)
1/128	.008	0.20	11/32	.344	8.73	43/64	.672	17.07
1/64	.016	0.40	23/64	.359	9.13	11/16	.688	17.46
1/32	.031	0.79	3/8	.375	9.53	45/64	.703	17.86
3/64	.047	1.19	25/64	.391	9.92	23/32	.719	18.26
1/16	.063	1.59	13/32	.406	10.32	47/64	.734	18.65
5/64	.078	1.98	27/64	.422	10.72	3/4	.750	19.05
3/32	.094	2.38	7/16	.438	11.11	49/64	.766	19.45
7/64	.109	2.78	29/64	.453	11.51	25/32	.781	19.84
1/8	.125	3.18	15/32	.469	11.91	51/64	.797	20.24
9/64	.141	3.57	31/64	.484	12.30	13/16	.813	20.64
5/32	.156	3.97	1/2	.500	12.70	53/64	.828	21.03
11/64	.172	4.37	33/64	.516	13.10	27/32	.844	21.43
3/16	.188	4.76	17/32	.531	13.49	55/64	.859	21.83
13/64	.203	5.16	35/64	.547	13.89	7/8	.875	22.23
7/32	.219	5.56	9/16	.563	14.29	57/64	.891	22.62
15/64	.234	5.95	37/64	.578	14.68	29/32	.906	23.02
1/4	.250	6.35	19/32	.594	15.08	59/64	.922	23.42
17/64	.266	6.75	39/64	.609	15.48	15/16	.938	23.81
9/32	.281	7.14	5/8	.625	15.88	61/64	.953	24.21
19/64	.297	7.54	41/64	.641	16.27	31/32	.969	24.61
5/16	.313	7.94	21/32	.656	16.67	63/64	.984	25.00
21/64	.328	8.33						

Conversion—Millimeters to Decimal Inches

mm	inches	mm	inches	mm	inches	mm	inches	mm	inches
1	.039 370	31	1.220 470	61	2.401 570	91	3.582 670	210	8.267 700
2	.078 740	32	1.259 840	62	2.440 940	92	3.622 040	220	8.661 400
3	.118 110	33	1.299 210	63	2.480 310	93	3.661 410	230	9.055 100
4	.157 480	34	1.338 580	64	2.519 680	94	3.700 780	240	9.448 800
5	.196 850	35	1.377 949	65	2.559 050	95	3.740 150	250	9.842 500
6	.236 220	36	1.417 319	66	2.598 420	96	3.779 520	260	10.236 200
7	.275 590	37	1.456 689	67	2.637 790	97	3.818 890	270	10.629 900
8	.314 960	38	1.496 050	68	2.677 160	98	3.858 260	280	11.032 600
9	.354 330	39	1.535 430	69	2.716 530	99	3.897 630	290	11.417 300
10	.393 700	40	1.574 800	70	2.755 900	100	3.937 000	300	11.811 000
11	.433 070	41	1.614 170	71	2.795 270	105	4.133 848	310	12.204 700
12	.472 440	42	1.653 540	72	2.834 640	110	4.330 700	320	12.598 400
13	.511 810	43	1.692 910	73	2.874 010	115	4.527 550	330	12.992 100
14	.551 180	44	1.732 280	74	2.913 380	120	4.724 400	340	13.385 800
15	.590 550	45	1.771 650	75	2.952 750	125	4.921 250	350	13.779 500
16	.629 920	46	1.811 020	76	2.992 120	130	5.118 100	360	14.173 200
17	.669 290	47	1.850 390	77	3.031 490	135	5.314 950	370	14.566 900
18	.708 660	48	1.889 760	78	3.070 860	140	5.511 800	380	14.960 600
19	.748 030	49	1.929 130	79	3.110 230	145	5.708 650	390	15.354 300
20	.787 400	50	1.968 500	80	3.149 600	150	5.905 500	400	15.748 000
21	.826 770	51	2.007 870	81	3.188 970	155	6.102 350	500	19.685 000
22	.866 140	52	2.047 240	82	3.228 340	160	6.299 200	600	23.622 000
23	.905 510	53	2.086 610	83	3.267 710	165	6.496 050	700	27.559 000
24	.944 880	54	2.125 980	84	3.307 080	170	6.692 900	800	31.496 000
25	.984 250	55	2.165 350	85	3.346 450	175	6.889 750	900	35.433 000
26	1.023 620	56	2.204 720	86	3.385 820	180	7.086 600	1000	39.370 000
27	1.062 990	57	2.244 090	87	3.425 190	185	7.283 450	2000	78.740 000
28	1.102 360	58	2.283 460	88	3.464 560	190	7.480 300	3000	118.110 000
29	1.141 730	59	2.322 830	89	3.503 903	195	7.677 150	4000	157.480 000
30	1.181 100	60	2.362 200	90	3.543 300	200	7.874 000	5000	196.850 000

To change decimal millimeters to decimal inches, position the decimal point where desired on either side of the millimeter measurement shown and reset the inches decimal by the same number of digits in the same direction. For example, to convert 0.001 mm to decimal inches, reset the decimal behind the 1 mm (shown on the chart) to 0.001; change the decimal inch equivalent (0.039″ shown) to 0.000039″.

Tap Drill Sizes

National Fine or S.A.E.

Screw & Tap Size	Threads Per Inch	Use Drill Number
No. 5	44	37
No. 6	40	33
No. 8	36	29
No. 10	32	21
No. 12	28	15
1/4	28	3
5/16	24	1
3/8	24	Q
7/16	20	W
1/2	20	29/64
9/16	18	33/64
5/8	18	37/64
3/4	16	11/16
7/8	14	13/16
1 1/8	12	1 3/64
1 1/4	12	1 11/64
1 1/2	12	1 27/64

Tap Drill Sizes

National Coarse or U.S.S.

Screw & Tap Size	Threads Per Inch	Use Drill Number
No. 5	40	39
No. 6	32	36
No. 8	32	29
No. 10	24	25
No. 12	24	17
1/4	20	8
5/16	18	F
3/8	16	5/16
7/16	14	U
1/2	13	27/64
9/16	12	31/64
5/8	11	17/32
3/4	10	21/32
7/8	9	49/64
1	8	7/8
1 1/8	7	63/64
1 1/4	7	1 7/64
1 1/2	6	1 11/32

Decimal Equivalent Size of the Number Drills

Drill No.	Decimal Equivalent	Drill No.	Decimal Equivalent	Drill No.	Decimal Equivalent
80	.0135	53	.0595	26	.1470
79	.0145	52	.0635	25	.1495
78	.0160	51	.0670	24	.1520
77	.0180	50	.0700	23	.1540
76	.0200	49	.0730	22	.1570
75	.0210	48	.0760	21	.1590
74	.0225	47	.0785	20	.1610
73	.0240	46	.0810	19	.1660
72	.0250	45	.0820	18	.1695
71	.0260	44	.0860	17	.1730
70	.0280	43	.0890	16	.1770
69	.0292	42	.0935	15	.1800
68	.0310	41	.0960	14	.1820
67	.0320	40	.0980	13	.1850
66	.0330	39	.0995	12	.1890
65	.0350	38	.1015	11	.1910
64	.0360	37	.1040	10	.1935
63	.0370	36	.1065	9	.1960
62	.0380	35	.1100	8	.1990
61	.0390	34	.1110	7	.2010
60	.0400	33	.1130	6	.2040
59	.0410	32	.1160	5	.2055
58	.0420	31	.1200	4	.2090
57	.0430	30	.1285	3	.2130
56	.0465	29	.1360	2	.2210
55	.0520	28	.1405	1	.2280
54	.0550	27	.1440		

Decimal Equivalent Size of the Letter Drills

Letter Drill	Decimal Equivalent	Letter Drill	Decimal Equivalent	Letter Drill	Decimal Equivalent
A	.234	J	.277	S	.348
B	.238	K	.281	T	.358
C	.242	L	.290	U	.368
D	.246	M	.295	V	.377
E	.250	N	.302	W	.386
F	.257	O	.316	X	.397
G	.261	P	.323	Y	.404
H	.266	Q	.332	Z	.413
I	.272	R	.339		

Anti-Freeze Chart

Temperatures Shown in Degrees Fahrenheit +32 is Freezing

Cooling System Capacity Quarts	Quarts of ETHYLENE GLYCOL Needed for Protection to Temperatures Shown Below													
	1	2	3	4	5	6	7	8	9	10	11	12	13	14
10	+24°	+16°	+ 4°	−12°	−34°	−62°								
11	+25	+18	+ 8	− 6	−23	−47								
12	+26	+19	+10	0	−15	−34	−57°							
13	+27	+21	+13	+ 3	− 9	−25	−45							
14			+15	+ 6	− 5	−18	−34							
15			+16	+ 8	0	−12	−26							
16			+17	+10	+ 2	− 8	−19	−34	−52°					
17			+18	+12	+ 5	− 4	−14	−27	−42					
18			+19	+14	+ 7	0	−10	−21	−34	−50°				
19			+20	+15	+ 9	+ 2	− 7	−16	−28	−42				
20				+16	+10	+ 4	− 3	−12	−22	−34	−48°			
21				+17	+12	+ 6	0	− 9	−17	−28	−41			
22				+18	+13	+ 8	+ 2	− 6	−14	−23	−34	−47°		
23				+19	+14	+ 9	+ 4	− 3	−10	−19	−29	−40		
24				+19	+15	+10	+ 5	0	− 8	−15	−23	−34	−46°	
25				+20	+16	+12	+ 7	+ 1	− 5	−12	−20	−29	−40	−50°
26				+17	+13	+ 8	+ 3	− 3	− 9	−16	−25	−34	−44	
27				+18	+14	+ 9	+ 5	− 1	− 7	−13	−21	−29	−39	
28				+18	+15	+10	+ 6	+ 1	− 5	−11	−18	−25	−34	
29				+19	+16	+12	+ 7	+ 2	− 3	− 8	−15	−22	−29	
30				+20	+17	+13	+ 8	+ 4	− 1	− 6	−12	−18	−25	

For capacities over 30 quarts divide true capacity by 3. Find quarts Anti-Freeze for the ⅓ and multiply by 3 for quarts to add.

For capacities under 10 quarts multiply true capacity by 3. Find quarts Anti-Freeze for the tripled volume and divide by 3 for quarts to add.

To Increase the Freezing Protection of Anti-Freeze Solutions Already Installed

Cooling System Capacity Quarts	Number of Quarts of ETHYLENE GLYCOL Anti-Freeze Required to Increase Protection													
	From +20° F. to					From +10° F. to					From 0° F. to			
	0°	−10°	−20°	−30°	−40°	0°	−10°	−20°	−30°	−40°	−10°	−20°	−30°	−40°
10	1¾	2¼	3	3½	3¾	¾	1½	2¼	2¾	3¼	¾	1½	2	2½
12	2	2¾	3½	4	4½	1	1¾	2½	3¼	3¾	1	1¾	2½	3¼
14	2¼	3¼	4	4¾	5½	1¼	2	3	3¾	4½	1	2	3	3½
16	2½	3½	4½	5¼	6	1¼	2½	3½	4¼	5¼	1¼	2¼	3¼	4
18	3	4	5	6	7	1½	2¾	4	5	5¾	1½	2½	3¾	4¾
20	3¼	4½	5¾	6¾	7½	1¾	3	4¼	5½	6½	1½	2¾	4¼	5¼
22	3½	5	6¼	7¼	8¼	1¾	3¼	4¾	6	7¼	1¾	3¼	4½	5½
24	4	5½	7	8	9	2	3½	5	6½	7½	1¾	3½	5	6
26	4¼	6	7½	8¾	10	2	4	5½	7	8¼	2	3¾	5½	6¾
28	4½	6¼	8	9½	10½	2¼	4¼	6	7½	9	2	4	5¾	7¼
30	5	6¾	8½	10	11½	2½	4½	6½	8	9½	2¼	4¼	6¼	7¾

Test radiator solution with proper hydrometer. Determine from the table the number of quarts of solution to be drawn off from a full cooling system and replace with undiluted anti-freeze, to give the desired increased protection. For example, to increase protection of a 22-quart cooling system containing Ethylene Glycol (permanent type) anti-freeze, from +20° F. to −20° F. will require the replacement of 6¼ quarts of solution with undiluted anti-freeze.

Index

Chilton's Repair & Tune-Up Guides

The complete line covers domestic cars, imports, trucks, vans, RV's and 4-wheel drive vehicles.

BOOK CODE	TITLE	BOOK CODE	TITLE
#7032	Arrow & D-50 Pick-Ups 79-81	#6980	Honda 73-80
#6637	Aspen & Volare 76-78	#5912	International Scout 67-73
#5902	Audi 70-73	#5998	Jaguar 69-74
#7028	Audi 4000 & 5000 77-81	#7136	Jeep CJ 45-81
#6337	Audi Fox 73-75	#6739	Jeep Wagoneer, Commando, and
#5807	Barracuda and Challenger 65-72		Cherokee 66-79
#6931	Blazer & Jimmy 69-80	#6634	Maverick/Comet 70-77
#6844	BMW 70-79	#6981	Mazda 71-80
#7045	Camaro 67-81	#7031	Mazda RX-7 78-81
#6695	Capri 70-77	#6065	Mercedes-Benz 59-70
#7041	Champ/Arrow/Sapporo 77-81	#5907	Mercedes-Benz 68-73
#6316	Charger, Coronet 71-75	#6809	Mercedes-Benz 74-79
#6836	Chevette 76-80	#6780	MG 61-79
#6840	Chevrolet Mid Size 64-79	#6542	Mustang 65-73
	Covers Chevelle, Laguna, El Camino,	#6812	Mustang II 74-78
	Monte Carlo & Malibu	#6963	Mustang & Capri 79-80 Inc. Turbo.
#7135	Chevrolet 68-81	#6845	Omni/Horizon 78-80
	All Full-Size Chevrolet Models	#5792	Opel 64-70
#6936	Chevrolet & GMC Pick-Ups 70-80	#6575	Opel 71-75
#6930	Chevrolet & GMC Vans 67-80	#6473	Pacer 75-76
#7051	Chevrolet LUV 72-81 Inc. 4 x 4 Models	#5982	Peugeot 70-74
#6841	Chevy II, Nova 62-79	#7027	Pinto & Bobcat 71-80
#7037	Colt & Challenger 71-80	#6552	Plymouth 68-76
#6691	Corvair 60-69	#5822	Porsche 69-73
	All Models and Engines, Inc. Turbo.	#6331	Ramcharger & Trail Duster 74-75
#6576	Corvette 53-62	#5985	Rebel/Matador 67-74
#6843	Corvette 63-79	#5821	Road Runner, Satellite, Belvedere,
#6933	Cutlass 70-80		GTX 68-73
#6962	Dasher, Rabbit, Scirocco, Jetta 74-80	#5988	Saab 99 69-75
#5790	Datsun 61-72	#6978	Snowmobiles 76-80
#6960	Datsun 73-80	#6982	Subaru 70-80
#7050	Datsun Pick-Ups 70-81	#5905	Tempest, GTO and Le Mans 68-73
#6932	Datsun Z and ZX 70-80	#5795	Toyota 66-70
#6554	Dodge 68-77	#7036	Toyota Corolla/Carina/Tercel/Starlet 79-81
#6486	Dodge Charger 67-70	#7043	Toyota Celica & Supra 71-81
#6934	Dodge & Plymouth Vans 67-80	#7044	Toyota Corona/Cressida/Crown/Mk II 70-81
#6320	Fairlane and Torino 62-75		
#6965	Fairmont & Zephyr 78-80	#6276	Toyota Land Cruiser 66-74
#6485	Fiat 64-70	#7035	Toyota Pick-Ups 70-81
#7042	Fiat 69-81	#5910	Triumph 69-73
#6846	Fiesta 78-80	#6326	Valiant and Duster 68-76
#5996	Firebird 67-74	#5796	Volkswagen 49-71
#7140	Ford Bronco 66-81	#6837	Volkswagen 70-81
#6983	Ford Courier 72-80	#6529	Volvo 56-69
#6842	Ford and Mercury 68-79	#7040	Volvo 70-81
	All Full-Size Models		
#6696	Ford and Mercury Mid-Size 71-78		**AUTOMOTIVE SPECIALITY BOOKS**
	Covers Torino, Gran Torino, Ranchero, Elite, LTD II, Thunderbird, Montego, and Cougar	#6754	Chilton's Diesel Guide
#6913	Ford Pick-Ups 65-80	#6942	Chilton's Guide to Consumers' Auto Repairs and Prices
#6849	Ford Vans 61-80	#6940	Chilton's Minor Auto Body Repair
#6935	GM Subcompact 71-80	#6908	Chilton's More Miles Per Gallon
	Covers Vega, Monza, Astre, Sunbird, Starfire, Skyhawk	#6867	Chilton's Motorcycle Owner's Handbook
#7049	GM X-Body 80-81	#6727	Chilton's Off-Roading Guide
	Covers Citation, Omega, Phoenix and Skylark	#6811	Chilton's Repair Guide for Small Engines - Covers 2 and 4-stroke air cooled gasoline engines up to 20 hp.
#6937	Granada/Monarch 75-80		

Chilton's Repair & Tune-Up Guides are available at your local retailer or by mailing a check or money order for **$9.95** plus **$1.00** to cover postage and handling to:

Chilton Book Company
Dept. DM,
Radnor, PA 19089

NOTE: When ordering be sure to include name & address, book code & title.